Timothy Leigh

Suite 283, The Water Tower
Johns Landing
Portland, OR 97201

.thy Leigh

Suite 283, The Water Tower
Johns Landing
Portland, OR 97201

A handbook for the WRITING *series*

*Along with the two writers whose names appear on the title page,
the following produced this series:*

Julian L. Maline, S.J., who, as executive editor, had everything
to do with every phase of the work.
John B. Amberg, S.J., who, as business editor and writer,
brought the books from the experimental stage to final production.
Wilfred M. Mallon, S.J., and Andrew C. Smith, S.J., who,
with Father Maline, formed an executive committee.
Frederick M. O'Connor, S.J., and Wilfred G. Lauer, S.J., who worked
on the series in the difficult days of the planning
and the experimental edition.
Wilburn A. Diebold, S.J., James E. Farrell, S.J.,
James K. Bopp, S.J., and Robert J. Kearns, S.J., who
contributed substantially to the present edition as writers;
Richard E. Tischler, S.J., who made the diagrams
and handwritten corrections;
William K. Schwienher, S.J., who prepared the copy
of the experimental edition,
and John A. Zollner, S.J., whose drawings enlivened it.

Writing handbook

Writing
handbook

MICHAEL P. KAMMER, S.J.

CHARLES W. MULLIGAN, S.J.

Loyola University Press

Chicago, Illinois

Contents

This table of contents lists matters by pages; but the index found at the back of the book lists them by rule, with letter and number.

A Parts of speech

Parts of speech, continued

B The sentence

Syntax, continued

D Punctuation

E Division of words

F Abbreviations

G Numbers

H Capitals

Capitals, continued

I Spelling

J   Diagraming

Contents, continued

P Variety of development

Q Interest and force

Interest and force, continued

R Exposition

S Description

T Narration

U Argument

Argument, continued

A Parts of speech

In general

A1 Words can be classified as parts of speech—to some extent according to what they mean outside of sentences but chiefly according to the way in which they are used in sentences.

A2 Nine parts of speech may be listed: nouns, pronouns, verbs, adjectives, adverbs, prepositions, conjunctions, exclamatory words, and dummy subjects. To this list may be added the three verbals—gerunds, participles, and infinitives—which combine the natures of two or more parts of speech.

A3 The parts of speech are here defined.

A *noun* is the name of a person, place, or thing.

Straighten the *calendar*.

A *pronoun* is a word that is used in place of a noun.

Crabtree was expected to object, but *he* didn't.
Helen said *she* would make ham sandwiches for us.

A *verb* is a word that puts action into a sentence. It expresses action, state, or being.

Millings *tied* the bundle to the crossbar.

An *adjective* is a word that modifies a noun or a pronoun.

I'm *afraid* that I'm the *ugly* duckling.

An *adverb* is a word that modifies a verb, an adjective, or another adverb.

A *very* high wall surrounded the place.

A *preposition* is a word that has a noun or pronoun as its object and forms with that object one modifying unit called a phrase.

The vertical lines *in* newspapers are called column rules.

1

A *conjunction* is a word or group of words whose main purpose is to connect sentence parts, sentences, and paragraphs. It does not take an object.

Joseph *and* I are the pleasantest people!

An *exclamatory word* is a word or group of words that expresses emotion but has no grammatical connection with the rest of the sentence.

Oh, someone will take care of it.

A *dummy subject* (expletive) is the word *it* or *there* used simply to indicate that the subject is coming after the predicate verb or to avoid awkward constructions.

It was plain that he was distressed.
There are no cars available.

A *gerund* is a verb-noun in *ing*. It names an action.

The pleasure of *waiting* is all yours.

A *participle* is a verb-adjective.

Carlson, *returning,* bolted the door.

An *infinitive* is a verb-noun, often introduced by *to,* that has *ing* only in the progressive form. It names an action.

It is too late to *run.*

A4 The same word, spelled the same way, can sometimes be several parts of speech in turn.

The *little* man was peering at me again.	*Little* is an adjective.
The cymbal player cared *little* for music of any kind.	*Little* is an adverb.
Let me have a *little,* please.	*Little* is a pronoun.

The noun

A5 A noun is the name of a person, place, or thing. ("Thing" includes not only objects, but also qualities or conditions, actions, ideas, and so on.)

2

KINDS OF NOUNS

A6 A common noun is a name shared by all persons or things of the same kind. It can be applied to every member of a group or class of things.

man	knife
house	dog

A7 A proper noun is a person's or thing's own name. It is the particular name of a particular person, place, or thing.

Daniel Boone   Chicago   Buick

A8 A concrete noun is the name of an object that exists by itself. Often, not always, such an object is perceived by the senses.

mountain	soul
violin	angel
flame	air

A9 An abstract noun names something that does not exist by itself: a quality or condition, an action, an idea.

courage	playing
dampness	sport

A10 A collective noun is a word that even in the singular names a group of persons or things.[1]

team	audience
army	chorus

GENDER OF NOUNS

A11 Nouns are said to be of the masculine gender when they carry with them the notion of the male sex.

The *boy* looked searchingly at me.
The *waiter* seemed to sneer without sneering.
My *uncle* really did intend to pay the rent.
The *stallion* reared his fine head.

---

[1] For predicate-verb agreement with collective nouns, see C14-15.

A12 Nouns are said to be of the feminine gender when they carry with them the notion of the female sex.

The *girl* says she heard no call.
The *waitress* sniffed and disappeared.
My *aunt* hopes to attend the classes for adults.
The *mare* was altogether proud of the colt and showed it.

A13 Nouns are said to be of the masculine-or-feminine (common) gender when they carry with them the notion of sex without distinguishing between male and female.

People are funny.

Parents often have no way of letting a child know how completely they understand the problems of young social life.

It is dangerous to take a bone from a *dog*.

A14 Nouns are said to be of the neuter gender when they name things that have no sex.

A great *rock* lay some yards to the left.
The *idea* was new to me.

A15 Some sexless things are always given masculine or feminine gender by tradition or necessity.

God has *His* plan for you.

My guardian *angel* has had *his* disappointments—if an *angel* can be disappointed.

A16 Some sexless things are sometimes given a gender in lively or poetic writing.

When you feed the body, you should remember to let the *soul* also have *her* food.

She was a graceful *ship*, much in love with speed.

Russia has made no move that would lead us to trust *her*.

The *moon* hid *herself* for a moment.

That ol' *man river, he* don't say nuthin'.

A17 The vegetable kingdom is ordinarily treated as neuter.

The *tree* lay in ruins, *its* upended roots high in the air.

Now here is a *blossom* that certainly has not wasted *its* sweetness on the desert air.

4

A18 Collective nouns naming groups as groups (not as individuals) are treated as neuter.

The *crowd* had *its* attention diverted by the frantically waving man on the fire escape.

As usual, the *army* overextended *its* supply lines.

A19 The common-noun names of very young children are often treated as neuter in passages where the sex of the child has no bearing on the thought.

A *child* [an *infant*, a *baby*] has *its* rights no less than an adult.

A20 The common-noun names of animals are often treated as neuter regardless of the thought of the passage.

A *hen* is perfectly happy trying to hatch a darning egg along with *its* own real eggs.

PERSON OF NOUNS

A21 A noun that designates the speaker is in the first person.

This revolver belongs to me, *James Horder.*

A22 A noun that designates the person or thing spoken to is in the second person.

I mean you, *Bill.*
For you, my *country,* I will gladly die; but I had rather live.

A23 A noun that designates the person or thing spoken of is in the third person.

St. Barbara is the *patron* of *gunners* and *miners.*

NUMBER OF NOUNS

A24 A singular noun names one person or thing; a plural noun names more than one person or thing.[2]

Singular	Plural
boy	boys
tree	trees

---

[2] For the correct spelling of plurals, see I4-10.

A25 Some nouns are plural in form but singular in meaning.

The *news is* all good.
Measles is catching.

The pronoun

A26 A pronoun is a word that is used in place of a noun.

Helen said *she* would make ham sandwiches for us.	*She* is used in place of *Helen.*
Tom made this bow. *He* is clever with tools but so hasty that *he* cut *himself* several times.	The two *hes* and *himself* take the place of *Tom.*
My uncle has an unconventional spaniel *that* does not sit up and beg.	*That* takes the place of *spaniel.*

A27 The noun whose place a pronoun takes is called the antecedent of the pronoun.

Helen said she would make ham sandwiches for us.	*Helen* is the antecedent of *she.*
Tom made this bow. He is clever with tools but so hasty that he cut himself several times.	*Tom* is the antecedent of the two *hes* and *himself.*

A28 Some words can be thought of as nouns, pronouns, or adjectives. They differ from ordinary pronouns in this, that they can modify[3] an implied but unexpressed noun.[4]

The *good* enjoy two worlds.	As an adjective, *good* modifies the absent noun *people.*
They enjoy two worlds.	*They* is a pronoun. It cannot modify *people. Good people* makes sense, but *they people* does not.

------

[3] For the meaning of *modify,* see A103.
[4] See A104.

PERSONAL PRONOUNS·

A29 The personal pronouns are called "personal" because, without looking at the sentence in which they stand, one can tell whether they indicate the speaker (first person), the person or thing spoken to (second person), or the person or thing spoken of (third person).

The personal pronouns are—[5]

First person

	Singular	*Plural*
Nominative	I	we
Possessive	mine	ours
Objective	me	us

Second person

	Singular	*Plural*
Nominative	you (thou)	you
Possessive	yours (thine)	yours
Objective	you (thee)	you

Third person

	Singular	*Plural*
Nominative	he, she, it	they
Possessive	his, hers, its	theirs
Objective	him, her, it	them

A30 *He, his,* and *him* are used when the antecedent is masculine or common; *she, hers,* and *her,* when the antecedent is feminine; *it* and *its,* when the antecedent is neuter; the rest of the personal-pronoun forms are used no matter what the gender of the antecedent.[6]

On the witness stand the policeman testified that *he* had fired in self-defense.

Grace decided to buy the orange hat, even though *she* thought *it* was rather expensive.

---

[5] The forms *my, our, your, her,* and *their* are not given here because, under the system followed in this book, they are considered possessive (pronominal) *adjectives,* not pronouns. *His* and *its* also, when they accompany and modify a noun, are considered adjectives, not pronouns.

[6] For the gender of antecedents, see A11-20.

DEMONSTRATIVE PRONOUNS

A31 The demonstrative pronouns are—

Singular	*Plural*
this	these
that	those

A32 The demonstrative pronouns are used to specify, to point out, to call attention to their antecedents with special emphasis.

This is my choice.
I did not say *that*.
Deliver *those* to my home; *these* I'll take with me.

A33 The demonstrative pronouns take the place of their antecedents; they do not accompany and modify nouns as the demonstrative adjectives do.

This is my home.	*This*—demonstrative pronoun —takes the place of *house* or *home* as subject of the predicate verb *is*.
This home is mine.	*This*—demonstrative adjective —is not the subject or object but accompanies and modifies the noun *home*.

A34 The demonstrative pronouns have the same forms for all persons, genders, and cases.

A35 *This* and *these* ordinarily refer to what is present, near, just referred to, or about to be referred to; demonstrative *that* and *those*, to what is more remote in time or place.

Look at *this* [referring to something near the speaker].
Look at *that* [referring to something across the room].

People call me the Worm. *This* would anger me if I did not reflect that they would call me worse if they knew me better.

And now *this* is what I am going to say to you.

Centuries ago someone first said, "An argument cannot batter down a fact." *That* is still true.

8

A36 Demonstrative *that* and *those* are used to refer to the thing or idea indicated or understood from the situation or context.

The writing is *that* of Claiborne, but the sentiments are not his.

[The first word spoken to a man who has just entered a room:] *That* is why I like you—you are always prompt.

[Boy meeting elderly lady carrying bundles:] I'll be glad to carry *those* for you, if there's nothing fragile in them.

Self-PRONOUNS

A37 The *self*-pronouns (compound personal pronouns) are—

First person

	Singular	*Plural*
Nominative and objective	myself	ourselves

Second person

	Singular	*Plural*
Nominative and objective	yourself	yourselves

Third person

	Singular	*Plural*
Nominative and objective	oneself[7]	
	himself	
	herself	themselves
	itself	

A38 *Himself* is used when the antecedent is masculine or common; *herself,* when the antecedent is feminine; *itself,* when the antecedent is neuter; but all the rest of the *self*-pronouns are used no matter what the gender of the antecedent may be.[8]

It has been said of Abe Lincoln that *he* pulled *himself* up by his own bootstraps.

My *sister* climbed the tree *herself* and rescued her kitten before the firemen arrived.

A large *boulder* detached *itself* from the mass atop the hill, and began to roll down toward us with increasing momentum.

---

[7] *Oneself* may also be written *one's self.*
[8] For the gender of antecedents, see A11-20.

9

A39 When a *self*-pronoun is used to show that the action is reflected upon the doer of the action, it is called a reflexive pronoun.

Fleavy hurt *himself.*

He wrote *himself* a note.

He wrote a note to *himself.*

They are sitting by *themselves.*

A40 As reflexives the *self*-pronouns can be used only in the objective case as direct objects, indirect objects, or the objects of prepositions.

Turner has betrayed *himself* [direct object].
That week Rossiter gave *himself* [indirect object] no peace.
Of *ourselves* [object of a preposition] we can do nothing.

A41 When a *self*-pronoun is not used as described in A39 but merely in apposition as reinforcement for another word in the sentence, it is called an intensive pronoun.[9]

He *himself* trained the seals.
He trained the seals *himself.*

A42 As intensives, the *self*-pronouns may be used in apposition with a word in the nominative or objective case.

He himself voted against the proposal twice.
We met none other than our *neighbors themselves* downtown.
Here is a picture of *John himself* when he was two.

RELATIVE PRONOUNS

A43 The relative pronouns are—

	Singular or plural		
Nominative	who	that	which
Possessive	whose		
Objective	whom	that	which

---

[9] Some grammarians call intensive pronouns adjectives. While you are in school, treat them as pronouns in apposition.

A44 The relative pronouns are so called because they not only take the place of nouns but join or relate a dependent (adjective) clause to an antecedent in another clause.

I know the girl *whom* you mean.

The moon, *which* was rising, looked huge and yellow.

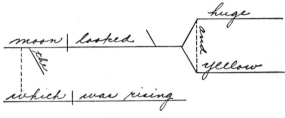

I want the one *that* I saw first.

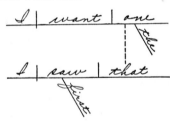

A45 In general, use relative *who* and *that*[10] when the antecedent is a person or a personification, and *which* and *that* when the antecedent is not a person.[11]

That *boy whom* I considered so worthless turned out to be the most reliable back on the team.

That *boy that* I considered so worthless turned out to be the most reliable back on the team.

The *wheel which* fell off rolled into the canal and sank.
The *wheel that* fell off rolled into the canal and sank.

---

[10] There is an increasing tendency, which you may follow if you like, to use *that* only when the antecedent is a thing.

[11] For the preferred use of *which* and *that* in restrictive clauses, see C322.

11

A46 Relative *which* is often preferred to *who* when the antecedent is a collective noun naming a group of persons as a group and not as individuals.

The committee, *which* met regularly, deserved its pay.
I consulted the family, *which* didn't like the idea at all.
The crowd, *which* had been quiet, broke into a roar.

A47 Where the antecedent nouns are both persons and things, use relative *that* when you can; use *which* when you cannot use *that*, or avoid the difficulty by rewording the sentence.

Where are the men and the money *that* will save our school?
Johnny Kerr and his dogs, of *which* I have spoken so often, have gone to Hollywood.
Johnny Kerr, of *whom* I have spoken so often, has gone to Hollywood with his dogs.

A48 The relative pronouns have the same form for all persons and numbers.

A49 A relative pronoun refers to an antecedent in another clause. This makes it easy to distinguish a relative pronoun and its adjective clause from an interrogative or indefinite pronoun or adjective and its noun clause, from demonstrative-pronoun and demonstrative-adjective *that*, and from the conjunction *that*.

Here are the *blueprints that* you were looking for.	*That* is a relative pronoun. It has an antecedent, *blueprints*, in the independent clause.
I was looking for the blueprints when I found *that* on the floor.	*That* has no antecedent in the independent clause. Demonstrative pronoun.
I was looking for something else when I found *that* blueprint on the floor.	*That* has no antecedent in the independent clause. Demonstrative adjective.
I knew *that* you were looking for the blueprints.	Once again, *that* has no antecedent in the independent clause. Conjunction.

12

I know the *girl whom* you mean.	*Whom* is a relative pronoun; it has an antecedent, *girl,* in the independent clause.
I know *whom* you mean.	*Whom* does not have an antecedent in this sentence. Indefinite pronoun.
Tell me, *whom* do you mean?	*Whom* does not have an antecedent in the independent clause. Interrogative pronoun.

INTERROGATIVE PRONOUNS

A50 The interrogative pronouns are—

		Singular or plural	
Nominative	who	which	what
Possessive	whose	whose	
Objective	whom	which	what

A51 The interrogative pronouns are so called because they ask questions.

Whom do you want?
No one asked me, *What* do you want?
No one asked me *what* I wanted.

A52 Use interrogative *who* in any kind of question when the antecedent is a person. Use interrogative *what* when the antecedent is not a person.

Whom do you want?
Whose is this pastrami sandwich?

What are you carrying?

A53 Use interrogative pronoun *which* whether or not the antecedent is a person, but only in questions involving a choice.[12]

Which did you choose (Myron or Clark)?
Which did you choose (the trip to Miami or the scholarship)?

---

[12] Many good writers will not use the interrogative pronoun *which* when the antecedent is a person, unless the pronoun is followed by an *of* phrase.

A54 The interrogative pronouns are all third person.

Who of us *is* brave enough to take Christ's dare?

INDEFINITE PRONOUNS

A55 Some common indefinite pronouns are—

Singular		*Plural*	*Singular or plural*
another	other	both	all
anybody	somebody	few	any
anything	someone	many	more
each	something	others	none
either	what	several	some
everybody	whatever		
everyone	whatsoever		
everything	which		
little	whichever		
much	whoever		
neither	whom		
nobody	whomever		
nothing	whose		
one	whosoever		

A56 The indefinite pronouns are so called because they often take the place of antecedents that are not named and that cannot be pinned down to particular persons, places, or things.

Anybody coming through the door would trip.
One of these has onions on it.
I found *nobody* with *whom* to play cricket.

A57 *All, any, some,* and *none* are singular if they indicate how much, plural if they indicate how many.[13]

All of the cake *was* burned.
All of the cakes *were* burned.

---

[13] *None* can indicate how many and yet be singular if there is good reason for stressing the notion of "not a single one." For example, "I went to the dog pound today and looked at every pooch there, but *none* of them *was* mine." The same is true of *any* when there is reason to stress the notion of "a single one": "*Any* at all—the red, the maroon, or the vermilion—*is* good enough."

Was any of the cake burned?
Were any of the cakes burned?

Some of the cake *was* burned.
Some of the cakes *were* burned.

We looked for crepe paper, but there *is none.*
None of the people you expected *have* come.

A58 If the antecedent is masculine, or masculine and feminine, treat the indefinite pronoun as masculine; if the antecedent is exclusively feminine, treat the indefinite pronoun as feminine.[14]

Everybody at the stag party made *his* contribution to the welfare fund.	Exclusively masculine.
Everyone has *his* own cross to bear.	Masculine and feminine.
Has *anybody* lost *her* purse?	Exclusively feminine.

A59 Singular indefinites are all third person. Plural indefinites get their person from their indefinite antecedents.

Each of you has a funny look on *his* face.
All of you have funny looks on *your* faces.
All of us have funny looks on *our* faces.

RECIPROCAL PRONOUNS

A60 The reciprocal pronouns are *each other* and *one another.* They are called reciprocal because they are used in pairs to show an interaction.

The twins helped *each other.*
Each helped the *other.*

The soldiers slaughtered *one another* mercilessly.
One slaughtered *another.*

A61 Use *each other* to refer to only two, *one another* to refer to more than two.

---

[14] For the gender of antecedents, see A11-20.

The verb

A62 A verb is a word that puts action into a sentence. It expresses action, state, or being.

[Action:] Who *dropped* that sundae?
[State:] Johnny *sleeps* very soundly.
[Being:] God *is*.

[Being:] This *is* a Nutty Delight without the nuts.

The verb *be* expresses, usually, not only being, but being complicated by something else—here, identity.

CONJUGATION OF VERBS

A63 Model conjugation of the verb *praise*:

ACTIVE VOICE

INDICATIVE MOOD

	Regular form	Progressive form
Present	I praise	I *am* ⎫
	you praise	you are
	he *praises*	he *is* ⎬ praising
	we praise	we are
	you praise	you are
	they praise	they are ⎭
Past	I ⎫	I *was* ⎫
	you	you were
	he ⎬ praised	he *was* ⎬ praising
	we	we were
	you	you were
	they ⎭	they were ⎭
Future	I ⎫	I ⎫
	you	you
	he ⎬ shall *or*	he ⎬ shall *or* will
	we ⎪ will praise	we ⎪ be praising
	you	you
	they ⎭	they ⎭

16

	Regular form	*Progressive form*
Present perfect	I have you have he **has** we have you have they have } praised	I have you have he **has** we have you have they have } been praising
Past perfect	I you he we you they } had praised	I you he we you they } had been praising
Future perfect	I you he we you they } shall *or* will have praised	I you he we you they } shall *or* will have been praising

SUBJUNCTIVE MOOD[15]

	Regular form	*Progressive form*
Present	I you he we you they } praise	I you he we you they } be praising
Past	I you he we you they } praised	I you he we you they } were praising

---

[15] Some word like *although, if, in order that, lest, that, though, till,* or *unless* is regularly used with the subjunctive mood. See C113-19.

	Regular form	Progressive form
Present perfect	I you he we you they } have praised	I you he we you they } have been praising
Past perfect	I you he we you they } had praised	I you he we you they } had been praising

IMPERATIVE MOOD

	Regular form	Progressive form
Present and future	(you) praise	(you) be praising

PARTICIPLES[16]

	Regular form	Progressive form
Present	praising	
Present perfect	having praised	having been praising

INFINITIVES[17]

	Regular form	Progressive form
Present	nom. praise obj. (to) praise	be praising (to) be praising

---

[16] Some grammars maintain that there is an active past participle, as, for instance, *returned* in the following sentence, "Recently returned from Denver, Mr. Alton had some interesting things to say about the western dispute over water rights." WRITING takes the traditional view that such a participle is the present-perfect active, with *having* implied but not expressed in the sentence.

The participles are verbals, half adjective and half verb. They are used in conjugating verbs, however, primarily in their verb sense, which stresses action, rather than in their adjective sense, which stresses modification—changing the meaning—of nouns.

[17] The infinitives are verbals, half noun and half verb. The nominative case is used chiefly in naming verbs, as in the sentence, "*Praise* is our model verb," or

	Regular form		Progressive form
Present *perfect*	nom. obj.	have praised (to) have praised	have been praising (to) have been praising

GERUNDS[18]

	Regular form		Progressive form
Present	nom. pos. obj.	praising praising's praising	
Present *perfect*	*and* *obj.*	having praised	having been praising

PASSIVE VOICE
INDICATIVE MOOD

	Regular form		Progressive form[19]	
Present	I *am* you are he *is* we are you are they are	} praised	I *am* you are he *is* we are you are they are	} being praised
Past	I *was* you were he *was* we were you were they were	} praised	I *was* you were he *was* we were you were they were	} being praised

---

as in dictionary listings. It does, however, turn up as subject noun or predicate complement, as, for example, in this sentence, "All he could do was praise me." The objective has many uses, one of which is to combine with helping verbs to produce changes of voice, mood, time, and so on; for example, I shall *praise*, I may *praise*, I ought to *praise*. The infinitive is very frequently the object of the preposition *to*.

[18] The gerunds are verb-nouns and are not used in the conjugation of verbs but only as subject nouns, predicate nouns, direct and indirect objects, and the objects of prepositions.

[19] The progressive forms that are not given in the passive paradigm do occasionally turn up in writing and speaking; but they sound so unpleasant and are so rarely used that it seems good to omit them here. For example, *I have been being praised* is so awkward that it is usually supplied by something like *I have been having my praises sung.*

19

Regular form

Future	I you he we you they	shall *or* will be praised

Present perfect	I have you have he **has** we have you have they have	been praised

Past perfect	I you he we you they	had been praised

Future perfect	I you he we you they	shall *or* will have been praised

SUBJUNCTIVE MOOD[20]

Regular form

Present	I you he we you they	be praised

---

[20] Some word like *although, if, in order that, lest, that, though, till,* or *unless* is regularly used with the subjunctive mood. See C113-19.

	Regular form	*Progressive form*
Past	I you he we you they } were praised	I you he we you they } were being praised
Present perfect	I you he we you they } have been praised	
Past perfect	I you he we you they } had been praised	

IMPERATIVE MOOD

Regular form

Present and future   (you) be praised

PARTICIPLES[21]

Regular form

Present   being praised

Past   praised

Present perfect   having been praised

---

[21] The participles are verbals, half adjective and half verb. They are used in conjugating verbs, however, primarily in their verb sense, which stresses action, rather than in their adjective sense, which stresses modification—changing the meaning—of nouns.

INFINITIVES[22]

| *Present* | *nom.* | be praised |
| | *obj.* | (to) be praised |

| *Present perfect* | *nom.* | have been praised |
| | *obj.* | (to) have been praised |

GERUNDS[23]

| *Present* | being praised |

| *Present perfect* | having been praised |

A64　Conjugation of the verb *be:*

INDICATIVE MOOD

Present	I *am* you are he *is* we are you are they are	*Past*	I *was* you were he *was* we were you were they were
Future	I shall be you will be he will be we shall be you will be they will be	*Present perfect*	I have been you have been he *has* been we have been you have been they have been
Past perfect	I you he we you they had been	*Future perfect*	I shall have been you will have been he will have been we shall have been you will have been they will have been

---

[22] The infinitives are verbals, half noun and half verb. The nominative case turns up chiefly in predicate complements, as in this sentence, "All I could do was be impressed and say nothing." The objective combines with helping verbs and is frequently the object of the preposition *to.*

[23] The gerunds are verb-nouns and are not used in the conjugation of verbs but only as subject nouns, predicate nouns, direct and indirect objects, and the objects of prepositions.

SUBJUNCTIVE MOOD[24]

Present	I you he we you they } be	*Past*	I you he we you they } were
Present perfect	I you he we you they } have been	*Past perfect*	I you he we you they } had been

IMPERATIVE MOOD

Present and future	(you) be

PARTICIPLES[25]

Present	being
Past	been
Present perfect	having been

INFINITIVES[26]

Present	(to) be
Present perfect	(to) have been

GERUNDS[27]

Present	being
Present perfect	having been

[24] Some word like *although, if, in order that, lest, that, though, till,* or *unless* is regularly used with the subjunctive mood. See C113-19.

[25] The participles are verbals, half adjective and half verb. They are used in conjugating verbs, however, primarily in their verb sense, which stresses action, rather than in their adjective sense, which stresses modification—changing the meaning—of nouns.

[26] The infinitives are verbals, half noun and half verb. The nominative of *be* has no particular use except to name the verb. The objective has many uses, one of which is to combine with helping verbs to produce changes of voice, mood, time, and so on; for example, I shall *be*, I shall *be* praised, I may *be*, I ought to *be*. The infinitive is very frequently the object of the preposition *to*.

[27] The gerunds are verb-nouns and are not used in the conjugation of verbs but only as subject nouns, predicate nouns, direct and indirect objects, and the objects of prepositions.

A65 A progressive form of the verb *be* (usually followed by a predicate adjective) exists, but as a general rule only in the following moods and tenses:

Present indicative	*Past indicative*	*Past subjunctive*[28]
I *am*	I *was*	I
you are	you were	you
he *is*	he *was*	he
we are } being	we were } being	we } were being
you are	you were	you
they are	they were	they

THE PRINCIPAL PARTS OF VERBS

A66 The principal parts of a verb are those forms from which, if known, the voices, moods, and tenses of the verb can be formed. They are the present infinitive active (nominative case); the past indicative active, first person singular; and the past participle.

Present infinitive active	*Past indicative active, first person singular*	*Past participle*
be	was	been
praise	praised	praised
begin	began	begun

A67 The greater number of verbs regularly form their past indicative active and past participle by adding *d, ed,* or *t* to the present infinitive active.

Present	*Past*	*Past participle*
praise	praise*d*	praise*d*
guide	guide*d*	guide*d*
rip	ripp*ed*	ripp*ed*
bless	bless*ed*	bless*ed*
bend	ben*t*	ben*t*
kneel	kneele*d or* knel*t*	kneele*d or* knel*t*

---

[28] Some word like *although, if, in order that, lest, that, though, till,* or *unless* is regularly used with the subjunctive mood. See C113-19.

A68 The principal parts of the following verbs sometimes cause difficulty.[29]

	Present	*Past*	*Past participle*
1	arise	arose	arisen
2	attack	attacked	attacked
3	awake	awaked *or* awoke	awaked
4	awaken	awakened	awakened
5	be	was	been
6	bear[30]	bore	borne *or* born[31]
7	beat	beat	beaten
8	become	became	become
9	begin	began	begun
10	bend	bent	bent
11	beseech	besought	besought
12	bid	bade *or* bid[32]	bidden *or* bid[32]
13	bind	bound	bound
14	bite	bit	bitten
15	bleed	bled	bled
16	blow	blew	blown
17	break	broke	broken
18	bring	brought	brought
19	broadcast	broadcast *or* broadcasted[33]	broadcast *or* broadcasted[33]
20	build	built	built
21	burn	burned *or* burnt	burned *or* burnt
22	burst	burst	burst
23	buy	bought	bought
24	carry	carried	carried
25	catch	caught	caught
26	choose	chose	chosen
27	climb	climbed	climbed

---

[29] Rhythmic recitation aloud is perhaps the only way of learning these verbs.

[30] Carry, suffer, tolerate, give birth to.

[31] When applied to pregnancy or birth, *borne* can be used as part of verbs in the passive only when they are followed by *by*, expressed or implied. *Born* means only brought into life, is always passive, and is never followed by *by*.

[32] Use *bid, bade, bidden* only in some sense of command or order; use *bid, bid, bid* in all senses—command, offer a price for something, name a number and a suit in cardplaying.

[33] Use either *broadcast* or *broadcasted* when speaking of television and radio; use only *broadcast* in all other senses.

Present	Past	Past participle
28 cling	clung	clung
29 come	came	come
30 deal	dealt	dealt
31 dig	dug *or* digged	dug *or* digged
32 dive	dived	dived
33 do	did	done
34 drag	dragged	dragged
35 draw	drew	drawn
36 drink	drank	drunk
37 drive	drove	driven
38 drown	drowned	drowned
39 eat	ate	eaten
40 fall	fell	fallen
41 feed	fed	fed
42 fight	fought	fought
43 find	found	found
44 flee	fled	fled
45 fling	flung	flung
46 flow	flowed	flowed
47 fly	flew	flown
48 forbid	forbade *or* forbad	forbidden
49 forget	forgot	forgotten *or* forgot
50 forsake	forsook	forsaken
51 freeze	froze	frozen
52 get	got	got *or* gotten
53 give	gave	given
54 go	went	gone
55 grind	ground	ground
56 grow	grew	grown
57 hang	hanged	hanged[34]
58 hang	hung	hung
59 hold	held	held
60 kill	killed	killed
61 kneel	knelt *or* kneeled	knelt *or* kneeled
62 know	knew	known

[34] *Hanged* is preferred to *hung* for putting to death by suspending.

	Present	Past	Past participle
63	lay[35]	laid	laid
64	lead	led	led
65	lean	leaned *or* leant	leaned *or* leant
66	leap	leaped *or* leapt	leaped *or* leapt
67	learn	learned	learned
68	leave	left	left
69	lend	lent	lent
70	let	let	let
71	lie[36]	lay	lain
72	lie[37]	lied	lied
73	light	lighted *or* lit	lighted *or* lit
74	loose	loosed	loosed
75	lose	lost	lost
76	mean	meant	meant
77	meet	met	met
78	pay	paid	paid
79	prove	proved	proved
80	raise[38]	raised	raised
81	read	read	read
82	ride	rode	ridden
83	ring	rang *or* rung	rung
84	rise	rose	risen
85	run	ran	run
86	say	said	said
87	seal	sealed	sealed
88	see	saw	seen
89	seek	sought	sought
90	sell	sold	sold
91	set[39]	set	set
92	sew[40]	sewed	sewed *or* sewn
93	shake	shook	shaken
94	shoot	shot	shot

---

[35] Transitive; to set or put something down.
[36] Intransitive; to recline.
[37] To tell an untruth.
[38] Do not confuse with *arise* or *rise*. (See Nos. 1 and 84 of this list.)
[39] Do not confuse with *sit*. (See No. 99 of this list.)
[40] As with thread.

Present	*Past*	*Past participle*
95 show	showed	shown *or* showed
96 shrink	shrank	shrunk
97 sing	sang	sung
98 sink	sank *or* sunk	sunk
99 sit	sat	sat
100 slay	slew	slain
101 sleep	slept	slept
102 slide	slid	slid *or* slidden
103 slink	slunk	slunk
104 smite	smote	smitten
105 sow[41]	sowed	sowed *or* sown
106 speak	spoke	spoken
107 split	split	split
108 spring	sprang *or* sprung	sprung
109 steal	stole	stolen
110 stick	stuck	stuck
111 sting	stung	stung
112 stink	stank *or* stunk	stunk
113 stride	strode	stridden
114 string	strung	strung
115 strive	strove *or* strived	striven *or* strived
116 swear	swore	sworn
117 sweat	sweat *or* sweated	sweat *or* sweated
118 swim	swam	swum
119 swing	swung	swung
120 take	took	taken
121 teach	taught	taught
122 tear	tore	torn
123 tell	told	told
124 throw	threw	thrown
125 tread	trod	trodden *or* trod
126 wake	waked *or* woke	waked
127 wear	wore	worn
128 weave	wove	woven
129 win	won	won
130 wring	wrung	wrung
131 write	wrote	written

[41] As, for example, seed.

A69 Do not use the past participle for the past indicative active.

drank
He ~~drunk~~ the poison.

saw
I ~~seen~~ it myself.

came
The cold drinks ~~come~~ earlier than we expected.

A70 Do not use the past indicative active but the past participle with helping verbs.

run
The ink had ~~ran~~ down the length of the paper.

fallen
Snow had ~~fell~~ all night.

A71 Do not invent parts for verbs.

brought
Rodney ~~brung~~ the beer.

thrown
The test papers were ~~throwed~~ out during the summer.

broke
The blast ~~busted~~ the window.

HELPING VERBS[42]

A72 Helping verbs are verbs that are used together with other verbs to express changes of thought such as voice, mood, tense, and other shades of meaning. The principal helping verbs are—

be	must
can *and* could	ought
do	shall *and* will
have	should *and* would[43]
may *and* might	

---

[42] Helping verbs are treated in detail in C39-95.

[43] *Should* and *would* are sometimes called past-tense forms of *shall* and *will*. But they are very frequently used to express a great deal more than mere past time. The same is true of *might* and *could*, which are considered past-tense forms of *may* and *can*. See C72-95.

29

FORMATION OF MOODS AND TENSES

A73 Tenses are the different forms that a verb takes to indicate the time of an action or state.

A74 To form the present indicative active of verbs (except *be*), use the present infinitive active and add *s* or *es* for the third person singular.

Present infinitive active	*Present indicative active*	
praise	I praise	we praise
	you praise	you praise
	he *praises*	they praise
go	I go	we go
	you go	you go
	he **goes**	they go

A75 The past indicative active is supplied in the principal parts of a verb.

A76 To form the future indicative active, use *shall* or *will* before the present infinitive.

Future indicative active

I shall *or* will praise	I shall *or* will be
you shall *or* will praise	you shall *or* will be
he shall *or* will praise	he shall *or* will be
we shall *or* will praise	we shall *or* will be
you shall *or* will praise	you shall *or* will be
they shall *or* will praise	they shall *or* will be

A77 To form the present-perfect indicative active, use *have* plus the past participle, except in the third person singular, where you must use *has*.

Present-perfect indicative active

I have praised	I have been
you have praised	you have been
he *has* praised	he *has* been
we have praised	we have been
you have praised	you have been
they have praised	they have been

A78 To form the past-perfect indicative active, use *had* plus the past participle.

Past-perfect indicative active

I had praised	I had been
you had praised	you had been
he had praised	he had been
we had praised	we had been
you had praised	you had been
they had praised	they had been

A79 To form the future-perfect indicative active, use *shall have* or *will have* plus the past participle.[44]

Future-perfect indicative active

I shall *or* will have praised	I shall *or* will have been
you shall *or* will have praised	you shall *or* will have been
he shall *or* will have praised	he shall *or* will have been
we shall *or* will have praised	we shall *or* will have been
you shall *or* will have praised	you shall *or* will have been
they shall *or* will have praised	they shall *or* will have been

A80 For the present subjunctive active, use the same form as the present infinitive active.[45] Note that the form does not change in the third person singular.

Present subjunctive active

I praise	I be
you praise	you be
he praise	he be
we praise	we be
you praise	you be
they praise	they be

[44] In the United States even the best writers tend to make *will* do *shall*'s work as well as its own. For the formal and careful distinction between *shall* and *will*, see C66-71.

[45] Some word like *although, if, in order that, lest, that, though, till,* or *unless* is regularly used with the subjunctive mood. See C113-19. The present subjunctive is not much used (see C113-15 and C121). The past subjunctive of *be* is still used to a great extent even in conversation to express what is contrary to fact or merely supposed (see C116). The past-perfect subjunctive is very much used; but, since it does not differ in form from the past-perfect indicative, its use involves no real problem.

A81 The past subjunctive active has the same form as the past indicative active (except for *be*).[46]

Past subjunctive active

I praised	I were
you praised	you were
he praised	he were
we praised	we were
you praised	you were
they praised	they were

A82 To form the present-perfect subjunctive active, use *have* (not *has*) plus the past participle.[46]

Present-perfect subjunctive active

I have praised	I have been
you have praised	you have been
he have praised	he have been
we have praised	we have been
you have praised	you have been
they have praised	they have been

A83 To form the past-perfect subjunctive active, use *had* plus the past participle.[46]

Past-perfect subjunctive active

I had praised	I had been
you had praised	you had been
he had praised	he had been
we had praised	we had been
you had praised	you had been
they had praised	they had been

A84 To form the present (also future) imperative active, use the same form as the infinitive.

Present and future imperative active

(you) praise   (you) be

A85 To form the present participle active, add *ing* to the present infinitive active. (Omit a final *e* except where the *e*

---

[46] Some word like *although, if, in order that, lest, that, though, till,* or *unless* is regularly used with the subjunctive mood. See C113-19.

is necessary to the pronunciation or distinguishing of a word, as in *being* and *dyeing* [coloring].)

Present participle active

praising   being

A86 To form the present-perfect participle active, use *having* plus the past participle.

Present-perfect participle active

having praised   having been

A87 The past participle (passive) is supplied in the principal parts of a verb.

A88 The present infinitive active is supplied in the principal parts of a verb.

A89 To form the present-perfect infinitive active, use *have* plus the past participle.

Present-perfect infinitive active

(to) have praised   (to) have been

A90 To form the present active of the gerund, add *ing* to the present infinitive active. (Omit a final *e* except where the *e* is necessary to the pronunciation or distinguishing of a word, as in *being* and *dyeing* [coloring].)

Present gerund active

praising   being

A91 To form the present-perfect active of the gerund, use *having* plus the past participle.

Present-perfect gerund active

having praised   having been

FORMATION OF THE PASSIVE VOICE

A92 Voice is that form which a verb takes to show whether the subject is acting or being acted upon.

Active voice, the subject is acting	*Passive voice, the subject is being acted upon*
Allen *bought* a car.	A car *was bought* by Allen.

A93 To change a verb from active to passive, use the proper mood and tense of the verb *be* plus the past participle of the verb in the active.

Active	*Passive*
Henry *has fed* the cow. [*Has fed* is present-perfect indicative of *feed*.]	The cow *has been fed* by Henry. [*Has been* is present-perfect indicative of *be. Fed* is the past participle of the verb used in the active.]

A94 To change a verb from passive to active, simply use the proper tense of the active.

Passive	*Active*
You *are upset* by the surprise.	The surprise *upsets* you.
The car *was being washed*.	The Finletter twins *were washing* the car.

VERB PERSON

A95 Verbs have person only to agree with their subjects; that is, in some moods and tenses verbs show a change of form to indicate that the subject noun or pronoun is the speaker (first person); the person or thing spoken to (second person); or the person or thing spoken of (third person).

> *I am* humble [first person].
> *You are* humble [second person].
> *He is* humble [third person].

A96 The verb *be* changes form to indicate person in—

A The present indicative singular.

> I *am* [first person]
> you *are* [second person]
> he *is* [third person]

B The past indicative singular.

> I was [first person]
> you *were* [second person]
> he was [third person]

c The present-perfect indicative singular.

> I have been [first person]
> you have been [second person]
> he *has* been [third person]

A97 Verbs other than *be* change form to indicate person by using an *s* or *es* form in—

A The present indicative singular (active).[47]

> I praise [first person]   I rush [first person]
> you praise [second person]   you rush [second person]
> he *praises* [third person]   he *rushes* [third person]

B The present-perfect indicative singular (active).[47]

> I have praised [first person]
> you have praised [second person]
> he *has* praised [third person]

VERB NUMBER

A98 Verbs have number only to agree with their subjects; that is, in certain moods and tenses verbs show a change of form to indicate that the subject noun or pronoun is singular or plural.

> *I am* humble [singular].
> *We are* humble [plural].

A99 The verb *be* changes form to indicate number in—

A The present indicative, first and third persons.

Singular	*Plural*
I *am*	we *are*
he *is*	they *are*

B The past indicative, first and third persons.

Singular	*Plural*
I *was*	we *were*
he *was*	they *were*

---

[47] The passive form, since it is made up of the verb *be*, is sufficiently described in A96.

c The present-perfect indicative, third person.

Singular	Plural
he **has** been	they **have** been

A100 Verbs other than *be* change form to indicate number by using an *s* or *es* form in—

A The present indicative singular (active), third person.[48]

he *praises*   he *hushes*

B The present-perfect indicative singular (active), third person.[48]

he **has** praised

THE EMPHATIC VERB-FORM

A101 Use helping verb *do* plus the present infinitive active of the main verb to make the emphatic form of verbs. The emphatic form is limited to the active voice and the following moods and tenses.

Present indicative	*Past indicative*
I do praise	I did praise
you do praise	you did praise
he *does* praise	he did praise
we do praise	we did praise
you do praise	you did praise
they do praise	they did praise

Present subjunctive[49]	*Past subjunctive*[49]
I do praise	I did praise
you do praise	you did praise
he do praise[50]	he did praise
we do praise	we did praise
you do praise	you did praise
they do praise	they did praise

---

[48] The passive form, since it is made up of the verb *be*, is sufficiently described in A99.

[49] Some word like *although, if, in order that, lest, that, though, till,* or *unless* is regularly used with the subjunctive mood. See C113-19.

[50] Note that there is no change in the third person singular.

Imperative[51]
do (you) praise

A102 The emphatic form of verbs is used, of course, for emphatic assertions; but its chief use is to substitute for regular forms of the verb when they would be awkward.

Regular form	Emphatic form
Went he?	*Did* he go?
You *paid* not.	You *did* not *pay*.
Cry not.	Don't *cry*.

The adjective

A103 In grammar *modify* means to add meaning to, to subtract meaning from, or to limit the meaning of a word.

[Unmodified:] dog

[Modified:] trained dog — Meaning has been added to the notion of dog.

[Unmodified:] hope

[Modified:] no hope — Meaning has been subtracted from the notion of hope.

[Unmodified:] men — This is a general notion, very indefinite.

[Modified:] two men — The notion has been somewhat limited, made somewhat more definite.

A104 An adjective is a word that modifies a noun or a pronoun.

That is *dangerous* fun.

Do you want to see something *strange*?

A105 An adjective can be distinguished from an adverb by this, that an adjective always modifies a noun or a pronoun, never a verb, an adjective, or an adverb.

---

[51] The emphatic form of the imperative is ordinarily used to persuade rather than to command.

A106 An adjective can be distinguished from a pronoun by this, that an adjective does not replace a noun but modifies it and accompanies it.

A107 In sentences like "The *good* die young," words ordinarily adjectives are sometimes said to be used as nouns or pronouns. They may be considered nouns, pronouns, or adjectives modifying an implied word like *people*.

DESCRIPTIVE AND LIMITING ADJECTIVES

A108 A descriptive adjective gives a word picture of (describes) the appearance or character or condition of the noun or pronoun it modifies.

> *green* apples   *young* thief   *sick* boy

A109 All the adjectives that are not descriptive adjectives are limiting adjectives.

A110 A limiting adjective modifies a noun or pronoun by narrowing down (limiting) or enlarging or multiplying the person or thing without describing it.

> *this* street   *five* boys
> *his* shirt   *triple* play
> *some* games   *second* trial
> *any* trick   *no* chance

A111 The limiting adjectives fall into these classifications: possessive, demonstrative, relative, interrogative, indefinite, and numeral (cardinal and ordinal) adjectives; and the articles (definite and indefinite).[52]

A112 The possessive, demonstrative, relative, interrogative, indefinite, and numeral adjectives are also called pronominal adjectives because they are part pronoun: they not only modify nouns and pronouns but take the place of other nouns and pronouns.

---

[52] Some grammarians of great authority speak of the *self*-adjectives in such sentences as "He himself spoke" and "He did it himself." Others consider these intensive pronouns. This book follows the latter.

POSSESSIVE ADJECTIVES

A113 The possessive adjectives are so called because they show ownership. They are part pronoun. These are the possessive adjectives:

First person		*Second person*	*Third person*	
Singular	*Plural*	*Singular and plural*	*Singular*	*Plural*
my	our	your	his	
			her	their
			its	

Here is *my* contribution.
Here is *our* contribution.
Your make-up is so heavy you look like a fugitive from a circus.
Its name is the Horror.
Their name is well known.

A114 Since the possessive adjectives are part pronoun they show person, number, and gender to agree with their antecedents as far as they can.

My plan is to train myself little by little to do without sleep altogether.	The first person is used because the antecedent is the speaker.[53]
As for Grace and me, *our* plan is to see Europe while there is something left of it.	*Our* is plural because the compound antecedent, *Grace and me,* is plural.
This stone has *its* story to tell to a man who can read it.	*Its* is neuter gender because the antecedent, *stone,* is neuter gender.

A115 Do not use the apostrophe with the possessive adjectives.

He spends ~~his~~ *his* holidays collecting and blowing eggs.

It's a friendly little beast. What's ~~it's~~ *its* name?

Is that ~~you're~~ *your* chignon?

---

[53] See A29.

A116   Do not use *there* or *they're* for *their.*

> *their*
> Isn't that ~~there~~ swimming pool?
>
> *Their*
> ~~They're~~ trouble is pride.

DEMONSTRATIVE ADJECTIVES

A117   The demonstrative adjectives are—

Singular	*Plural*
this	these
that	those

A118   The demonstrative adjectives are so called because they not only modify nouns (or, rarely, pronouns) but also specify them, point them out, or call attention to them.

> *These* people around us, I feel, are not friendly.
> No, *those* permits; not the ones in your hand.

A119   *This* and *these* ordinarily refer to what is present, near, just referred to, or about to be referred to; demonstrative *that* and *those,* to what is more remote in time or place.

> Look at *this* exhibit [referring to an exhibit near the speaker].
>
> Look at *that* new Chrysler [referring to an automobile passing in the street].
>
> People call me the Worm. *This* nickname would anger me if I did not reflect that they would call me worse if they knew me better.
>
> And now *this* proverb may interest you: God's help is nearer than the door.
>
> Centuries ago someone first said, "An argument cannot batter down a fact." *That* statement is still true.

A120   Do not use *them* as a demonstrative adjective.

> *those*
> Give me ~~them~~ taws that you borrowed from me.

A121   Do not say *this here* and *that there, these here* and *those there.*

> This ~~here~~ bed is not nearly so comfortable as that ~~there~~ one.

A122 Use *this* and *that* with singular nouns, *these* and *those* with plural nouns.

That makes
~~These~~ sort of people ~~make~~ me ill.

This is an
~~These~~ kind of word~~s~~ ~~are~~ adjective~~s~~.

This turns
~~These~~ make of automobile~~s~~ ~~burn~~ alcohol.

Those sorts of candy—peppermints and chocolates—make me ill.

These kinds of words are called adjectives and pronouns.

These makes of automobile—Daimler and Isotta—are foreign.

RELATIVE ADJECTIVES

A123 The relative adjectives are—

         which   whose[54]

A124 Relative adjectives are so called because they not only modify a noun (or, rarely, a pronoun) but also connect the dependent clause in which they stand with an antecedent in another clause.

The man *whose* window we broke just went into the police station.

We spent more than seven years in Juárez, in *which* city, by the way, we met Tracy.

A125 The relative adjectives are used with nouns of any gender and number.

A126 The relative adjective *which* seldom makes for pleasant reading. It is usually best to avoid it when you do not have to use it.

[Unpleasant:] I met a stranger in Miami, *which stranger* turned out to be a man with a Christlike attitude toward money.

[Better:] I met a stranger in Miami who turned out to be a man with a Christlike attitude toward money.

---

[54] The distinction between the relative pronouns *which* and *whose* and the relative adjectives *which* and *whose* is, of course, that the latter accompany and modify a noun.

INTERROGATIVE ADJECTIVES

A127 The interrogative adjectives are—

      whose   which   what

A128 The interrogative adjectives are so called because they not only modify a noun (or, rarely, a pronoun) but also ask questions.

Whose picture is that?

Vickie asked *which* show we intended to see.

What sort of technician is your friend?

A129 The interrogative adjectives are used with nouns of any gender and number.

What man would dare to think that he can plan better for himself than God has planned for him?

He stormed into my office and asked *which ladies* had taken his hat and coat for the rummage sale.

INDEFINITE ADJECTIVES

A130 Some common indefinite adjectives are—

Singular	Singular or plural	Plural
a, an[55]	all	both
another	any	few
each	no	many[56]
either	other	several
every	such	
neither	what	
	whatever	
	whatsoever	
	which	
	whichever	

---

[55] *A, an* are indefinite adjectives; but they may also be called indefinite articles.
[56] In the expression *many a* ("Many a boy has been a hero"), *many* may most conveniently be considered an adverb modifying *a.*

A131 The indefinite adjectives are so called because they modify nouns (or, rarely, pronouns) but do so by limiting the nouns somewhat vaguely, saying indefinitely which one, how many, or how much.

Let me have *another* chance.

Any kind of yacht will do.

Both eyes are blue, of course.

No one has ever seen the *other* sisters.

Someone should have told the general *what* password was being used that night.

Slice it in any way *whatsoever*, it's still cold pheasant.

Whichever road you take, you will be lonely as long as you run from Christ.

NUMERAL ADJECTIVES

A132 A numeral adjective limits a noun by stating its number.

A133 The cardinal numeral adjectives give the amount, tell how many. They are *one, two, three,* and so on.

I have *six* dollars.

A134 The ordinal numeral adjectives give the rank or place in an order or line-up.

Franklin, by carefully concealing his brilliance, managed to rank *twenty-ninth* in a class of thirty.

By the *sixth* day we were getting a little weary of pork chops.

If you sail from New York on the *fifth,* you should dock at Southampton on the *eleventh.*

The archers, under Henry V, overwhelmed the French.

ARTICLES

A135 The articles are limiting adjectives. *The* might be called a definite adjective, somewhat akin to demonstrative *this* and *that,* since it tends to specify or point out the noun it modifies. *A* and *an* can be grouped with the indefinite adjectives, since they specify very vaguely.

43

A136 Today it is common always to use *a* before a word beginning with a consonant sound, *an* before a word beginning
with a vowel sound.

a drugstore   an apple
a hawk   an hour [sound of *o (ou)*]
a union [sound of *y*]
a one [sound of *w*]

The adverb

A137 An adverb is a word that modifies a verb, an adjective,
or another adverb.[57]

Ferdinand growls *fiercely.*

A *very* high wall surrounded the place.

Jeanne was *not* entirely surprised.

A138 Whether a word is an adverb or not depends upon the
work it does. Thus not every word that ends in *ly* is an
adverb, nor must every adverb end in *ly; lovely* is an adjective, for instance, and *slow* may be an adverb. Again,
a word ordinarily used as an adverb may sometimes be
used as an adjective or a noun.

Here [adverb] is the man who rules baseball.
The cloister runs to *here* [noun].

A139 An adverb adds affirmation, negation, degree, manner,
time, place, doubt, conclusion, and so on, to the word that
it modifies.

[Affirmation:] yes, surely, certainly, indeed
[Negation:] no, not, hardly, scarcely, never
[Degree:] almost, barely, hardly, scarcely, completely, entirely,
merely, only, partially, mainly, little, much, more, less, very
[Manner:] well, fast, slowly, lazily, busily, badly
[Time:] now, yesterday, immediately, always, recently, daily

---

[57] For the meaning of *modify*, see A103.

[Place:] here, there, within, behind, everywhere

[Doubt:] maybe, perhaps, possibly, probably

[Conclusion:] consequently, therefore, hence, wherefore [but these words are usually conjunctive adverbs][58]

A140 Some adverbs have two forms, one like the adjective and the other in *ly;* for example, *slow, slowly; sharp, sharply; cheap, cheaply.* You may use the briefer form where it does not sound awkward, usually in imperative sentences.

Drive *slow.*

Look *sharp!*

Slowly the marquis mounted the guillotine.

Scrooge looked *sharply* at Marley's ghost.

A141 An adverbial noun is a word that both names a person, place, or thing and also modifies a verb, an adjective, or an adverb.

Ronald went *home.*

Eileen is fourteen *years* old.

Our tunnel is six *feet* high.

The preposition

A142 A preposition is a word that has a noun or pronoun as its object and forms with that object one modifying unit (called a phrase).

The vertical lines *in* newspapers are called column rules.	*In* has an object, *newspapers,* and together with *newspapers* makes one adjective phrase modifying *lines.*
He left *with* me.	*With* has an object, *me,* and together with *me* makes one adverb phrase modifying *left.*

[58] See A154-55.

A143 A preposition always takes an object. That object is always a noun or pronoun and should always be put in the objective case.

Did you send for *him* and *me?*

No one wants to *drive* [infinitive, verb-noun].

This came from *underneath the stage* [noun phrase].

A144 Some of the more common prepositions are—

about	besides	notwithstanding	through
above	between	of	throughout
across	beyond	off	till
after	but [except]	on	to
against	by	out	touching
along	concerning	outside	toward
among	considering	over	towards
around	despite	past	under
at	down	pending	underneath
barring	during	regarding	until
before	except	respecting	up
behind	in	round	upon
below	inside	save	with
beneath	into	saving	within
beside	like	since	without

A145 Some words are called participial prepositions because they are participles given a prepositional use but keeping the *ing* form. Some common participial prepositions are *concerning, including, notwithstanding, pending.*[59]

I should like to talk to you *concerning* your passport.

Everyone, *including* the captain, thought the ship had sailed.

We shall have to proceed *notwithstanding* your objections.

Why don't you write your memoirs, *pending* your release from the penitentiary?

A146 As a rough test to determine whether you are dealing with a participial preposition or a verbal, substitute *about* for *concerning; with* for *including; in spite of* for *notwithstanding;* and *until* for *pending.* If the sentence makes

---

[59] See A146.

46

sense after the substitution, the chances are good that you have a participial preposition.

We shall have to proceed *notwithstanding* your objections.	Substitute *in spite of* for *notwithstanding* and the sentence makes good sense. *Notwithstanding* is here a participial preposition.
I am afraid, sir, that we shall have to proceed, your objections *notwithstanding*.	Substitute *in spite of*. The substitution makes nonsense of the end of the sentence. *Notwithstanding* is not a participial preposition here.

A147 Some prepositions are called compound because they are made up of more than one word. Such, for example, are *because of, on account of, along with, together with, in spite of, in order to, with a view to*.[60]

The conjunction

A148 A conjunction is a word or group of words whose main purpose is to connect sentence parts, sentences, and paragraphs. It does not take an object.

Joseph *and* I are the pleasantest people!

The rest, I'm afraid, is up to you. *For* you will be alone, quite alone, with no one to turn to.

At length it was decided to strike for Kotuk afoot. ¶ *But* that decision turned out to be a mistake and a bad one.

A149 A conjunction may be distinguished from a preposition by this, that the conjunction does not govern an object.

Go in *before* me.	*Me* is the object of *before*. *Before* is a preposition.
Go in *before* I do.	*Before* has no object. It is a conjunction here.

---

[60] It is equally common, however, to treat *on account, in spite, in order,* and *with a view* as preposition and object followed by another phrase.

A150 A co-ordinating conjunction connects paragraphs or sentences or sentence parts that are of the same order or rank: two subject nouns, two predicate verbs, two adjective modifiers, two independent clauses, two dependent clauses, and so on.

A151 The common simple co-ordinating conjunctions are—

and	but not	neither	or
but	for	nor	

Raphael *and* Michael were originally Jewish names.	*And* connects the two subject nouns.
It should rain, *for* the wind has shifted to the south.	*For* connects the two independent clauses.
They do not toil, *neither* do they spin.	*Neither* connects the two independent clauses.
The explanation was not that Austin was cold *but* that he was bashful.	*But* connects the two dependent clauses.

A152 The correlative co-ordinating conjunctions are so called because they are used in split pairs. The common correlatives are—

both . . . and	neither . . . nor
either . . . or	not only . . . but (also)
if [in the sense of *whether*] . . . or	whether . . . or

Both the children *and* the adults of the tribe are adept in the use of the blowgun.

Not only did we lose the supplies, *but* our guide came down with cholera just beyond Mamba.

Either Carmichael is telling the truth, *or* we have been cruelly unjust to Williams.

It is difficult to decide *whether* to abandon the prisoners *or* to send them back with an inadequate guard.

A153 Use *neither . . . nor*, not *neither . . . or*.

Gilbert was neither strong ~~or~~ *nor* intelligent.

A154 Conjunctive adverbs are adverbs that have a tying-up force. The common ones are—

accordingly	furthermore	so
again	hence	still
also	however	then
besides	indeed	therefore
consequently	moreover	thereupon
finally	nevertheless	thus
further	nonetheless	yet

The job had to be done; *consequently,* the Marines did it.

Whirligig beetles can skitter fast across the surface of the water; *furthermore,* they can dive.

Verano likes flattery; *indeed,* he thrives on it.

Averil is not clever; *yet* he makes friends more easily and keeps them longer than I do.

A155 Do not confuse conjunctive adverbs with subordinating conjunctions[61] or relative adverbs.[62] Conjunctive adverbs are never used in dependent clauses unless some subordinating connective is also expressed or implied.[63]

Now you contradict yourself; *before,* you said that you could not possibly have overheard the accused.	Conjunctive adverb. Independent clause.
The experiment took place on the day *before* Mr. Kenna and his son disappeared.	Relative adverb. Dependent adjective clause.
We had left *before* you and Aleck arrived.	Subordinating conjunction. Dependent adverb clause.

A156 Subordinating conjunctions are those that connect sentence parts that are not of the same order or rank. Most importantly, they connect noun and adverb clauses with independent clauses or subordinate them to other dependent clauses.

---

[61] See A156.

[62] See A159.

[63] *So* is an exception. In very informal speech, *so* is sometimes used in place of the subordinating conjunction *so that.*

A157 The following subordinating conjunctions are commonly used to connect noun clauses with independent clauses or with other dependent clauses.

how	when
if [in the sense	where
of *whether*]	whether
that	why

I don't know *whether* Alfred has the popcorn concession.

Tell me *where* we can vote.

A strutting, apoplectic little man in a rusty black suit asked *why* the doors had been locked and *how* he was supposed to get home in time for dinner.

A158 The following subordinating conjunctions are commonly used to connect adverb clauses with independent clauses or with other dependent clauses.

after	if	till
although	in order that	unless
as	lest	until
as . . . as	now that	when
as if	provided (that)	whence
as though	since	whenever
because	so as (so . . . as)	where
before	so that (so . . . that)	wherever
even if	that	while
even though	though	whither

No one looked up *when* I tripped on the kneeler.

I feel a kinship with Achilles *because* he also had difficulty with a heel.

Everything was fine *until* the dog, excited by the jarring start of the train, barked once and attracted the attention of the conductor.

A159 Relative adverbs are a kind of subordinating conjunction. They are adverbs so used that they introduce a dependent (adjective) clause and at the same time refer to a noun or pronoun in another clause. Some common relative adverbs are—

after	since	whence	whither
before	when	where	why

50

I have been quite busy in the time *since* I committed my last murder.

This is the place *where* I always hide the bodies.

Holt told us the reason *why* the fan belt had broken.

The exclamatory word

A160 An exclamatory word is a word or group of words that expresses emotion but has no grammatical connection with the rest of the sentence.[64]

Ah! There's the sniveling little ape.

A161 Some common exclamatory words are—

ah   for heaven's sake   oh   oh my

A162 *O*, without *h*, is nowadays capitalized and used almost exclusively with nouns in direct address in rather formal and poetic contexts.

O Diana, these are your forests!

The dummy subject

A163 A dummy subject (expletive) is the word *it* or *there* used simply to indicate that the subject noun or pronoun is coming after the predicate verb or to avoid awkward constructions. It is a filler.

It is evident that your rifle needs cleaning.	*That your rifle needs cleaning* is the subject noun clause.
There will be a field Mass tomorrow.	*Mass* is the subject noun.
How many cats *there* are in Farrell's cabin!	*Cats* is the subject noun.
Was *it* very difficult to scrape the paint off?	*To scrape the paint off* is the subject noun phrase.

---

[64] Some grammars call both exclamatory words and dummy subjects "expletives."

A164 It is easy to distinguish dummy-subject *it* from personal-pronoun *it* or impersonal *it*, for the latter two are the subject pronouns of their predicate verbs.

I received your letter. *It* disappointed me.	Personal-pronoun *it*, subject pronoun of *disappointed*.
It snowed heavily.	Impersonal *it*, subject pronoun of *snowed*.
It is weak to lie.	Dummy-subject *it: to lie* is subject noun of *is*.

The gerund

A165 A gerund is a verb-noun in *ing*.[65] It names an action.

The pleasure of *waiting* is all yours.
Smoking is not permitted here.
To begin *sending*, flick this switch and set this dial.
My husband devotes a great deal of time to *bowling*.

A166 Because a gerund is part verb, it has active and passive voice and some tenses.[65]

A167 Because a gerund is part verb, it may have a subject noun or pronoun.

We can count on *several objecting* to our motion.
Hal's coming home was a surprise.

A168 Because a gerund is part verb, it may take a direct or indirect object or a complement.

There is no question of his *having given me help*.	*Me* is indirect object, *help* direct object, of *having given*.
I had no suspicion at all of your *being Superman*.	*Superman* is predicate noun after *being*.

A169 Because a gerund is part verb, it may be modified by an adverb.

God gave Fritzl the equipment for *talking loudly*.

---

[65] For the various forms of the gerund, see pages 19, 22, and 23.

A170 Because a gerund is part noun, it may do what a noun ordinarily does in a sentence: be subject noun, object, or complement, and take an adjective modifier.

> The Nazi breakthrough depended on careful *planning*.

> *Planning* is the object of *on* and is modified by the adjective *careful*.

The participle

A171 A participle is a verb-adjective.[66]

> Carlson, *returning*, bolted the door.
> A *roaring* wind tumbled down the valley.

PARTICIPLES AS PART OF PREDICATE VERBS

A172 When the participle is used to produce changes of voice, mood, and tense in predicate verbs, it loses almost all of its adjective force and should be considered simply part of the predicate verb.[67]

A173 Occasionally it is difficult to know whether the participle is being used with adjective force or merely as part of the predicate verb. In such cases only the writer's intention or the context can decide.

> Florence was surprised.

PARTICIPLES OUTSIDE PREDICATE VERBS

A174 Because a participle is part verb, it has active and passive voice and some tenses.[68]

---

[66] For the various forms of the participle, see pages 18, 21, and 23.
[67] See, for example, A77.
[68] See footnote 66, above.

A175 Because a participle is part verb, it may take a direct or indirect object or a complement.

There sat Siegel *selling Itzy* the eight *beatitudes*.	*Itzy* is indirect object, *beatitudes* direct object, of *selling*.
Fleetwood, *feeling embarrassed*, cleared his throat.	*Embarrassed* is predicate adjective after *feeling*.

A176 Because a participle is part verb, it may be modified by an adverb.

Rising slowly, the old man put out a hand to accept the paper.
Gaulbert, *much distressed*, made an ineffectual little gesture.

A177 Because a participle is part adjective, it may modify a noun or a pronoun, be a predicate complement, or take an adverb modifier.

Grover says that the principal is not *quite satisfied*.	*Satisfied*, as predicate adjective, completes *is* and modifies *principal*. The adverb *quite* modifies *satisfied*.
The others, *highly dissatisfied with the result*, stalked off the field, bad losers.	*Dissatisfied* modifies *others* and is modified by the adverb *highly* and the adverb phrase *with the result*.

The infinitive

A178 An infinitive is a verb-noun, often introduced by *to*, that has *ing* only in the progressive form. It names an action.

It is too late to *run*.

INFINITIVES AS PART OF PREDICATE VERBS

A179 When the objective of the infinitive without *to* is used to produce changes of meaning in predicate verbs (like *go* in *I may go*), it loses almost all of its noun force and should be considered part of the predicate verb.[69]

---

[69] See, for example, A76.

INFINITIVES OUTSIDE PREDICATE VERBS

A180 Because an infinitive is part verb, it has active and passive voice and some tenses.[70]

A181 Because an infinitive is part verb, it may have a subject noun or pronoun (in the objective case).[71]

We considered *him to be* negligible.

A182 Because an infinitive is part verb, it may take a direct or indirect object or a complement.

If you want *to give yourself* a *fright*, look down.	*Yourself* is indirect object, *fright* direct object, of *give*.
It was thought *to be he*.	*He* is predicate noun after *be*.

A183 Because an infinitive is part verb, it may be modified by an adverb.

It had better *be done quickly*.

A184 Because an infinitive is part noun, it can be used as subject noun (rarely), object, or complement (rarely); (it cannot, however, take an adjective modifier).[72]

B The sentence

Definition

B1 A sentence is a word or group of words that expresses a complete statement, question, or command (plea, and so on).

Garry says yes but means no.
Did you find Halsted Street?
Give me back my bubble gum.

---

[70] For the various forms of the infinitive, see pages 18-19, 22, and 23.
[71] See C224.
[72] What is said here refers only to the infinitive itself and not to an infinitive phrase, for which see C394-96.

B2 An elliptical sentence is a sentence from which words have been omitted that can be *easily and naturally* supplied by the reader or listener.

Meeting tonight at eight-fifteen.
A smart boy!
Anybody home?
Happy birthday!
[In answer to a question:] Three o'clock.
[In answer to a question:] No.
O to be in England, now that April's there!

B3 Do not use elliptical sentences often. When you doubt whether you have written an elliptical sentence or merely a half-sentence, substitute a complete one.

Sentence sense

B4 A half-sentence is a word or group of words that does not express a complete statement, question, or command.[1] It does not contain an independent subject and predicate either expressed or easily and naturally supplied by the reader or listener.

You mean that you have not read the famous Father Brown detective stories? Father Brown, a jovial, keen-witted little priest, being one of the great fictional detectives, much beloved not only by readers but by writers of mysteries.

A nominative absolute poses as a complete sentence.

Damon Runyon made himself a national reputation as a newspaperman. Before writing the now-famous stories of the bandits of Broadway and adding many a word to the American language.

A prepositional phrase poses as a complete sentence.

---

[1] The half-sentence is also known as the incomplete sentence, the sentence fragment, the no-sentence, and the period-fault sentence.

Although he was born in the humblest surroundings and reared almost without schooling, Mark Twain lived to achieve world-wide fame. To be honored by generations of men, many of whom never noted his pessimism.

An infinitive phrase poses as a complete sentence.

From boyhood Howard Pyle was captivated by the daredevil spirit of pirates. Being able, moreover, to express his dreams with the pen.

A participial phrase poses as a complete sentence.

I found Mr. Canterbury at work in his place at the very end of Fordham Road. A peculiar establishment, uncluttered by anything but Mr. Canterbury and a telephone.

An appositive poses as a complete sentence.

Treason and loyalty, mystery and adventure, tragedy and comedy—all play their part in making *Ivanhoe* a romantic book. Which should be read by everyone.

An adjective clause poses as a complete sentence.

The Nigger of the Narcissus is one of the greatest sea stories ever written. Because Conrad, the author, put into this novel all his love and understanding of ships, seamen, the winds, and the great sea.

An adverbial clause poses as a complete sentence.

He claims that there are dramatic stories behind the invention of the streamlined train, the radio, the typewriter. That an interesting story lies behind every invention in the world.

A noun clause poses as a complete sentence.

B5 Write only sentences; do not write half-sentences.

B6 A common way of correcting a half-sentence is to expand to completion the phrase or clause that poses as a sentence. Another good way is to change the punctuation and capitalization.

It is a

Jamieson is proud of his new car. ⋏ bright red roadster.

for

I am ordering tomato plants⟍ Fʳˣ the children's garden.

You should meet him.

Mertz is a great golfer. ~~Whom you should meet~~

B7 A runover is a sentence that runs over into the next sentence, being stopped only by a comma or by no punctuation at all.[2]

He enjoyed reading *Captain Blood,* it is a book of adventure.

B8 Do not write runovers.

B9 Correct runovers by putting a period and a capital between the sentences.

. It

He enjoyed reading *Captain Blood*⟍ ⋏ is a book of adventure.

B10 Correct runovers by inserting a semicolon, if there is sufficient unity in the thought.

;

He enjoyed reading *Captain Blood*⟍ it is a book of adventure.

B11 Correct runovers by inserting *and, or, nor, but,* or *for* and preceding it with the proper punctuation.[3]

for

He enjoyed reading *Captain Blood,*⋏it is a book of adventure.

---

[2] The runover is also known as the run-together or run-on sentence or the comma-splice sentence.

[3] Use a comma before *and, or, nor, but,* and *for* when they join independent clauses of a compound sentence. Use a semicolon rather than a comma if either clause is long, say three or four lines, or if either clause contains punctuation. And use a semicolon rather than a comma if *and, or, nor, but,* or *for* is not present (D30-32). (Do not mistake an inverted *that* clause for a runover. See D33.)

B12 Correct runovers by subordinating the less important idea, when this can reasonably be done.

which

He enjoyed reading *Captain Blood*, ~~it~~ is a book of adventure.

Sentences according to use

B13 According to use, sentences are classified as declarative, interrogative, imperative, and exclamatory.

B14 A declarative sentence makes a statement.

The noises began at midnight.

Charles asked when the noises began.

"When did the noises begin?" asked Charles.

"The man is dangerous!" cried Evanston with what seemed to be genuine alarm; and, I must admit, I was inclined to agree.

"Go at once," said Emily, quietly but with unmistakable determination; so Charles went—at once.

B15 An interrogative sentence asks a direct question.[4]

When did the noises begin?

Now that I come to think of it, why would anyone wish to fish the snapper banks at a season when the snappers will not bite?

B16 An imperative sentence in general gives a command. The command may be an entreaty, a warning, a prohibition, and so on.

Stop.

Come.

Save me!

Please come!

Proceed at your own risk.

Thou shalt not kill.

You shall not pass.

---

[4] A direct question is a question expressed in the words of the speaker; for example: "Where is the wampum?" An indirect question gives the sense of the speaker's question without quoting him; for example: "He asked where the wampum was." An indirect question does not make an interrogative sentence, since it involves rather a statement about a question than the mere question itself.

B17   An exclamatory sentence expresses a sudden or strong emotion.

Mother!

Patriots, arise!

Must I see this!

Yes! Essex still rebels!

[But declarative:] "Oh, no!" he shouted; and, jumping into the command car, pulled away at top speed from under the startled noses of the border guard.

Sentences according to structure

B18   According to structure, sentences are classified as simple, compound, complex, and compound-complex.

B19   A simple sentence is a sentence that has only one subject and one predicate.

Witchmen howled.

Herman Melville published *Moby Dick,* his greatest and best-known novel, in 1851.

Starvation affects a man's mind as well as his body.

It was a peculiar place of business, uncluttered by furniture, files, secretaries, or anything but Mr. Canterbury and a telephone.

B20   The subject of a simple sentence may be a noun or any noun substitute except a clause.

Frogs [noun] croak.
They [pronoun] croak.
To croak dismally [noun phrase] is natural to frogs.

B21   The subject of a simple sentence may be simple or compound. The predicate of a simple sentence may be simple or compound.[5]

Chieftains pranced.
Witchmen and chieftains howled.
Witchmen pranced and howled.
Witchmen and chieftains pranced and howled.

_____
[5] See C4 and C6.

B22 A compound sentence is a sentence made up of two or more independent clauses properly connected.[6]

The cougar looked down, and I shot him.	Independent clause: *The cougar looked down.* Independent clause: *and I shot him.*
The cougar looked down; I shot him.	Independent clause: *The cougar looked down.* Independent clause: *I shot him.*

B23 A complex sentence is a sentence made up of one independent clause and one or more dependent clauses.[7]

When the cougar looked down, I shot him.	Independent clause: *I shot him.* Dependent clause: *when the cougar looked down.*
I shot the cougar as he looked down and before he was aware of the child.	Independent clause: *I shot the cougar.* First dependent clause: *as he looked down.* Second dependent clause: *and before he was aware of the child.*

B24 It is sometimes difficult to explain the independent clause in complex sentences that have a noun clause as subject, complement, or object. Looked at one way, such a noun clause is the subject, complement, or object in the independent clause. Looked at another way, it is a distinct dependent clause; and the sentence is complex.

What you are going to say to my proposal interests me.	*What you are going to say to my proposal* is the subject noun (clause) of *interests.*
It should be clear that a boy will either associate with Catholic girls or never marry a Catholic girl.	*That a boy will either associate with Catholic girls or never marry a Catholic girl* is, of course, the subject noun (clause) of *should be.*

---

[6] For independent clauses see C400-401. For proper connection of the clauses of compound sentences, see D30-32.

[7] For independent and dependent clauses, see C400-405.

B25 A compound-complex sentence is a sentence that contains two or more independent, and one or more dependent, clauses.[8]

Magellan was killed in the Philippines; nevertheless, his companions, eager to prove that the world is round, continued their westward journey until their ships at length cast anchor off the coast of Spain.	Independent 1: *Magellan was killed in the Philippines.* Independent 2: *nevertheless, his companions, eager to prove . . . continued their westward journey.* Dependent 1: *that the world is round.* Dependent 2: *until their ships at length cast anchor off the coast of Spain.*

C Syntax

Subjects and predicates

C1 The subject is the part of a clause or sentence that is talked about. The predicate is the part of a clause or sentence that talks about the subject.[1]

	Subject | *Predicate*
Jim prays.	Jim | prays.
Were you waiting for me?	You | were waiting for me?
The man in the bowler hat was leaning against the lamppost, waiting for me.	The man in the bowler hat | was leaning against the lamppost, waiting for me.
Go!	[You] | go!

---

[8] For independent and dependent clauses, see C400-405.

[1] Many grammars call subject and predicate in this general sense *complete subject* and *complete predicate*. This series distinguishes between *subject* and *subject noun* or *pronoun* and between *predicate* and *predicate verb*. In one-word subjects and predicates, of course, *subject* and *subject noun* will coincide, as will *predicate* and *predicate verb*.

There is something strange about you tonight, Count Dracula.	Something strange | is about you tonight, Count Dracula.
Squatting on the sandy ground, his eyes looking off beyond us to the hills, the wrinkled old Indian took the drum between his knees and began to beat a hypnotic rhythm.	Squatting on the sandy ground, his eyes looking off beyond us to the hills, the wrinkled old Indian | took the drum between his knees and began to beat a hypnotic rhythm.

C2 The subject noun or pronoun is the noun or pronoun that the predicate talks about most directly.[2]

Subject noun | Predicate

Jim prays.	*Jim* | prays.
Marcia sneered.	*Marcia* | sneered.
Is the train waiting for me?	*train* | is waiting for me?
The man in the bowler hat was leaning against the lamppost, waiting for me.	*man* | was leaning against the lamppost, waiting for me.
Squatting on the sandy ground, his eyes looking off beyond us to the hills, the wrinkled old Indian took the drum between his knees.	*Indian* | took the drum between his knees.

C3 Do not insert immediately after a subject noun a subject pronoun meaning exactly the same thing.[3]

Jules ~~he~~ wants to be a chemical engineer.
Willa Cather and Edna Ferber ~~they~~ are American novelists.

---

[2] Many grammars call the subject noun or pronoun simply the *subject*.
[3] This does not affect those constructions in which a speaker is represented as mulling over names; for example, "Willa Cather and Edna Ferber—they were American novelists, weren't they?"

C4 A compound subject is a subject that has only one predicate but contains two or more subject nouns.

Johnson and *Powers* disappeared.
Men, women, and *children* fainted.

C5 The predicate verb is the verb (not verbal) in the predicate.[4]

	Subject noun | *Predicate verb*
Jim prays.	Jim | *prays*
Marcia sneered.	Marcia | *sneered*
Were you waiting for me?	you | *were waiting*
The man in the bowler hat was leaning against the lamppost, waiting for me.	man | *was leaning*
Squatting on the sandy ground, his eyes looking off beyond us to the hills, the wrinkled old Indian took the drum between his knees.	Indian | *took*

C6 A compound predicate is a predicate that has only one subject but contains two or more predicate verbs.

Johnson *bowed* and *disappeared.*
Johnson and Powers *bowed* and *disappeared.*
Men, women, and children *screamed, pointed,* and *fainted.*

VERB AGREEMENT IN GENERAL

C7 In general, make a predicate verb agree with its subject noun or pronoun in person and number.[5] (Practically speaking, this means: use the *s* or *es* form of the predicate verb only when the subject noun or pronoun is in the third person, singular number.)

John sing*s* like an excited bullfrog.
This machine crush*es* rock.

---

[4] Many grammars call the predicate verb simply the *predicate* or the *verb.*
[5] For the notion of person, see A21-23. For the notion of number, see A24-25.

My dog loves to swim.
This is hardtack.
Bucky goes on the air at four.
What does sanctifying grace do?
Paul has a live platypus.
Salt water has rusted the cooling system.

say
Everybody is to be inoculated, ~~says~~ the authorities.

Were
~~Was~~ you on Mertau's team?

Doesn't
~~Don't~~ he go to De Paul?

C8 Make predicate verbs agree with subject nouns or pronouns only. (In most noninterrogative sentences and clauses the subject comes before the verb. Some sentences, however, are inverted; and you will have to ask yourself, What am I really trying to say?)

An excellent athlete and a good
is
student ~~are~~ Jonathan.

You do not want to talk about an athlete and a student; you want to talk about Jonathan. *Jonathan* is the subject noun.

C9 Make the predicate verb agree with the real subject noun or pronoun after the dummy subject *there.*[6] (But see C36.)

There is only one glass.

are
There ~~is~~ others besides you.

There are more than two confessors available before Mass.

C10 Make the predicate verb agree with the subject noun or pronoun and not with words in apposition.

order
I, your commanding officer, ~~orders~~ this retreat.

has
The doubles team, Ogden and McCarthy, ~~have~~ not won a set.

---

[6] For the notion of dummy subjects, see A163. For sentences like "There *is* more than one way to skin a cat" and "There *are* more than two ways to skin a cat," see C19.

C11 Make the predicate verb agree with the subject noun or pronoun and not with words introduced by *with, along with, including, as well as, no less than, of,* and so on.

I, together with my dog, ~~has~~ *have* hunted these woods for five years.

Joe, as well as I, ~~have~~ *has* stayed up, getting the annual ready for the printer's deadline.

Bad health, along with many years, ~~have~~ *has* weakened poor Featherstonhaugh.

The light on the new Raleigh bicycles ~~have~~ *has* a generator.

C12 The number and person of a relative pronoun depend upon its antecedent. Make sure that you have the right antecedent, according to the sense of the sentence, before you make the predicate verb agree with a relative-pronoun subject.

Pasteur was one of those men who ~~is~~ *are* not easily discouraged.

Pasteur was the only one of those men who ~~were~~ *was* not easily discouraged.

The only one of his stories that ~~were~~ *was* amusing was a tale of three men locked in an elevator.

One of the people who ~~was~~ *were* present was a Don Q.

The number of members, which runs [*or* who run] into the thousands, surprised me.

The number of members ~~which was~~ *who were* absent was truly deplorable.

C13 Always use a third-person singular predicate verb after dummy-subject or pronoun *it.*

It *is* fun swimming and sailing.
It *was* they; it *was* not I.
It *was* two hours before he returned.

C14 When a collective noun names a group acting as a unit, use a singular predicate verb with it.[7]

The committee ~~are~~ *is* angry.

The jury ~~have~~ *has* been out an hour and a half.

The congregation ~~sing~~ *sings* badly.

C15 When a collective noun names a group acting as individuals, use a plural predicate verb with it.[8]

The jury ~~has~~ *have* disagreed among themselves.

The crew ~~is~~ *are* not yet all in their places.

The senior class ~~was guest~~ *were guests* of the Stoneleighs.

C16 Use a singular predicate verb with the singular indefinite pronouns and adjectives.

Each of the thieves ~~were~~ *was* caught.

Everyone ~~are~~ *is* asked to be there.

Neither plan is worth anything.

Each wave and ripple ~~sparkle~~ *sparkles*.

C17 Use a plural predicate verb with expressions like *the rest, a part, half, two thirds, all, any, none,* and *some* when they indicate how many, and a singular predicate verb when they indicate how much.

Half of the exercises *were burned* by the janitor.
Half of the exercise *was burned* by the janitor.

---

[7] There are times when it is difficult to decide whether in a given sentence a collective noun names a group acting as a unit. In your own writing, decide in such borderline cases what you would like to say and use a singular or plural verb accordingly.

[8] (See footnote 7, just above.) Often it is better to change the sentence than to admit such awkward expressions as this: "The class are sitting each in a different seat." Say rather something like this: "Each member of the class is sitting in a different seat."

The rest of the books *are* trash.
The rest of the book *is* trash.

Part of the horses *were shipped* to Miami.
Part of the horse *was shipped* to the glue factory.

C18 Use a plural predicate verb with *a number* (meaning several, quite a few), but a singular predicate verb with *the number*.

have
A number of people ~~has~~ asked us for the recipe.

has
The number of people ~~have~~ increased greatly.

C19 If a noun or pronoun following *more than* is singular, use a singular predicate verb. If it is plural, use a singular predicate verb if it indicates how much, a plural predicate verb if it indicates how many.

There *is* more than one way to skin a cat.
There *are* more than two ways to skin a cat.
There *is* more than two gallons in the tank.
There *are* more than ten one-dollar bills on the counter.

C20 Use a plural predicate verb when adjectives connected by *and* so modify a subject noun or pronoun as to show that it means more than one thing.

are
Both good and bad butter ~~is~~ sold here.

have
The chocolate and the pound cake ~~has~~ been won.

C21 Use a singular predicate verb with words that are plural in form but singular in meaning.[9]

was
The gallows ~~were~~ erected beside the road.

is
Measles ~~are~~ catching.

was
The news ~~were~~ good.

was
Physics ~~were~~ my easiest subject.

---

[9] See C22-25.

C22 Ordinarily use a singular predicate verb with the names of sciences like *mathematics, physics,* and *economics.*

Mathematics *is* my downfall.
Physics *is* the study of matter and motion.
Economics *is required* in third year.

C23 Ordinarily use a plural predicate verb with the names of practical affairs like *politics* and *athletics.*

Athletics *are* much *fostered* at North High.
Politics *play* havoc with a policy based on principle.
Gymnastics *have been* highly *developed* by some nations.
Foreign affairs *are* much *debated* in the Senate.

C24 In sentences where the notion of one thing is emphasized, use a singular predicate verb even with words like *politics* and *athletics.*[10]

Politics *has become* a complicated study.
Athletics *wastes* too much of a student's time.
Foreign affairs *offers* real opportunity for a fascinating career.

C25 When doubt arises about the use of words such as those described in C21-24, consult the dictionary.

C26 Use a singular predicate verb with plural nouns that are felt to express a single unit.[11]

Four gallons ~~aren't~~ *isn't* much gas.

Ten miles ~~are~~ *is* too far on worn-out tires.

There ~~were~~ *was* five hundred dollars in his pocket.

C27 Use a singular predicate verb with a word that is discussed as a word.

They is a pronoun.
Lilacs has a very pleasant sound.

---

[10] See C25.

[11] Occasionally—but not always—the predicate complement will indicate that the plural subject noun is expressing a single unit. In some sentences, however, the singular or plural predicate verb is a matter of writer's choice; for example, "Clothes absorb [or absorbs] too much of a girl's thinking and planning."

69

C28 Use a singular predicate verb with plural titles and plural proper names used to designate one person or one thing.

has
The United States ~~have~~ great responsibilities.

is
The Fishermen ~~are~~ an interesting book.

has
The *Times* ~~have~~ a full sports coverage.

has
Shelley, Shark, and Shumack [one business firm] ~~have~~ gone into bankruptcy.

Twin Oaks *is* a ramshackle house at the bend of the river.

VERB AGREEMENT WITH COMPOUND SUBJECTS

C29 Ordinarily use a plural predicate verb with a compound subject.

have
Johnson and Powers ~~has~~ disappeared.

were
The water polo and the diving contest ~~was~~ called off.

Three sandwiches and a quart of milk *are* waiting for you.

C30 When a compound subject has affirmative and negative parts, make the predicate verb agree in person and number with the affirmative.[12]

am
I, not you, ~~are~~ deciding.

are
You, not I, ~~am~~ deciding.

are
Terry and Bill, hardly Kenneth, ~~is~~ to be relied on.

C31 When awkwardness results from carrying out C30, rewrite the sentence.

I am deciding, not you.
You are deciding, not I.
Terry and Bill are to be relied on. Kenneth seems less trustworthy.

---

[12] See C31.

C32 When the parts of a compound subject are connected by *or, either . . . or, not only . . . but also, neither . . . nor,* and other disjunctives, make the predicate verb agree in person and number with the nearer part.[13]

am
Either they or I ~~are~~ to go.

was
Not only you but also Jim ~~were~~ mistaken.

C33 When awkwardness arises from carrying out C32, rewrite the sentence.

If they don't go, then I must.
You were not the only one who was mistaken; Jim was too.

C34 When the parts of a compound subject represent one person or thing, or are felt to make up one collective idea, use a singular predicate verb.

plays
My friend and neighbor, Kittredge, ~~play~~ the flute.

was
A coach and four ~~were~~ rattling down the King's Road.

is
The hop, skip, and jump ~~are~~ no longer a common event at track meets.

Rioting and violence often leads [*or* lead] to tyranny.

He was of the old school, and maintained that a blackboard and a switch was [*or* were] all that any teacher needed to turn dullards into scholars.

[Singular verb would be incorrect:] A destroyer and a cruiser were standing by.

C35 When each of the singular parts of a compound subject is considered separately, make the predicate verb agree with the nearest. (To decide whether or not you have such a case, mentally insert *or* before the last part. If *or* makes

---

[13] See C35. Disjunctives are conjunctions that separate, or offer a choice between, the words that they connect. They connect in one way, because they show that words go together as subject nouns or objects and so on; but they also separate, offer a choice between, or break into units, the meanings of those same words. Naturally, therefore, they affect predicate-verb agreement.

sense in the sentence, each part of the subject is being considered separately. If it does not, then they are being taken together.)

A shred of a tune, a face vaguely familiar, the *odor* of a hallway *unleashes* a flood of memory to sicken or delight us.

A shred of a tune, a face vaguely familiar, *or* the odor of a hallway *unleashes* a flood of memory to sicken or delight us.

Or makes good sense here.

A pitcher, a catcher, a batter, *or* a fielder-baseman *is* all one needs to play a simple form of baseball.

Or makes nonsense of this sentence. Change *is* to *are.*

C36 When several words (at least four) separate the subject nouns or pronouns of a compound subject, the predicate verb after dummy subject *there* may agree with the nearer subject noun or pronoun.

There *was* a plain, unpainted wooden *table* in a corner of the kitchen under the window and, near the stove, two ancient and scabrous wicker *chairs* of doubtful comfort and uncertain strength.

A good many words intervene between *table* and *chairs.*

C37 When a whole compound subject is modified by *each* or *every,* use a singular predicate verb.

Each man, woman, and child ~~have~~ *has* received some sort of souvenir to take home with ~~them~~ *him.*

Every officer and member ~~were~~ *was* there to answer to ~~their~~ *his* name at the roll call.

Each back, *each* lineman, and *each* coach ~~were~~ *was* quizzed before the ruling was changed.

Verb use

HELPING VERBS IN GENERAL

C38 Helping verbs are verbs that are used together with other verbs to express changes of thought such as voice, mood, tense, and other shades of meaning. The principal helping verbs are—

be	must
can *and* could	ought
do	shall *and* will
have	should *and* would[14]
may *and* might	

C39 Helping verbs together with the verb they help, form **one** predicate verb—even when the helpers are separated **from** the rest of the verb.

Poison was mentioned.	One predicate verb: *was mentioned.*
The three tethered horses must have been frightened.	One predicate verb: *must have been frightened.*
Did he call?	One predicate verb: *did call.*
Isn't all this mournful talk depressing you?	One predicate verb: *is depressing.*
Copperheads have often been seen in this swamp.	One predicate verb: *have been seen.*
May I—excuse this interruption—make a remark?	One predicate verb, exclusive of the clause between dashes: *may make.*
This code has twice been completely lost.	One predicate verb: *has been lost.*
Should not Del have been more quickly alerted?	One predicate verb: *should have been alerted.*

---

[14] *Should* and *would* are sometimes called past-tense forms of *shall* and *will*. But they are used to express a great deal more than mere past time. The same is true of *might* and *could*, called past-tense forms of *may* and *can*.

C40 Do not separate parts of the predicate verb when awkwardness results.

[Awkward:] They referred to the speech which the president *had* late this past summer *delivered.*

[Better:] They referred to the speech which the president *had delivered* late this past summer.

C41 Do not use the past indicative active but the past participle with helping verbs.

The ink had ~~ran~~ *run* down the length of the paper.

Snow had ~~fell~~ *fallen* all night.

I had never before *swum* so far.

HELPING VERB *be*

C42 Helping verb *be* is used to make up its own progressive form[15] and the progressive form of other verbs.[16]

C43 The progressive form of a verb presents the action not merely as something that happens, but as something that continues to happen or that progresses.

[Regular form:] She *sews.*
[Progressive form:] She *is sewing.*

C44 The progressive form of the present tense of verbs is commonly used as a substitute for the future tense.

[Future:] I *will return* tomorrow.
[Progressive present:] I *am returning* tomorrow.

C45 The progressive present of the verb *go* is commonly used as a substitute for the future tense.

[Future:] You *will regret* this.
[Progressive present of *go:*] You *are going* to regret this.

[Future:] I *will go.*
[Progressive present of *go:*] I *am going* to go.

---

[15] See A65.
[16] See A63.

C46 The progressive form of the present tense active is used to avoid awkwardness or archaic formality in asking direct questions.

[Regular form, to be avoided:] *Swim* you with us today?
[Progressive form:] *Are* you *swimming* with us today?

C47 The progressive form of the past tense active of *go* is sometimes used to express supposition, expectation, intention, or purpose.

Hilton *was going* with us, but at the last moment he found that he could not go.

I thought Reinke *was going* to scream.

C48 Helping verb *be* is used to form the passive voice.[17]

C49 Helping verb *be*, followed by an infinitive with *to*, is used to express futurity, obligation, expectation, supposition, or an indirect command.

[Futurity:] I *am to be* queen of the May.

[Obligation:] We *are to obey* God in all things.

[Expectation:] A department store *is to be built* on the site of the finest old theater that this section of the country possessed.

[Supposition:] You are basing your investment on the guess that there *is to be* a new market for automobile cranks.

[Indirect command:] You *are* all *to be* up and dressed by four-thirty tomorrow morning.

HELPING VERB *do*

C50 Helping verb *do* is used to make up its own emphatic form and the emphatic form of other verbs.[18]

C51 The emphatic form of a verb lends insistence or emphasis to what the verb asserts.[19]

[Regular form:] I *finished* my homework.
[Emphatic form:] I *did finish* my homework.

---

[17] See pages 19-22 and A93.
[18] See A101-2.
[19] In old verse and in some modern verse, helping verb *do* is often used with no note of emphasis simply for rhythm or sound.

C52 Helping verb *do* is used with the present and past active to avoid awkwardness or archaic formality when *not* is used with regular forms of *do*.

[Regular form, to be avoided:] I *did* not what I was told.
[With helping verb:] I *did* not *do* what I was told.

[Regular form, to be avoided:] Did she complain? No, she *complained* not.
[With helping verb:] Did she complain? No, she *didn't*.

C53 Helping verb *do* is used with the present and past active to avoid awkwardness or archaic formality when asking direct questions.

[Regular form, to be avoided:] *Play* you the saxophone?
[With helping verb:] *Do* you *play* the saxophone?

[Regular form, to be avoided:] *Heard* you Buster calling?
[With helping verb:] *Did* you *hear* Buster calling?

C54 Helping verb *do* is used in the imperative to express polite insistence.

Do sit down, Mr. Topeavy.

Do tell us, Father Smithers, whether we will have to associate with, well, all sorts of people in heaven.

Do have a fifth helping of the turkey, Alfred; we weren't really planning on serving it cold for supper this evening.

HELPING VERB *have*

C55 Helping verb *have* is used to form the present-perfect, the past-perfect, and the future-perfect (in short, the perfect) tenses.[20]

C56 Helping verb *have*, followed by an infinitive with *to*, is used to express obligation or necessity.

We *have to leave* everything just as we found it.

Ray, please try to understand that Eric *had to do* what he did.

If you *had had to earn* your money as a boy, you might now have more respect for other people's property.

---

[20] See A63, A77-79, A82-83, A86, A89, and A91.

C57 Do not use *of* for *have* or *'ve,* and do not insert an *of* after *had.*

have
You should ~~of~~ seen the crowd at Dinny's last night.

have
They ought to ~~of~~ gone to a vocational school.

would've
If Duke had ~~of~~ let go, the rest of us ~~would of~~ fallen.

HELPING VERB *must*

C58 Helping verb *must* has only one form for all tenses, persons, and numbers.

C59 Helping verb *must* is most commonly used to express obligation or necessity.

Someone *must stay* with Phineas until the doctor comes.

When you increase the pressure to that point, then something *must give* somewhere.

To win the jackpot you *must answer* at least four out of the five questions correctly.

C60 Since helping verb *must* has only one form, it is often wise to substitute another verb for it in order to avoid ambiguity or awkwardness.

[Ambiguous and awkward:] Ray, please try to understand that Eric *must have done* what he did.

[Better:] Ray, please try to understand that Eric *had to do* what he did.

C61 Helping verb *must* is used with the present-perfect infinitive (without *to*) of other verbs to express supposition or speculation.

Someone *must have broken* the news to my father before the report card arrived.

The window *must have been broken* by the storm.

Whoever it was *must have worn* gloves.

It *must have been* about three before the mailman finally brought it to the house.

HELPING VERB *ought*

C62 Helping verb *ought* has only one form for all tenses, persons, and numbers.

C63 Use the infinitive with *to* after *ought;* without *to* after *ought not.*

C64 Do not use *had ought.*

ought to have seen
You ~~had ought to see~~ the crowd at the puppet show.

ought not
You ~~hadn't ought to~~ be disrespectful.

C65 Helping verb *ought* expresses obligation, supposition, expectation, speculation, or fitness.

[Obligation:] You *ought to set* an example to your children.

[Supposition, expectation, speculation:] There *ought to be* another train in ten minutes.

[Fitness:] I *ought to have been told* of the family's plans.

HELPING VERBS *shall* AND *will*

C66 Helping verbs *shall* and *will* have only one form for all tenses, persons, and numbers.

C67 Helping verbs *shall* and *will* are used to form the future and the future-perfect tenses.[21]

C68 Use *shall* with the first person and *will* with the second and third to express simple futurity or expectation, a mere statement of fact.[22]

At this rate *I shall graduate* before Barney leaves second high.

If things happen as they usually do, *you will* someday *regret* your silly threat.

Tchaikovsky, the copyright owner, *will give* no trouble.

---

[21] See A63-64, A76, and A79.

[22] In the United States even the best writers frequently pay scant attention to this rule but rather tend to make *will* do *shall's* work as well as its own. You may ignore the rule too, unless your teacher directs otherwise.

C69 Use *will* with the first person and *shall* with the second and third to express intention, purpose, or determination on the part of the speaker.[23]

I will cut right through all this red tape.	Clearly determination, intention, or purpose.
You shall go where you're told!	Spoken in reprimand.
They shall not *pass.*	Spoken by a general rallying his troops against an enemy.
What kind of dinner *shall they give* us?	This indicates that we have control over the dinner.
What kind of dinner *will they give* us?	This indicates that we do not have control over the dinner but are merely asking what the menu will be.

C70 In questions, always use *shall* with the first person; use *shall* with the second and third person if *shall* is expected in the answer, but use *will* if *will* is expected in the answer. (What is expected in the answer is, of course, determined by C68-69.)[23]

Shall I or *shall I* not *eat* another peanut?
Shall we dance, or are you tired?

Will you be quiet?	Answer expected: *I will* or *I will not*—for this is a matter of intention or willingness.
Shall good old *Joe be made* to eat crow?	Answer expected: *he shall* or *he shall not*—for this is a matter of determination.
Shall you graduate this June?	Answer expected: *I shall* or *I shall not* (C68)—for this is a matter of mere futurity or of expectation.

---

[23] In the United States even the best writers frequently pay scant attention to this rule but rather tend to make *will* do *shall*'s work as well as its own. You may ignore the rule too, unless your teacher directs otherwise.

C71 In conditions that carry no notion of "contrary to fact," but are simple, straightforward conditions, use *shall* with the first person and *will* with the second and third in the *if* clause. (Use *shall* or *will* in the independent clause according to C68-69.)[24]

If *I shall get* home in time, I shall have first chance at the paper.
If *you will* come, we shall be delighted.

HELPING VERBS *should* AND *would*

C72 Helping verbs *should* and *would* have only one form for all moods, tenses, persons, and numbers.

C73 Use *should* after *if* in all persons to express a supposition or imagined condition or a condition contrary to fact.[25]

C74 If *if . . . should* has been used in a condition, then in the conclusion use *should* with the first person and *would* with the second and third to express a simple future result.[26]

If Barbara should sing, *I should be* sure to have another sleepless night afterwards.

If Tom should not return, then *you would be* one of the six to share the pie.

If Rome should fall, *would* the *pope* still *be* bishop of Rome?

C75 If *if . . . should* has been used in a condition, then in the conclusion use *would* with all three persons to express intention or willingness.

If Barbara should sing, *I would make* for that exit.
If I should ask you, I'm sure *you would oblige* me.
If Bill should hit Stein, *Stein would hit* him.

---

[24] In the United States even the best writers frequently pay scant attention to this rule but rather tend to make *will* do *shall*'s work as well as its own. You may ignore the rule too, unless your teacher directs otherwise.

[25] This rule holds, of course, in conditions where *if* is implied but not expressed; for example, "*Should he come*, we would be delighted."

[26] In the United States even the best writers frequently pay scant attention to this rule but rather tend to make *would* do *should*'s work as well as its own. You may ignore the rule too, unless your teacher directs otherwise.

C76 Use *would* after *if* in all persons to express imagined or supposed willingness or a condition of willingness that is contrary to the facts.

If *I would* [usually expressed today by *if I wanted to*], I could be a saint.

If *you would try,* you could become a very effective speaker.

If *Evans would* only *talk* to me, I think I could persuade him to buy an advertisement in the annual.

C77 Use *should* with the first person and *would* with the second and third to express a modest opinion.[27]

I should say that this oyster is asserting itself.
You would hardly *say,* would you, that I look like a criminal?
One would imagine that O'Leary dislikes talking in public.

C78 Use *should* with the first person and *would* with the second and third with verbs like *prefer, care, like, be glad, be inclined.*[27]

I should prefer, of course, to breathe.

You would be inclined, I think, to consider mayhem good fun.

The *Millers would* not *care* to have their goldfish pond used as a wading pool.

C79 Use *should* with all persons to express duty, obligation, desirability, expectation, doubtful necessity.

[Duty or obligation:] If you are going to follow Christ, *you should be* joyous.

[Desirability:] *You should have seen* the crowd at Macy's after the price war was announced.[28]

[Desirability:] I think it better that *someone* known to the family *should attend* the funeral.

[Expectation:] There *should be* another *car* in ten minutes.

[Doubtful necessity:] Ordinarily, a *rock* of that size *should fall* with terrific force.

---

[27] In the United States even the best writers frequently pay scant attention to this rule but rather tend to make *would* do *should*'s work as well as its own. You may ignore the rule too, unless your teacher directs otherwise.

[28] The notion of desirability has been all but lost in many such sentences. In this example, for instance, the *should* form is hardly more than an emphatic way of saying "There was a large crowd at Macy's after the price war was announced."

C80 Use *would* with all persons to express habit or inclination (except in the case considered in C78).

I would put my foot in the bucket every time at bat.

Even as a baby, *you would take* Homer down from the shelf and gaze at the beautiful Greek words.

But an *American would think* that there is nothing more delicious than steak and potatoes.

C81 Use *would* as a softer, more polite, more indirect form of *will*.

Would you *hand* me the butter, please.
Would you *take* the wheel a while?

C82 Questions with *should* and *would* are governed by C73-81.

C83 Use *should* as a past of *shall* and *would* as a past of *will*.[29]

At that time I was sure that *I should be* a lawyer some day.
At that time you were sure that *you would be* a lawyer some day.
At that time he was sure that *he would be* a lawyer some day.

HELPING VERBS *may* AND *might*

C84 Helping verbs *may* and *might* have only one form for all tenses, persons, and numbers.

C85 Use *may* to express permission.[30]

Please, Ma, *may* I *keep* the puppy?
We *may stay* in swimming until the car comes back.

C86 Use *might* as a past of *may*.

Mother said that I *might keep* the puppy; but when I returned to look for it, it was gone.

The moderator had told us that we *might stay* in swimming until the car came back.

---

[29] In the United States even the best writers frequently pay scant attention to this rule but rather tend to make *would* do *should's* work as well as its own. You may ignore the rule too, unless your teacher directs otherwise.

[30] In the United States even the best writers frequently pay scant attention to this rule but rather tend to make *can* do *may's* work as well as its own. You may ignore the rule too, unless your teacher directs otherwise.

C87 When no *if* clause is involved, use *may* to express a near, *might* to express a remote, possibility.

> It *may rain.* [The sky is cloudy.]
> It *might rain.* [The climate is treacherous.]

> They *may go;* in fact, I should not be surprised if they did.
> They *might go;* but, judging by the way that Irma was talking at lunch, I don't think they will.

C88 When an *if* clause expresses a supposition, an imagined condition, or a condition that is contrary to fact, use *might* in the independent clause even to express a near possibility. Do not use *may.*

> If you were more careful, you *might be allowed* to use the drill press on Saturdays.
> If Creon would control his temper, we *might be* able to use him as the father in the play.
> If someone could invent a way of putting two colors, red and black, on paper typewriter-tapes, he *might make* a fortune.

C89 When an *if* clause does not fall under C88, use either *may* or *might* in the independent clause.

> If someone invents a way of putting two colors, red and black, on paper typewriter-tapes, he *may* [or *might*] *make* a fortune.

C90 Use *may* and *might* (*might* for the past) to express purpose or intention.

> I'm working in order that I *may encourage* the others.
> I worked in order that I *might encourage* the others.

HELPING VERBS *can* AND *could*

C91 Helping verbs *can* and *could* have only one form for all tenses, persons, and numbers.

C92 Use *can* to express power, ability, skill.[31]

> I don't know whether I *can sail* so large a boat by myself.

---

[31] In the United States even the best writers frequently use *can* and *could* to express permission. See C85.

C93   Use *could* as a past of *can.*

> I didn't know whether I *could sail* so large a boat by myself.

C94   When an *if* clause expresses a supposition, an imagined condition, or a condition that is contrary to fact, use *could* in the independent clause.

> If there were less talk, we *could finish* the cracker-eating contest.
>
> He really believes that he *could sing* the title role [if he should be asked to do so].
>
> If we had had a third, we *could have played* three-man territory, a game invented by my brother.
>
> If nobody would object, we *could leave.*

C95   Use *could* as a softer, more polite, more indirect form of *can.*

> *Could* you *get* me another job, Dad?

ACTIVE AND PASSIVE VOICE[32]

C96   Voice is that form which a verb takes to show whether the subject is acting or being acted upon.

Allen *bought* a car. They *grow* tulips in Michigan.	*Bought* and *grow* are in the active voice. The subjects, *Allen* and *they,* are acting.
A car *was bought* by Allen. Tulips *are grown* in Michigan.	*Was bought* and *are grown* are in the passive voice. *A car* and *tulips* are acted upon.

C97   The active voice is the form of the verb that shows that the subject is acting.

> Herbert *teased* the lion.

C98   The passive voice is the form of the verb that shows that the subject is being acted upon.

> Herbert *was teased* by the lion.

C99   Do not confuse passive voice with past time (tense).

---

[32] For the forms of the active and passive voice, see pages 16-22 and A93-94.

C100 Avoid awkward passives.

[Awkward:] The streets *are being walked* by restless crowds.
[Use the active:] Restless crowds *are walking* the streets.

C101 A verb used in an intransitive sense cannot usually be changed into the passive voice. But sometimes a preposition and an intransitive verb are so closely associated that together they are felt to equal a transitive verb and can be put into the passive.[33]

[Active:] The truck *ran into* the bus.
[Passive:] The bus *was run into* by the truck.

[Active:] Tim's friends *thought* well *of* him.
[Passive:] Tim *was* well *thought of* by his friends.

C102 When the doer of the action is present in the passive, it is the object of the preposition *by* and is commonly called the agent.

[Active:] *Everybody* drank the strange concoction.
[Passive:] The strange concoction was drunk *by everybody*.

C103 A verb in the passive may have a predicate complement; that is, a predicate noun or predicate adjective.[34]

Mervin was elected *treasurer*.
Ursula is considered *clever*.

C104 A predicate complement results in the passive when the verb in the active has an objective complement.[35]

The committee elected Mervin *treasurer* [objective complement in the active].
Mervin was elected *treasurer* [predicate noun in the passive].

Everyone considers Ursula *clever* [objective complement in the active].
Ursula is considered *clever* [predicate adjective in the passive].

[33] When this takes place, it is sensible to think of the word that was a preposition in the active as part of the verb in the passive and to analyze it and diagram it accordingly. However, it may justly be considered a preposition retained from the active and diagramed to one side as a phrase without an object.
[34] For predicate complements see C167.
[35] For objective complements see C158.

C105 Although a verb cannot have an ordinary direct object while it is in the passive, yet it can have an object held over from the active and called a "retained object."[36]

We were asked the *price*.

We were given *joy* by Christ.

Someone must have been given a *warning*, for the enemy artillery was waiting for us.

C106 A retained object results in the passive when the verb in the active has two direct objects, one of which is made the subject noun or pronoun of the active.[37]

[Active:] The customer immediately asked *us* the *price*.	*Us* and *price* are the double object of *asked*. (Do not confuse with compound object.)
[Passive:] *We* were immediately asked the *price*.	*Us* has been made the subject pronoun *(we)*, and *price* is the retained object, held over from the active.

C107 A retained object results in the passive when the indirect object of the active (or the object of *to* or *for* acting as an indirect object) is made the subject noun or pronoun in the passive.[38] For then the direct object is retained in the passive.

[Active:] Christ gave us *joy* [*or* gave joy to us].

[Passive:] We were given *joy* by Christ.	Indirect object *us* has been made the subject pronoun *(we)*, and *joy* is the retained object, the direct object held over from the active.

[Passive:] Just outside the library, I was handed a *summons*.

---

[36] Ordinarily retained objects are not pronouns; but, if one were, it should of course be put in the objective case. Since retained objects are so seldom pronouns, and hence case is not involved, the retained object is of no consequence in English and, along with a good number of other finical points of grammar, is treated in this book only because it may give difficulty from time to time in the analysis of a sentence.

[37] For the notion of two direct objects, or double object, see C156.

[38] For the notion of indirect object, see C161.

THE THREE MOODS

C108 The mood of a verb is the manner in which a verb puts action into a sentence. It is the way in which a verb expresses action, state, or being.

C109 In English there are three moods: the indicative, the imperative, and the subjunctive.[39]

C110 Use the indicative mood to state a thing as a fact, to deny that a thing is a fact, or to ask questions about it as a fact.[40]

Robert W. Service *was born* in England in 1874.
The sun *is* not *shining.*
Will the dog *bite?*
I wonder whether there *is* any use in waiting.

C111 Use the imperative mood to give commands.[41] (*Command* is here taken to include direct second-person orders, pleas, warnings, instructions, and so on.)

Stop.
Save me!
Proceed at your own risk.
Let's go.[42]

C112 The present and future indicative are frequently used as substitutes for the imperative mood.

This is my command; Malcolm Guerny *dies.*	Substitute for *execute Malcolm Guerny.*
Thou *shalt* not *kill.*	Substitute for *do not kill.*
You *shall be* here tomorrow at eight.	Substitute for *be here at eight.*

---

[39] Many grammars list also an optative mood, a potential mood, and so on. This book acts on the principle that all the manners of expression of a verb are well accounted for by the three moods given here and by the helping verbs.

[40] For indicative forms see pages 16-17, 19-20, and 22.

[41] For imperative forms see pages 18, 21, and 23.

[42] Many grammars treat this as a hortatory (exhorting) subjunctive. They do this apparently because such an expression is translated by a subjunctive in Latin. It seems more realistic and accurate to call it an imperative.

C113 In general, use the subjunctive mood[43] to show that conditions, concessions, and wishes are contrary to the facts. It indicates that what is said is in some way not actual or certain but is imagined or wished or desired or conceived as possible. However, since some subjunctive forms have fallen into rather general disuse, keep the following particular rules.

C114 Use the present subjunctive after verbs of ordering, willing, resolving, and proposing and after expressions of necessity when these are followed by the conjunction *that*.

The principal *has ordered that* Fleming *take* another examination on Friday.

God *wills that* all men *be saved*.

We *are determined that* no one *be admitted* this year who cannot speak persuasively.

The law *requires that* a boy *reach* his sixteenth year before he may apply for an apprentice license.

It *is necessary that* Igor *play* loud enough to cover the noise of shifting the set.

Mrs. Reingold *asks that* a guest not only *enjoy* her parties but also *work* hard at doing so.

C115 If you like and especially if you want to avoid all formality, in place of *that* and the subjunctive use an infinitive phrase with the verbs of C114.

The principal has ordered Fleming *to take* another examination on Friday.

God wills all men *to be saved*.

We are determined *to admit* no one this year who cannot speak persuasively.

The law requires a boy *to reach* his sixteenth year before he may apply for an apprentice license.

It is necessary for Igor *to play* loud enough to cover the noise of shifting the set.

Mrs. Reingold asks her guests not only *to enjoy* her parties but also *to work* hard at doing so.

---

[43] For subjunctive forms see pages 17-18, 20-21, and 23.

C116 Use *were* (past subjunctive) to indicate that what you are saying is contrary to present or future fact.

If only I *were* class president. [I'm not.]

Even if he *were* to beg me, I wouldn't drive. [And he hardly will.]

If I *were* you, I would apologize. [But I'm not.]

Were Christ here, He wouldn't like it. [But Christ is not here, in the sense of this sentence.]

C117 Use *had* plus the past participle (past-perfect subjunctive) to indicate that what you are saying is contrary to past facts.

If only I *had been* class president. [But I was not.]

Even if he *had begged* me, I wouldn't have driven. [But he didn't.]

Had Christ *been* there, He wouldn't have liked it. [But He was not there, in the sense of this sentence.]

C118 Do not use *would have* (for *had* plus the past participle) to express a wish, a concession, or a condition that is contrary to past facts.

had

If the apartment ~~would have~~ been on the first floor, we would have taken it.

C119 When using the subjunctive after *as if* and *as though,* use *were* to express action or state simultaneous with that of the main verb; use *had* plus the past participle to express action or state that is prior to that of the main verb.

Simultaneous

Douglas { acts / acted / will act / has acted / had acted } as if he *were* owner of the place.

Prior

Douglas { acts / acted / will act / has acted / had acted } as if he *had been* owner of the place.

C120 Nowadays the present and present-perfect subjunctives are scarcely used. The indicative, the past and the past-perfect subjunctive, and helping verbs are used instead.

Instead of—	*Ordinarily use—*
If Karl *be* here, he will answer for me.	If Karl *is* here, he will answer for me. [Indicative.]
If Karl *have been* here, he will have left a note.	If Karl *has been* here, he will have left a note. [Indicative.]
	If Karl *had been* here, he would have left a note. [Past-perfect subjunctive.]

C121 When they carry the sense and do not sound awkward, helping verbs may be substituted for the subjunctive forms of C114, C116-17, and C119.

Instead of—	*You may find—*
Even if you *were* to pay me, I would have to tell the truth.	Even if you *should pay* me, I would have to tell the truth.
If Tooky *were* here, he would prove that I caught that fish.	If Tooky *could be* here, he would prove that I caught that fish.
We are determined that no one *be admitted* who cannot speak persuasively.	We are determined that no one *shall be admitted* who cannot speak persuasively.
If you *played* [past subjunctive] your cards right, you might get Mr. Acton to equip the darkroom.	If you *should* [or *would,* depending on the meaning] *play* your cards right, you might get Mr. Acton to equip the darkroom.

THE TENSES

C122 The tenses are the different forms that a verb takes to indicate the time of an action or state.

C123 In general, the present tense indicates that something is happening now.

I *eat* now.
I *am eating* now.
I *do eat* now.

C124 The present (indicative, chiefly) is used to express facts and truths that are independent of time.

Man's soul *is* immortal.
He said that blue and yellow *make* green.

C125 The present (indicative) is used to indicate habitual action that still continues.

He *takes* a nap in the afternoon.
Alison *is* always here by four o'clock.

C126 The present (indicative) is sometimes used for vividness in narratives about the past. Once introduced into a narrative, this present-for-past device must be kept until there is a reason within the narrative for changing to a past tense.

Booth *shoots* Lincoln and *leaps* to the stage.

C127 The present tense of all moods, and of the participle, gerund, and infinitive is frequently used with a future meaning.

When *does* this morning's mail *get* in?

Max's ship *sails* at midnight.

Henry plans to *escape* next month.

We *may*—we're not sure—*have* a holiday next Monday.

Someone said that we *might be asked* to repeat the performance for the Ursuline nuns, who haven't seen it.

I suggest that he *see* Mr. Carroll, who handles all quaint complaints.

C128 In general, the past tense (indicative) is used to indicate that something happened in the past and is no longer happening now.

I *came*; I *saw*; I *conquered*.

I *was hoping* to find a small helicopter for my youngest son.

The wailing *began* yesterday at sunset and *stopped* just a moment or two ago.

C129 The past (indicative), usually the progressive form, may indicate an action or state that was the background of another action or state in the past.

I *was swimming* alone just past the outer reef when the shark attacked me.

C130 The past (indicative) may indicate past habitual action.

Moreland *prayed* twice a day.
Moreland *used* to pray twice a day.

C131 The past subjunctive is used to express present and future time.

If you *were* interested, I would show you a quicker method of factoring.

If you *sang* the song with the same naturalness during the performance tomorrow, we would have a hit. But I'm afraid you will be a little tense.

C132 The future tense indicates that something will take place later.[44]

The rest *will be sent* out later.
I *will phone* for a taxi this minute.

C133 The present perfect (indicative) indicates that something has taken place in the past but continues into the present or has consequences that continue into the present. In short, use the present perfect when you wish to stress a link between the present time and what happened in the past.

No one *has heard* from Bud since he went away.
The examinations *have begun.*
I *have been* ill for two months.
There *has been* a riot.

Obviously the war *has been* a sorry failure.

The war is definitely over, but the writer wishes to stress that it was recent and that its consequences are still present.

---

[44] For the present as a common substitute for the future, see C127.

C134 The past perfect (indicative) indicates that an action or state took place prior to some other past action or state.

Father De Smet learned that the tribe *had retreated* farther west.

The fire *had been burning* briskly for an hour or more when we began to see some change in the glowing metal.

Mr. Kane *had* already *bought* his ticket before he went to the depot.

C135 The past perfect (indicative) is used with *before* to indicate that an action or state that was begun in the past and that might, could, should, or would have been completed in the past was not completed.

He was interrupted before he *had finished* the story.

We were ready an hour before anyone *had arrived.*	The past perfect implies that people might, could, or should have arrived. If a mere statement of fact is wanted, the past should be used: *before anyone arrived.*

C136 The past may properly be used for the past perfect when it is not important to show that one action has preceded another.

Mother punished me because I *washed* the dishes too hastily.	Although the dishwashing preceded the punishing, the statement is clear without using the past perfect.
We changed our plans after we *got* the message.	Although receiving the message preceded the changing of plans, the statement is clear without the past perfect.

C137 The past should be used for the past perfect when the latter would detract from the thought of the sentence.

Men *heard* the news and leaped into the air for joy.	"Men *had heard* the news" would be distracting here. The writer wants to stress the sudden impact of the news and the men's almost simultaneous reaction to it.

C138 The future perfect is used to indicate that something will already have happened before something else will happen.

I *shall have finished* this weaving before night [falls].
They *will have left* before you arrive.

C139 Sometimes the future perfect is used in a sentence to go with a future thought that is not expressed but merely implied.

If Tom has been here, he *will have left* a note.	Implied thought: as we *shall discover* later.
By now Grandmother Webster *will have arrived* at the farm.	Implied thought: as we *shall find* out later. (Here the future perfect also carries a connotation of *should* or *ought to have arrived*.)

C140 The future perfect is not much used in America today. For it are substituted the present, the future, or the present perfect.

Instead of—	*You may find—*
I *shall have finished* the weaving before night.	I *shall finish* the weaving before night.
Please telephone me as soon as you *will have heard*.	Please telephone me as soon as you *hear*.
	Please telephone me as soon as you *have heard*.

SEQUENCE OF TENSES[45]

C141 The tense of verbals and subordinate predicate verbs frequently depends on the tense of the main verb.

C142 If the main verb is present, the subordinate verbs are usually present, present perfect, or future.

Jane *says* that tea *is* ready.	Both the saying and the being ready occur at the same time.

---

[45] Various helping-verb and subjunctive-mood situations are not accounted for in these rules. For them see C73-83, C86-90, C93-94, and C113-21.

Buddy *won't talk* now, because he *is* afraid.

The talking and the being afraid occur at the same time. *Won't talk* is present here.

The examination *seems* easy because we *have studied* hard.

The studying preceded the examination; so the present perfect is used.

We *have* some fine indoor games ready, so that the rain *will* not *spoil* our fun.

The rain is a future possibility; so the future is used here.

[Exception:] The examination *seems* easy because we *studied* hard.

The rule is not ironclad. Here the past is used rather than the present perfect because the writer does not wish to present the studying as something recent or not yet over.

[Exception:] I *believe* that Columbus *discovered* America in 1492.

The rule is not ironclad. Here the sense simply demands the past rather than the present-perfect tense.

C143 If the main verb is past or past perfect, make the subordinate verbs past or past perfect if you can do so and still express your meaning fully and accurately.[46]

Margate *said* that he *was* too busy to come and hear what you *might propose* at the meeting. So don't expect him.

Was indicates the same time as the main verb, *said*. And the past, *might propose*, is better than the present, *may propose*, after the past.

Margate *said* that he *would be* out of town and hence *could* not *attend* tomorrow's meeting. So don't expect him.

Would and *could* are better than *will* and *can* to express the proper time relation.

Whenever he *heard* the owl hoot, he *shuddered*.

Hears would be quite incorrect, as it would give no hint of the time relation of one act to the other.

---

[46] See C144.

| Josue *could conquer* the city only after God *had come* to his aid. | At the time Josue was able to conquer the city, God's help had already been given. |
| [Exception:] Tavitt *ordered* that I *report* for KP. | The present, *report,* is required by C114 after verbs of ordering, and so on. Of course, if you wanted to use the less elegant helping verb, you could say *should report* (past). |

C144 Do not keep the sequence of tenses asked for in C143 if the dependent clause is intended to present something as usual, characteristic, or always true.

Did you *ask* when the eastbound train *comes* in?

It *was reported* that Nigel *studies* hard, *plays* hard, and *is making* a good record in school.

Junior *had* never *heard* that the earth *is* round.

C145 In a single sentence or in a series of sentences or paragraphs connected by one line of thought, do not change the verb time unless you have to.

[Wrong:] When first we meet him, he is lying on the cropped grass in front of the grandstand watching with an idle eye the afternoon scrimmage of the football team. His pose is altogether graceful and seems to imply relaxed power rather than lethargy or weakness. He *had* a good head, strong, with features cleanly but not sharply chiseled.

[Right:] When first we meet him, he is lying on the cropped grass in front of the grandstand watching with an idle eye the afternoon scrimmage of the football team. His pose is altogether graceful and seems to imply relaxed power rather than lethargy or weakness. He *has* a good head, strong, with features cleanly but not sharply chiseled.

[Right:] When first we met him, he was lying on the cropped grass in front of the grandstand watching with an idle eye the afternoon scrimmage of the football team. His pose was altogether graceful and seemed to imply relaxed power rather than lethargy or weakness. He *had* a good head, strong, with features cleanly but not sharply chiseled.

C146 Use the present participle if the action of the participle takes place at the same time as that of the predicate verb.

Working for thirty-six hours hand running, that single shift cleared the ways of three oil tankers.

Being a little uncomfortable even in my sleep, I tore great slits in the bedclothes with my toenails.

Leaving the parking lot, you will hand your ticket to the attendant.

I am without a care in the world, *sailing* along between the islands that wall off the sound.

C147 Use the present-perfect participle if the action of the participle is prior to the action of the predicate verb.

Having scuttled the clipper, Johannsen sat in the dory planning his next move.

Having been rejected by every publisher in the city, Schmidt bought his own printing press.

Having paced sixty feet from the shore, we came to the mound and began to dig feverishly.

C148 Use the past participle regardless of the time of the predicate verb.

Delighted with my job, I see no reason to change.

Wearied with waiting, the dog had curled up on a seat of the ferris wheel and gone to sleep.

Given half a chance, he will win the TV contest hands down.

Frightened by the deafening crash, she jumped from her chair and ran to the window.

C149 Use the present-perfect infinitive if the action of the infinitive is prior to that of the predicate verb. Use the present infinitive in all other cases.

He is said to *have died* of apoplexy while delivering a frenzied television commercial.

The doctor was reported to *have come* to Tranquillity Beach to study the effects on the human body of sand in picnic lunches.

I want to *leave* now.

I wanted to *leave* yesterday.

I had expected to *leave* tomorrow.

C150 Use the present or present-perfect gerund if the action of the gerund is prior to that of the predicate verb. Use the present gerund in all other cases.

Noble was accused of *having written* a ditty lampooning Stalin.
Noble was accused of *writing* a ditty lampooning Stalin.
"I have no intention of *budging*," said the immovable object.

TRANSITIVE VERBS AND OBJECTS

C151 A transitive verb is a verb whose action goes over to a receiver or target.

The Ford▷—hit—▷Jimmy.   *Hit* is transitive; *Jimmy* is the receiver or target.

We▷— enjoy —▷music.   *Enjoy* is transitive; *music* is the receiver or target.

C152 The same verb may be transitive in one sentence and intransitive in another.

Jack▷— is dancing—▷ the minuet.
Jack▷— is dancing—↘.

C153 The subject noun or pronoun is the receiver or target of the action of a transitive verb in the passive voice.[47]

Jimmy was hit by the Ford.
I was much struck by your argument.

C154 A direct object is the noun or pronoun that receives the action of a transitive verb in the active voice.

The Ford hit *Jimmy*.   The Ford hit whom? Jimmy.

We enjoy *music*.   We enjoy what? Music.

I hate *lying*.   I hate what? Lying (gerund).

I like *to loaf*.   I like what? To loaf (noun phrase).

I prefer *that you remain*.   I prefer what? That you remain (noun clause).

---

[47] See C98.

C155 A direct object may be compound.

We bought *caramels* and *liverwurst*.

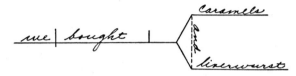

C156 In some sentences, some verbs—like *ask, teach, lead,* and *hear*—take two direct objects. (Do not confuse two **direct** objects with a compound object.)

You led *us* a merry *dance*.

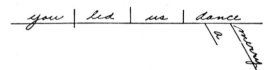

Ask *me* my *name*.

Hear *me* my *lessons*.

You can teach *yourself* to *swim*.

You made *me* go.

C157 In some sentences, some verbs—like *name, choose, elect, deem,* and *find*—take both a direct object and an objective complement.

C158   An objective complement is a noun, pronoun, or adjective referring to the direct object and completing the meaning of the verb.

We elected Dorothy *captain*.

we | elected | Dorothy / captain

My parents named me *Bottomley*.

parents | named | me / Bottomley

I find this paint *sticky*.

I | find | paint / sticky

C159   Put a pronoun used as direct object in the objective case.[48]

I rather like *him*.

Did I miss anyone? Yes, ~~he~~ *him* and ~~she.~~ *her.*

I don't know ~~who~~ *whom* I invited.

C160   Expressions like *I believe* and *do you suppose* complicate the use of the proper case of *who* or *whom*. Whenever you are in doubt, diagram the sentence and see where *who* or *whom* falls in the diagram.

This is the gentleman whom,   *Whom* is the direct object of
I believe, you distrust.   the verb *distrust*.

---

[48] In spoken conversation, in informal writing, and in conversation reported in written stories, it is quite all right to use *who* instead of *whom* as direct object. In fact, where the atmosphere is informal, it is frequently better manners. However, use the objective in high school except when reporting conversation.

Who do you suppose ate the icing?

Who is the subject pronoun of the verb *ate*.

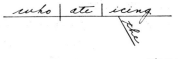

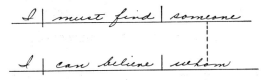

I must find someone whom I can believe.

Whom is the direct object of the verb *can believe*.

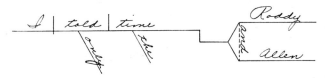

C161 The indirect object of a transitive verb names the person or thing that receives the direct object. In other words, the indirect object names the person or thing to, for, or toward whom the action is done.

Professor Trinkle gave *me* a retort.

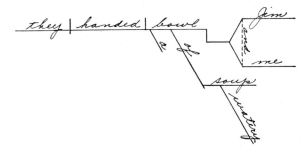

I only told *Roddy* and *Allen* the time.

They handed *Jim* and *me* a bowl of watery soup.

C162 Insert the preposition *to* or *for* before a likely object. If the insertion makes good sense, the chance is excellent that you have an indirect object.

Father Burns brought Mother Holy Communion.

Insert *to* before *Mother,* and you make sense. *Mother* is the indirect object.

A taxi brought Mother home.

Insert *to* before *Mother,* and you do not make good sense. *Mother* is not the indirect object in this sentence.

C163 Put a pronoun that is the indirect object in the objective case.

[Answering the question, "Did Ralph give anybody a bite?":] Not *me.*

INTRANSITIVE VERBS AND COMPLEMENTS

C164 An intransitive verb is a verb that does not have a direct object.[49]

Who *is singing?*
The plot *thickens.*
My blood *boiled* when he told me to bring him his slippers.

C165 Some verbs—like *be* and *seem*—cannot be used transitively; other verbs may be transitive in one sentence and intransitive in another.

[Transitive:] Jack▷—is dancing—▷the minuet.

[Intransitive:] Jack▷—is dancing—◡ .

C166 A linking verb is an intransitive verb that connects its subject noun or pronoun with a noun, pronoun, or adjective that completes the meaning of the verb.

---
[49] For direct objects see C154.

Pete *is* president.

Is connects *Pete* with *president* and uses *president* to complete its own meaning.

Pete | is \ president

You *seem* strange.

you | seem \ strange

C167 A predicate complement is a word that is used to complete the meaning either of a linking verb or of a transitive verb in the passive voice and that represents, describes, or refers to the subject noun. Predicate complements are divided into predicate nouns, predicate pronouns, and predicate adjectives.

They are *brothers.*	Predicate noun.
That is *what I asked.*	Predicate noun (clause).
You do not seem *yourself.*	Predicate pronoun.
The iron is becoming *red.*	Predicate adjective.
Kurt was appointed *waterboy.*	Predicate noun after a passive predicate verb.

C168 Put the predicate pronoun of a predicate verb in the nominative case.[50]

It is *I.*
This should be *he.*
Was it *they?*

C169 All linking verbs carry some sense of the verb *be.* So, in deciding whether you should use an ordinary intransitive verb with an adverb modifier, or a linking verb with a predicate adjective, do this: Substitute a corresponding form of the verb *be* for the predicate verb and use an

---

[50] In informal writing and talking, it is quite proper to ignore this rule and use the objective case of the predicate pronoun after *it is, it was,* and so on. However, so that you may have facility in correct usage for your more formal writing, use the nominative after *it is* and *it was* in your high-school work except when you are reporting conversation.

adjective complement. If the substitution carries the sense you want, then the linking verb plus a predicate adjective is probably the correct construction.

Suppose you are deciding whether to say "A rose smells sweet" or "A rose smells sweetly." Say "A rose is sweet." Does that carry the rough sense of what you want to say? Yes. So "A rose smells sweet" is quite correct. (As a matter of fact, "A rose smells sweetly" would mean that a rose looks charming when it is smelling something else.)

Suppose you are deciding whether to say "The flames burn blue" or "The flames burn bluely." Say "The flames are blue." Does that carry the rough sense of what you want to say? Yes. So "The flames burn blue" is quite correct.

Suppose you are deciding whether to say "You looked strange" or "You looked strangely." Say "You were strange." Does that carry the sense of what you want to say? It does—if you mean *look* in the sense of *appear*. It does not—if you mean *look* in the sense of *gaze*.

C170   Say *feel bad, ill, well, good, right* (adjectives after linking verb). Do not say *feel badly, rightly* (adverbs).

I don't feel ~~badly~~ *bad* about voting the Republican ticket.

After working all afternoon laying pipes, I had a swim off the point that felt very good indeed.

C171   Say *do well, badly* (adverbs), since *do* in the sense of *succeed* is not a linking verb. Do not say *do good, bad, nice.*

I did pretty ~~good~~ *well* in my examination.

This will do [succeed, fill the bill] very ~~nice~~ *nicely.*

C172   The following verbs are frequently used as linking verbs.

act [*in the sense of* pretend to be] (stupid)	become (wise)
	break (free)
appear (strange)	burn (blue)
bang (shut)	burst [out] (singing)
be (sure)	continue (agreeable)

104

fall (dead *or* sick)	remain (puzzled)
feel (bad)	rest (assured)
flame (red)	ring (true)
get (sick)	rise (triumphant)
go (mad)	run (true [to form])
go [on] (studying)	seem (odd)
grow (ridiculous)	shine (golden)
hold (true)	show (cowardly [*adjective*])
keep (honest)	smell (sweet)
lie [*in the sense of* remain]	sound (harsh)
(quiet)	stand (corrected)
look (funny)	stay (united)
loom (large)	take (sick)
prove (worth while)	taste (strong)
rank (fifth)	turn (white)

VERBS CONFUSED

C173 Do not confuse—

Lie—meaning to recline. (Intransitive.)[51]

Present	Past	Past participle
lie	lay	lain

lie

People ~~lay~~ down when they're tired.

lay

The bicycle ~~laid~~ in the weeds for three days.

lain

I had scarcely ~~laid~~ down on my bed when the alarm rang.

Lay—meaning to put *something* down. (Transitive.)

Present	Past	Past participle
lay	laid	laid

lay

Now I ~~lie~~ me down to sleep.

laid

Hollings ~~lay~~ his big hand on my rifle.

laid

Christ has ~~lain~~ down His life for His friends.

---

[51] There is, of course, another intransitive verb *lie*, meaning to tell an untruth; but it is not a source of confusion. Its principal parts are *lie, lied, lied.*

C174 Do not confuse—

Sit—meaning to rest upon the haunches. (Intransitive.)

Present	Past	Past participle
sit	sat	sat

sit
Don't ~~set~~ in that chair; that's the cat's.

sat
Imperturbable Jones has ~~set~~ so long in front of Cornby's Drugstore that people think that he and the wooden Indian are related.

sat
Kings have ~~set~~ on that bench you are polishing your boots on, soldier.

sat
[Exceptional, transitive use:] Ichabod ~~set~~ his horse like a loose-jointed scarecrow athwart a great beer barrel.

sat
[Exceptional, transitive use:] Mr. Northrup ~~set~~ himself down and chatted for an hour.

Set—meaning to put, place, or fix *something*. (Transitive.)

Present	Past	Past participle
set	set	set

set
Gubbins had ~~sat~~ a pail of water on the lowest step to catch a thief but had caught his own astonished father.

Set the coffeepot on the stove, Sam.

Set your watches to agree with mine; we attack in exactly six minutes.

Set—meaning chiefly to sit on eggs as does a fowl. (Intransitive.)

Present	Past	Past participle
set	set	set

set
Hens will ~~sit~~ on darning eggs or light bulbs.

C175 Do not confuse—

Hang—meaning to suspend or be suspended (but preferably not used of putting to death by suspending).

106

Present	Past	Past participle
hang	hung	hung

Hang your clothes on a hickory limb; the water's fine.

We ~~hanged~~ *hung* our clothes on a hickory limb but found crocodiles in the water.

You should have ~~hanged~~ *hung* your clothes on a higher limb where the goat couldn't have reached them.

That suit ~~hanged~~ *hung* on Longjohn like a slack tepee around a tent pole.

Hang—meaning to put to death by suspending.

Present	Past	Past participle
hang	hanged	hanged

Hang your friend from a hickory limb; he used up all the hot water.

Tommers was ~~hung~~ *hanged* from a hickory limb for confusing other ranchers' brands with his own.

Before they ~~hung~~ *hanged* him, they put Edmund Campion through a mock trial whose verdict was set before its date.

C176 Do not confuse—

Rise—meaning to ascend, to get up, or to emerge. (Intransitive.)

Present	Past	Past participle
rise	rose	risen

The sun ~~raised~~ *rose* at about four-thirty that morning.

Come on, marine; ~~raise~~ *rise* and shine!

There we saw peak ~~raising~~ *rising* above peak sharply, till the last seemed a pinnacle upon which a man could never stand—though an angel might dance there.

We had ~~raised~~ *risen* early, for fish greet the dawn hungry.

You could almost see the dough *rising* in the pan.

Raise—meaning to make *something* rise. (Transitive.)

Present	Past	Past participle
raise	raised	raised

The sun had ~~risen~~ *raised* itself for a look over the rim of the world.

Our Lord ~~rose~~ *raised* Lazarus from the tomb.

Here's a story that may ~~rise~~ *raise* a laugh.

C177   Do not confuse—

Lose—meaning to fail to keep, to suffer defeat.

Present	Past	Past participle
lose	lost	lost

I am afraid you are going to ~~loose~~ *lose* a hubcap.

Leoville should ~~loose~~ *lose* to Damien by six points.

Loose and *loosen*—meaning to free, to untie, to relax.

Present	Past	Past participle
loose	loosed	loosed
loosen	loosened	loosened

Loose ~~Lose~~ the prisoners and let them go.

Loosen ~~Losen~~ the girth on the black stallion.

C178   Do not confuse—

Teach—meaning to cause or attempt to cause someone else to learn.

Miss McBride ~~learned~~ *taught* us how to square dance.

Christ had a difficult time ~~learning~~ *teaching* the apostles.

Learn—meaning to acquire knowledge or skill.

We *learn* that Richelieu had some good points.
Why should a boy *learn* to cook?

C179 Do not confuse—

Effect—meaning to bring about or cause something.

Present	Past	Past participle
effect	effected	effected

effected

My white mouse, Squeaky, has ~~affected~~ his escape.

effect

If McCoy will keep his temper, we can ~~affect~~ a compromise.

The minute we saw the bull glaring at us from the far corner of the pasture we *effected* a quick retreat to the other side of the fence.

Affect—meaning to influence, to move the emotions; to pretend or feign something.

Present	Past	Past participle
affect	affected	affected

affected

Too much sun has ~~effected~~ poor Maddern's brain.

affected

All the coarse louts in the crowd were visibly ~~effected~~ by the sentimental movie.

affect

Mr. Pringle tried to ~~effect~~ surprise; but he was a poor actor, and so he deceived nobody.

C180 These are the principal parts of *let* and *leave*:

Present	Past	Past participle
let	let	let
leave	left	left

C181 Use *let*, not *leave*, with *be*.

Let

~~Leave~~ me be.

C182 Use *let*, not *leave*, in the sense of *permit*.

Let

~~Leave~~ me tell you.

Let

~~Leave~~ them enter.

Let

~~Leave~~ us know if there are any changes.

C183 Use *let*, not *leave*, to give a sense of exhortation to a verb.

Let
~~Leave~~ us go to the matinee.

Let
~~Leave~~ us answer tyranny with a smile.

C184 Use *leave*, not *let*, in the sense of *abandon, forget.*

left
I must have ~~let~~ the keys in the car.

left
Who ~~let~~ his ice cream on top of the stove?

C185 Ordinarily use either *let* or *leave* with *alone.*

Let me *alone.*
Leave me *alone.*

[Exception:] Two men, *let alone* one, would be unable to budge him if he fell down.

Only *let alone* may be used in this peculiar, idiomatic sense of *not to mention.*

Case[52]

C186 Nouns, pronouns, and the possessive and relative adjectives (which are part pronoun) have case.

C187 Case is the form of a noun or pronoun that indicates its sense relation to other words in a sentence. The nominative shows that a noun or pronoun is subject or predicate complement of a verb; the objective, that it is object of some other word; and so on.

C188 There are three cases in English, the nominative, the possessive, and the objective.

C189 Nouns in English have a distinctive form only for the possessive case. Sense and position indicate the nominative and objective relationships.

---

[52] The possessive of nouns and pronouns is treated in C191-200. The nominative, possessive, and objective cases of pronouns are treated in A29, A37, A40, A42-43, A50, and C221-33.

C190 Some pronouns have distinctive forms for all three cases.

Nominative	I	we
Possessive	mine	ours
Objective	me	us

Possessive of nouns and pronouns[53]

THE POSSESSIVE CASE

C191 If a noun or pronoun denotes ownership, put it in the possessive case.[54]

Mr. Witherspoon's car is here.
Sorry, they are not *mine.*

C192 Ownership in the sense of C191 is a broad notion containing concepts of source, right, responsibility, and so on.

Michael's jokes are dull.	Michael does not strictly own the jokes, but he tells them or originates them.
That father of *mine* delights in doing the unexpected.	In the strict sense I do not own my father, and yet he does belong to me.
This is all *Hillman's* fault.	In the strict sense Hillman does not possess the fault; and yet it does belong to him, for he is responsible for it.

C193 The possessive case is an adjective case; that is, it frequently makes adjectives out of nouns.

This is all *Hillman's* fault.

---

53 For the formation of the possessive case, see D128-38.
54 For the *of* possessive, more common with nonliving things, see C195-200.

111

C194   A noun or pronoun may be in the possessive case and at the same time, from another point of view, in the nominative or objective case.

That hat is *mine*.

Mine is the possessive case of *I*, but also predicate pronoun in the sentence and therefore nominative case.

That old hat of *Father's* might fit you.

Father's is possessive case, but also object of *of* and therefore objective case.

THE *of* POSSESSIVE[55]

C195   *Of* followed by a noun or pronoun is frequently used to show ownership.

The clamor *of the alarm* finally awakened them.

The alarm's clamor.

The Mohicans tortured the brother *of Andaiuga*.

Andaiuga's brother.

That old Model T *of Henry's* should be laid to rest in a junk yard.

Henry's old Model T.

C196   When the owner is a living thing, the *of* possessive is used where it sounds better or is clearer than the ordinary possessive.

For the life *of me*, I could not think of the answer [rather than *for my life*].

---

[55] This is commonly called the possessive genitive.

C197 A combination of the *of* possessive and the ordinary possessive is very common, especially when the object possessed is modified by a demonstrative.

He is a friend *of mine.*
He is a friend *of John's.*
Those remarks *of Colby's* have cost us a holiday.
A cousin *of the Joneses'* painted that—er—picture.

C198 The *of* possessive is the more common form when the owner is not a living thing.[56]

[Common:] the back *of the chair*
[Less common:] the *chair's* back

[Common:] the pleasure *of reading*
[Unusual, because awkward and ambiguous:] *reading's* pleasure

[Common:] the call *of the sea*
[Unusual, because awkward:] the *sea's* call

[Common:] the end *of the line*
[Unusual, because awkward:] the *line's* end

C199 Inanimate objects that are personified use the possessive case and the *of* possessive with equal ease.

the *wind's* murmur
the murmur *of the wind*

death's cold fingers
the cold fingers *of death*

the *rose's* breath
the breath *of the rose*

C200 The possessive case is more common than the *of* possessive with the following expressions and some others.

the law's delay	a year's leave
for pity's sake	the year's events
half an hour's walk	six months' interest
a stone's throw	the world's work
a day's work	fifty cents' worth
a month's notice	a dollar's worth

---

[56] See C199.

Nominative absolutes[57]

C201 A nominative absolute is a word group related to the rest of the sentence in sense but not in grammar and made up of a noun or pronoun plus a participle or a participial phrase.

Classes having been dismissed, we found time heavy on our hands.

C202 Elliptical nominative absolutes, with the participle omitted but understood, are rather common.

(kneeling)
An acolyte at his feet, the priest was saying Mass.

(being)
The game over, Marty collapsed in the locker room.

C203 Put the "subject" pronoun of a nominative absolute in the nominative case.

He
~~Him~~ absent, there was no one to play the piccolo.

Direct address[58]

C204 A noun in direct address is a noun used to address someone or something, or to attract his attention. A noun in direct address is related to the rest of the sentence in sense but not in grammar; that is, it is not subject noun, object, modifier, and so on.

Drop that, *brother!*
Pulasko, where's your story?
Remember, *sister dear,* the times I've done the dishes for you.

C205 Words that are usually adjectives may be used as nouns in direct address.

Turn on the ignition, *stupid.*
Where, my *sweet,* did you hide my pipe?
Those are my feet you're stepping on, *graceful.*

---

[57] Set off a nominative absolute by commas (D44).
[58] Set off words in direct address by commas (D34).

C206 Impolite persons sometimes use the pronoun *you* in direct address.

Hey, *you,* here's your nickel.

Appositives

C207 An appositive noun or pronoun is a word used only to explain another noun or pronoun and meaning practically the same thing.

Our neighbors, the *Tuttles,* raise vultures.	The head word[59] is *neighbors;* the appositive noun, explaining *neighbors,* is *Tuttles.*
Bwana has gone with my brother, the witch *doctor.*	The head word is *brother;* the appositive noun, explaining *brother,* is *doctor.*
Whom did you forget—*me?*	The head word is *whom;* the appositive pronoun, explaining *whom,* is *me.*
His favorite sport, *hunting,* cost him his life.	The head word is *sport;* the appositive noun (gerund), explaining *sport,* is *hunting.*
My job, *to sing,* is pleasant.	The head word is *job;* the appositive noun phrase, explaining *job,* is *to sing.*
The fact *that you are here* proves your innocence.	The head word is *fact;* the appositive noun clause, explaining *fact,* is *that you are here.*

C208 Except for the cases in C209, put appositive nouns and pronouns into the same case as the head word.[59]

This is Stoat's [possessive], the catcher's [possessive], expensive new chest protector.

Whose [possessive] is this—yours [possessive]?

Whom [objective] did you forget—me [objective]?

---

[59] For convenience, the noun that is explained by an appositive noun is called the head word.

C209 Do not use the possessive case for both head word and appositive when (*a*) agreement would sound awkward or (*b*) head word and appositive are treated as a unit.

The next two meetings will be held at *Smith's*, the best *host* among us.	*Host's* would sound awkward.
I bought this pith helmet at *Carlton* the *Hatter's*.	*Carlton the Hatter's* is the trade name used by the company; therefore it is a unit.
Have you seen *Brando* the *Great's* new trick—the one in which he pulls a hat out of a rabbit?	*Brando the Great's* is a unit. *Brando's the Great's* would be altogether absurd.

C210 Some appositives are introduced by *or, namely,* and similar expressions.

A pirogue, or *dugout,* is the main means of transportation on some bayous.	*Dugout* is used to explain *pirogue* and means practically the same thing; therefore it is clearly an appositive.
A pirogue or a *raft* was what we needed.	*Raft* does not explain *pirogue* nor mean the same thing; therefore it is clearly not an appositive.
There is only one person for whom I would vote; namely, my *uncle.*	*Uncle* explains *person* and in this sentence means the same thing; therefore it is clearly an appositive.

C211 An appositive noun or pronoun taken together with its objects, modifiers, and other words closely associated with it is called simply an appositive.

His favorite sport, *hunting,* nearly cost him his life.	*Hunting* is an appositive noun (gerund) all by itself.
His favorite sport, *hunting lost documents,* nearly cost him his life.	The whole noun phrase, *hunting lost documents,* is called an appositive.

RESTRICTIVE AND NONRESTRICTIVE APPOSITIVES[60]

C212 Appositives are called restrictive when the writer wants them joined very closely in sense to the head word.

My cousin *John Keating* is brighter than all the rest of my cousins put together.

Suppose that you have several cousins and you want the reader to know that none of the others is meant but only John Keating. Then you must join *John Keating* very closely to the head word *cousin*. In other words, the noun *John Keating* is restrictive.

At that moment, someone at the back of the hall raised the cry *"Down with Carrigan!"*

Suppose that you have not previously told the reader what the cry was; the sense would be incomplete without *down with Carrigan*. So you want *down with Carrigan* joined very closely to the head word. The noun phrase, therefore, is restrictive.

The very fact *that you are here* proves that you did not telephone me from Washington just now.

Suppose that you have not told the reader previously what fact you are talking about; *that you are here* is necessary to the sense. Therefore you want *that you are here* joined very closely to the head word. The noun clause is restrictive.

---

[60] Set off an ordinary nonrestrictive appositive by commas (D35). Do not set off restrictive appositives (D36). Do not set off appositives or adjectives that are part of a proper name (D37). Use a colon to introduce formally any matter that follows—usually matter in apposition (D59). Dashes may be used occasionally to set off nonrestrictive appositives more emphatically than commas do; and they should be used if the appositives are long (say, more than ten words) or contain their own punctuation (D71). A dash is more emphatic than a comma but less formal than a colon before an appositive at the end of a sentence (D72). For dashes with figures see D73; for parentheses with appositives see D78.

C213 Appositives are called nonrestrictive when the writer wants them joined loosely to the head word—as added information, as a point worth bringing in but not very necessary to the thought.[61]

A young cousin of mine, *John Keating,* stumbled upon the hide-out quite by accident.

Suppose that you add the information that your cousin is named John Keating simply because the addition might please a reader who knows him or might brighten the sentence by adding a bit of identification. Then you do not want *John Keating* joined very closely to the head word *cousin.* The noun *John Keating* is nonrestrictive.

This cry, *"Down with Carrigan!"* was taken up first by one throat, then by another, until it swelled into a hoarse, frightening chant.

Suppose that you have told what the cry was in an earlier sentence (not given here). Here you mention it only to remind the reader what it was and to emphasize it. So you do not want *down with Carrigan* joined very closely to the head word. The noun phrase is just added information and hence nonrestrictive.

Let me tell you how lucky is your presence here at this moment. This fact, *that you are here,* proves that you did not telephone me from Washington just now.

Suppose that you have already told the reader what fact you mean and only add *that you are here* for emphasis and unmistakable clearness or even just for better rhythm. Then you want *that you are here* joined only loosely to the head word. In this case the noun clause is nonrestrictive.

---

[61] For the punctuation of restrictive and nonrestrictive appositives, see page 117, footnote 60.

C214 Often context or circumstances force a writer to use an appositive restrictively.

[If there has been no previous mention of the word *garrison,* then it must be restrictive in this sentence:] The word *garrison* does not sound Anglo-Saxon to me.

[If *novelist* and *statesman* were nonrestrictive in this sentence, the result would be nonsense:] I believe you are talking about Churchill the *novelist* rather than Churchill the *statesman.*

C215 Use this test: Read the sentence without the appositive. If the sentence still says most of what you want it to, the appositive is nonrestrictive. If the sentence is changed— if it does not say most of what you want it to but something else—the appositive is restrictive.

The butcher, Abell Miller, won't give us any credit.

[Without the appositive:] The butcher won't give us any credit.

Suppose that you are chiefly interested in saying that the butcher cut off your credit. You add *Abell Miller* not from need but as an extra. The omission does not change the sense. The appositive noun is nonrestrictive.

Dominic was very fond of the expression "on the nose."

[Without the appositive:] Dominic was very fond of the expression.

Suppose that you chiefly intend to tell which expression Dominic was fond of. The omission changes the sense entirely. The appositive noun phrase *on the nose* is clearly restrictive.

I dropped the rescue note from the window on the chance that someone might be passing below.

[Without the appositive:] I dropped the rescue note from the window on the chance.

Suppose that you chiefly wish to state what it was that made you drop the rescue note from the window. The omission changes the sense entirely and leaves the sentence puzzling and incomplete. The appositive noun clause *that someone might be passing below* is clearly restrictive.

119

Pronoun use

PRONOUNS IN GENERAL

C216 A pronoun is a word that is used in place of a noun.

Crabtree was expected to object, but *he* didn't.

C217 Do not use *same* as a pronoun unless you wish to stress identity or similarity.

I have received your letter and thank you for ~~same~~ *it*.	Here there is no reason to stress identity. *It* carries the full meaning perfectly.
Water seeks its own level. The *same*, I think, may be said of mean characters.	Here there is reason to stress identity or similarity.

C218 Do not insert immediately after a subject noun a subject pronoun meaning exactly the same thing.[62]

Jules ~~he~~ wants to be a chemical engineer.
Willa Cather and Edna Ferber ~~they~~ are American novelists.

C219 Do not say *let's us*, which is the same as saying *let us us*.

~~Let's us~~ *Let us* be very careful in using contractions.

C220 Politeness usually requires that the personal pronouns *I* and *we* be placed last in a compound subject.

Mary and I [*not* I and Mary] have a suggestion.

PRONOUN SUBJECTS, OBJECTS, AND COMPLEMENTS[63]

C221 Since a pronoun takes the place of a noun, it does the same things in a sentence that nouns do; hence there are subject pronouns, predicate pronouns, direct- and indirect-object pronouns, appositive pronouns, and so on.

---

[62] Not affected by this rule are those rare constructions in dialogue in which a person is represented as thinking over names and then breaking off into a statement about them. Such a construction requires a dash; for example, "Willa Cather and Edna Ferber—they were American novelists, weren't they?"

[63] For the possessive case of pronouns, see D137-38.

C222 Put the subject pronoun of a predicate verb in the nominative case.

He   she
~~Him~~ and ~~her~~ will come at eight.

they
Would Charles or his brother take a catfish off a hook? Not ~~them~~.[64]

C223 Put the "subject" pronoun of a nominative absolute in the nominative case.[65]

He
~~Him~~ absent, there was no one to play the piccolo.

They being what they are, I'm afraid that you will simply have to make allowances for them.

C224 Put the subject pronoun of an infinitive in the objective case.

The judges expected *him* to be nervous.

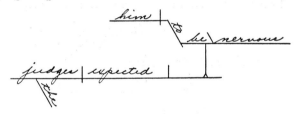

For *her* to object is unusual.

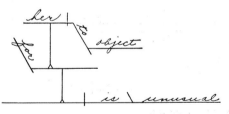

C225 In general, put the subject noun or pronoun of a gerund in the possessive case, or use the possessive adjective. Where this is impossible or awkward, use the objective case.

---

[64] In informal talking and writing, it is good form to use the objective case in elliptical answers to questions. However, to make sure that you master the nominative case, make no use of this exception in your high-school written work.

[65] For nominative absolutes see C201-3.

Hal's coming home was a surprise.

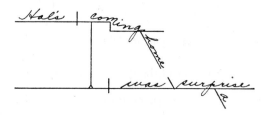

There is no doubt about *his* being elected.

I can't conceive of *him,* a man we trusted, saying such a thing.

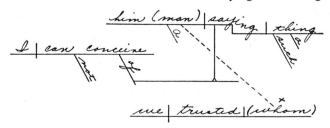

C226 Put the predicate pronoun[66] of a predicate verb in the nominative case.[67]

It is *I.*

This should be *he.*

---

[66] For predicate pronouns see C167.

[67] In informal writing and talking, it is quite proper to ignore this rule and use the objective case of the predicate pronoun after *it is, it was,* and so on. However, so that you may have facility in correct usage for your more formal writing, use the nominative after *it is* and *it was* in your high-school work except when you are reporting conversation.

C227 Put the predicate pronoun of an infinitive in the nominative case if a nominative precedes the infinitive; put it in the objective case if an objective precedes the infinitive.

It [nominative] seemed to be *he* [nominative].

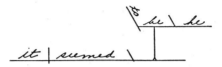

The assistant principal took him [objective, subject of the **infinitive**] to be *me* [objective].

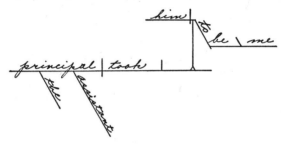

C228 Put the predicate pronoun of a gerund in the nominative case if a possessive precedes the gerund; put it in the objective case if an objective precedes the gerund.

There is little chance of *its* being *she*.

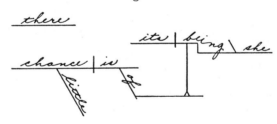

There is no doubt about *this* being *her*.

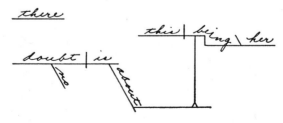

123

C229 Put a pronoun used as direct object of a predicate verb or of a verbal in the objective case.[68]

Did I miss anyone? Yes, ~~he~~ *him* and ~~she~~ *her*.

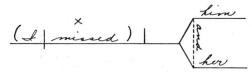

Whom
~~Who~~ did you invite?

C230 Expressions like *I believe* and *do you suppose* complicate sentences containing *who* or *whom* and make it difficult to apply C229. Whenever you are in doubt, mentally diagram the sentence and see where *who* or *whom* falls in the diagram.

This is the gentleman *whom,* I believe, you distrust.	*Whom* is the direct object of the verb *distrust.*

This | *is* \ *gentleman*

you | *distrust* | *whom*

I | *believe*

Who do you suppose ate the icing?	*Who* is the subject pronoun of the verb *ate.*

who | *ate* | *icing*

you | *do suppose*

---

[68] In spoken conversation, in informal writing, and in conversation reported in written stories, it is quite all right to use *who* instead of *whom* as direct object. In fact, where the atmosphere is informal, it is frequently better manners. However, use the objective in high school except when reporting conversation.

I must find someone *whom* I can believe.

Whom is the direct object of the verb *can believe.*

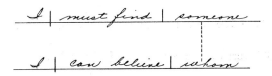

C231 Put a pronoun that is the indirect object in the objective case.

Generous though he usually is, Ralph did not give *me* a bite of the olive.

[Answering the question, "Did Ralph give anybody a bite?":] Not *me.*

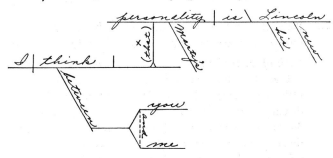

C232 Put the object pronoun of a preposition in the objective case.

Between you and ᴍᴇ, I think Marty's personality is his new Lincoln.

I'm sure I gave the carbolic acid to someone. Now to *whom?*

125

C233 In order to use the right case of a personal pronoun after *than* or *as*, mentally complete the elliptical sentence.

Tush! You are much stronger than ~~him~~ *he* [is strong].

I'd trust Marcus sooner than [I'd trust] ~~she~~ *her*.

I'd trust Marcus sooner than ~~her~~ *she* [would trust Marcus].

There is no other as strong as ~~him~~ *he* [is].

PRONOUNS AND ANTECEDENTS

C234 The noun whose place a pronoun takes is called the antecedent of the pronoun.

Helen said she would make ham sandwiches for us.

Helen is the antecedent of *she*.

C235 Sometimes a pronoun takes the place of another pronoun. The latter is then called the intermediate antecedent.

Each of the boys has his own way of making a bed.

Each is the intermediate antecedent of *his*. *His* is a possessive (pronominal) adjective in this sentence.

C236 Except for the cases discussed in C237, make sure that every pronoun and possessive adjective has an antecedent.

Lack of antecedents

I want to tell you about a little experience I had while driving from Albuquerque to Santa Fe last week. They don't have culverts to carry off rain under the road. They just dip, and rain rushes down from the hills and over the road, usually leaving a lot of sand and gravel on them. We were driving too fast, I'll admit, when he shouted, "Look

Proper use of antecedents

I want to tell you about a little experience I had while driving from Albuquerque to Santa Fe last week. There are no culverts to carry off rain under the road. The highway just dips, and rain rushes down from the hills and over the road, usually leaving a lot of sand and gravel in the depressions. My companions and I were driving too fast, I'll

126

out! There's a dip." Well, the other didn't see the dip in time; and so it plowed right into the sand, skidded off the road, and stopped on the brink of a ravine some twenty feet deep. It is certainly dangerous, and I'll tell you it taught us a lesson.

admit, when one of them— not the driver—shouted, "Look out! There's a dip." Well, the driver didn't see the dip in time; and so the car plowed right into the sand, skidded off the road, and stopped on the brink of a ravine some twenty feet deep. Driving fast, especially over such roads, is certainly dangerous; and I'll tell you it taught us a lesson.

C237 In some expressions it is impossible and undesirable to give a definite antecedent for a pronoun; for instance, this is the case with the interrogative pronouns, the indefinite pronouns, and with *they* or *we* when it means "people in general," or *one* when it means "a man" or "a person."

I say, *somebody* knocked.	The antecedent must be kept indefinite until it is disclosed who did knock.
Who is behind you?	It is impossible to give the antecedent of *who*—at least until the question is answered.
[Right:] *It* is raining.	This is impersonal *it*, an idiomatic use. No antecedent can be named.
[Wrong:] *It* explains radar in this book.	*It* lacks an antecedent, and there is no reason for the construction. Say "This book explains radar."
[Wrong:] *It* says in the paper that the game was rained out.	Say "The paper says."
[Right:] *They* say that Mr. Hawkins had money that his heirs never discovered.	*They* does not have to have an antecedent here, because it means "people in general."

127

[Wrong:] *They* have a new gadget down at the plant that can read letters without opening them.

They does not mean "people in general" here. It must have an antecedent, or *they have* must be replaced by *there is*.

[Right:] *We* are all inclined to like people who like us.

We needs no antecedent here, because it means "people in general."

[Wrong:] Some people may not select their friends with care, but *we* do.

We does not mean "people in general" here. It must have an antecedent in an earlier sentence, or it must not be used.

[Right:] *One* does not notice the rapid calculations the eye makes when one is guiding a bulky automobile through close-packed traffic.

One means "a man" or "a person" here; hence no antecedent is needed.

[Wrong:] A pronoun is *one* that takes the place of a noun.

One should have a clear antecedent here, or it should be replaced by *a word*.

[Right:] *He* who prays is certainly blessed.

He needs no antecedent here, for it is the equivalent of "any person" or "people in general."

[Wrong:] I went down to the newspaper, and *he* gave me my name on a slug of type.

He should have an antecedent in an earlier sentence.

C238 *You* is quite commonly used in the sense of "people in general," but it is so frequently confusing that it should be avoided in this sense as far as it can be without considerable awkwardness.

C239 Except for the cases discussed in C237, make sure that your reader can easily know what the antecedent of each pronoun is.[69]

---

[69] "Easily" means without hesitation or rereading.

Vague reference

"That old pinchbeak, Mrs. Snoop, and the other two neighborhood busybodies, Miss Small and Miss Prim, caught us just as we were about to leave."

"I'll bet she told you off about teasing her old cat."

"Yes. Well, you know what I told her? I told her if she didn't stop scratching my dog when she's asleep and harming nobody, I'd take her to the quarry pond and drown her in a sack."

"The old cat!"

"She is. She's an old cat."

Clear reference

"That old pinchbeak, Mrs. Snoop, and the other two neighborhood busybodies, Miss Small and Miss Prim, caught Johnny and me just as we were about to leave."

"I'll bet Mrs. Snoop told you two off about teasing her old cat."

"Yes. Well, you know what I told her? I told her that if her cat didn't stop scratching my dog when the dog is asleep and harming nobody, I'd take the cat to the quarry pond and drown her in a sack."

"Mrs. Snoop is an old cat herself."

"She is. She's an old cat."

C240 If there is a chance that a pronoun might cause confusion, do one of these things:

A Put the pronoun so close to its antecedent that the reader must see without any trouble that the two go together.

B Repeat the antecedent or use another noun.

C Avoid the antecedent-pronoun arrangement altogether.

[Wrong:] On my last visit to Seaux, before it was bombed off the map, I saw a thing that moved me very much. *It* was a little town in the South of France, hardly more than a village. *It* moved me so deeply because *it* was very Christlike and at the same time unexpectedly American.

It is not immediately clear whether *it* refers to Seaux or to the thing that moved the writer so much.

[Correction by moving antecedents and pronouns closer together:] I remember my last visit to *Seaux* before it was bombed off the map. *It* was a little town in the South of France, hardly more than a village. My recollection is vivid because while I was there I saw a *thing* that moved me very much. *It* moved me so deeply because it was very Christlike and at the same time unexpectedly American.

[Correction by repeating the antecedent or using another noun:] On my last visit to Seaux, before it was bombed off the map, I saw a thing that moved me very much. *Seaux* was a little town in the South of France, hardly more than a village. The *incident* moved me so deeply because it was very Christlike and at the same time unexpectedly American.

[Correction by rewriting so as to avoid the antecedent-pronoun arrangement:] On my last visit to Seaux (until it was bombed off the map, Seaux was a little town in the South of France, hardly more than a village), I saw a thing that moved me very much. *I was moved* so deeply because what happened was very Christlike and at the same time unexpectedly American.

C241 The case of a pronoun has nothing to do with the antecedent but depends on how the pronoun is used in the clause or sentence.

We met an Eskimo ~~whom~~ *who* had been converted by Father Buliard.

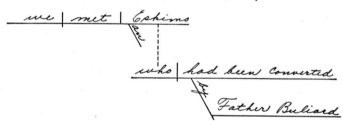

The Eskimo *whom* we met had been converted by Father Buliard.

C242 Make a pronoun agree with its antecedent in person, number,[70] and gender.[71]

---

[70] For the person and number of personal pronouns, see A29; of demonstrative pronouns, see A31 and A34; of *self*-pronouns, see A37; of relative pronouns, see A43 and A48; of interrogative pronouns, see A50 and A54; of indefinite pronouns, see A55, A57, and A59; and of reciprocal pronouns, see A61.

[71] For the gender of antecedents, see A11-20; of personal pronouns, see A30; of demonstrative pronouns, see A34; of *self*-pronouns, see A38; of relative pronouns, see A45-47; of interrogative pronouns, see A52-53; and of indefinite pronouns, see A58.

Jim [second-person antecedent], you [second person] put those books behind you [second person].

My fellow *officers* and *I* [plural antecedents (*I* is an intermediate antecedent)] promise that we [plural] will give safe-conduct to any messenger sent to us [plural].

The *tree* [neuter antecedent], strong as it [neuter] looked, splintered as it [neuter] fell.

C243 When the antecedent is the context or situation, make the pronoun third person, singular number, neuter gender.

It's Anna coming up the stairs, isn't *it?*
It's twenty miles to St. Louis.
It was another magazine salesman at the door.

C244 Use a singular pronoun or possessive adjective with a singular collective noun, unless the group is clearly acting as separate individuals.

its
The *team* lost ~~their~~ second game through sheer nervousness.

their
The *team* were either standing, kneeling, or lying at ~~its~~ ease in the end zone.

C245 Use a singular pronoun or possessive adjective when the antecedent is two or more singular nouns or pronouns joined by *or, nor, either . . . or, neither . . . nor,* or other disjunctives.[72]

his
Have you no pen? *Joe or Ted* will lend you ~~theirs~~.

hers
Whose hat is this? *Neither Lou nor Meg* left ~~theirs~~.

C246 Use a plural pronoun or possessive adjective when the antecedent is made up of a plural and a singular word.

My *brothers* and *I* have *our* quarrels, but *we* get along.

If *Mary* and her *friends* come in after school to make fudge, tell *them* not to use all the sugar.

[72] Disjunctives are conjunctions that separate, or offer a choice between, the words that they connect. When singular antecedents connected by disjunctives are of different persons or genders, either use a pronoun (for example, *that*) that does not show gender or person or else recast the sentence.

C247 When an antecedent is made up of words in the first and the second or third persons, put the pronoun or possessive adjective in the first person.

You, your *sister,* and *I* are to wait for *our* group captain on the corner of Washington and Beloit.

You and *I* are to wait for *our* group captain on the corner of Washington and Beloit.

My *teammates* and *I* met *our* match at bowling last night; *we* lost.

C248 When an antecedent is made up of words in the second and third persons, put the pronoun or possessive adjective in the second person.

You and *Clifford* ought to wait for *your* group captain on the corner of Washington and Beloit.

You and your *teammates* certainly met *your* match at bowling last night; *you* lost.

C249 When agreement is complicated by an *of* expression, make sure that you select the right antecedent according to the sense.

The only one of his stories that ~~were~~ *was* amusing was a tale of three men locked in an elevator.

One is the antecedent, not *stories,* since all of the stories but one were dull.

One of the people who ~~was~~ *were* present was a Don Q.

People is the antecedent, not *one.*

This was the best of the stories which ~~was~~ *were* told.

Stories is the antecedent, not *best* or *this.*

The number of members, *which runs* [or *who run*] into the thousands, surprises me.

Either *number* or *members* may be the antecedent.

The number of members who ~~was~~ *were* absent was truly deplorable.

Members is the antecedent, not *number.*

132

C250 Except for the case in C251, make a pronoun or possessive adjective agree in person, number, and gender with an indefinite pronoun that is the (intermediate) antecedent.[73]

As for schedule cards, *everyone* must show ~~theirs~~ *his* to me.

All of us lost *ours*.

I remembered my lines, but *several* forgot *theirs*.

Does *anyone* want to buy *his* ticket now?

Someone left *her* earrings at our house.

C251 In cases where singular reference, called for by C250, is awkward or silly, rewrite the sentence or use the plural.

When I came up out of the dark cellar, ~~everybody was~~ *all the boys and girls were* laughing at me; but even so I was glad to see ~~him~~ *them*.

The candidate made an excellent impression on everyone, and ~~he~~ *they* cheered him wildly.

C252 When the indefinite pronoun *one* is the (intermediate) antecedent, put the pronoun or possessive adjective in the third person, singular number.

[Wrong:] One does *their* [or *your*] best in life by serving God.

[Right:] One does *one's* best in life by serving God.

[Right:] One does *his* best in life by serving God.

C253 Put a pronoun or possessive adjective in the third person singular when its antecedent is modified by a singular indefinite adjective.[74]

Each truck must have ~~their~~ *its* proper license. So, too, every automobile and trailer must have ~~theirs~~ *its*.

Neither one looks like *his* father.

If *another* man throws *his* hat in the ring, the campaign should be a lively one.

---

[73] For the person, number, and gender of indefinite pronouns, see A55 and A57-59.

[74] For the singular indefinite adjectives, see A130.

PERSONAL-PRONOUN USE[75]

C254 Do not write *theres* or *there's* for *theirs*.

The money is *theirs*, belongs to them.

There's [there is] food enough for everybody. Please take your time.

These must be friends of ~~theres~~ *theirs*.

DEMONSTRATIVE-PRONOUN USE[76]

C255 Do not use *them* where you should use a demonstrative.

Housewife, pointing to the cheapest grapefruit on the counter: "I'll take a dozen of ~~them~~ *those*."

~~Them~~ *Those* are just the words I expected to hear, Clarence.

C256 Do not say *this here, that there, these here,* and *those there*.

These ~~here~~ will fit, but those ~~there~~ will not.

C257 If you insert words between the demonstrative and *here* or *there,* the expression can stand in good writing but should not be used unless the rhythm or some other quality of the sentence will be helped.

"Now *these melons here,*" said Mr. Grover, leading me down the row of exhibits, "are about the size of a healthy California grape."

Self-PRONOUN USE[77]

C258 Do not use a *self*-pronoun where a personal pronoun can carry the full meaning without sounding awkward.

[Wrong:] John and *myself* were here at seven-thirty.
[Right:] John and *I* were here at seven-thirty.

---

[75] For personal pronouns see A29-30.
[76] For demonstrative pronouns see A31-36.
[77] For *self*-pronouns see A37-42.

[Wrong:] Robert gave the old bicycle to my brother and *myself*.
[Right:] Robert gave the old bicycle to my brother and *me*.

[Wrong:] *Ourselves* and the others made twenty people.
[Right:] *We* and the others made twenty people.

[Right:] There goes Careless Smith hurting *himself* again.	If you used the personal pronoun here, you would change the meaning of the sentence to something else.
[Right:] Finally the guard left us to *ourselves*.	*Left us to us* would sound strange indeed.
[Right:] They are quite able to get along by *themselves*.	*By them* would sound strange and mean nothing.

C259 Do not write *ourselfs* for *ourselves, hisself* for *himself,* or *theirselves* for *themselves.*

We are proud of ~~ourselfs~~ *ourselves*.

I think he hurt ~~hisself~~ *himself* badly.

I say let them take care of ~~theirselves~~ *themselves*.

RELATIVE-PRONOUN USE[78]

C260 The relative pronouns are used only to introduce (dependent) adjective clauses.[79]

I know the girl *whom* you mean.	*Whom you mean* is an adjective clause modifying the noun *girl* in the other clause.
We found the weapon *that* he probably used.	*That he probably used* is an adjective clause modifying *weapon*.
The newspaper account, *which* I read last night, didn't give his name.	*Which I read last night* is an adjective clause modifying *account*.

---

[78] For relative pronouns see A43-49.
[79] For adjective clauses see C411.

C261 A relative pronoun refers to an antecedent in another clause. This makes it easy to distinguish a relative pronoun and its adjective clause from an interrogative or indefinite pronoun or adjective and its noun clause, from demonstrative-pronoun and demonstrative-adjective *that,* and from the conjunction *that.*[80]

I know the *girl whom* you mean.

Whom is a relative pronoun. It has an antecedent in the independent clause: *girl.*

I know *whom* you mean.

Whom is not a relative pronoun. It does not have an antecedent in the independent clause.

Here are the *blueprints that* you were looking for.

That is a relative pronoun. It has an antecedent in the independent clause: *blueprints.* So the dependent clause is an adjective clause.

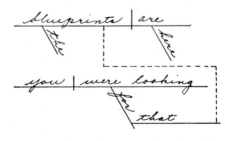

---

[80] A relative pronoun sometimes has as its antecedent the whole idea expressed in the independent clause; for example, "She sang badly, which made the maestro wince." But it is difficult to use this construction without awkwardness and confusion. Avoid it while you are an apprentice writer in high school.

136

I was looking for the blue-prints when I found *that* on the floor.

That is not a relative pronoun. It has no antecedent in the other clause (the independent clause).

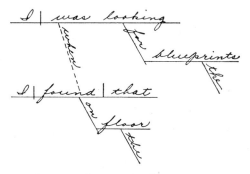

I was looking for something else when I found *that* blueprint on the floor.

That is not a relative pronoun. It has no antecedent in the other clause (the independent clause).

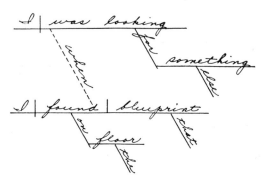

I knew *that* you were looking for the blueprints.

That is not a relative pronoun. It has no antecedent in the other clause (the independent clause).

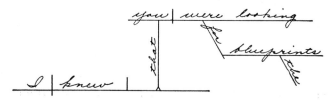

137

C262 While it is by no means a matter of obligation, for the sake of clarity *that* is usually preferred to *which* in restrictive adjective clauses;[81] *which* is preferred to *that* in nonrestrictive adjective clauses. (If awkwardness results, simply ignore this rule.)

[Restrictive:] The bike *that* I sold is very different from the bike *that* you sold.

[Nonrestrictive:] The bike, *which*, by the way, I sold the other day, had become a matter of envy between my two children.

C263 The case of the relative pronoun has nothing to do with the antecedent but depends on how the relative is used in its own clause.

We met an Eskimo ~~whom~~ *who* had been converted by Father Buliard.

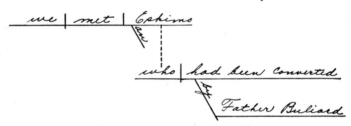

C264 Parenthetical clauses that come in between the relative pronoun and the rest of its own clause do not affect the case of the relative.

Tim was a man ~~whom~~ *who* we thought would fight for us.

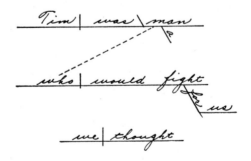

---

[81] For restrictive and nonrestrictive adjective clauses, see C312-15.

138

C265 To determine whether a clause is parenthetical or not, cancel it. If the sentence still makes easy, good sense, the clause is parenthetical.

Tim was a man who ~~we thought~~ would fight for us.	Cancel *we thought* and the sentence still makes easy, good sense. Therefore *we thought* is parenthetical.

INTERROGATIVE-PRONOUN USE[82]

C266 Do not use an apostrophe with *whose* and do not confuse *whose* (of whom) with *who's* (who is).

Whose
~~Who's~~ are you wearing?

INDEFINITE-PRONOUN USE[83]

C267 Use *less* to indicate how much, *fewer* to indicate how many.

Fewer   *are*
~~Less~~ than five instructions ~~is~~ insufficient.
Less than a bushel is insufficient.

Adjective and adverb use

ADJECTIVE USE[84]

C268 An adjective that is not a predicate adjective or an objective complement[85] is called an attributive or an appositive adjective.

C269 An attributive adjective is an adjective that precedes the noun it modifies.

Don't eat *green* apples.
There is a *sick* boy.

---

[82] For interrogative pronouns see A50-54.
[83] For indefinite pronouns see A55-59.
[84] For adjectives see A103-36.
[85] For predicate adjectives see C167 and C169-72. For adjectives as objective complements, see C157-58.

C270 An appositive adjective is an adjective that is not a predicate adjective or an objective complement, yet follows the noun it modifies.

Simpson dropped his chin like a man *shot.*
The wind, *mournful* and *desolate,* howled all night.

C271 Clarity often requires that the article be used with each noun or adjective to show that more than one person or thing is meant.

The secretary and *the* treasurer were arrested. [Two men.]
The secretary and treasurer *was* arrested. [One man.]

A black and *a* white purse *were* lost. [Two purses.]
A black and white purse *was* lost. [One purse.]

ADVERB USE[86]

C272 Do not use *most* (to the maximum degree) for *almost* (not quite).

The milk is ~~most~~ *almost* gone.

C273 Do not use two negatives.

I didn't do ~~nothing~~ *anything* wrong!

C274 In connection with C273 remember that words like *scarcely, hardly, barely, nothing, nobody,* and *never* are negative.

There ~~wasn't~~ *was* scarcely any recoil.

His face was so battered I ~~didn't barely recognize~~ *barely recognized* him.

There was hardly ~~no~~ *any* water in the radiator.

No, sir, I didn't see ~~nobody~~ *anybody.*

In his whole life he never did ~~nothing~~ *anything* worth while.

---

[86] For adverbs see A137-41.

C275 Do not use *never* when you mean simply *not*.

I ~~never took~~ *didn't take* those letters for you this afternoon.

C276 Do not add an *s* to *somewhere, anywhere, nowhere,* or *anyway*.

Let's go ~~somewheres~~ *somewhere* else.

C277 Do not use *kind of* or *sort of* as an adverb; use *somewhat, rather, fairly,* and so on.

I'm ~~kind of~~ *a little* tired.

C278 Do not use *real* for *really* or for *very* or *extremely*.

The coffee is ~~real~~ *very* hot.

C279 Do not use *some* for *somewhat* or *a little*.

He reads ~~some~~ *somewhat* faster than he used to.

I'm *a little* perplexed by your argument.

C280 Do not use *sure* but *surely* to mean undoubtedly, indeed, yes indeed.

You ~~sure~~ *surely* told him.

Will I work for a dollar an hour? ~~Sure~~ *Surely*!

C281 Do not place *too* or *very* immediately before a past participle that usage has not as yet established as an adjective. Between *very* or *too* and the past participle insert an appropriate adverb, like *deeply, genuinely, greatly, much*.

Questionable	Preferable
Yes, indeed, we were *very* impressed.	Yes, indeed, we were *very much* impressed.
But, sir, I am *too* indebted to you already.	But, sir, I am *too deeply* indebted to you already.

[Quite all right:] You could hardly expect him to admit that he is a *very* distinguished man.

141

C282 It is preferable, ordinarily, not to use *up* after such verbs as *ascend, connect, cripple, divide, end, finish, open, rest,* and *settle.*

> Our Lord ascended ~~up~~ into heaven.
> Please connect me ~~up~~ with the superintendent.
> Poor Mother is all crippled ~~up~~ with rheumatism.
> Let's divide ~~up~~ the candy now!
> Where does this highway end ~~up~~?
> At last Angus has finished ~~up~~ drying the dishes.
> Don't open ~~up~~ this package until Christmas.
> It will take me a long time to rest ~~up~~ completely.
> Why don't these people settle ~~up~~ their bills?

[Not affected by this rule, because *up* is necessary:] On the seventh day we broke *up* several packing cases for fuel.

CONFUSION OF ADJECTIVE AND ADVERB

C283 Do not use adjectives to modify verbs, adjectives, or adverbs.[87]

I didn't do very ~~good~~ *well* in the physics test.

This is a ~~good~~-*well-*built house.

---

[87] For "I feel bad" and the use of adjectives with linking verbs, see C169-72.

142

She played a bit of Chopin very ~~nice~~. *nicely*

Don't walk about so ~~heavy~~. *heavily*

Robert behaved very ~~bad~~ at Mrs. Snifton's tea. *badly*

C284 Do not use *this* or *that* for the adverbs *so* or *very*.

He was ~~that~~ happy he could only cry. *so*

I have never seen the lake ~~this~~ blue∧ *so* *as this.*

Comparison of adjectives and adverbs

THE THREE DEGREES OF COMPARISON

C285 Comparison is the change made in the form of adjectives and adverbs to show that the word they modify is greater or less in quantity or quality than some other word.

C286 The positive degree indicates that the word modified is not being compared with any other word. The comparative and superlative degrees indicate that the word modified is being compared with some other word.[88]

[Positive degree:] A hamburger is a *beautiful* thing.

[Comparative degree:] A hamburger is *more beautiful* than anything else I know.

[Superlative degree:] A hamburger is the *most beautiful* thing in the world.

[Positive degree:] What a *large* onion that is.

[Comparative degree:] Bermuda onions are a great deal *larger* than chives.

[Superlative degree:] This is the *largest* onion of the three.

[Positive degree:] Mr. Marble closed the store *early.*

[Comparative degree:] Mr. Marble closed the store *earlier* than Mr. Kemp closed his.

[Superlative degree:] Of all the merchants on Clay Avenue, Mr. Marble closed his store *earliest.*

FORMING THE COMPARATIVE AND SUPERLATIVE

C287 Many adjectives and adverbs of one and two syllables form the comparative by adding *er,* and the superlative by adding *est,* to the positive.

Positive	Comparative	Superlative
dull	dull*er*	dull*est*
small	small*er*	small*est*
large	larg*er*	larg*est*
few	few*er*	few*est*
humble	humbl*er*	humbl*est*
flighty	flight*ier*	flight*iest*
high	high*er*	high*est*
near	near*er*	near*est*
early	earl*ier*	earl*iest*

---

[88] The superlative degree of an adjective or adverb (usually with *most*) may be used without any suggestion of comparison to express a high degree of perfection, imperfection, and the like (C311).

C288 If the adjective or adverb ends in *e*, drop that *e* before *er* and *est*. If the adjective ends in *y* preceded by a consonant, change the *y* to *i*.

humble	humbler	humblest
flighty	flightier	flightiest

C289 If the adjective or adverb is of one syllable, double a final consonant after a vowel that is short in sound.

fat	fatter	fattest
wet	wetter	wettest
thin	thinner	thinnest
hot	hotter	hottest

C290 Many adjectives and adverbs of one and two syllables and all adjectives and adverbs of more than two form the comparative by placing *more* or *less,* and the superlative by placing *most* or *least,* before the positive.

Positive	*Comparative*	*Superlative*
dull	*more* dull	*most* dull
dull	*less* dull	*least* dull
humble	*more* humble	*most* humble
humble	*less* humble	*least* humble
softly	*more* softly	*most* softly
softly	*less* softly	*least* softly
absurdly	*more* absurdly	*most* absurdly
absurdly	*less* absurdly	*least* absurdly
delightfully	*more* delightfully	*most* delightfully
delightfully	*less* delightfully	*least* delightfully
elaborate	*more* elaborate	*most* elaborate
elaborate	*less* elaborate	*least* elaborate
joyously	*more* joyously	*most* joyously
joyously	*less* joyously	*least* joyously
admirable	*more* admirable	*most* admirable
admirable	*less* admirable	*least* admirable
near	*less* near	*least* near
close	*less* close	*least* close

145

C291 The following adjectives and adverbs form the comparative and superlative irregularly as shown.

ADJECTIVES

Positive	Comparative	Superlative
good	better	best
well	better	best
bad	worse	worst
ill	worse	worst
little	⎰ smaller [size] ⎱ less [quantity]	smallest [size] least [quantity]
much	more	most
many	more	most
far	⎰ further ⎨ farther ⎱ [distance only]	furthest farthest [distance only]

ADVERBS

well	better	best
ill	worse	worst
badly	worse	worst
much	more	most
little	less	least
far	⎰ further ⎨ farther ⎱ [distance only]	furthest farthest [distance only]

C292 Note that the comparison of *few* is *fewer* and *fewest,* not *less* and *least.* Do not say "Less people came than were expected." Say "Fewer people came than were expected."

C293 Do not use counterfeit comparative or superlative forms. When in doubt, consult a dictionary.

more curious
You are ~~curioser~~ than any other boy I ever saw.

more legibly
I expect to write ~~legiblier~~ now that I have a new ribbon in the typewriter.

C294 Of their very nature some adjectives and adverbs have, strictly speaking, no comparative or superlative. Such are *unique, dead, circular, triangular.* Some of them, however,

146

are used in loose or figurative comparisons; for example, *deader than a doornail*. But it is considered a blunder to attribute any degree whatever to *unique* or *peerless*, since *unique* means the only one of its kind and *peerless* means without equal. So do not say "very unique" or "more peerless."

USING THE COMPARATIVE

C295 Use the comparative with *than*.

Horrowitz is a *better* quarterback *than* Flugel.
Chetwood was hurt *less severely than* Tracy or Cameron.
Schmidt proved *more obstreperous* than we expected.

C296 Do not use the comparative if you are comparing more than two persons or things or more than two groups of persons or things.

Geraldine is clearly the ~~more~~ *most* bashful of the three Hollingsworth girls.

If you are talking about the Sneeds, the Clarks, and the Lapierres, the Clarks are to my mind the ~~more~~ *most* Christlike couple of the three.

C297 Finish a comparison involving *than* before beginning one involving *as* or *so*, and vice versa.

[Wrong:] She is prettier but not so entertaining as her sister.
[Right:] She is prettier *than* her sister but not so entertaining.

C298 Keep balance in a comparison.

[Wrong:] The freshmen's awards are far, far handsomer than the sophomores.	Awards are compared with sophomores.
[Right:] The freshmen's awards are far, far handsomer than the sophomores'.	Freshmen's awards are compared with sophomores' awards.

C299 Do not use double comparatives.

Wait! I know a ~~more~~ better way.

C300 When using the comparative with things of the same group, use *other, else,* or an equivalent word.

[Wrong:] Dr. Black has more elaborate gadgets than any dentist in his town.

This compares Dr. Black with himself and says that he has more elaborate gadgets than he himself has.

[Right:] Dr. Black has more elaborate gadgets than any *other* dentist in his town.

This compares Dr. Black with the rest of his group—the dentists in his town. *Other* keeps the doctor from being compared with himself.

[Wrong:] I have made smaller contributions to the mission drive than anybody in my class.

[Right:] I have made smaller contributions to the mission drive than anybody *else* in my class.

[Wrong:] I like tutti-frutti better than any flavor.

[Right:] I like tutti-frutti better than any *other* flavor.

C301 When using the comparative with things of different groups, do not use *other, else,* or an equivalent word.

[Wrong:] This steam engine develops as much power as any *other* diesel.

This statement implies that a steam engine is a diesel engine. The word *other* illogically puts the two engines in the same group or class.

[Right:] This steam engine develops as much power as any diesel.

[Wrong:] Without training, Stani sings as well as somebody *else* with years of music school behind him.

This statement implies that the untrained Stani has had years of music school. *Else* puts Stani in the group of those who have had training.

[Right:] Without training, Stani sings as well as somebody with years of music school behind him.

[Wrong:] This plane is as big and as comfortable as any *other* moderate-sized ocean liner.

[Right:] This plane is as big and as comfortable as any moderate-sized ocean liner.

C302 In order to use the right case of a personal pronoun after *than* or *as,* mentally complete the elliptical sentence.

he
Tush! You are much stronger than ~~him~~ [is strong].

her
I'd trust Marcus sooner than [I'd trust] ~~she~~.

she
I'd trust Marcus sooner than ~~her~~ [would trust Marcus].

he
There is no other as strong as ~~him~~ [is].

C303 Do not substitute *all the farther, all the further, all the faster, all the longer, all the quicker,* and similar expressions for *as far as, as fast as, as long as, as quick as,* and similar expressions of comparison.

as long as
This is ~~all the longer~~ I can wait.

the fastest
Four knots an hour is ~~all the faster~~ that the Q will sail.

[Right, since it is not a substitute for *as soon as:*] If you leave now, you will get to Covington all the sooner.

USING THE SUPERLATIVE

C304 Use the superlative degree when *than* is not used and more than two persons or things or groups of persons or things are compared.

greatest
There are faith, hope, and charity, of which the ~~greater~~ is charity.

fattest
Which was the ~~fatter~~—Cassius, Casca, or Caesar?

C305 When an *of* phrase limits an adjective or adverb in the superlative degree, do not use *other, else,* or an equivalent word.

[Wrong:] That suggestion is the most cowardly of all the *others.*
[Right:] That suggestion is the most cowardly of all.

[Wrong:] I am the least known of all the *other* poets in my class.
[Right:] I am the least known of all the poets in my class.

149

C306 When an *of* phrase limits an adjective or adverb in the superlative degree, make the object of *of* a plural noun or a collective noun.

[Wrong:] Paul has the sincerest friends of any *boy* in our class.
[Right:] Paul has the sincerest friends of all the *boys* in our class.

[Wrong:] You are the least responsible person of *anybody* I know.
[Right:] Of all the people I know, you are the least responsible.

C307 When an *of* phrase limits an adjective or adverb in the superlative degree, make sure that the object of *of* includes the person or thing to be compared.

[Wrong:] Nolan Kane is the most talented of his brothers, Kerry and "Sugar" Kane. | This sentence says that Nolan is one of his two brothers, which is absurd.

[Right:] Of the three Kane brothers—Nolan, Kerry, and "Sugar"—Nolan is the most talented.

[Wrong:] Of all the *cities* along the Mississippi, the *people* of Natchez seem to me the most charming. | This sentence compares cities with people, instead of people with other people.

[Right:] Of all the *dwellers* in the cities along the Mississippi, the *people* of Natchez seem to me the most charming.

[Wrong:] You are the least responsible of all the *others* I know.
[Right:] You are the least responsible of all the boys I know.

C308 Do not use a superlative where the comparative is called for and is sufficient.

less
Of the two plans, this is the ~~least~~ effective.

C309 Do not use double superlatives.

You do the ~~most~~ oddest things!

C310 Make all comparisons grammatical and complete.

[Wrong:] She maintained that Rudolph Valentino was one of the handsomest actors, if not the handsomest, of modern times.
[Right:] She maintained that Rudolph Valentino was one of the handsomest actors, if not the handsomest *actor,* of modern times.

150

[Wrong:] Salmon is one of the greatest, if not the greatest, export articles of Alaska.

[Right:] Salmon is probably the greatest export article of Alaska.

[Wrong:] One of, if not the oldest, priests of the diocese is Father Jim Hardy.

[Right:] Father Jim Hardy is either the oldest priest of the diocese or one of the oldest priests.

C311 The superlative degree of an adjective or adverb (usually with *most*) may be used without any suggestion of comparison to express a high degree of perfection, imperfection, and the like.

This cowardly remark is *most unworthy* of you.
I must say he was a *most unruly* little boy.
And, of course, all of your teachers have treated you *most kindly?*

Restrictive and nonrestrictive modifiers[89]

C312 Modifiers are classified as restrictive and nonrestrictive. By modifiers are meant adjectives (including participles used adjectivally) and adjective phrases and clauses, adverbs and adverb phrases and clauses.

C313 Modifiers are called restrictive when the writer wants them joined very closely in sense to the words that they modify.

The girl *that I marry* will have to support me in the manner to which I am accustomed.

C314 Modifiers are called nonrestrictive when the writer wants them joined loosely to the words that they modify—as added information, as a by-the-way thought, as a point worth bringing in but not very necessary to the chief notions of the sentence.

A comb—*which, by the way, costs very little*—is equipment that you should have and even use.

---

[89] For the punctuation of restrictive and nonrestrictive modifiers, see D38-40, D74, and D79.

C315 Use this test: Read the sentence without the modifier. If the sentence still says most of what you want it to, the modifier is nonrestrictive. If the sentence is changed—if it does not say most of what you want it to but something else—the modifier is restrictive.

I prefer freshmen, enthusiastic and willing.

[Without the modifier:] I prefer freshmen.

Suppose that you wish mainly to say that you had rather teach freshmen than other classes. Suppose you add *enthusiastic and willing* as extra and secondary information explaining why you prefer freshmen. The adjectives, then, are nonrestrictive.

I prefer freshmen enthusiastic and willing.

[Without the modifier:] I prefer freshmen.

Suppose you wish to say that you like freshmen better when they are enthusiastic and willing than when they are lazy. The omission of *enthusiastic and willing* would change this sense. Here the adjectives are restrictive.

Johnson, blubbering, was a sight to behold.

[Without the modifier:] Johnson was a sight to behold.

Suppose your chief thought is that Johnson was a sight to behold. You add *blubbering* as an interesting detail, unnecessary to the main idea. In this sentence the participial adjective is nonrestrictive.

Johnson blubbering was a sight to behold.

[Without the modifier:] Johnson was a sight to behold.

Suppose that you wish to say that it was an astonishing thing to see an ordinarily brave man like Johnson mumbling tearfully. Omit *blubbering* and the sentence no longer expresses your meaning. In this sentence the participial adjective is restrictive.

Joan Drew was, probably, the only person at the table who had ever tasted enchiladas.

[Without the modifier:] Joan Drew was the only person at the table who had ever tasted enchiladas.

Joan Drew was probably the only person at the table who had ever tasted enchiladas.

[Without the modifier:] Joan Drew was the only person at the table who had ever tasted enchiladas.

Suppose that your main point is that Joan was the only one who had tasted enchiladas. You add *probably* as an afterthought, just to be accurate. Omit *probably* and your chief thought is unchanged. The adverb is nonrestrictive.

Suppose that you want it part of your chief thought that you are not certain but nearly so that only Joan had tasted enchiladas. Omit *probably*. The sentence is not what you intend. The adverb is restrictive.

That column of Allen's, about fast driving, made Oliver Hornsby angry.

[Without the modifier:] That column of Allen's made Oliver Hornsby angry.

Suppose your chief thought is that Allen's column made Hornsby angry. Your reader knows the column you refer to. You add *about fast driving* only to make sure that he remembers. The adjective phrase is nonrestrictive.

That column of Allen's about fast driving made Oliver Hornsby angry.

[Without the modifier:] That column of Allen's made Oliver Hornsby angry.

Suppose you are sure that your reader will not know which column you are talking about unless you name it. *About fast driving* is necessary to your chief thought. The adjective phrase is restrictive.

I did take the car back, right after the dance.

[Without the modifier:] I did take the car back.

Suppose your chief thought is that you took the car back. You add *right after the dance* only as some extra information that might impress your reader. In this sentence the adverb phrase is nonrestrictive.

153

I took the car back right after the dance.

[Without the modifier:] I took the car back.

Suppose your chief purpose is to tell *when* you took the car back. In this sentence the adverb phrase is restrictive.

Mr. Ruhlman, who was here less than an hour ago, has just died.

[Without the modifier:] Mr. Ruhlman has just died.

Suppose your chief thought is that Mr. Ruhlman just died. *Who was here less than an hour ago* is an interesting, but extra, detail. The adjective clause is nonrestrictive.

The Mr. Ruhlman who was here less than an hour ago just died.

[Without the modifier:] The Mr. Ruhlman just died.

Suppose that you are using the dependent clause to distinguish the dead Mr. Ruhlman from another Mr. Ruhlman. It is necessary to your thought. In this sentence the adjective clause is restrictive.

No one will be in the office on the Fourth, because that's a holiday.

[Without the modifier:] No one will be in the office on the Fourth.

Suppose that you add *because that's a holiday* only to emphasize what has already been made clear. The adverbial clause is nonrestrictive.

No one would commit murder just because he did not like a hat.

[Without the modifier:] No one would commit murder.

Suppose that you are discussing motives for murder. The motive is then part of the chief thought. Omit *just because he did not like a hat* and you say something you do not intend—something silly, in fact. The adverbial clause is restrictive.

C316 Adjectives that precede their nouns must, in most cases, be restrictive if they are to make any sense at all. But there are exceptions.

[Restrictive:] The *perfect* friend is the Man who is God.
[Restrictive:] Someone played a *cracked* and *asthmatic* record.

[Nonrestrictive:] *Unafraid,* he faced the crowd.
[Nonrestrictive:] The last balloon popped and, *dismayed,* he burst into tears.

C317 Articles are always restrictive.

The solution did not appeal to Blackbeard.
A bat and *an* eagle should not be kept in *the* same cage.

C318 Almost all adverbs that precede and modify adjectives or adverbs must be restrictive if they are to make sense at all.

The fumes were *quite* strong.
I have never seen you behave *more* disagreeably.

C319 *Possibly, probably, certainly, perhaps, therefore, consequently, doubtless,* and some other adverbs expressing certainty, doubt, or conclusion almost always modify verbs and hence may be used restrictively or nonrestrictively.

[Restrictive:] The boy was tall and *probably* strong.
[Nonrestrictive:] The boy was tall and, *probably,* strong.

C320 Introductory phrases have their own rules of punctuation (D46-48), regardless of whether they are restrictive or nonrestrictive.

C321 Adverb clauses that precede their independent clause have their own rule of punctuation (D45), regardless of whether they are restrictive or nonrestrictive.

C322 While it is by no means a matter of obligation, for the sake of clarity *that* is usually preferred to *which* in restrictive adjective clauses; *which* is preferred to *that* in nonrestrictive adjective clauses. (If awkwardness results, simply ignore this rule.)

[Restrictive:] The bike *that* I sold is very different from the bike *that* you sold.

[Nonrestrictive:] The bike, *which,* by the way, I sold the other day, had become a matter of envy between my two children.

Dangling, misplaced, and squinting modifiers

DANGLING MODIFIERS

C323 Modifiers that seem to modify the wrong word or no word at all are called dangling modifiers.

[Dangling adjective:] *Restless,* the forbidden door seemed to taunt the two little children.

[Right:] The forbidden door seemed to taunt the two restless little children.

[Dangling participle:] *Exhausted,* the bench looked inviting.
[Right:] Since I was exhausted, the bench looked inviting.

[Dangling participial phrase:] *Peeling onions,* our eyes watered.
[Right:] Peeling onions, we found that our eyes watered.

[Dangling participial phrase:] An hour later, *strolling the beach and climbing the sand dunes,* an outrigger canoe emerged from behind Starvation Point.

[Right:] An hour later, while Mary and Ronald were strolling the beach and climbing the sand dunes, an outrigger canoe emerged from behind Starvation Point.

[Dangling phrase with gerund:] *Before rising,* a cup of coffee is comfortable indeed.

[Right:] It is comfortable to have a cup of coffee before rising.

[Dangling phrase with gerund:] *After having been in the sun for two hours,* the punch tasted cool and refreshing.

[Right:] After having been in the sun for two hours, Tom and Janet found the punch tasted cool and refreshing.

[Dangling infinitive phrase:] Water wings are silly *to swim.*
[Right:] It is silly to use water wings to swim.

[Dangling infinitive phrase:] *To sing well,* the diaphragm should be extended.

[Right:] To sing well, extend your diaphragm.

[Dangling elliptical dependent clause:] *When two days old,* my father died.

[Right:] When I was two days old, my father died.

C324 Make sure that every modifier modifies a definite word that is expressed in the sentence.

C325 Do not use a dangling elliptical dependent clause. The omitted subject noun or pronoun of an introductory elliptical dependent clause must be the same as the subject noun or pronoun of the independent clause.

When~~,~~ *I was* two days old, my father died.

C326 An introductory infinitive used as an adverb expressing purpose must logically refer to the subject noun or pronoun even though grammatically the infinitive modifies the predicate verb.

To be educated, *one must read books* ~~books must be read~~.

C327 A few participial and infinitive phrases are said to be used in the absolute construction when they have no grammatical connection with the rest of the sentence. But do not make use of such a construction unless you are certain that it is common in good writers.

Talking of football, who won the Army game?

Coming to the point, the answer is no.

He may be wrong—*granting,* of course, his truthfulness.

Granted that he is a persuasive speaker, will he make a steady worker?

Allowing for minor errors, the experiment can be called a success.

To judge from her looks, she's about forty years old.

To think you'd be so unmannerly!

MISPLACED MODIFIERS

C328 Misplaced modifiers are modifiers—whether words, phrases, or dependent clauses—so placed in a sentence that they seem to modify the wrong word.

[Misplaced adjectives:] *Orange and crimson,* the poet gazed long at the sunset.

[Right:] The poet gazed long at the orange and crimson sunset.

157

[Misplaced adjective phrase:] *With the face of a dinosaur,* the hunter killed the prehistoric monster.

[Right:] The hunter killed a prehistoric monster with the face of a dinosaur.

[Misplaced adjective clause:] He hid the oriental jewel in a fragile cigar box, *which was worth many fortunes.*

[Right:] He hid the oriental jewel, which was worth many fortunes, in a fragile cigar box.

C329 Place modifying words, phrases, and clauses as near as you reasonably can to the words that they modify.

SQUINTING MODIFIERS[90]

C330 Squinting modifiers—often adverbs, adverb phrases, or adverb clauses—are modifiers so placed that they seem to modify either of two expressions.

frequently
I was ˄ advised ~~frequently~~ to review Latin.

Without the correction it is difficult to tell whether *frequently* modifies *advised* or *to review.*

On the following day
˄ Frank was told ~~on the following day~~ to enlist.

Without the correction it is difficult to tell whether *on the following day* modifies *was told* or *to enlist.*

When I was too tired to think,
˄ I agreed ~~when I was too tired to think~~ to work on Saturdays.

Without the correction it is difficult to tell whether *when I was too tired to think* modifies *agreed* or *to work on Saturdays.*

C331 Place a modifier so that it unmistakably modifies only the word or expression that you want it to.

---

[90] Squinting modifiers are simply one special kind of misplaced modifier. A modifier is said to squint when one cannot tell whether it is looking toward the expression that precedes it or toward the expression that follows it. It is corrected by a change of position.

Preposition use[91]

CORRECT PREPOSITION USE

C332 Prepositions are used to indicate relationships between the noun or pronoun they govern and some other word in the sentence.

C333 You may end a sentence with a preposition.

I can tell you what the shouting is *about.*
Craig has nobody to eat lunch *with.*

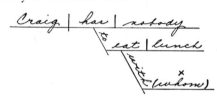

C334 Do not make a preposition do its own work and that of a different preposition as well.

He is willing to listen to but not to argue with you.

C335 Do not omit a preposition when the omission dulls the parallel between the sentence elements or makes the sentence a little difficult to understand at first reading.

Seven of us will be back by nine if not by eight.

C336 Do not use *of* for *have* or *'ve,* and do not insert an *of* after *had.*

You should have seen the crowd at Dinny's last night.

They ought to have gone to a vocational school.

If Duke had let go, the rest of us would've fallen.

C337 *Upon* and *on* may be used interchangeably, except where one or the other sounds unpleasant.

---

[91] For prepositions see A142-47.

C338 Use *into* for entrance, not *in*.

Boris *dropped* the corpse's clothing ~~in~~ *into* the well.
That Crosley has been *parked in* the same place all day.

C339 Use *beside* when you mean at the side of or next to; use *besides* when you mean in addition to.

~~Besides~~ *Beside* the ice cream there stood a mountain of cookies.
~~Beside~~ *Besides* ice cream there were mountains of cookies.

C340 Use *from,* not *than* or *to,* after *different*.

Oh, she is entirely different ~~than~~ *from* other girls.

Smollett's reply was very different ~~to~~ *from* what the chemist expected.

C341 When *differ* means to be different, use *from* after it.

You differ a great deal *from* your studious brother.

C342 When *differ* means to disagree, use *with* for persons and *on, about,* and so on, for things.

I differ *with* you *about* the oddest things!

C343 Use *part from* to mean leave or bid farewell to; use *part with* to mean give up.

He parted *from* his parents.
He parted *with* his last cent.

C344 Use *agree with* with persons; use *agree on, to,* and so on, with things.

I don't agree *with* you.
Let us all agree *to* his nomination.

C345 Do not use *at* or *to* after *where*.

Now where on earth can he have gone ~~to~~?
I don't know exactly where I am ~~at~~.

C346 Do not use *off* where *from* will make sense.

Jerry bought the motorcycle ~~off~~ *from* a friend.

C347 Do not use *of* after *remember, recollect,* or *recall.*

I don't remember ~~of~~ hearing him say that.

Do you recollect ~~of~~ the days when we used to gig frogs in this same pool?

C348 Use *between* in reference to two; use *among* in reference to more than two.

among

The old man divided his wealth ~~between~~ his four sons.

C349 Do not use the expression *want in* (*out, off, through, up, down,* and so on), or one like *want next the window.*

to get

This man wants∧off at the next stop.

to sit

Does little Herbie want∧near the window?

POLISHED PREPOSITION USE[92]

C350 Use *like* as a preposition, not as a conjunction. (In other words, always use *like* with an object.)

mine

You have a jacket like ~~I have~~.

as

Put a little alcohol into the tank ~~like~~ he told you.

C351 Do not use *inside of* for *within* in reference to time, or *outside of* for *aside from.*

within

We should finish ~~inside of~~ a day.

aside from

~~Outside of~~ a month of zero weather, the winter has been mild.

C352 Do not use *around* to mean nearly or about.

about

The baby weighs ~~around~~ eight pounds.

nearly

We had to paddle ~~around~~ seven miles for food.

---

[92] These rules are rather frequently ignored, even by writers and speakers of note. If, however, you keep them, your writing will gain in simplicity, clarity, and elegance.

C353 Do not use *on* after *continue* unless you need it to make sense.

> Then we continued ~~on~~ walking for another day.
> Paul continued *on* the road to Damascus.

C354 Say *forbid to* and *prohibit from*.

> *to hold*
> The constitution forbids a man ~~from holding~~ two offices at once.
> *from parking*
> People are prohibited ~~to park~~ their cars in the schoolyard except during the eleven o'clock Mass.

C355 Do not use *of* after *off*.

> The maid knocked the picture off ~~of~~ the table.

C356 Do not use *of* after *inside* and *outside*.

> Dent was trapped inside ~~of~~ the burning hotel.
> We had locked ourselves outside ~~of~~ the house.

C357 Omit the prepositions in such expressions as these: *cover over, over with,* and *start in*.

> Cover ~~over~~ the stew.
> Thank the Lord the war is over ~~with~~.
> John had better start ~~in~~ to read his book.

C358 Use *at* or *about* but not *at about*.

> [Inelegant:] This snapshot was taken at about ten o'clock.
> [Nice:] This snapshot was taken at ten o'clock.
> [Nice:] This snapshot was taken about ten o'clock.

C359 In expressions like *angry with* and *angry at* use *with* for persons, *at* for things.

> The block leader was angry *with* me *at* my carelessness.

C360 Since *due* is an adjective, use it only as a predicate complement or the modifier of a noun; do not use it as a preposition.

> *Because of*
> ~~Due to~~ Cardinal Schmidt's visit, there will be no school tomorrow.
> [Predicate complement:] The applause was *due* to him.
> [Adjective:] I am waiting for the discount *due* to me.

162

C361 Do not say *back behind;* and use *behind* rather than *back of* or *in back of.*

Behind
~~Back behind~~ me sat the Martins.

Behind
~~Back of~~ me sat the Martins.

Behind
~~In back of~~ me sat the Martins.

Conjunction use[93]

C362 Use *neither . . . nor,* not *neither . . . or.*

nor
Gilbert was neither strong ~~or~~ intelligent.

C363 Do not use *because* for *that* or *the fact that* to introduce the subject of a sentence.

That
~~Because~~ you are sleepy does not exempt you from the examination.

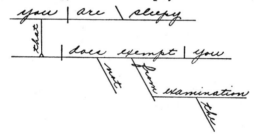

The fact that
~~Because~~ you are sleepy does not exempt you from the examination.

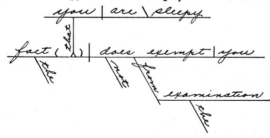

[93] For conjunctions see A148-59. For the punctuation of compound sentences, see D30-32. For the conjunctions that connect the various kinds of dependent clauses, see A150 and A156-59.

C364 Do not use *because* for *that* or *the fact that* to introduce a predicate complement after *the reason is.*

The reason for his broad smile is ~~because~~ *that* he won the essay contest.

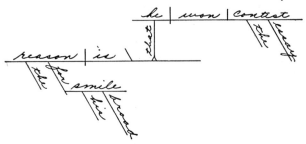

The reason for his broad smile is ~~because~~ *the fact that* he won the essay contest.

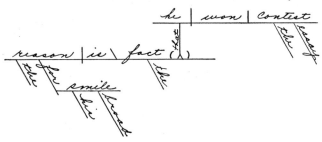

The reason why I've changed my mind is *that* this horse is absolutely uncontrollable.

The reason why I've changed my mind is *the fact that* this horse is absolutely uncontrollable.

C365 Do not use *when* or *where* to introduce a predicate complement in definitions or explanations.

The big event of the year is ~~when the seniors have their dance~~ *the senior dance*.

A rainbow is ~~when the sun's rays are refracted and reflected~~ *the refraction and reflection of the sun's rays* by raindrops.

The jackknife is *a dive in which you bend from the waist and touch your ankles while keeping your knees unflexed.*

Most people will agree that one of the loveliest times of the year is *the coming of spring.*

164

C366 Do not use *where* for *that* in object clauses.

that
I saw in the bulletin ~~where~~ Jones was appointed.

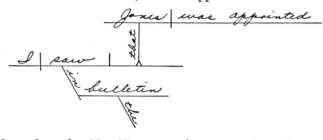

Did you hear *that* Mrs. Wipperman keeps more than fifty cats in her house?

C367 Do not use *as, as if,* or *as though* to introduce an object or predicate noun clause after verbs of thinking, saying, or feeling. Use *that.*

It seems to me [same as *I*
that
think] ~~as if~~ that's a great deal of automobile for so small a boy.

That that's a great . . . a boy is the predicate noun of *seems.*

that
Well, he didn't say ~~as~~ he agreed with me.

That he agreed with me is the object of *say.*

that
Mother doesn't feel ~~as though~~ she should go without a particular invitation.

That she should go without a particular invitation is the object of *does feel.*

C368 Do not use *being as* or *being that* for *since* or *because.*

Since
~~Being as~~ you are my brother, you should lend me the tie.

Because
~~Being that~~ I have no ticket, I shall have to watch from the doorway.

C369 Do not use *except* for *unless.*

unless
You will get nowhere ~~except~~ you talk to a powerful man like Rooney.

165

C370   Do not use *without* as a conjunction.

Don't leave ~~without~~ *before* you pay your dues.

There's no hope ~~without~~ *unless* they find another halfback.

I seldom eat peanuts ~~without I~~ *that I do not* think of going to the circus with my dad when I was a kid.

C371   Do not omit the second *as* when expressing a comparison.

[Wrong:] Cleve's average is as good if not better than mine.
[Right:] Cleve's average is as good *as,* if not better than, mine.
[Right:] Cleve's average is as good *as* mine if not better.

C372   Do not omit *than* when it is needed to complete a comparison.

[Wrong:] Your explanation is more convincing but altogether different from his.

[Right:] Your explanation is more convincing *than,* but altogether different from, his.

C373   Do not use *as* ambiguously, so that it could indicate either time or cause.

[Ambiguous:] *As* Blackie was   Time or cause.
being pommeled, Mary was
smiling coldly.

[Clearly time:] *When* Blackie was being pommeled, Mary was smiling coldly.

[Clearly cause:] *Because* Blackie was being pommeled, Mary was smiling coldly.

[Ambiguous:] *As* I was talk-   Time or cause.
ing, my wife left the room.

[Clearly time:] *While* I was talking, my wife left the room.
[Clearly cause:] *Because* I was talking, my wife left the room.

[Clearly time:] *As* I lay on the beach, someone stole my watch and class ring.

[Clearly cause:] *As* I was very late, I took a short cut through Forest Park.

C374 Do not use *on account of* or *on account of because* as a conjunction.

I play the oboe ~~on account of~~ *because* I like to play the oboe.

Olive fell ~~on account of because~~ *because* the stairs were slippery.

C375 Do not use *while* in place of *although* unless the meaning is perfectly clear.

although
~~While~~ John was only two months old, his aunt read him the Bible.

C376 Do not use *directly* or *immediately* in place of the conjunction *as soon as.*

As soon as
~~Immediately~~ volunteers were called for, Jud stepped forward.

As soon as
~~Directly~~ the painters left, little Maury, with a gleam in his eye, raised his dirty hands to the wall.

C377 *So that* is preferred to *so* in expressing purpose.

[Doubtful:] Chris built a shelter up in the tree, *so* he could have a place to himself.

[Better:] Chris built a shelter up in the tree, *so that* he could have a place to himself.

C378 *When* is preferred to *than* after *scarcely, hardly, barely.*

when
The Greshams had *scarcely* met her ~~than~~ she began to rearrange their lives for them.

C379 *And* is clearer and is considered better usage than *while* for expressing addition.

and
A book lay open on his knees, ~~while~~ a blanket was wrapped about his feet.

C380 Use *from,* not *than* or *to,* after *different.*

from
Oh, she is entirely different ~~than~~ other girls.

from
Smollett's reply was very different ~~to~~ what the chemist expected.

167

Phrases[94]

IN GENERAL

C381 A phrase is a group of words not containing a predicate verb and used as a noun, an adjective, or an adverb.

C382 According to their form phrases are divided into prepositional, gerund, participial, and infinitive phrases.

PREPOSITIONAL PHRASES

C383 A prepositional phrase consists of a preposition plus its object and whatever modifiers there may be.

Caesar was certainly a master *of men.*

C384 A prepositional phrase can be used as an adjective to modify a noun or pronoun, or as an adverb to modify a verb, an adjective, or an adverb.[95]

[Adjective phrase:] The girl *in blue* is Sid's cousin.

[Adjective phrase:] The house *to the left* is going to be the parish youth center.

---

[94] For dangling, misplaced, and squinting phrases, see C323-31. For the punctuation of adjective and adverb phrases, see D38-40, D46-48, D74, and D79. For the punctuation of appositive noun phrases, see D35-37, D59, D71-72, and D78.

[95] Prepositional phrases are sometimes nouns rather than modifiers. In "Over the fence is out," *over the fence* names something and is subject of the predicate verb. But this is not the common use of a prepositional phrase.

[Adverb phrase:] Mr. Clark lost his billfold *in the rain barrel.*

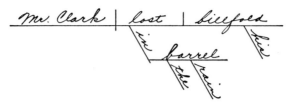

[Adverb phrase:] This is very good *of you.*

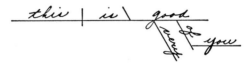

[Adverb phrase:] Where *in the world* are they?

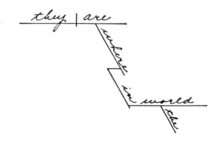

GERUND PHRASES

C385 A gerund phrase is a gerund plus a subject noun or pronoun, an object, or a predicate noun, pronoun, or adjective.[96]

Ellen's crawfishing has disgraced her.

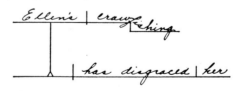

---

[96] For gerunds see A165-70. For the case of the subject, object, or predicate noun or pronoun of a gerund, see C225 and C228-29.

Fighting sharks is unpleasant.

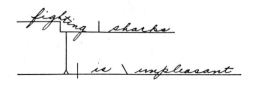

Volpone was punished for *playing sick*.

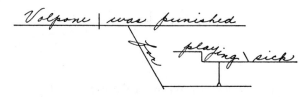

She resents *his having been a butler*.

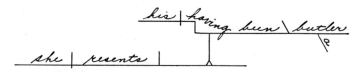

C386   By tradition a possessive adjective can be called the "subject" of a gerund and diagramed as the subject. That is the system followed in this series in the various rules, descriptions, and diagrams.[97]

There is no question of *our leaving* today.

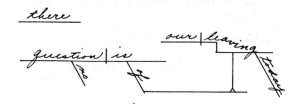

---

[97] It is, of course, by no means wrong to consider a possessive adjective or a noun in the possessive case as the modifier of a gerund rather than its subject. Indeed, though such is the less traditional view, yet it is by far the more logical. In order, however, that there may be uniformity of understanding and terminology throughout your school and in order that all the rules in this handbook may make ready sense to you, follow C386.

C387 Any modifiers that accompany a gerund phrase are considered part of the phrase.

There is no question of our leaving *today*.

C388 Gerund phrases are used only as nouns.

[Noun, subject of predicate verb:] *Fighting sharks* is unpleasant.

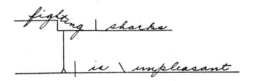

[Noun, object of a verb:] She resents his *having been a butler*.

[Predicate noun:] One witch's occupation was *killing swine*.

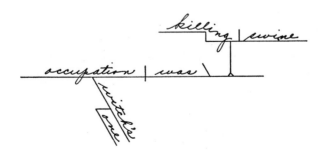

171

[Noun, object of preposition:] Volpone was punished for *playing sick*.

C389 After a preposition, use the possessive with the gerund rather than the objective with the participle, when this can be done and when it will not hurt the sense that you intend.

[Not very good:] There is some hope of *him* paying what he owes.

His could be used instead of *him* without awkwardness and without loss.

[Better:] There is some hope of *his* paying what he owes.

[Bad:] The sight of *his* waiting so coolly infuriated me.

One sees a person waiting, not the waiting itself.

[Better:] The sight of *him* waiting so coolly infuriated me.

PARTICIPIAL PHRASES

C390 A participial phrase is a participle plus an object, a predicate noun, or a predicate adjective.[98]

A man *fighting an octopus* gets wrapped up in his work.

---

[98] For participles see A171 and A174-77. Put the pronoun object of a participle in the objective case. (C229)

It is difficult at times to discover whether one is dealing with a gerund phrase or with a participle or participial phrase; for example, "With this new pitcher there is no danger of *any being wasted*." *Being wasted* could be conceived as a participle modifying *any*. As a matter of fact, it is the gerund; for the writer wishes primarily to name the action of wasting (a gerund names an action) and say that that action constitutes no danger. When you come across such academic puzzlers, do not trouble yourself about them. Only make sure that your sentence is clear and correct.

Fargrave, *looking rather pale*, stepped back from the balcony.

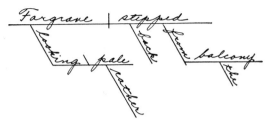

C391 Any modifiers that accompany a participial phrase are considered part of the phrase.

Fargrave, looking *rather* pale, stepped back from the balcony.

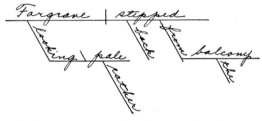

C392 Participial phrases are used only as adjectives.

A man *fighting an octopus* gets wrapped up in his work.

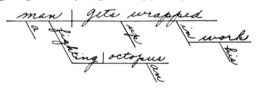

C393 After a preposition, use the possessive with the gerund rather than the objective with the participle, when this can be done and when it will not hurt the sense that you intend.

[Not very good:] There is some hope of *him* paying what he owes.

His could be used instead of *him* without awkwardness and without loss.

[Better:] There is some hope of *his* paying what he owes.

[Bad:] The sight of *his* waiting so coolly infuriated me.

One sees a person waiting, not the waiting itself.

[Better:] The sight of *him* waiting so coolly infuriated me.

173

INFINITIVE PHRASES

C394 An infinitive phrase is either an infinitive introduced by the preposition *to* or an infinitive—with or without *to*—that has a subject noun or pronoun, an object, or a predicate complement.[99]

The other choice is *to fight.*

Adam Boyd planned *to betray John Ogilvie.*

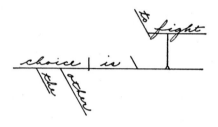

I never manage *to look neat.*

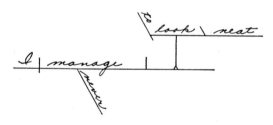

---

[99] For infinitives see A178 and A180-84. Put the subject pronoun of an infinitive in the objective case (C224). Note that the subject pronoun of an infinitive is quite often preceded by the preposition *for,* as, for example: "*For* her to lose courage now would be fatal." Put the predicate pronoun of an infinitive in the nominative case if a nominative precedes the infinitive; put it in the objective case if an objective precedes the infinitive (C227). Put a pronoun used as direct object or as indirect object of an infinitive in the objective case. (C229, C231)

174

C395 Any modifiers that accompany an infinitive phrase are considered part of the phrase.

This is a day to remember *always*.

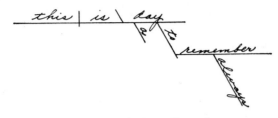

It is absurd for you to like *only funeral* marches.

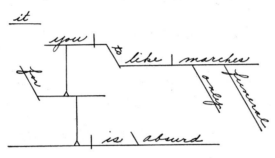

C396 Infinitive phrases are used as nouns, as adjectives, and as adverbs.

[Noun phrase:] *To return* would be impossible.

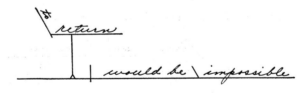

[Noun phrase:] The other choice is *to fight*.

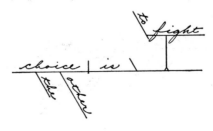

[Noun phrase:] Make him *give an answer.*

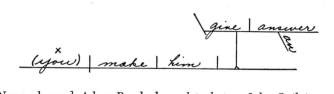

[Noun phrase:] Adam Boyd planned *to betray John Ogilvie.*

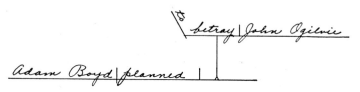

[Adjective phrase:] A desire *to run* took hold of me.

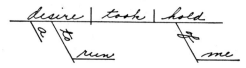

[Adjective phrase:] I don't doubt your ability *to thrash me.*

[Adverb phrase:] The filly was eager *to run.*

[Adverb phrase:] The little fellow slipped from his horse *to retrieve the gun.*

176

Clauses[1]

IN GENERAL

C397 A clause is one subject and predicate in a sentence that has more than one subject and predicate.

Three men left last night,	and three will leave today.
Clause 1	*Clause 2*
My hope has sickened,	but it has not died.
Clause 1	*Clause 2*

C398 The predicate of a clause must contain a predicate verb, not merely a verbal.

Three men left last night, *and three will leave today.*	*And three will leave today* is a clause. *Will leave* is the predicate verb.
Three men left last night, *slipping away in the dark.*	*Slipping away in the dark* is not a clause. There is no predicate verb, merely the participle *slipping*.
Three men left last night *to destroy the main span.*	*To destroy the main span* is not a clause. There is no predicate verb, merely the infinitive *to destroy*.

C399 The one subject and the one predicate of a clause may either or both be compound.

| *Three men and a child left last night,* and another man will leave today. | *Three men and a child left last night* is one clause. It has only one (compound) subject: *three men and a child*. |
| *Three men and a child packed and left last night,* and another man will leave today. | *Three men and a child packed and left last night* is one clause. It has only one (compound) subject and one (compound) predicate. |

---

[1] For the relationship between clauses and compound, complex, and compound-complex sentences, see B22-25.

INDEPENDENT CLAUSES

C400 An independent clause is a clause that could be used alone as a simple sentence.

> Three men left last night, | and three will leave today.
> *Independent clause*   *Independent clause*

[*Three men left last night* could make a simple sentence by itself. *And three will leave today* could make a simple sentence by itself.]

> While we were sleeping, | three of the men left.
>   *Independent clause*

[*Three of the men left* could make a simple sentence by itself: independent clause. *While we were sleeping* could not make a simple sentence by itself. It is a clause, but not an independent clause.]

C401 A second independent clause may be connected to the first by punctuation alone or by punctuation and co-ordinating conjunctions or conjunctive adverbs.[2]

DEPENDENT CLAUSES

C402 A dependent clause is one subject and predicate which makes only a half-sentence when standing alone. It is used in a sentence as a noun, adjective, or adverb.

> While we were sleeping, | three of the men left.
> *Dependent clause*   *Independent clause*

[*While we were sleeping* is one subject and predicate in a sentence that has more than one subject and predicate. It is, therefore, a clause. But were it standing alone, it would make only a half-sentence; so it is a dependent clause.]

C403 An essential part of every dependent clause is either a subordinating conjunction; a relative or interrogative pronoun, adjective, or adverb; or indefinite *who, which, what,* or *whose.* Never leave them out when you are reading a clause to see whether it is dependent or not.

---

[2] For such punctuation see D30-32. For co-ordinating conjunctions see A150-53. For conjunctive adverbs see A154-55.

178

Elias didn't say *that* he would return.
Elias didn't say *when* he would return.
This is *what* I want.
Ask him *what* he is doing here.
We paid five dollars, *which* price was not exorbitant.
There is the car *that* I want.

C404 Since the connective is often omitted from an elliptical sentence, be sure to insert it mentally before deciding whether a clause is independent or dependent.

that
I say‸you're not going.

that
That little box‸you hold contains death.

The other box, he said, would not hold so much.	*He said* is independent. No connective can be inserted.

C405 Dependent clauses are always used as nouns, as adjectives, or as adverbs.

NOUN CLAUSES[3]

C406 A noun clause is a dependent clause that does the work ordinarily reserved to a noun.

[Noun clause, subject:] *What you are saying* does not interest me.

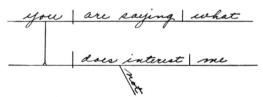

[Noun clause, direct object:] I see *that you are determined.*

---

[3] For restrictive and nonrestrictive appositive noun clauses, see C212-15. For the punctuation of such clauses, see D35-36, D59, D71-72, and D78.

[Noun clause, object of a preposition:] Nothing is clear but *that Flau has escaped.*

C407 The following subordinating conjunctions are commonly used to connect noun clauses with independent clauses or with other dependent clauses.[4]

how	when
if [in the sense	where
of *whether*]	whether
that	why

I don't know *whether* Alfred has the popcorn concession.
Tell me *where* we can vote.
It is certain *that* ground-controlled approach was inadequate.
Where he could have hidden is the question.

C408 The interrogative and indefinite pronouns and adjectives *who, whose, whom, which,* and *what* introduce noun clauses.[5]

What you mean is not clear.

The question is, *who* has the chipmunk?

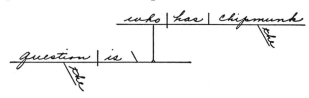

---

[4] For the correct use of subordinating conjunctions in noun clauses, see C363-67.
[5] For the correct use of these, see A52-54, C222, C226, and C229-33.

Russ would not say to *whom* he had given his ring.

We had an argument about *whose* snapshot should be submitted.

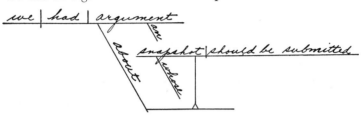

Mr. Ebbetts couldn't decide *which* was the worst.

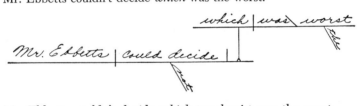

Mr. Ebbetts couldn't decide *which* trombonist was the worst.

C409 Subject noun clauses are frequently preceded by dummy subject *it.*

It is clear *that a crowbar was used.*

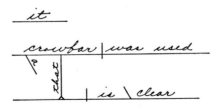

C410 It is a peculiarity of some sentences that the independent clause cannot be stated without the inclusion of the noun clause.

What you have said to me is frightening.

Noun clause: *what you have said to me.*
Independent clause: *what you have said to me is frightening.*

ADJECTIVE CLAUSES[6]

C411 An adjective clause is a dependent clause that modifies a noun or pronoun.

The one *that sneezed* is a penguin.

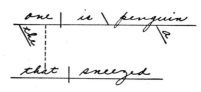

C412 Adjective clauses are relative clauses; that is, they are introduced by relative adverbs, relative pronouns, and relative adjectives.[7]

[Relative adverb:] I have been quite busy in the time *since* I committed my last murder.

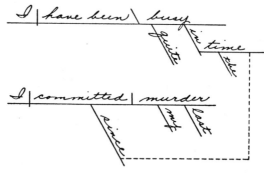

---

[6] For restrictive and nonrestrictive adjective clauses, see C312-15. For the punctuation of such clauses, see D38-40, D74, and D79.

[7] For relative adverbs see A159. For relative pronouns see A43-49, C260, and C262-65. For relative adjectives see A123-26. For the preferred use of *which* and *that* in restrictive clauses, see C262.

182

[Relative pronoun:] I know the girl *whom* you mean.

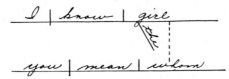

[Relative adjective:] We spent more than seven years in Juarez, in *which* city, by the way, we met Mark Tracy.

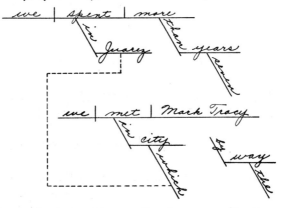

C413 You do not have a relative adverb or an adjective clause unless the adverb refers to a noun or pronoun in another clause.

I don't know *why* you should worry.	*Why* is not a relative adverb here. It does not refer to a noun in the independent clause; so the dependent clause is not an adjective clause.
There was a great deal of talk *when* you left.	*When* is not a relative adverb. It does not refer to a noun in the independent clause; so the dependent clause is not an adjective clause.
I can remember the *period* *when* no one took the telephone seriously.	*When* is a relative adverb. It refers to the noun *period* in the independent clause. The dependent clause is an adjective clause.

C414 A relative pronoun refers to an antecedent in another clause. This makes it easy to distinguish a relative pronoun and its adjective clause from an interrogative or indefinite pronoun or adjective and its noun clause, from demonstrative-pronoun and demonstrative-adjective *that*, and from the conjunction *that*.

I know the *girl whom* you mean.

Whom is a relative pronoun. It has an antecedent in the other clause (the independent clause): *girl*. So the dependent clause is an adjective clause.

I know *whom* you mean.

Whom is not a relative pronoun. It does not have an antecedent in the independent clause.

Here are the *blueprints that* you were looking for.

That is a relative pronoun. It has an antecedent in the independent clause: *blueprints*. So the dependent clause is an adjective clause.

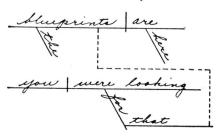

184

I was looking for the blueprints when I found *that* on
the floor.

That is not a relative pronoun.
It has no antecedent in the
independent clause.

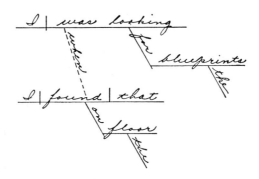

I was looking for something
else when I found *that* blueprint on the floor.

That is not a relative pronoun.
It has no antecedent in the
independent clause.

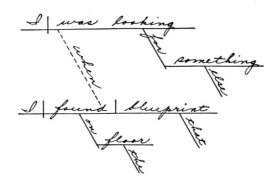

I knew *that* you were looking
for the blueprints.

That is not a relative pronoun.
It has no antecedent in the
independent clause.

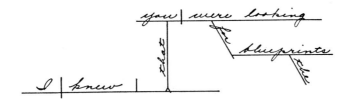

185

C415 The case of the relative pronoun has nothing to do with the antecedent but depends on how the relative is used in its own clause.[8]

who
We met an Eskimo ~~whom~~ had been converted by Father Buliard.

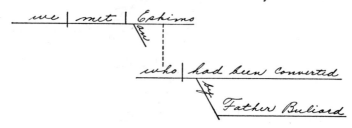

C416 The relative adjective *which* seldom makes for pleasant reading. It is usually best to avoid it when you do not have to use it.

who
I met a stranger in Miami ~~which stranger~~ turned out to be a man with a Christlike attitude toward money.

[All right, because it somehow increases the humor:] Demarre made a bombastic speech about Demarre; and then Horner proclaimed him the modern Aeolus, *which* term Demarre did not understand and so took for a compliment.

ADVERB CLAUSES[9]

C417 An adverb clause is a dependent clause that modifies a verb, an adjective, or an adverb.

[Modifying a verb:] *When he had revived,* he said a strange thing.

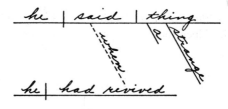

---

[8] For the case of pronouns, see C222, C226, and C229-32.

[9] For restrictive and nonrestrictive adverb clauses, see C312-15. For the punctuation of such clauses, see D38-40, D74, and D79. For the punctuation of an adverb clause that precedes an independent clause, see D45.

[Modifying an adjective:] Television long remained unsatisfactory *because it could be transmitted only some fifty miles.*

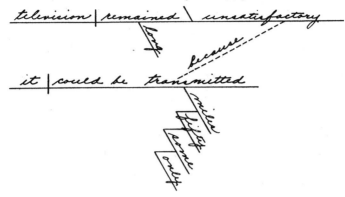

[Modifying an adverb:] Charles behaved so badly *that we had to put him into a strait jacket.*

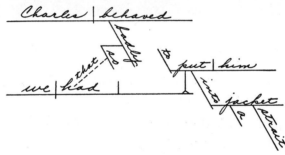

C418 Adverb clauses are introduced by subordinating conjunctions.[10]

Because Fonder had the only automobile, we elected him president of our motor club.

You will surely get into trouble *unless* you put in supplies now for the long, harsh winter ahead.

C419 Do not confuse subordinating conjunctions with conjunctive adverbs, which cannot be used in dependent clauses unless a subordinating connective is present; or with relative adverbs, which have an antecedent in another clause.[11]

---

[10] For subordinating conjunctions with adverb clauses, see A158 and C363-80.
[11] For conjunctive adverbs see A154-55. For relative adverbs see A159.

C420 If an elliptical adverb clause dangles—modifies or seems to modify nothing or the wrong thing—simply fill in the missing words.

the pot is   *it*
When simmering, carefully remove from the stove.

C421 *If* is sometimes omitted from conditional clauses, and the subject noun or pronoun is put after the predicate verb.

Had Father the means, he most certainly would give us children an education.	Same as *if Father had the means.*
Should you ever come West, be sure to visit us.	Same as *if you should ever come West.*

D Punctuation

End punctuation

D1 Every sentence must end with a period, a question mark, or an exclamation point.[1]

D2 Put a period at the end of a declarative sentence.

The sun is shining.

D3 Put a period at the end of an imperative sentence if the feeling expressed is mild.

Do what I tell you.
Close the door when you leave.
Don't forget to remind me.

D4 Put a period at the end of a request, order, or command that—for the sake of courtesy—is phrased as a question.

Will you please see me before you go home.
Would you type this letter before any of the others.
May I have a reply by tonight.
Will the witness take the stand, please.

---

[1] For punctuation of sentences that are interrupted or that trail off, see D11-13.

D5 Put a period at the end of an indirect question.[2]

A man asked me where I was going.

D6 Put a question mark at the end of a direct question.[2]

Where are you going?
He had no answer to the question, Where are you going?
"Where are you going?" a man asked me.

D7 Words or phrases or clauses in a series may each be followed by a question mark if each is equivalent to a fully expressed question.

Where did you come from? why? how?
Where did you find this dog? at what time of day?
Shall I tell Mother you called? that you will return again?

D8 Put an exclamation point after a word, a phrase, a statement or command or question to indicate strong feeling.

What! You wouldn't dare!
Jump!
How splendid!
The safe was empty!
The ghost was gone!

D9 Put an exclamation point at the end of an imperative sentence if the feeling expressed is strong.[3]

Do what I tell you!
Help!
Call the police!
Drop it!

D10 Do not use exclamation points often.

D11 Use a dash (—) to show that a sentence is interrupted before its close.

Besides, I see no reason for thinking that we must have the Merkels over just because—You are not listening to me, George Lindquist!

---

[2] A direct question is a question expressed in the words of the speaker; for example: "Where is the wampum?" An indirect question gives the sense of the speaker's question without quoting him; for example: "He asked where the wampum was." Indirect questions are frequently introduced by *whether* and by *if* in the sense of *whether*.

[3] For imperative sentences see B16.

D12 Use marks of ellipsis (. . .) to show that a sentence, while not abruptly interrupted, trails off with words left unsaid.

Trevor was there when the letter was stolen. Trevor was recognized by old Marsden, and now Marsden has been killed. Trevor spends a good deal of money, but never seems to earn any. I'm beginning to wonder whether Mr. Trevor . . .

D13 Use the sentences described in D11 and D12 only rarely.

D14 Do not use any punctuation to mark the end of the lines in the various headings and addresses of a letter or envelope.[4]

The Donner Publishing Co.	709 Webster Street
1544 Banks Street	Pitt, Maine
Salem, Massachusetts	January 18, 1956

D15 Use a comma or a colon—but preferably a comma—after the salutation of an informal letter.[5]

Dear Joe,	Dear Father Raymond,
Dear Mother,	Dear Grandpa,

D16 Use a comma after the complimentary close of a letter.

Yours truly,	Sincerely yours,
Very truly yours,	Yours sincerely,

D17 Do not use a period or a comma at the end of a literary title that is set off on a line by itself (for example, at the beginning of a theme). You may use a question mark, or, if it is really needed, an exclamation point.

They Live on a Volcano

A Short Dissertation
On Buying Pigs in a Poke
By Norman Coles

Did Nero Burn Rome

Did Nero Burn Rome?

A Rat! A Rat!

---

[4] It was formerly common to use a comma after every line except the last.
[5] Use a colon after the salutation of a formal letter (D65).

The comma

D18   If words, phrases, and dependent clauses occur in the form *a, b, c*—if, that is, there are no conjunctions between them—then use commas between them.

A long, gleaming, two-edged knife stuck in the wall.

This is a government of the people, by the people, for the people.

The charges against you are that you were driving without a license, that you were exceeding the speed limit, that you drove through a red light.

D19   Separate by a comma only adjectives equal in rank. (They are equal in rank if they can be joined by *and*.)

a truthful, courageous answer [truthful *and* courageous]

a dingy, evil-smelling hallway [dingy *and* evil-smelling]

[Wrong:] a variety of small, Alaskan salmon

D20   Often an adjective is so closely united to a noun that the two are equivalent to one word. If such an expression is preceded by another adjective, do not separate the two adjectives by a comma.

fur coat—cheap fur coat

white man—bearded white man

brick house—new brick house

D21   If there is a conjunction between only the last two words, phrases, or dependent clauses in a row—if, that is, they occur in the form *a, b, and c*—separate them by commas, placing the last comma before the conjunction.[6]

Were they red, yellow, *or* white roses?

She was always running from office to office, laughing uproariously at nothing, *and* shouting at the top of her voice.

If you are back here by four o'clock, if you have half of the money with you, *and* if you have a note from Mr. Farmer that he will take the rest from your wages, then you may have the drawing board and the compass and the dividers.

---

[6] This is not the only system used in the United States, but it seems to be the more common and has the advantage of clarity.

D22 If all the words, phrases, or dependent clauses in a row are connected by conjunctions—if, that is, they occur in the form *a and b and c*—do not separate them by commas.

Men *and* women *and* children wandered through the ruins looking for scraps that might be sold to buy food.

If you mean that Heflin was negligent *or* that the radar was defective *or* that your information was incomplete, then we shall have to ask you for evidence.

D23 Where a conjunction makes one unit of two things, use no comma before the conjunction.

I ordered soup, a salad, and *ham and eggs.*

Ham and eggs is considered one dish, one unit.

Sink or swim, fail or succeed, and *live or die,* for all I care.

D24 Do not put a comma before a co-ordinating conjunction that connects only two words, two phrases, or two dependent clauses.

[Wrong:] To the end of the line he attached a wire leader, *and* a hook about two and a half inches long.

[Right:] To the end of the line he attached a wire leader *and* a hook about two and a half inches long.

[Wrong:] He was a tall, *and* gawky lad.
[Right:] He was a tall *and* gawky lad.

D25 Do not separate the last adjective of a series from the noun it modifies.[7]

[Wrong:] The boatswain of the *Cleopatra* was a squat, shifty-eyed, *soft-spoken, fellow.*

[Right:] The boatswain of the *Cleopatra* was a squat, shifty-eyed, *soft-spoken fellow.*

[Wrong:] Hers is a merry, wholesome, *hearty, laugh* that makes you want to laugh too.

[Right:] Hers is a merry, wholesome, *hearty laugh* that makes you want to laugh too.

---

[7] However, if a series of adjectives is nonrestrictive, the comma before the noun may be needed (D38): "*Humble, happy, and kind, Philip* brought out the best in all of us."

D26 Unless an interrupter occurs, do not separate a conjunction from what follows it.

[Wrong:] Mr. Sutherland was riding a sleek, young, *and,* spirited palomino.

[Right:] Mr. Sutherland was riding a sleek, young, *and* spirited palomino.

[Right:] Mr. Sutherland was riding a sleek, young, *and*—unless it was merely restless—spirited palomino.

[Wrong:] They said they wouldn't come, *but,* they did.

[Right:] They said they wouldn't come, *but* they did.

[Right:] They said they wouldn't come; *but,* if Alcide is to be believed, they did.

D27 Use commas to set off the second and subsequent items in a reference, a geographical name, a date, an address, personal titles.[8]

Look up Shakespeare's *Hamlet,* Act III, scene 2, line 14.

Shreveport, Louisiana, is very different from New Orleans.

Earthquakes shook Los Angeles on Friday, November 14, 1941.

John Dickson lives at 2115 Pershing Drive, Watertown, Maryland, in a walk-up apartment on the second floor.

William Watson, Jr., will speak at the luncheon.

The Reverend John Blake, O.P., S.T.D., Ph.D.

D28 Do not use a comma before the first item of a series.

[Wrong:] Bilstein was thinking of, *driving home,* getting out of his wet clothes, taking a hot bath, and going directly to bed.

[Right:] Bilstein was thinking of *driving home,* getting out of his wet clothes, taking a hot bath, and going directly to bed.

[Wrong:] Graves grew up in, *Elsford,* Rhode Island.

[Right:] Graves grew up in *Elsford,* Rhode Island.

[Wrong:] All you have to do is, *dial this number,* ask for Mr. Scribner, and mention my name.

[Right:] All you have to do is *dial this number,* ask for Mr. Scribner, and mention my name.

---

[8] For semicolons with items in a series, see D57.

D29 Unless an interrupter occurs, do not use a comma to separate a subject from its predicate verb or a predicate verb from its complements or objects.

[Wrong:] *Fishing, swimming, and woodcraft, took* a lot of our time.

[Right:] *Fishing, swimming, and woodcraft took* a lot of our time.

[Right:] Fishing, swimming, and woodcraft, *all under the direction of the cabin counselors,* took a lot of our time.

[Wrong:] His particular aversions *are, work, study, and exercise.*

[Right:] His particular aversions *are work, study, and exercise.*

[Right:] His particular aversions are, *as you know,* work, study, and exercise.

D30 Use a comma before *and, or, nor, but,* and *for* when they join independent clauses of a compound sentence.[9] (But see D31.)

The siren cried out, *and* instantly a narrow lane was opened for the ambulance.

Neither was the coffee hot, *nor* were the doughnuts fresh.

D31 Use a semicolon rather than a comma before *and, or, nor, but,* and *for* in a compound sentence if—

A Either clause is long—say, three or four lines.

B Either clause contains a comma, colon, dash, or parentheses.

Ted was reared in the country and lived on a farm for eighteen years; but in spite of that he cannot recognize the common trees and flowers and seems to know nothing of the care and feeding of livestock and poultry.

You may take the six-o'clock local train, slow-traveling but comfortable; or you may take the express, less convenient, perhaps, but faster.

It all came to one thing: mutiny; but some of the crew were not quite ready for that.

---

[9] Exception: you may omit the comma before *and, or, nor, but,* and *for* if both clauses are short—say, three or four words. For example, "I shall go but you must stay." (Do not make use of this exception in your school work.)

The town—a little one-street affair suddenly cropping up on the prairie—was not the place to look for Reggie; nor did our first day of inquiry there achieve any results.

Millhaven has suffered a number of epidemics (see Gilchrist's *Terror in Millhaven*); and so it seemed an ideal place to begin our investigation.

D32 Use a semicolon rather than a comma between independent clauses if *and, or, nor, but,* or *for* is not present.[10]

John Markey was supposed to arrive this morning; he arrived last night instead.

Pat is the sort to plan a thing thoroughly; moreover, she has the personality to win support for the new constitution.

There was no point in taking a loss year after year; so we sold the presses and the equipment in the bindery.

I bowled 225; however, I don't do that every day.

D33 In a sentence beginning with a *that* clause from which the *that* is omitted, a comma is sufficient between the *that* clause and the principal clause.

Our vacation is over, I am sorry to say.	[Usual phrasing:] I am sorry to say that our vacation is over.
He will stay a week longer, he tells me.	[Usual phrasing:] He tells me that he will stay a week longer.
She did not understand a word of his talk, it could clearly be seen.	[Usual phrasing:] It could clearly be seen that she did not understand a word of his talk.
You are really not at fault, you know.	[Usual phrasing:] You know that you are really not at fault.

D34 Set off words in direct address by commas.

Dick, I want to apologize for what I said.

Come this way, *my friend,* to see the giraffe.

---

[10] Under three strict conditions a comma may be used even when *and, or, nor, but,* or *for* is not present: (*a*) if the clauses are short (say, three or four words); (*b*) if neither of them contains a comma, colon, dash, or parentheses; (*c*) if they are closely allied in thought and construction. For example, "United we stand, divided we fall" or "I came, I saw, I conquered." (Do not make use of this exception in your school work.)

D35 Set off an ordinary nonrestrictive appositive by commas.[11]

The first letter of the alphabet, *a,* was all that Marko learned in the first eight weeks.

The Turkish government sternly forbade the wearing of the fez, *or tarboosh.*

This ambition you mentioned, *to make people notice you,* is selfish and will make you unhappy.

You are simply repeating the most important of all truths, *that there is a God.*

D36 Do not set off restrictive appositives.[12]

I mean Churchill *the novelist,* not Churchill *the statesman.*
The word *affect* is often confused with the word *effect.*
He made the claim *that he was not responsible for his brother.*

D37 Do not set off appositives or adjectives that are part of a proper name.

Robert *the Strong* was a great warrior.
This is a statue of Alexander *the Great.*
We call him Wilfred *the Destroyer.*

D38 Set off ordinary nonrestrictive modifiers by commas.[13]

A young man, *tall and handsome,* waved to me from his table across the room.

There is no point in asking, *probably.*

Baker will be the first to avoid punishment, *begging off somehow.*

Mr. Pierce is as pleasant a man as you would care to meet, *in his own odd way.*

The second abstract picture we came to, *which I liked well enough,* Laury said looked like a red cow wearing a bathing suit and blowing a peashooter.

There had been no Mass said in the town for fifty years, *although some sort of service was held on Sundays and holydays by a handful of Catholic laymen.*

---

[11] For restrictive and nonrestrictive appositives, see C212-15. For dashes, especially with long nonrestrictive appositives or those that contain their own punctuation, see D71-73; for colons see D59; for parentheses see D78.

[12] For restrictive and nonrestrictive appositives, see C212-15.

[13] For restrictive and nonrestrictive modifiers, see C312-21. For dashes and parentheses with nonrestrictive modifiers, see D74 and D79.

D39 Before setting off a modifier, make sure that you intend it to be nonrestrictive. If you are in doubt, use no punctuation. Too many commas are worse than too few.

D40 Do not set off restrictive modifiers.[14]

Someone played *a cracked* and *asthmatic* record.
It was *quite* cold.
The perfect friend is the Man *who is God*.

D41 Ordinarily use commas (or an exclamation point) with *oh* and other exclamatory or parenthetical words, phrases, and clauses.[15]

Oh, what's the use?
It was a deep, blue pool in a kind of grotto; and, *oh,* was the water cold.
If you don't have the car—*oh!* you do have it.
Well, that's just about it.
It seemed like a short swim; and, *well,* I certainly didn't want to seem a coward.
Next, there is a little matter of timing that I want to take up with the sound man.
Try the recipe for, *say,* a week.
Where, *pray tell,* are the keys?
Red, *to be sure,* never knew that he had been cheated.
You have a reason, *I suppose,* for the charges you make?
He would have come, *he explained,* if his aunt had not hidden his clothes.
Then you do agree with me, *don't you?*
John Hamilton, *Jr.,* is nauseated.
Father Basil, *O.F.M.,* is on the forum.
A James Peck, *M.A., Ph.D.,* wants to sell you and me a carload of breakfast food.
The contracts, blueprints, *etc.,* call for a room without doors.
Flowers, magazines, ash trays, *and so on,* cluttered every available table and chair.

---

[14] For restrictive and nonrestrictive modifiers, see C312-21.
[15] For dashes and parentheses with parenthetical expressions, see D69 and D77.

D42 Punctuation may be omitted if a parenthetical expression can be clearly and easily read without pause.

Oh what's the use?
Well that's just about it.

It seemed like a short swim; and, *well,* I certainly didn't want to seem a coward.	*Well* cannot be clearly and easily read without pause. It requires commas.
He had no right, *she asserted,* to do another man out of a job.	Parenthetical *he said* expressions always require a pause and commas.
This happened when I was, *say,* fifteen years old.	Parenthetical *say* almost always requires a pause, however slight, and commas.
You did go, *didn't you?*	Repetitive parenthetical expressions always require a pause and commas.

D43 Do not set off *O* (which is nowadays always capitalized and reserved for rather poetic use with nouns in direct address).

O Diana, these are your forests!

D44 Set off a nominative absolute by commas.[16]

The danger signal ringing, we stopped the car.

I cannot tell you, *my parents being away,* whether I can go bowling or not.

Nothing extra was served at dinner, *the supplies being lower than they had been for months.*

D45 When an adverb clause precedes an independent clause, set off the adverb clause by commas.[17]

---

[16] A nominative absolute is a word group related to the rest of the sentence in sense but not in grammar and made up of a noun or pronoun plus a participle or a participial phrase (C201-3).

[17] The comma may be omitted if the adverb clause is short (say, three or four words) and the meaning is clear, or if the subject of the adverb clause and the subject of the principal clause are the same. For example: "After Mr. Murphy died his wife moved to Canada." "Since Mr. Crane came to Maryvale last year he has made many friends." (Do not make use of this exception in your school work.)

Although the road was icy and snow was falling, the doctor got to our house in time.

Finally, *when order had been completely restored,* the cowardly judge crept from behind his desk.

While you are baiting my hook, I'll dig for more worms behind the boathouse.

D46 Use a comma after an introductory phrase or series of phrases unless it is short—four words or less.

To see the real West, drive your own car and spend several days in each place.

Returning from a walk late last night, I heard the angry voices of some neighbors quarreling in their back yard.

Quite a while before dark, bats began to dip, circle, and glide through the long avenue of oaks.

After dinner we plan to entertain you with some home movies we took last summer.

D47 Even if it is only four words or less, use a comma after an introductory phrase that is only loosely connected with the sentence (for example, a bridging phrase like *after all* or *for that matter*).

After all, I'm only human.

For that matter, Russia was a dictatorship too.

For one thing, grey and *gray* are spelled differently.

In the next and last place, strikes have brought serious hardship to hundreds of men and women.

For heaven's sake, go ahead and sign!

For the last time, the answer is no.

D48 Do not confuse a phrase that is really the subject or object with an introductory phrase.

Bringing wood into the house every evening is a sheer waste of time.	Subject of the sentence. No comma here.
Bringing wood into the house every evening, she used up what little strength and energy she had left.	Introductory phrase. Use a comma here.

D49 Set off by commas a contrasting expression introduced by *not, but not, certainly not, never,* and so on, if you want it read with a preceding or following pause.

Only a lawyer or a doctor, *but not a tradesman,* would so pepper his language with Latin expressions.

Because he had power, *not of course because he was astute,* Tag's word was received with respect by the Randall politicos.

I have decided to lend the car to Jim *but not to you.*

He is very kind *not because he is a king;* many a man has been a king and has not been kind.

D50 Use commas to set off a suspended expression.

During, *and for a long time after,* the famine, the people were desperately poor.

In his fright the man began swimming away from, *not toward,* the dock.

Joe looks like, *but is quite different from,* his twin brother.

Our old house was as large as, *but less conveniently arranged than,* this new one.

D51 Use a comma before a single, complete, directly quoted sentence that occurs within another sentence.[18]

Herbert answered, "I don't know."

D52 Do not use a comma before an indirect quotation or an indirect question.

[Wrong:] Herbert answered, that he didn't know.
[Right:] Herbert answered that he didn't know.

[Wrong:] He asked, whether anybody else had noted a change in the frequency.
[Right:] He asked whether anybody else had noted a change in the frequency.

D53 Separate by a comma those parts of a sentence that would be confusing if read together without pause.

Two hours before, the fire broke out.

Within, the box was lined with satin.

---

[18] Use a colon to introduce a quotation of more than one sentence (D60).

Frightened, he licked his lips.

Whatever is, is not necessarily right.

A man, that is what we need.

Instead of hundreds, thousands came.

To John, Matthew was always kind.

When the cyclone hit, the Ryans were away from home.

By striking, the members of the union forced a reluctant recognition of their rights.

There was a small dog with the man, barking in miniature frenzy.

To deceive, a man must go against his nature.

To escape, a small, enterprising mouse chewed his way through *Mrs. Rancy's Cookbook.*

Fifteen people loaded with Christmas presents and bustling about exchanging greetings and inquiries about friends, and five neighbors cutting sandwiches in the tiny kitchen crammed the capacity of the little cottage to bursting.

The assistant dean wants Winterhalter, Ravel, Fosdick, Burns, to clean up the hall.

Adelbert, Ethelred, Warren, are impatiently waiting for you in the butler's pantry.

I like ribs and sauerkraut, and enjoy other heavy foods.

A man, not a mouse, is what we need.

He's going to go, crazy or not crazy.

D54 Do not use unnecessary commas; that is, commas for which you cannot cite a rule or give a good reason.

The semicolon

D55 Use a semicolon rather than a comma before *and, or, nor, but,* and *for* in a compound sentence if—

A Either clause is long—say, three or four lines.

B Either clause contains a comma, colon, dash, or parentheses.[19]

Ted was reared in the country and lived on a farm for eighteen years; but in spite of that he cannot recognize the common trees

---

[19] For the full treatment of the punctuation of compound sentences, see D30-32.

and flowers and seems to know nothing of the care and feeding of livestock and poultry.

You may take the six-o'clock local train, slow-traveling but comfortable; or you may take the express, less convenient, perhaps, but faster.

It all came to one thing: mutiny; but some of the crew were not quite ready for that.

The town—a little one-street affair suddenly cropping up on the prairie—was not the place to look for Reggie; nor did our first day of inquiry there achieve any results.

Millhaven has suffered a number of epidemics (see Gilchrist's *Terror in Millhaven*); and so it seemed an ideal place to begin our investigation.

D56 Use a semicolon rather than a comma between independent clauses if *and, or, nor, but,* or *for* is not present.[20]

John Markey was supposed to arrive this morning; he arrived last night instead.

Pat is the sort to plan a thing thoroughly; moreover, she has the personality to win support for the new constitution.

There was no point in taking a loss year after year; so we sold the presses and the equipment in the bindery.

I bowled 225; however, I don't do that every day.

D57 Use a semicolon to set off the items of a series if the items contain commas.

The Dana Company has branch offices in Billings, Montana; Santa Fe, New Mexico; and Tucson, Arizona.

Tell what is significant about these dates in the life of Julian Randolph: January 4, 1900; September 27, 1902; March 1, 1904; and December 9, 1908.

D58 Use a semicolon before *namely, for example, for instance,* and similar expressions when they occur as an extra at the end of a sentence.

Chrysler introduced something new in 1951; *namely,* the spark plug in the center of the cylinder.

---

[20] For the full treatment of the punctuation of compound sentences, see D30-32.

Rodent is a name that includes a number of little beasts besides rats; *for instance,* squirrels.

Tippy has quite redeemed himself; *for example,* he behaved like a human being at lunch today.

The colon

D59 Use a colon to introduce formally any matter that follows—usually matter in apposition.

All the difficulty is due to just one little man: *James Nelson.*

The headings of the report are these: *the cause of the flood in Fremont County, the damage done by the flood, and the help given to the farmers by the Red Cross.*

I have been trained in three skills: *double-entry bookkeeping, typing, and shorthand.*

The next question that came up for discussion was: *Are the requirements for membership strict enough?*

She felt as you would expect: *worried, frightened, perplexed.*

D60 Use a colon to introduce a quotation of more than one sentence.

Boswell wrote of Oliver Goldsmith: "Goldsmith's incessant desire of being conspicuous in company was the occasion of his sometimes appearing to such disadvantage as one should hardly have supposed possible in a man of his genius. . . . One evening, in a circle of wits, he found fault with me for talking of Johnson as entitled to the honor of unquestionable superiority. 'Sir,' said he, 'you are for making a monarchy of what should be a republic.' "

D61 Use a colon to introduce a clause that summarizes what has gone before.[21]

You are to appear at the Vendôme at precisely four o'clock; you are to select a table near the door; you are to leave at precisely four-fifteen: *these things you must do exactly and without fail.*

A shred of wet, muddy tweed coat; a scrap of paper torn from a railroad timetable; a hat carefully placed on the head of the stone Audubon in the park: *that was all we had to go on.*

---

[21] A dash can be used in the same way (D68).

D62 Use a colon to introduce items that are indented like paragraphs, provided that the introductory statement could stand as a sentence by itself. If the introductory statement is incomplete, use a dash.

These things should be kept in mind:

We are not obliged to repress our intelligence and try to persuade ourselves that an evil man is a saint.

On the other hand, we are obliged to try to give him the benefit of any reasonable doubt when assessing his character.

We must not decide for ourselves that he is certainly destined for heaven or hell.

If it will help, we may divide the whole problem into these three topics for discussion:

The usefulness of an electronics club.

The difficulties of founding an electronics club.

The usefulness weighed against the difficulties.

To tabulate our reasons, Milton was admitted because—

He has the draftsmanship we need.

He is a worker.

He can work with others.

The charges made against him by Mosser were accompanied by not one solid bit of evidence.

D63 Use a colon to separate items that contain semicolons.

Trains leave in the morning at seven, eight, and nine from the Euston Station; at seven, eight-fifteen, and ten from the Paddington Station: in the afternoon at one, two, and three from the Euston Station; at twelve-ten, one, three, and four-thirty from the Paddington Station.

D64 Use a colon to divide hours from minutes when time is written in figures.

10:20 A.M.   1:07 P.M.   5:00 P.M.

D65 Use a colon after the salutation of a formal letter.[22]

Dear Miss Smithers: Very Reverend and
Gentlemen: dear Monsignor:
Dear Sir: Dear Mr. Thorn:

[22] Use a comma after the salutation of an informal letter. See D15.

D66 Use a colon to divide Psalm or chapter from verse when these numbers are indicated by figures alone.

Ps. 32:1 [meaning Psalm 32, verse 1]

II Cor. 5:1 [meaning the Second Epistle to the Corinthians, Chapter 5, verse 1]

The dash

D67 Use dashes to show that a sentence is broken up, interrupted, unfinished, or suddenly changed.

Tell me—tell me the truth—are you my brother?

I came upstairs and entered the room to find—

When I think how your life has been spent—how old did you say you were?

D68 Use a dash before that part of a sentence which summarizes what has gone before.[23]

Mr. Micawber warned that a person will be worried and unhappy who, making ten pounds a week, spends fifteen; who buys clothes and flowers and theater tickets heedlessly; who spends tomorrow's salary today—*who, in short, lives beyond his income.*

D69 Dashes may be used for emphasis instead of commas to set off a parenthetical expression, and they are preferred if the construction of the parenthetical expression does not fit the rest of the sentence or itself contains punctuation.[24]

A man named Will Due—*what a name*—is waiting to see you.

Didn't Joe Cain—*he went to law school after college, you remember*—become a noted attorney in New York?

D70 If a parenthetical remark is a direct question or an exclamation, you may put a question mark or exclamation point before the final dash.

Joe Cain—he went to law school after college, *don't you remember?*—became a noted attorney in New York.

---

[23] A colon may be used in the same way but is a little more formal (D61).
[24] For parentheses with parenthetical expressions, see D77.

The second man—*plucky little fellow!*—was not to be intimidated by Mr. Robble's rumbling and grumbling.

D71 Dashes may be used occasionally to set off nonrestrictive appositives more emphatically than commas do; and they should be used if the appositives are long (say, more than ten words) or contain their own punctuation.[25]

The first letter of the alphabet—*a*—was all that Marko learned in the first eight weeks.

Tod's brothers—*Jake, Harry, and Al*—are all as pleasant as he.

The plot of the play—*the story of a mortgage, a sick father, a beautiful daughter, and a villain*—is trite, unblushing melodrama; but the actors enjoy themselves.

Everything—*whatever he earned as wages and whatever came to him as tips*—went anonymously to the men he had wronged.

When you admit what I say—*that some kind of discipline in speaking and acting is necessary for every growing boy and girl*—then we can make plans together.

D72 A dash is more emphatic than a comma but less formal than a colon before an appositive at the end of a sentence.

One thing I do not like—*spinach*.

A friend of mine telephoned me today, a man I haven't spoken to for ten years—*Jim Burke*.

D73 Do not use dashes to set off an expression containing only figures.

[Wrong:] The year of the crash—1929—made no change in Paulinus.
[Right:] The year of the crash, 1929, made no change in Paulinus.
[Right:] The year of the crash (1929) made no change in Paulinus.

D74 Dashes may be used occasionally to set off nonrestrictive modifiers more emphatically than commas do, especially if the modifiers contain their own punctuation.[26]

Mr. Pierce is as pleasant a man as you would care to meet—*in his own odd way*.

[25] For restrictive and nonrestrictive appositives, see C212-15. For commas, colons, and parentheses with nonrestrictive appositives, see D35, D59, and D78.
[26] For restrictive and nonrestrictive modifiers, see C312-21. For parentheses with nonrestrictives see D79.

Agnes answered with a giggle—*which infuriated me, startled Higgins, and made Cleo guffaw*—but did not offer any useful information.

D75 Use a dash instead of a colon to introduce items that are indented like paragraphs when the introductory statement could not stand by itself as a complete sentence.[27]

> To tabulate our reasons, Milton was admitted because—
> He has the draftsmanship we need.
> He is a worker.
> He can work with others.
> The charges made against him by Mosser were accompanied by not one solid bit of evidence.

D76 Use dashes sparingly. Their too-frequent use results in restless and childish writing.

Parentheses and brackets

D77 Use parentheses to enclose a parenthetical remark, an aside, or extra information only when commas or dashes are not emphatic enough, when the parenthetical expression already contains a dash, or when one or more independent sentences are parenthetical.

> Enclosed please find my check for twelve dollars ($12).
>
> The author confuses James Mill (1773-1836) with his son, John Stuart Mill (1806-73).
>
> One of the earliest detective stories (Collins's *The Moonstone*) is better constructed than many later examples.
>
> The hero of my story (I write this for your private information) was not an honest man.
>
> If the phrase is short (say, four or five words), the comma may be omitted.
>
> The figures (78, 76, and 75—Roland adds 74, but no one else agrees with him) turned up 180 times in 4 hours.
>
> Feuerbach tore the paper to shreds. (As we have said, he loves drama.) Then he burst into tears.

---

[27] Do not apply this rule to outlines. See R32.

D78 Use parentheses to enclose a nonrestrictive appositive only when commas or dashes are not emphatic enough or when the appositive already contains a dash.[28]

Enclosed is my check for twelve dollars ($12).

Jonathan Crespy (a friend—and a loyal friend, I may say) reluctantly admitted that Julius should go.

D79 Use parentheses only rarely to set off nonrestrictive modifiers when commas or dashes are not emphatic enough.[29]

We were offered some milk (which was fresh) and some wine (which was sour); there was no solid food in the inn.

D80 Place in parentheses letters or figures used to mark the divisions of an enumeration in a sentence, a paragraph, or other continuous text.[30]

I maintain (1) that Watson did not come to London; (2) that, even if he had come, he could not have met Holmes; and (3) that Watson's letter to Holmes was actually written by Vance.

There were two possibilities: (*a*) to go home and (*b*) to fight.

D81 Do not use periods with the figures or letters described in D80.

D82 In business letters and commercial and technical documents, figures are sometimes given in parentheses after written numbers.

Send me twenty-five (25) pairs of basketball shorts and a dozen (12) handballs, for which I enclose one hundred dollars ($100).

D83 When a sentence in parentheses interrupts another sentence, do not capitalize the first word of the parenthesis.

Though I have often been tempted to quit (such thoughts surely come to every man), the example of More's fortitude has always given me courage to go on.

Here the sentence in parentheses interrupts another sentence. No capitals.

---

[28] For restrictive and nonrestrictive appositives, see C212-15.
[29] For restrictive and nonrestrictive modifiers, see C312-21.
[30] Do not apply this rule to outlines. See R39 and R46.

They say he was a wealthy man. (That was in 1860, of course, when a dollar bought more than it buys now.) Whether or not he was is beside the point.

Here the sentence in parentheses does *not* interrupt another sentence.

D84 If a period, comma, semicolon, or dash is needed at the end of a parenthesis that interrupts a sentence, place the mark outside the parentheses.

Karen did not know (or so she said).

Here he gave his strange, though accurate (and handsomely delivered), account of the disaster.

Tilton was born the year of the flood (1894); he doesn't remember much about it.

D85 If a colon, question mark, or exclamation point belongs only to the parenthesis, place the mark inside the parentheses and end the sentence with another mark.

(Helen:) There is something you are forgetting!
Karen did not know (or did she?).
Yates absconded with my fishing tackle (the scoundrel!).

D86 If a colon, question mark, or exclamation point belongs only to the rest of the sentence or to both the parenthesis and the rest of the sentence, place the mark outside the parentheses.

Perón mentions three *ladrones* (robbers): Gonzales, Trega, and the nameless butcher.

Would you care to join us (in other words, will you take the dare)?

Chesterton said the most startling thing (on page 7)!

D87 Enclose independent parenthetical sentences in parentheses. They are punctuated and capitalized just like other sentences. The end punctuation, of course, is placed inside the parentheses.

I had just met the man. (Oldenburg insists I met him a year earlier. Oldenburg, however, remembers things more or less as he pleases.) We had been introduced by Clesi, a mutual friend.

Staub took the floor. (It has never been explained how the chair happened to recognize him; no alert presiding officer would have done so.) He began a speech that ran three days and nights.

Staub took the floor. (Why did the chair recognize him? That has never been satisfactorily explained.) He began a speech that lasted three days and nights.

D88 Use brackets [ ] to enclose a remark that is inserted into a quotation.

"So they [that is, Christian and Hopeful] were forced to go, because he [Giant Despair] was stronger than they. They had also but little to say, for they knew themselves in a fault. The giant, therefore, drove them before him, and put them into his castle [Doubting Castle], into a very dark dungeon."

—BUNYAN

Quotation marks

D89 Put a direct quotation in double quotation marks.[31]

"I have no intention of budging," he said.

He answered, "I have no intention of budging."

"I have no intention of budging," he answered, "until you have given me your promise."

D90 Put in single quotation marks a quotation within a quotation.

"We must remember," said the orator, "the immortal words of a great patriot, 'Give me liberty or give me death!' "

D91 Do not use quotation marks if words are directed by a person to himself or are merely unexpressed thoughts (but capitalize the first word).

I thought to myself, They did not expect me.
No doubt you have asked yourself, Why am I here?
He said to himself, Here we go again!
They were thinking, We will have to pay.

---

[31] A direct quotation is a quotation in the speaker's or writer's own words that is not introduced by the conjunctions *whether, if,* or *that* either expressed or implied.

D92 Put an indirect quotation in double quotation marks if you want it unmistakable that you are using another's own words; if you do not want it so, then do not use quotation marks.[32]

St. Paul declared that "our citizenship is in heaven."
St. Paul declared that our citizenship is in heaven.

It is an old saying that "a penny saved is a penny earned."
It is an old saying that a penny saved is a penny earned.

D93 Put all sentences belonging to a single uninterrupted quotation in one set of quotation marks.

Trafford replied: "I don't think you understand my position. I am not here to defraud you people. But I cannot return your money just now without defrauding others."

Erin warned me: "Don't you dare pass this time, partner. I made a demand bid, and you have to answer. I said two spades, and Eil said three clubs. Come on, you have to say something."

"Mickey and I want to go duckhunting out at Scheller's slough today. Can I go, and can I take Dad's shotgun, and can I stay out until five?" Richard asked.

D94 When a continuous quotation falls into paragraphs, place quotation marks at the beginning of each paragraph, but at the end of only the last.

"I was ten years old at the time," began Joe Manning. "My brother and I lived in a shanty near the docks. I say 'lived,' but really we only slept there; we lived in the streets. We ate when and where we could; we got money anyhow; and we made friends of vicious boys and girls as abandoned as we.

"Then one day I was taken to the hospital badly hurt. Mrs. Parkham saw me there, adopted me, and took me West to live. My whole life was changed. I never heard from my brother, never saw him again.

"All that happened twenty years ago. How can you expect me to recognize this murderer as my brother? It's some kind of trick to get money out of Mrs. Parkham."

---

[32] An indirect quotation is a quotation introduced by the conjunctions *whether, if,* or *that* either expressed or implied.

D95 In dialogue, use a new paragraph and a new set of quotation marks every time the speaker changes.

> "It seems to me," said Dr. Nichols, "that you ought to sell the farm and buy yourself a college education. You want an education, don't you?"
>
> "Yes, sir," I said; "but would the sale fetch enough money to pay all my expenses?"
>
> "Why, yes, I should think so. As a matter of fact, I myself am prepared to offer you twenty thousand for the place. That's perhaps a bit more than you would get if you put it on the market. But we are good friends, and the property is worth it. Will you sell it to me?"
>
> "No, sir," I said, "I wouldn't sell it to you unless you were the last person who wanted it."
>
> "Why, my boy, you surprise and embarrass me. Why wouldn't you sell it to me?"
>
> "Because you just front for a big syndicate that buys up farms, works the land to death with the same money crop for about ten years, and then moves on, leaving dead dust and Johnson grass. I'll sell to a man who respects the earth and wants a home."

D96 Capitalize the first word of a directly quoted sentence, even when it appears within another sentence.

> Cecil replied, "My mother is a very determined person."
>
> "My mother," replied Cecil, "is a very determined person." [*Is* is not the first word of the directly quoted sentence.]
>
> Then, "Don't you worry," she whispered. "For an old woman I'm feeling very fit indeed. Why, I've many a song in me yet, and many a quarrel, too."

D97 Do not capitalize the first word of a directly quoted sentence fragment unless the fragment begins the sentence in which it stands.

> Margaret won't speak to "those common Kellys," as she calls them.
>
> He is always talking about "roughing it"; by which he means putting up at a luxury cabin not more than ten miles from town.
>
> "My mother," replied Cecil, "is a very determined person." [Note that *is* is not capitalized, since it is the first word of only a fragment, not of a sentence.]

She said, "For an old woman I'm feeling very fit indeed." But her "very fit" sounded unconvincing, spoken as it was in a rather feeble voice.

"Crazy as a loon," he called me.

"If wishes were horses," we could overtake Selwyn.

D98 Place periods and commas always inside the second quotation mark.[33]

As usual, the newspapers denounced the strikers as "roughnecks," "hoodlums," and "traitors."

"It seems," said the traveler, "that there is nobody here."

Packer replied glumly, "All he said to *me* was, 'No, I won't.'"

No, you're thinking of the "Johnson Rag," not the "Tiger Rag."

D99 Place colons and semicolons always outside the second quotation mark.

These were included under "necessary expenses": theater tickets, four new novels, and a foot-long taxi bill.

Curtiss said, "I don't think so"; but it was obvious that he *did* think so.

D100 Place marks other than periods, commas, colons, and semicolons (*a*) inside the second quotation mark if they belong to the quoted matter or to both the quoted matter and the rest of the sentence; (*b*) outside, if they belong to the rest of the sentence only.

Pilate asked, "What is truth?"	These marks belong to the quoted matter only; hence, inside the quotation marks.
I thought of the famous cry, "They shall not pass!"	
Who asked "What is truth?"	These marks belong to both the quoted matter and the rest of the sentence; hence, inside.
How stupid of you to keep shouting "Police!"	
Who wrote "Miniver Cheevy"?	These marks belong to the rest of the sentence only; hence, outside.
Yet these men, thieves and murderers, prate of "decency"!	

---

[33] There is more than one system of writing quotation marks with other marks of punctuation. The one followed in this book is common in the United States.

D101 If a direct quotation is broken by an expression like *he said,* and if the part before the break would ordinarily be followed by a semicolon, use a comma instead and put the semicolon after the *he said* expression.[34]

"That was thoughtless—incredibly so," he said; "but I forgive you."

D102 Put in quotation marks (but do not italicize) the title of something that is mentioned as part of a larger work.[35]

"Hamlet" in *The Seven Greatest Tragedies*	"Hamlet" would ordinarily be italicized, since it is a play. But here it is put in quotation marks as part of a larger work that is also named.
Marquand's "The Late George Apley" in *A Marquand Reader*	"The Late George Apley" would ordinarily be italicized, since it is ordinarily published as a book by itself.

D103 Put in quotation marks (but do not italicize) the title of an article, short story, essay, chapter; or of a poem, musical work, or story that is not long enough to make a book by itself—whether or not these are mentioned as part of a larger work.[36]

"Ode to a Nightingale" in *The Oxford Book of English Verse*
"Ode to a Nightingale"

"On Leisure" from *Essays in Idleness*
"On Leisure"

"Summertime" from *Porgy and Bess*
"Summertime"

"St. Louis Blues"

D104 Put in quotation marks the title of a whole series of books.

"Problems of the High-School Boy," Vol. II, *Homework*

---

[34] For commas with *he said* expressions and with direct and indirect quotations, see D41-42 and D51-52. For colons with quotations of more than one sentence, see D60.

[35] For italic with titles of books, see D115.

[36] For italic with titles of longer literary and musical works, see D115-21.

D105 Do not put in quotation marks (or italicize either) the titles of dictionaries, encyclopedias, indexes, directories, almanacs, and similar reference works.

Webster's New Collegiate
   Dictionary
Catholic Encyclopedia
Cumulative Book Index
the Official Catholic Direc-
   tory

Information Please Almanac
Americana Annual
the Roman Ritual
Reader's Guide
Code of Canon Law
Who's Who

D106 Do not put in quotation marks (or italicize either) the titles of charters, acts, statutes, reports, and so on, or of alliances and treaties.

Act of Supremacy
Articles of Confederation
Declaration of Independ-
   ence

Emancipation Proclama-
   tion
Stamp Act
Treaty of Versailles

D107 Do not put in quotation marks (or italicize either)—

A The names of the Bible or of its books, divisions, parts, or versions.

the Septuagint
the Synoptic Gospels
the Gospel According to
   St. John

the Book of Psalms
the Sermon on the Mount
the Lord's Prayer
the Reims-Douay Version

B The titles of prayers.

the Lord's Prayer

the Ave Maria

C The titles of the Breviary, Missal, Book of Common Prayer, or the parts of these books.

the Breviary
the Office
the Roman Missal
the Proper

the Book of Common Prayer
Lauds
the Canon
the Common

D The names of creeds, confessions of faith, and catechisms.

the Apostles' Creed
the Augsburg Confession

the Baltimore Catechism
the Thirty-nine Articles

215

E The names of the Mass or of any of its parts.

the Mass   the Gloria
the Asperges   the Preface

F The titles of church services and devotions.

Benediction   First Friday devotions

G The titles of the mysteries of the rosary.

The fourth glorious mystery is the Assumption of the Blessed Virgin Mary into Heaven.

D108 Put in quotation marks words that need setting off for clearness.

"I said—incorrectly—that my brother and I 'lived' in a shanty near the docks."

"Ngaio Marsh" is not the name of an African swamp, but of a woman detective-story writer.

What a gap there is between "ought" and "is"!

D109 Put in quotation marks words followed by their definition or explanation.

"Geometer" means a person skilled in geometry.
"At your service" signifies that the speaker is ready to obey orders.

D110 An occasional technical word or term, which can be misunderstood by the reader or which is unknown to him, may be put in quotation marks the first time that it occurs in a work.

The money was borrowed from the bank by an "entrepreneur."

D111 An expression on a different language level from that of the rest of the composition (for example, a slang expression in a rather formal context) may be put in quotation marks. (If you find yourself using this rule a great deal in the course of a theme, then you are probably changing language levels too often, or the language level is not what you think it is.)

The man had no residence, no employment, no prospect of it, and no desire for any of these things. He was a "bum."

D112 It is usually bad taste to put in quotation marks a word that is used ironically or given a forced meaning. It is all right to do so, however, when there is a real chance that intelligent readers might otherwise be misled.

For Brutus is an honorable man.	Not: For Brutus is an "honorable" man.

I have had quite enough of your remarkable "hospitality," Cyril.

D113 Use brackets [ ] to enclose a remark that is inserted into a quotation.

"So they [that is, Christian and Hopeful] were forced to go, because he [Giant Despair] was stronger than they. They had also but little to say, for they knew themselves in a fault. The giant, therefore, drove them before him, and put them into his castle [Doubting Castle], into a very dark dungeon."

—B<small>UNYAN</small>

Italic

D114 To indicate in typescript or manuscript that a word is italicized, draw a line under it.

D115 Although the titles of books, pamphlets, plays, motion pictures, and radio and television programs may be put in quotation marks, good usage prefers to write them in italic. Write them in italic.[37]

Thackeray's *Vanity Fair* [book]
Lord's *I Can Read Anything* [pamphlet]
Shakespeare's *The Tempest* [play]
The Birth of a Nation [motion picture]
Invitation to Learning [radio program]
Meet the Press [television program]
Milton's *Paradise Lost* [a long poem, often printed as a book][38]

---

[37] But see D116-18.

[38] For such a work when mentioned as part of a larger work, see D102. For titles of articles, short stories, essays, chapters; or of poems, musical works, or stories that are not long enough to make a book by themselves, see D103. For titles of whole series of books, see D104.

D116 Do not italicize (or put in quotation marks either) the titles of dictionaries, encyclopedias, indexes, directories, almanacs, and similar reference works.

Webster's New Collegiate Dictionary	Information Please Almanac
	Americana Annual
Catholic Encyclopedia	the Roman Ritual
Cumulative Book Index	Reader's Guide
the Official Catholic Directory	Code of Canon Law
	Who's Who

D117 Do not italicize (or put in quotation marks either) the titles of charters, acts, statutes, reports, and so on, or of alliances and treaties.

Act of Supremacy	Emancipation Proclamation
Articles of Confederation	
Declaration of Independence	Stamp Act
	Treaty of Versailles

D118 Do not italicize (or put in quotation marks either)—

A The names of the Bible or of its books, divisions, parts, or versions.

the Septuagint	the Book of Psalms
the Synoptic Gospels	the Sermon on the Mount
the Gospel According to St. John	the Lord's Prayer
	the Reims-Douay Version

B The titles of prayers.

the Lord's Prayer	the Ave Maria

C The titles of the Breviary, Missal, Book of Common Prayer, or the parts of these books.

the Breviary	the Book of Common Prayer
the Office	Lauds
the Roman Missal	the Canon
the Proper	the Common

D The names of creeds, confessions of faith, and catechisms.

the Apostles' Creed	the Baltimore Catechism
the Augsburg Confession	the Thirty-nine Articles

E The names of the Mass or of any of its parts.

the Mass the Gloria

the Asperges the Preface

F The titles of church services and devotions.

Benediction First Friday devotions

Novena of Grace Forty Hours devotion

G The titles of the mysteries of the rosary.

The fourth glorious mystery is the Assumption of the Blessed Virgin Mary into Heaven.

D119 Italicize the titles of newspapers and magazines (but do not italicize or capitalize the initial article).

the St. Louis *Post-Dispatch*

the London *Times*

the *Queen's Work*

America

Fortune

Holiday

Variety

D120 Do not italicize the name of the city in which the newspaper or magazine is published.

the Baltimore *Sun*

the Omaha *World-Herald*

the Manila *Philippines Herald*

the Chicago *Tribune*

the Hankinson *News*

D121 Although the titles of works of art such as paintings, statues, and lengthy musical works, including operas and ballets, may be put in quotation marks, good usage prefers to write them in italic. Write them in italic.

Raphael's *Sistine Madonna* [painting]

Praxiteles' *Hermes* [statue]

Beethoven's *Emperor Concerto* [lengthy musical work]

Gilbert and Sullivan's *Iolanthe* [opera]

Oklahoma! [musical comedy]

Swan Lake [ballet]

D122 Italicize the names of ships, aircraft, and trains (but do not italicize or capitalize the initial article).

> the *Queen Mary* [ship]
> the *China Clipper* [airplane]
> the *Empire Builder* [train]
> the *Flying Fish* [submarine]
> the *Mary Ann* [rowboat]

D123 Do not italicize the name of a steamship line, airline, or railroad.

> the Louisville and Nashville Railroad
> the Cunard Steam-Ship Company
> the Burlington *Zephyr*

D124 Italicize foreign words and phrases not yet adopted into English.

> *dolce far niente*   *advocatus diaboli*
> *Mimosa pudica*   *bon voyage*
> *passim*   *supra*
> *op. cit.*   *ibid.*
> *en passant*   *enfant terrible*

D125 Italicize a word used only as a word, a letter used only as a letter, and a figure (number) used only as a figure.

Jimmy, spell *measles*.

Write *ought to be* where you have *is*.

Both *grammar* and *glamour*, curiously enough, came originally from the same word.

Your *os* and *as* look too much alike.

Use a capital *S* there.

All the *8s* on this page are in the wrong type.

D126 Do not italicize (or put in quotation marks either) letters used for names.

The house was sold by A to his brother, B.
Father L—— will say the Mass.
Who is the mysterious Mr. X?

D127 Use italic for emphasis very sparingly.

Menge has *not* been retaken.

The apostrophe

D128   Use 's to form the possessive of singular nouns (except those in D129).[39]

Edison's inventions	James's coat
Byrd's discoveries	man's shoes
Dickens's novels	fox's brush
Keats's sonnets	cow's horns

D129   Use the apostrophe (') alone to form the possessive singular of the following:

A The expressions *for conscience' sake, for acquaintance' sake, for goodness' sake.*

B Foreign names ending in *es,* like *Xerxes (Xerxes'), Socrates (Socrates'), Alcibiades (Alcibiades').*

C Our Saviour's name (*Jesus'*).

D130   Use 's to form the possessive of plural nouns that do not end in *s.*

alumnae's card party	men's shoes
alumni's wishes	oxen's yoke
children's clothing	women's gloves

D131   Use only the apostrophe (') to form the possessive of plural nouns that end in *s.*

Davises' fence	boys' caps
Joneses' front yard	cows' horns
Smiths' garage	foxes' brushes

D132   Add the apostrophe or 's to the last word of compound words in the possessive. (Compound words follow D128-31 according as the last word of the compound is singular or plural, ends in *s* or not.)

your daughter-in-law's success	the herdsmen's cries
the emperor of Japan's palace	the master of ceremonies' jokes

---

[39] There are other, equally common systems of showing possession. The one used in this book, however, has the advantage of simplicity, which seems to outweigh the disadvantage of an occasional awkward expression like *Dickens's novels.*
For the possessive case, see C191-94.

D133 Add the apostrophe or *'s* to the last word of titles in the possessive case (except those in D134).

> Pope Leo XIII's encyclicals
> the district attorney's office
> Henry VIII's disobedience
> the Standard Oil Company's boats
> the Lord Mayor of London's cat
> the Guild of Goldsmiths' annual exhibit

D134 Some titles in the possessive case are "frozen"; they omit the apostrophe or *'s*.

Bankers Association	St. Marys, Kansas
Governors Island	Teachers College

D135 If two or more nouns possess something together (joint possession), add the apostrophe or *'s* to the last only.

> Abercrombie and Fitch's clothing for men
> Gilbert and Sullivan's operas
> Beaumont and Fletcher's plays
> the juniors and seniors' poor-relief work

D136 If two or more nouns possess something separately, add the apostrophe or *'s* to each.

> Tom's, Dick's, and Harry's overcoats
> Wordsworth's and Shelley's poetry

D137 Use an apostrophe or *'s*[40] to form the possessive case of those indefinite and reciprocal pronouns[41] that have a possessive case (except *who, which, what,* and their compounds).

another's idea	someone's umbrella
others' ideas	somebody else's
anyone's guess	each other's clothes
nobody's business	one another's eyes

D138 Do not use an apostrophe with the personal, interrogative, relative, and possessive pronouns or adjectives.

> mine   ours   yours   his   hers   its   theirs   whose

---

[40] According to D128 and D130-31.
[41] For indefinite and reciprocal pronouns, see A55-56 and A60.

D139 Use an apostrophe in a contracted word to indicate the omission of a letter or letters.

can't [*not* ca'nt]	ev'ry
doesn't [*not* does'nt]	he's
don't [*not* do'nt]	I'm
isn't [*not* is'nt]	o'
it's [*for* it is]	o'clock
who's [*for* who is]	th'

D140 In the number of a year, the first two numerals are sometimes replaced by an apostrophe.

the spirit of '76	the class of '48
vintage of '02	the events of '65
depression of '32	the Panic of '93

D141 Use either an unitalicized *s* or an unitalicized *'s* to form the plural of letters, figures, and words used as words.

Mind your *ps* and *qs*.
Mind your *p's* and *q's*.

Your 7s look just like your 9s.
Your 7's look just like your 9's.

Is and *mes* are too prominent in your talk.
I's and *me's* are too prominent in your talk.

D142 Except for the cases in D141, do not use the apostrophe to form the plural of a word.

two ~~book's~~ *books* on the table   long, pointed ~~snout's~~ *snouts*

D143 Do not use an apostrophe for which you cannot give a rule or solid precedent.

The hyphen

D144 When two nouns not ordinarily used in combination are used as one word, connect them with a hyphen.

Father Abram Ryan was the *poet-priest* of the South.
He is the only *philosopher-statesman* in Washington.
Some modern painters might be classified as *artist-salesmen*.

D145 Hyphen a compound modifier preceding a noun (except in those cases mentioned in D146-47).[42]

do-as-I-please manner	saber-toothed tiger
door-to-door canvass	so-called geniuses
eleventh-century art	well-phrased sentences

D146 Do not hyphen (*a*) compound proper adjectives or (*b*) compound proper nouns that are used as adjectives.

| East Indian spices | New Orleans restaurants |
| Lake District scenery | North American savages |

D147 Do not hyphen an adverb in *ly* and the adjective or adverb it modifies.

Mike's *badly swollen* hand pained him a great deal.
This factory was *extraordinarily well* planned.

D148 Do not hyphen a compound modifier following a noun.

[Preceding:] This is a *well-chosen* adverb.
[Following:] This adverb is *well chosen*.

D149 Use a hyphen after *re* where it will help to distinguish two words that might otherwise be easily confused.

Mr. Antonescu *re-covered* the stolen chair.
Christianity could partly *re-create* the Garden of Eden.

D150 Use a hyphen between words when it will help to keep the reader from falsely combining them with other words.

Dr. Cox is president of the *insane-hospital* board.
Twelve *foot-soldiers* walked up the path.

D151 Hyphen compound numbers from twenty-one to ninety-nine.

I'll be *twenty-one* next Tuesday.

D152 Hyphen a fraction when it is used as an adjective or adverb.

Can I get lumber in *one-half* and *two-thirds* lengths?
The gas tank is *three-fourths* full.

---

[42] Note the difference in meaning between *red and white roses* (two kinds of roses) and *red-and-white roses* (one kind).

D153 Do not hyphen a fraction when it is used as a noun. (If, however, the fraction contains a compound number from twenty-one to ninety-nine, that number must be hyphened according to D151.)

Crumbock lost *one half* of his savings.
Two thirds of the distance remains.
I was airsick for *three fourths* of the trip.

Five thirty-seconds is not very much of an error.
This bottle contains almost *twelve twenty-sevenths* of the acid.
Why, *twenty-one thirty-seconds* is more than half!

D154 No general rules can be given here for hyphening ordinary compound words, because usage varies so widely. Consult a recent dictionary.

D155 Whenever you doubt about a hyphen and these rules or a dictionary cannot help you, do not use the hyphen.

E Division of words

E1 The following rules apply chiefly to matter that is hand-written or typed, rather than to printed matter.

E2 Do not divide a word at the end of a line when you can reasonably avoid doing so.

E3 Use a dictionary in order to be sure what the syllables of a word are.

E4 If a word must be divided at the end of a line, make the division between syllables only.

Autumn is the season of *frui-*
fulness.

His sickness is only an *imag-*
inary ailment.

E5   If a word begins with a prefix, divide after the prefix.

> Casey was said to be an ~~intrac~~- *in-*
> *tractable*
> ~~table~~ young rebel.

E6   Do not divide (*a*) one-syllable words (like *golf, thought,* and *praised*) or (*b*) words of less than seven letters (like *inner, useful,* and *filial*).

E7   Do not divide a word after one letter.

> It seems that we live in ~~e~~-
> *eventful*
> ~~ventful~~ days.

E8   Do not carry only two letters of a divided word to the next line.

> Mark has protested ~~violent~~-
> *violently*
> ~~ly~~ to the chaplain.

E9   Do not divide the syllables of a proper noun or adjective.

> Here is an issue of the ~~Atlan~~-
> *Atlantic*
> ~~tic~~ Monthly.

F Abbreviations

F1   Abbreviate these Latin words: *id est (i.e.); exempli gratia (e.g.); et cetera (etc.); et alibi, et alii (et al.); ibidem (ibid.); opere citato (op. cit.); videlicet (viz.).* (It is now very common to write *that is* in place of *i.e.; for example* in place of *e.g.; and so forth* or *and so on* in place of *etc.; and others* or *and elsewhere* in place of *et al.; and namely* in place of *viz.*)

[Right:] We found paper, kindling, *etc.,* all laid ready for a fire.

[Better:] We found paper, kindling, *and so forth,* all laid ready for a fire.

F2 Abbreviate eras of time and A.M. and P.M. when these are accompanied by figures.[1]

There is not a scrap of evidence before 10 B.C.
There is not a scrap of evidence until ten years before Christ.

In A.D. 1300 the university was still rather small.
Anno Domini thirteen hundred dawned on a university that was still rather small.

The masking stops at 6:00 P.M.
The masking stops at six in the evening.

F3 Abbreviate these titles always and only when they precede proper names: *Mr., Messrs.; Mrs.; saint (St.), saints (Sts.); doctor (Dr.), doctors (Drs.).*

That must be *Mr.* Clark in the closet.
See here, *mister,* that's airline property.

According to you, *St.* Thomas must have been jolly just because he was fat.
The *saint* spent a peculiar week in Denver.

I can guarantee that *Drs.* Pell and Nive will find something wrong with you.
I'm sorry, but the *doctors* are both ill.

F4 Abbreviate *reverend* and *honorable* only in the addresses and headings of letters, and not even then if they are preceded by *the.*

Rev. Francis X. Clements
St. Ignatius Rectory
502 Seward Avenue
Clifton, North Carolina

We were harangued by the *Honorable* Cyrus R. Schumacher.

The Reverend Francis X. Clements
St. Ignatius Rectory
502 Seward Avenue
Clifton, North Carolina

---

[1] Spell out the time of day when A.M. or P.M. is not used (G8). Put in figures the hours of the day if A.M. or P.M. is used, except at the beginning of a sentence (G16).

F5   Abbreviate *junior, senior,* academic degrees, the names of religious orders, and other standard tags when they are used after a person's name, and set them off by commas.

Does anybody here know an Andrew Johnson, *Jr.?*
James B. Fall, *Ph.D.,* held us in his drowsy spell for four hours.
Father Patrick Donovan, *O.S.B.,* blessed the new fire engine.

F6   Except in technical lists, do not abbreviate first and last names but only middle names, unless the person himself uses initials.

Mr. ~~Chas.~~ *Charles* Dyke   ~~Geo.~~ *George* O. Pickton
~~Wm.~~ *William* Colgrave   ~~J.~~ *Joseph* R. Connaught

He signs his name *J. V. Train.*
The register is signed *M. Moresby Mult.*

F7   Except in technical lists or the headings and addresses of letters (where abbreviation is optional), do not abbreviate but spell out the names of the months and of the days of the week.

There is going to be a class night on ~~Tues., Feb.~~ *Tuesday, February* 9.

F8   Except in technical lists and references or the headings and addresses of letters (where abbreviation is optional), do not abbreviate but spell out such words as *street, boulevard, avenue, page, chapter, company, manufacturing, brothers, consolidated, limited, incorporated, building, university,* and *railroad.*

The first shift at Able Seal ~~Mfg. Co.~~ *Manufacturing Company* comprises about five hundred men.

The clubroom, a two-by-four affair on Wellston ~~St.,~~ *Street* could hold a typewriter and an upright hand press.

In ~~Ch.~~ *Chapter* 2, ~~p.~~ *page* 22, there is a remark about the mystical body which may indicate that the author is a Catholic.

F9 Do not abbreviate *Father, Brother,* or *Sister.*

> *Father* LaFarge
> *Fathers* Engstrom and Smith
> *Brother* Martin de Porres
> *Brothers* Anselm and Basil
> *Sister* Teresa
> *Sisters* Frances and Emilda

F10 Use a period after abbreviations, except the titles of government agencies, labor unions, athletic associations; the call letters of broadcasting stations; and those abbreviations like CARE, NATO, and UNESCO that are pronounced like words.[2]

> At 9:00 P.M. there will be a cakewalk.

FBI	CIO	WAVES
NATO	AAU	WACS
AMG	WWL	SPARS
WDAY	NBC	CYO

F11 Use no comma after the period of an abbreviation unless a comma is required for clarity or by one of the rules of punctuation listed elsewhere in this book.

> [Wrong:] I have a 7:00 P.M., class.
> [Right:] I have a 7:00 P.M. class.[3]

> [Wrong:] In A.D., 64 Nero fiddled while Rome burned.
> [Right:] In A.D. 64 Nero fiddled while Rome burned.

If the schedule says P.M., P.M. is what it means.	Here the comma is required for clarity.
Planes leave at 7:00 P.M., at 11:00 P.M., and at 1:00 A.M.	Here the commas are required by D21.
Pencils, sketching pads, binoculars, etc., will have to be provided by the bird watchers themselves.	*Etc.* is generally considered to be parenthetical, and so the comma is required by D41.

---

[2] There is an increasing tendency to use no period with abbreviations. Until this becomes more general, the above rule is the one to follow.

[3] While printed matter uses small capitals for the abbreviations A.M. and P.M., you may write and type them a.m. and p.m. if you like.

F12 Except in the cases provided for in these rules and a few others for which you can find good authority, do not use abbreviations.

G Numbers

G1 Always spell out numbers at the beginning of a sentence.

Nineteen forty-three

~~1943~~ was not a bad year for wheat.

G2 When it would be awkward to spell out a number at the beginning of a sentence, recast the sentence.

Instead of—

Four million, two hundred and forty-six thousand, five hundred and forty-two dollars was the company's gross in the first five years of operation.

Write this—

In the first five years of operation, the company grossed $4,246,542.

G3 In general, spell out all numbers expressed in only one or two words, provided they are not affected by some other rule in this section.

He was in the hospital *three* months and *seventeen* days.
With bones and feathers, this is about a *five*-pound chicken.
In *sixty-eight* cities, *ten thousand* people gave *two* dollars each.
At *seven-fifty* the *three* golf clubs were a bargain.

G4 Spell out numbers from 2,100 to 9,900 when they are expressed only in hundreds.

[Wrong:] The auditorium held *two thousand one hundred* people.
[Right:] The auditorium held *twenty-one hundred* people.
[Right if intended to be read as *two thousand one hundred:*] The auditorium held 2,100 people.

[Wrong:] The auditorium held *twenty-three hundred and forty* people.
[Right:] The auditorium held 2,340 people.

230

G5 Spell out the numbers of streets up to twenty, of centuries, of sessions of Congress, of military bodies, and of political divisions and subdivisions.

> East Twentieth Street
> the seventeenth century
> Eightieth Congress, second session
> One Hundred and Sixty-seventh Infantry
> Ninth Congressional District, Fifty-second Ward

G6 Spell out the ages of persons and things (except in the cases treated in G10).

> a one-hundred-and-four-year-old tree
> men between thirty and forty

G7 Spell out the names of particular decades and hundreds.

Display was typical of the *nineties;* the *eighties* were not so lavish. The *eighteen-hundreds* were years of savage economic warfare.

G8 Spell out the time of day when A.M. or P.M. is not used.

I'll see you at *four-thirty* this afternoon [*but* at 4:30 P.M.]. We adjourned at *ten o'clock* [*but* at 10:00 P.M.].

G9 Spell out sums in cents up to one hundred (except for the cases treated in G10).

> four cents   ninety-eight cents

G10 In technical, statistical, and business writing—where it is important that the reader be able to work with figures— put in figures dimensions, degrees, distances, weights, measures, sums of money, and the like, even though they could be expressed in one or two words. (But do not put them in figures if they begin a sentence.)

> Decimals and percentages: .05 of an inch, 7 per cent
> Dimensions: 8 by 11 inches, 3 by 5 by 9 feet
> Degrees: 70° F., 30° C.
> Distances: 15 miles, 9 yards, 2 inches
> Weights: 3 tons, 15 pounds, 5 ounces
> Measures: 5 gallons, 2 pints, 50 bushels, 1 peck
> Sums of money: $5.00, $43.85, $.85, 85¢
> Ages: 18 years, 1 month, and 3 days

G11 In general, put in figures numbers expressed in more than two words, provided they are not affected by some other rule in this section.

1,556 hospitals	101 airplanes
1,250,000 people	514 pennies
123 times	28,634,878 Catholics

G12 Put years and dates in figures except for the case in G1 and except when, in text, the day precedes the month or the month is omitted.

1820	June 3
March 1, 1820	April 1

Nineteen forty-three was not a bad year for wheat.

The *fifth* of May is a day of much celebration in Mexico, for on the *fifth* the revolution is commemorated.

G13 Put in figures (Roman or Arabic as required) the page numbers, chapter numbers, and other divisions of books.

page 39	column 4	Volume III
pp. 39-72	line 18	Vol. 3
Chapter V	section 1	Book I
Chap. 5	verse 3	No. 16

G14 Put in figures the numbers of houses and of streets above twenty (except for the case in G1).

3648 Fifth Avenue
29 East 60th Street
Fifteen [*or* 15] Rosalind Drive

G15 Put in figures the numbers in abbreviated measurements (except for the case in G1).

75 m.p.h.	700 ft/sec
8 mi.	2 ft., 9 in.

G16 Put in figures the hours of the day if A.M. or P.M.[1] is used (except for the case in G1).

6:00 P.M.	11:45 A.M.

----

[1] Printed matter uses small capitals for the abbreviations A.M. and P.M.

G17 If similar numbers come under conflicting rules in the same sentence or in neighboring sentences, write them all in figures or spell them all out according to G1, G18, and G19, if you can do so without awkwardness.

G18 If all the numbers could be expressed in two words or less, spell all of them out or put them all in figures.[2]

[Wrong:] I arrived at 8:00 A.M. and began the operation about *nine o'clock.*

[Right:] I arrived at *eight* in the morning and began the operation about *nine.*

[Right:] I arrived at 8:00 A.M. and began to operate about 9:00.

G19 If some of the numbers would have to be expressed in more than two words, put them all in figures.[2]

[Wrong:] The number of accidents recorded in the three-year period were *fifty-five, seventy-three,* and 108, respectively.

[Wrong:] The number of accidents recorded in the three-year period were *fifty-five, seventy-three,* and *one hundred and eight,* respectively.

[Right:] The number of accidents recorded in the three-year period were 55, 73, and 108, respectively. [Note that *three* of "three-year" is not affected because it is not, according to the sense of the sentence, a number similar to the others.][2]

G20 In hyphening figures, omit hundreds from the second figure unless the first ends in two zeros or the hundreds change.

> 7640-95 [*not* 7640-7695]
> pp. 223-26 [*not* pp. 223-226]
>
> *But—*
> 1900-1914 [because of the two zeros]
> 487-504 [because of the changing hundreds]

G21 In hyphening figures, if the second-last figure of the first number is a zero, do not repeat the zero in the second number.

> pp. 1207-9 [*not* 1207-09]

---

[2] See G17.

G22 In hyphening dates before Christ, repeat the hundreds, since the numbers diminish rather than increase.

494-426 B.C. [*not* 494-26]

H Capitals

Line and sentence capitals

H1 Capitalize the first word of a sentence.

> *They* say he was a wealthy man. (*That* was in 1860, of course, when a dollar bought more than it buys now.) *Whether* or not he was is beside the point.

H2 When a sentence in parentheses interrupts another sentence, do not capitalize the first word in parentheses.

> Though I have often been tempted to quit (*such* thoughts surely come to every man), the example of More's fortitude gives me courage.

In this example the sentence in parentheses interrupts another sentence.

> They say he was a wealthy man. (*That* was in 1860, of course, when a dollar bought more than it buys now.) Whether or not he was is beside the point.

In this example the sentence in parentheses does *not* interrupt another sentence.

H3 Within a sentence you may capitalize, if you like, the first word of a question that is put in the form of a direct question but is not quoted.[1] The capital makes the question rather formal and emphatic.

> The big question is, *Will* this help a man to find Christ?
> Miss Ford's invariable morning question was, *did* you sleep well?

---

[1] A direct question is a question expressed in the words of the speaker; for example: "Where is the wampum?" An indirect question gives the sense of the speaker's question without quoting him; for example: "He asked where the wampum was." Indirect questions are frequently introduced by *whether* and by *if* in the sense of *whether*.

H4 If words are directed by a person to himself or are merely unspoken thoughts, capitalize the first word. (Do not use quotation marks.)

> I thought to myself, *Where* is all this going to end?
> No doubt you have asked yourself, *Why* am I here?
> She said to herself, *Here* we go again!

H5 Capitalize the first word of a directly quoted sentence, even when it appears within another sentence.[2]

> Cecil replied, "*My* mother is a very determined person."
>
> "*My* mother," replied Cecil, "is a very determined person." [*Is* is not the first word of the directly quoted sentence.]
>
> Then, "*Don't* you worry," she whispered. "*For* an old woman I'm feeling very fit indeed. *Why*, I've many a song in me yet, and many a quarrel, too."

H6 Do not capitalize the first word of a directly quoted sentence fragment, unless the fragment begins the sentence in which it stands.[3]

> Margaret won't speak to "*those* common Kellys," as she calls them.
>
> "My mother," replied Cecil, "*is* a very determined person." [Note that *is* is not capitalized, since it is not the first word of a sentence but of a fragment.]
>
> She said, "For an old woman I'm feeling very fit indeed." But her "*very* fit" sounded unconvincing, spoken as it was in a rather feeble voice.
>
> "*Crazy* as a loon," he called me.
>
> "*If* wishes were horses," we could overtake Selwyn.

---

[2] A direct quotation is a quotation in the speaker's or writer's own words that is not introduced by the conjunctions *whether, if,* or *that* either expressed or implied.

[3] Do not confuse a sentence fragment or half-sentence with an interrupted sentence or elliptical sentence. In the following, the quoted sentence is an interrupted sentence, not a sentence fragment, and hence is capitalized.

> Margot was stopped just as she began to say, "Then you mean that the ghost isn't—"

In the following, the quoted portion is an elliptical sentence, not a sentence fragment, and hence is capitalized.

> Shelley turned around and said very carefully, very deliberately, "Not a chance."

H7 Do not capitalize the first word of an indirect quotation, whether you use quotation marks around it or not.[4]

St. Paul declared that *"our* citizenship is in heaven."
St. Paul declared that *our* citizenship is in heaven.

H8 Capitalize the first word of every line of poetry.[5]

> Being your slave, what should I do but tend
> Upon the hours and times of your desire?
> I have no precious time at all to spend,
> Nor services to do, till you require.
> —SHAKESPEARE

H9 Do not capitalize a line of poetry that simply runs over from the preceding line for lack of room.

> The cloud shadows of midnight possess their
> own repose,
> For the weary winds are silent, or the moon
> is in the deep;
> Some respite to its turbulence unresting ocean
> knows
> Whatever moves or toils or grieves hath its
> appointed sleep.
> —SHELLEY

H10 When the beginning of a line of poetry is omitted, do not capitalize the first word.

> . . . hast thou golden slumbers?
> O sweet content!
> . . . is thy mind perplexed?
> O punishment!
> —THOMAS DEKKER

---

[4] See D92. An indirect quotation is a quotation introduced by the conjunctions *whether, if,* or *that* either expressed or implied.

[5] In some modern poetry this rule (as well as many others) does not apply. If you quote such poetry, follow copy exactly.

> I am afraid, dear friend,
> that something trivial will come
> of men
> with dollars.
> —MICHEL CHAMBRE

See H9.

H11 Capitalize the first word after a colon whenever you want to introduce formally a complete sentence following the colon.

My advice to you is this: *Stay* in bed Monday and Tuesday, and stay in the house at least until noon Saturday.

They asked me the same old tiresome question over and over again: *Where* were you, and whom with, last Thursday afternoon?

This is the problem we must talk over: *The* woman is old and getting feeble, has no money, cannot stay any longer at her niece's, and has gotten into trouble at the police station.

H12 Do not capitalize the first word after a colon when you are (*a*) merely giving an example or amplifying a preceding clause or (*b*) adding brief items that do not make a complete sentence.

Everything was perfect for our walk to Corona: *the* day was sunny and clear; the air grew cooler and scented as we climbed the Divide; and we seemed to have the whole mountain to ourselves.

Peace is not an accident: *it* is built of law and self-restraint.

Be sure to bring these things with you: *slacks,* swimming trunks, tennis shorts, tennis shoes, crew socks, and plenty of T shirts.

One thing the human heart requires: *love.*

H13 Capitalize the first word of each line in the heading and addresses of a letter.

The Narrows	The Shorthorn
Pawhasset, New York	Arlington State College
February 15, 1954	Arlington, Texas
The Roberts Family	The Debate Team
326 Westwood	Elspeth High School
Briarly, Maine	Wotan, Nevada

H14 Capitalize the first word in the salutation of a letter. Do not capitalize *dear* unless it is the first word.

Dear Sir:	Reverend and dear Father:
Dear Aunt Marie,	Very Reverend and dear
My dear Aunt Marie,	Monsignor:
Dear Reverend Father:	My dear Senator:

237

H15 Capitalize only the first word in the complimentary close of a letter.

Yours truly,   Sincerely yours,
Very truly yours,   Yours sincerely,

H16 When a title is set in two or more lines (for example, on a title page or at the beginning of a theme), capitalize the first word of each line.[6]

A Short Dissertation
On Buying Pigs in a Poke

Marius
The King's Henchman

Proper nouns and adjectives

H17 In general, capitalize proper nouns—the particular names of particular persons, places, animals, and other things.

May I have an appointment with Mr. *Anthony Powers*, please?
Let's stop off at *Niagara Falls.*
The lobby of the *Statler Hotel* will be a good place to meet.
Wasn't *Man o' War* one of the greatest race horses?
They say *Blackie* is a vicious dog.

H18 In general, capitalize proper adjectives; that is, adjectives derived from proper nouns.

American   North Korean
Christian   Olympian
Napoleonic   South American

H19 Do not capitalize the combining forms *un, non, pro,* and *anti* when they are used with proper nouns and adjectives.

un-American   pro-British
non-Jewish   anti-Bolshevik

Is it *un-American* [adjective] to want God in the schools?
For a *non-Catholic* [noun] he shows a remarkable knowledge of the Mass.

---

[6] For the capitalization of other words in titles, see H120.

H20 Do not capitalize words that, though derived from proper nouns, have lost almost all of the proper noun's original meaning.

apache [Parisian gangster], from Apache Indian

artesian well, from Artesium in ancient France

babel of opinion, from the Tower of Babel

bedlam [uproar, confusion], from Bedlam [Bethlehem] Hospital for lunatics

china [porcelain ware], from China

gothic type, from Gothic

italic type, from Italic, pertaining to ancient Italy

macadam [a road finishing], from John L. McAdam, Scots engineer

mulligan stew, from Mulligan

pasteurize, from Pasteur

quisling, from Vidkun Quisling

roman type, from Roman

venetian blinds, from Venetian, pertaining to Venice

watt [volt-ampere], from James Watt, Scots inventor

If you tear another *jersey*, you'll have to play in an overcoat.

The *bedlam* at Bedlam could never have been more wildly noisy than dinnertime at Miss Willick's school.

Religious terms

RELIGIOUS BOOKS, PRAYERS

H21 Capitalize the word *Bible* and its synonyms, and the titles of the sacred writings of all religions.[7] (Do not use italic or quotation marks.)

the Bible	the Koran
the Book of Life	Mishna
God's Word	the Scriptures
the Holy Bible	the Talmud
Holy Writ	the Written Word

---

[7] Do not capitalize initial *the* or conjunctions, articles, prepositions, within such names or titles.

H22 Do not capitalize words derived from those in the preceding rule.

biblical   scriptural
koranic   talmudic
mishnaic

H23 Capitalize all texts, versions, and revisions of the Bible and all canons (that is, lists of inspired books).[8] (Do not use italic or quotation marks.)

the American Translation   the Roman Catholic Canon
the King James Version   the Septuagint
the Reims-Douay Version   the Vulgate

H24 Capitalize all parts and books of the Bible.[8] (Do not use italic or quotation marks.)

the Acts of the Apostles   the New Testament
the Apocalypse   the Old Testament
the Book of Psalms   the Pentateuch
Deuteronomy   Proverbs
the Epistles   the Psalms
Genesis   the Psalter
the Letter to Philemon   the Synoptic Gospels

H25 Capitalize the nouns *gospel* and *gospels* when they refer to one or more of the first four books of the New Testament, but not otherwise.[8] (Do not use italic or quotation marks.)

Everyone should read the Gospels and know them.
This passage is from the Gospel According[9] to St. John.

Preach the *gospel* to every creature.
"Oh," he said, "big business has its own *gospel*."

H26 Do not capitalize the adjective *gospel*.

Millions of men have never heard the *gospel* message.
Businessmen should act upon *gospel* principles.
I'm telling you the *gospel* truth.

---

[8] Do not capitalize initial *the* or conjunctions, articles, prepositions, within such names or titles.
[9] For *According* see H149.

H27 Capitalize the titles of Christ's and others' discourses that are known by names equivalent to the titles of literary works.[10] (Do not use italic or quotation marks.)

> the Angelic Salutation
> the Discourse at the Last Supper
> the Eight Beatitudes
> the Sermon on the Mount

The Sermon on the Mount and the Discourse at the Last Supper were addressed to different audiences.

But—
Our Lord gave a *discourse* at the Last Supper.
There are *eight beatitudes*.

H28 Capitalize the titles of Christ's parables.[10] (Do not use italic or quotation marks.)

> the Faithful Steward   the Ten Virgins
> the Five Talents   the Unjust Steward
> the Good Samaritan   the Unmerciful Servant

The Prodigal Son is one of the greatest of all short stories.

The *prodigal son* [the person, not the parable, here] asked for less than his father gave him.

H29 Capitalize the titles of prayers.[10] (Do not use italic or quotation marks.)

> Ave Maria   Litany of the Saints
> Benedictus   Lord's Prayer
> Gloria [Gloria Patri]   Magnificat
> Glory Be to the Father   Memorare
> Hail Mary   Pater Noster

We always recited the Memorare to ask for good weather on picnics and holidays.
Say the Glory Be to the Father at the end of each mystery.

Let *glory be to the Father*, not to me, for this day's manful work. [Not the title of a prayer here.]

---

[10] Do not capitalize initial *the* or conjunctions, articles, prepositions, within such names or titles.

H30   Do not capitalize *rosary* or *beads.*

The complete *rosary* has fifteen decades.

Most Catholics say their *beads* every day.

H31   Do not capitalize descriptive names of real or imaginary biblical characters.

The *good thief* was saved.

Repent as the *prodigal son* did.

The *faithful steward* was commended.

H32   Capitalize the words *Breviary* and *Missal* and the names of the parts of these books.[11] (Do not use italic or quotation marks.)

Breviary	Missal
Canon	Office
Compline	Office of the Dead
Divine Office	Preface
Lauds	Psalter
the Little Hours	Roman Missal
Matins	Second Nocturn

The new translation of the Psalms has made reading the Breviary a more pleasant and more intelligent duty than it was.

Is today's Office a double or a simple?

The prayers of the Canon say so much so beautifully that I should like to memorize them.

The Missal was almost as big as the altar boy.

St. Chrysostom says that (in his day) the priest would not proceed with the Mass until the people had responded to the Preface.

H33   Capitalize the names of all creeds, confessions of faith, and catechisms.[11] (Do not use italic or quotation marks.)

the Apostles' Creed

the Augsburg Confession

the Baltimore Catechism

the Nicene Creed

the Thirty-nine Articles

---

[11] Do not capitalize initial *the* or conjunctions, articles, prepositions, within such names or titles.

NAMES OF GOD

H34 Capitalize the names of God.[12]

Allah	Jehovah
Christ	Jesus
Divine Persons	Logos
Father	Messias [Messiah]
First Person	Paraclete
God	Second Person
God-Man	Third Person
Holy Ghost	Trinity

H35 Capitalize the following names whenever they are used as proper names of God—whenever they are substitute names, that is.

Advocate	Lord
the Bread of Angels	the Lord of Lords
the Child Jesus	Maker
Comforter	Master
the Creator	the Prince of Peace
the Good Shepherd	the Redeemer
the Infant	the Sanctifier
the Infant Jesus	Saviour
the King of Heaven	the Son
the King of Kings	the Son of God
the Lamb of God	the Son of Man

Adore your *Maker*.
The *Son of God* is Jesus Christ.
Simeon was glad because he saw his *Redeemer* and *Saviour*.

H36 Do not capitalize names such as those in H35 when they are used simply as descriptive predicates or appositives.

God is our *maker*.
[But:] Adore your *Maker*.

Christ is the *son* of Mary.
[But:] The *Son of God* is Jesus Christ.

---

[12] Do not capitalize initial *the* or conjunctions, articles, prepositions, within such names or titles.

All nations have longed for a *redeemer,* a *savior.*
[But:] Simeon was glad because he saw his *Redeemer* and *Saviour.*

Christ came into the world as an *infant.*
[But:] The Magi adored the *Infant.*

Our Lord proved Himself the *master* of His enemies.
[But:] "Peace!" cried Martha. "The *Master* is coming."

Christ, the *good shepherd,* searched for the lost sheep.
[But:] Teach us, *Good Shepherd,* to be kind.

Jesus is the *lord* of the world.
[But:] You can heal me, *Lord,* if You will.

Christ, as *lord of lords* and *king of kings,* has all power.
[But:] Jesus, *King of Kings,* have mercy on me!

Jesus is the *bread of angels.*
[But:] O *Bread of Angels,* be our strength!

The Holy Ghost is our *comforter.*
[But:] Courage comes from the grace of the *Comforter.*

God is the one true *sanctifier* of souls.
[But:] Pray that the *Sanctifier* may give light to men's minds.

H37 Do not capitalize adjectives accompanying the names of
God (unless the adjectives combine with the name to
form a descriptive substitute name—an epithet, that is).[13]

all-wise Creator	loving Saviour
almighty God	merciful Father
eternal Father	our Lord
Father almighty	our Saviour

H38 Capitalize adjectives and adverbs in descriptive substitute
names of God (in epithets for God, that is) whenever
such names would lose their meaning if the adjective or
adverb were left out.

the First Cause	the Most High
Immutable One	the Only Begotten

Such reasoning brings one back to the *First Cause.*
It is the *Only Begotten* who is altogether pleasing to His Father.

---

[13] See H38.

244

H39 Capitalize *divinity, providence,* and *deity* when they are used as names of God.

> May the *Divinity* guide your steps!
> Christ proved His *divinity* by His miracles.

> Place your hope in *Providence.*
> God's *providence* directs all things.

> All men must worship the *Deity.*
> The ancient Egyptians had their *deities.*

H40 Do not capitalize *name, holy name, fatherhood,* or *sonship.*

> Judge with mercy, in the *name* of God!
> Show reverence for the *holy name.*
> The thought of God's *fatherhood* will comfort you.
> Christ was conscious of His divine *sonship.*

H41 Capitalize *body* or *blood* only when it is a synonym for the Eucharist.

> Every second day Eric received the *Body* of Christ.
> Catholics always genuflect to the most precious *Body* and *Blood.*

> The *body* of Christ in the tomb could be adored.
> Christ gave His *blood* for us.

H42 Capitalize *heart* only in the name *Sacred Heart* or when it is used as an abbreviation for the name. Do not capitalize the words for any other part of Christ's body.

> The *Sacred Heart* is our refuge and our hope.
> His *Heart* is our refuge and our hope.

> Jesus was meek and humble of *heart.*
> They pierced His *hands* and His *feet;* they counted all His *bones.*

H43 Do not capitalize *humanity, hypostatic union, mystical body, mystical union, cross.*

> We shall meditate on Christ's *humanity.*

> What is meant by the *hypostatic union?*

> We are all members of Christ's *mystical body.*

> Some saints have been granted the unusual grace of *mystical union* with God.

> In the *cross* of Christ is our salvation.

H44 Capitalize *he, his, him, himself, we, our, ours, us, ourselves, me, my, mine, myself, you, your, yourself, thee, thine, thou, thyself, they, their, them,* and *themselves* when they refer to God.[14]

Christ went *Himself* to raise *His* friend Lazarus from the dead.

The Father and I are one, and *We* will keep *Our* faithful safe from the world.

All *My* sheep know *Me,* and I know *Mine.*

The three Persons of the Trinity are one in *Their* nature.

H45 Do not capitalize *it* when referring to God.

The Sacred Heart will bless all who trust in *it.*

H46 Do not capitalize *one, who, whose, whom, that* referring to God unless the reference to God would otherwise be obscure.

Our hope is in Christ, *who* redeemed us.

[If there is no other indication that *who* refers to God:] I know *Who* has care of me.

H47 Do not capitalize *god* when it refers to a false deity, or *gods, goddess,* and *goddesses.*

The Romans built a temple to Mars, the *god* of war.

Juno was queen of all the *gods* and *goddesses.*

NAMES OF THE BLESSED VIRGIN

H48 Capitalize the names of the Blessed Virgin; but do not capitalize *blessed* when it is preceded by another adjective and *and,* or by an adverb.

Blessed Virgin	our Lady
Blessed Virgin Mary	our Queen
Immaculate Conception	Queen
Lady	Virgin
Mother of Mercy	Virgin Mary

Let us pray to the *glorious and blessed* Virgin.

Let us pray to the *ever-blessed* Virgin.

---

[14] See H45-46.

H49 Do not capitalize *virgin* when it is not used as a proper name or part of a proper name.

Mary was a *virgin* before, during, and after the birth of her son.

H50 Capitalize the following names of the Blessed Virgin (and all such names as are found in the Litany of Loretto) whenever they are used as proper names—whenever they are descriptive substitute names (that is, epithets).

Mother of Christ	Refuge of Sinners
Star of the Sea	Help of Christians

H51 Do not capitalize the names in H50 when they are used as simple descriptive predicates or appositives.

Mary, the *mother of Christ,* was also asked to the wedding.
[But:] O *Mother of Christ,* be my mother!

The Blessed Virgin shines like the *star of the sea.*
[But:] Hail, bright *Star of the Sea!*

Mary has always been the *refuge of sinners.*
[But:] Let us pray to the *Refuge of Sinners.*

H52 Do not capitalize adjectives accompanying the names of the Blessed Virgin.[15]

What an ugly statue of *our* Lady!

Mary, *immaculate* and *holy,* never knew sin.

St. Bernard wrote many sermons in praise of his *gracious* and *loving* Queen.

H53 Capitalize *mother* when it is a substitute for the proper name of the Blessed Virgin or in the expression *His Mother,* not otherwise.

Then, *Mother,* pray for me.

Remember, Jesus worked His first recorded miracle at the suggestion of *His Mother.*

Jesus had a human *mother* but not a human father.

---

[15] This rule does not apply to *blessed,* for which see H48.

There are a few "frozen" titles like *Our Lady of Good Counsel, Our Lady of Lourdes, Our Lady of Mercy,* in which the *our* is considered part of the title and is capitalized. Make use of this exception.

HOLY FAMILY, EVENTS OF THE REDEMPTION

H54 Capitalize *Holy Family.*

Quickly the *Holy Family* fled into Egypt.

H55 Do not capitalize the names of events and states of being in the life of our Lord and the Blessed Virgin except for the following, which long usage has decided should be capitalized.

the Advent [of Christ]	the Last Supper
the Ascension	the Nativity
the Assumption	the Passion
the Crucifixion	Pentecost
the Immaculate Conception	the Resurrection
the Incarnation	the Sermon on the Mount
the Last Judgment	the Visitation

The *flight* into Egypt took place during that part of our Lord's life of which we know almost nothing.

The *public life* of Christ lasted a scant three years.

Our *redemption* was accomplished with the death of the Redeemer.

The *descent* of the Holy Ghost was followed by the first general manifestation of the new Church to the world.

At the *circumcision* Jesus received His name.

Christ endured a *passion* all the more horrible because He was utterly innocent.

Surely, after the *Passion* Christ knows our sufferings very well.

Mary's *Immaculate Conception* sheds glory on us too when we are in the state of grace.

Note 1. Many terms similar to the ones listed in the columns above are not capitalized. When in doubt, consult the most recent edition of a good dictionary.

Note 2. Of course, when names not ordinarily capitalized fall under some other rule, they are capitalized. For example, *scourging at the pillar* is capitalized when it is used as the name of a mystery of the rosary; *circumcision* is capitalized when it is used as the name of a feast.

H56 When two or more of the names indicated in H55 are used together in the same sentence and one is not capitalized, do not capitalize the others.

> It is surprising how many people confuse the *virgin birth* with the *immaculate conception.*
>
> We read of the *passion, death,* and *resurrection* of Christ.

H57 Capitalize *redemption* when it is preceded by *the* and refers to the entire series of events constituting our redemption by Christ.

> The second volume treats of *the Redemption.*
>
> We should be grateful to God for our *redemption.*

ANGELS, HOLY SOULS, DEVILS

H58 Capitalize *angel, archangel,* and *guardian angel* only when they are used as titles in direct address in place of proper names, or as titles followed by proper names. Do not capitalize the classes of angels, like *seraphim* or *principalities.*

> O *Archangel* Michael, defend us from evil!
> Help and protect me, *Guardian Angel.*
>
> Pray to your *guardian angel* every day.
> I always think of the *seraphim* as bigger than the *cherubim.*

H59 Do not capitalize *holy souls* or *souls in purgatory.*

> November is the month of the *holy souls.*
> O *holy souls,* pray for us!
> Mass will be said tomorrow morning for the *souls in purgatory.*

H60 Capitalize all synonyms for *Satan* except *devil.*[16]

the Archfiend	His Satanic Majesty
Beelzebub	Lucifer
the Evil One	the Prince of Darkness

The *devil* goes about like a roaring lion.

---

[16] Do not capitalize initial *the* or conjunctions, articles, prepositions, within such names or titles.

HEAVEN, HELL, PURGATORY

H61 Capitalize *Gehenna, Hades, Elysian Fields, Garden of Eden, Pearly Gates,* and *Tartarus,*[17] but not *Abraham's bosom, beatific vision, heaven, hell, purgatory, nether regions,* and *nirvana.*

Christ sometimes spoke of *hell* as *Gehenna.*

If we cannot be perfectly happy in *heaven* without football, then we shall have football in *heaven.*

H62 Capitalize *paradise* only when it is used as a synonym for *Garden of Eden.*

God talked familiarly with Adam in *Paradise.*

Everyone's hope is to reach *paradise* some day.

CHURCHES, CHURCH MEMBERS, CHURCH

H63 Capitalize the names of all religions and their adherents.[17]

Anglican Church	Lutheran Church
Anglicans	Lutherans
Catholic Church	Protestantism
Catholicism	Protestants
Catholics	Roman Catholic Church

H64 Capitalize *church* standing alone when it means the Roman Catholic Church.[17]

A great many prominent persons have been received into the *Church* recently.

H65 Do not capitalize *church* standing alone when it indicates a building, when it is used as an adjective, or when it does not necessarily refer to the Roman Catholic Church. And do not capitalize it when it is used as part of the description, rather than as part of the proper name, of a building.

There seems to be a *church* on every corner.

It is *church* law that everyone must help support his pastor.

---

[17] Do not capitalize initial *the* or conjunctions, articles, prepositions, within such names or titles.

The question of *church* and state is much argued.

That is the Baptist *church*.	Here *church* is part of a description rather than part of a proper name.
On the corner is the First Baptist *Church*.	Here *church* is part of a proper, particular, name.

MASS, THE SACRAMENTS

H66 Capitalize *Mass* and all the parts of the Mass, even when used as adjectives.[18] (Do not use italic or quotation marks.)

Asperges	Introit
Canon	Ite Missa Est
Communion of the Priest	Last Gospel
Consecration	Offertory
Credo	Ordinary
Elevation [of the Host]	Postcommunion
Epistle	Proper

I went to early Mass this morning.
No one has put away the Mass vestments.
The congregation stands during the reading of the Gospel.
The storm struck while the priest was at the Offertory.
Look up the Collect in your Missal.

H67 Do not capitalize adjectives modifying *Mass.*

low Mass	requiem Mass
Missa cantata	solemn high Mass

H68 Do not capitalize *sacrament* or the names of the sacraments (except the Eucharist, for which see H69).

Ted has received the *sacrament* of *baptism,* but he has never received *confirmation.*

I have been given *extreme unction* five times.

Christ Himself instituted *penance;* that is, *confession.*

My uncle has returned to the *sacraments.*

---

[18] Do not capitalize initial *the* or conjunctions, articles, prepositions, within such names or titles.

H69 Capitalize the names of the Holy Eucharist and the Eucharistic Sacrifice.[19]

Blessed Eucharist	Holy Communion
Blessed Sacrament	Holy Sacrament
Communion	sacrament of the Eucharist
Eucharist	Viaticum

H70 Do not capitalize adjectives and adverbs modifying the terms listed in H69.

Every night there will be devotions in honor of the *most adorable* Sacrament of the Altar.

H71 Do not capitalize *real presence, host, sacred host, sacred species, transubstantiation.*[20]

All Catholics believe in the *real presence.*
Vandals scattered the *sacred species* all over the sanctuary.

SERVICES, DEVOTIONS

H72 Capitalize the following church services and devotions (but not *service* and *devotion*).[21]

Benediction [of the Blessed Sacrament]	Mass
Compline	Novena of Grace [of the Sorrowful Mother, of the Sacred Heart, *and so on*]
Exposition [of the Blessed Sacrament]	Stations of the Cross
First Friday devotions	Tenebrae
Forty Hours devotion	Three Hours devotion
Holy Hour	Tre Ore [service, devotion]
Litany of Loretto [of the Sacred Heart, *and so on*]	Vespers
	Way of the Cross

There will be rosary and *Benediction* at 8:15 P.M.
Many churches still have *Vespers* on Sunday afternoon.

---

[19] Do not capitalize initial *the* or conjunctions, articles, prepositions, within such names or titles.
See H70.

[20] Of course, the words should be capitalized if they come under some other rule; for example, *Elevation of the Host,* in accord with H66.

[21] See footnote 19, above.
See H73.

H73 Do not capitalize the following words except when they appear as part of the names in H72 or come under some other rule.

benediction	prayers
blessing	retreat
day of recollection	rosary
exposition	sermon
grace	thanksgiving
litany	triduum
novena	veneration

The priest raised his hand in *benediction* [blessing].

There will be a *sermon* and *prayers,* followed by *exposition* and *veneration* of the relic.

This *novena* is the Novena of Grace.

There will be *rosary* and Benediction at 8:15 P.M.

After the *litany* the clergy and the laity marched in procession to the bishop's house.

H74 Capitalize the titles of the mysteries of the rosary: the *Carrying of the Cross,* the *Crowning of the Blessed Virgin Mary,* the *Crowning with Thorns,* the *Crucifixion,* the *Descent of the Holy Spirit,* and so on.[22]

The fourth glorious mystery is the *Assumption of the Blessed Virgin Mary into Heaven.*

CLASSES AND ORDERS OF PEOPLE IN THE CHURCH

H75 Do not capitalize the names of classes of men such as *patriarchs, prophets, doctors* and *fathers of the Church, apostles,* and *disciples.*

The greatest of the *prophets* was John the Baptist.

St. Robert Bellarmine is a *doctor of the Church.*

Give me the name of the earliest church *father.*

The *apostles* were simple, not stupid, men.

Christ's grace produced Peter, the *apostle.*

There were all sorts of men among the *disciples.*

---

[22] Do not capitalize initial *the* or conjunctions, articles, prepositions, within such names or titles.

H76 Capitalize the names of religious orders and the names by which their members are known.[23]

Brothers of Mary	Benedictines
Christian Brothers	Cistercians
Daughters of Divine Charity	Dominicans
Institute of Charity	Eudists
Order of Preachers	Jesuits
Order of St. Benedict	Oblates
Society of Jesus	Trappists

H77 Do not capitalize *congregation, order,* and so on, unless they are used as part of an official title.

The Jesuit *order* [the Society of Jesus] considers the foreign missions one of its primary works.

The *Order of Preachers* was founded by St. Dominic.

This *congregation* numbers more than two thousand religious.

The *Congregation of the Missions,* whose members are known as Vincentians, has three parishes in our town.

Three *religious* were caught in the rain, and you should have seen what happened to those white things they wear.

She joined the *Religious of the Missions* and was sent to New York, and there she spent the rest of her life.

H78 Do not capitalize such words as *priest, monk, nun,* and so on, when they are used as common nouns; that is, not as a title or part of a title.

abbot	deacon	nun
archbishop	dean	pope
bishop	evangelist	priest
canon	friar	rabbi
cardinal	minister	religious
catechumen	monk	scholastic
cleric	novice	theologian

What is the difference between an *archbishop* and a *bishop?*
A *deacon*, unlike a *priest*, may not say Mass.
The *ministers* of the Mass will vest in the east sacristy.

---

[23] Do not capitalize initial *the* or conjunctions, articles, prepositions, within such names or titles.

APOSTOLIC SEE, PAPACY

H79 Capitalize *Apostolic See, Holy See,* and *Chair of Peter,* meaning the supreme governing authority of the Church.[24]

All Catholics must obey the *Apostolic See.*

The last two popes in the *Chair of Peter* understood America very well.

H80 Do not capitalize *papacy.*

Personal titles

H81 Capitalize all religious, civil, military, and social titles that are followed by a proper name.[24]

Pope Pius XII	Monsignor Fleckler
His Holiness, Pope Pius XII	Canon Appleby
Cardinal Spellman	Father Thomas Reid
His Eminence, Cardinal Stritch of Chicago	Brother Jonathan
	Mother Marie
Bishop Manning	Sister Mary Helen
Alderman Porter Smith	General Heath
Ambassador John J. Archer	Governor Herman Long
Chairman Kelly	Judge J. Robert Regan
Chief Justice Fred M. Vinson	Lieutenant Seldon Wadsworth
Commissioner Walker	Mayor James G. Fogarty
Director Cecil B. de Mille	Professor Walter Briggs
Mr. Rollins	Miss Helen McIntyre
Mrs. James B. Sellen	Master John Smithers

At this point *Bishop* Manning rose in protest.

The *Abbot* Marmion would hardly agree with *Miss* Kelly.

I believe the last speaker was *Ambassador* John J. Archer.

General Chennault urged that Chiang Kai-shek's forces be allowed to attack the Chinese on the mainland.

The lady in question is a *Mrs.* James B. Sellen.

---

[24] Do not capitalize initial *the* or conjunctions, articles, prepositions, within such names or titles.

H82 Capitalize titles indicating position or occupation when they are followed by a proper name.

Architect Riley	Designer Adrian
Catcher Hargrave	Halfback Steiner
Chairman Walker	Singer Mary Martin
Coach Wilson	Treasurer Lambert

His brief encounter with *Halfback* Steiner left him crippled for life.

As usual, there was some disagreement between *Architect* Riley and *Treasurer* J. Charles Lambert.

I hear that *Designer* Adrian is not going along with Paris this year.

H83 Do not capitalize words indicating position or occupation when they are not used as titles.

His brief encounter with the *halfback,* Steiner, left him crippled for life.

As usual, there was some disagreement between the *architect,* Riley, and the *treasurer,* J. Charles Lambert.

Do you mean the *poet* Wordsworth or the *poet* Longfellow?

H84 Except for those mentioned in H85, capitalize titles that are used in direct address. (Such titles are a substitute for a proper name and identify the person addressed.)

Please, *Mr. Secretary,* will you read the minutes of the last meeting?
Welcome, *Senator,* to our banquet.
Your position, *Judge,* is perfectly clear.
Will *Your Excellency* please sign this?
Be so kind, *Your Eminence,* as to sit over here.

H85 Do not capitalize *sir, madam,* and broad general terms (like *gentlemen, ladies,* and *children*) that can be applied to wide classes of persons, unless they are followed by a proper name or are used in the salutation of a letter.

Yes, *sir,* you'll find him in.
No, *madam;* the boat has sailed.
Listen carefully, *gentlemen,* to this hypocrite.
But, *lady,* that's the only hat I own!
See here, my dear *child,* that's my nose!

Dear Sir:	Gentlemen:
Dear Madam:	Dear Ladies:

H86 Do not capitalize *mister, master,* and *miss* when they are not followed by a proper name; nor terms of address used opprobriously, like *nitwit, slowpoke,* or *stupid.*

You don't know the half of it, *mister.*

Indeed, *master,* the third camel does have an irresponsible expression on its face.

You'll find flat silver on the third floor, *miss.*

Hurry up, *slowpoke!*

H87 In general, do not capitalize a title not followed by a proper name unless it is in direct address or is affected by another of the rules of capitals.

The *pope* spoke on the radio today.

The *cardinal* asked the *pope* what to do.

Pius XII, the present *pope,* is tall and thin.

Henry IV, *king* of England, had not yet been heard from.

I'm sorry, but the *governor* will not see you.

Should the *president* carry his complaint to Congress?

Was Fred Vinson ever *chief justice* of the United States?

Cardinal Spellman, *archbishop* of New York, hurried to Rome.

H88 Always capitalize *father* (a priest) and *brother* and *sister* (religious), whether or not they are used in direct address or before a proper name.[25]

Father Thomas Reid   Brother Jonathan   Sister Mary Helen

I have two *Sisters* and a *Brother* in my class.

Bucky has an uncle who is an Oblate *Father.*

The *Fathers'* birettas are on the sedile.

H89 Capitalize such titles as *His Holiness, His Eminence, His Excellency,* and *His Honor* even when they are used without the person's name.

You have just heard a broadcast by *His Holiness.*

I wasn't able to see *His Eminence.*

I wasn't able to see *His Eminence,* the cardinal.

Gentlemen, *His Honor* is detained.

Gentlemen, *His Honor,* the mayor, is detained.

[25] Do not abbreviate *Father, Brother,* or *Sister.*

H90 Capitalize all epithets and nicknames.[26]

Apostle of the Gentiles	Lone Eagle
Father of His Country	Maid of Orleans
the Holy Father	Richard the Lionheart
Iron Chancellor	St. Leo the Great
Ivan the Terrible	Sunshine State
Leo XIII, the Pope of Labor	William the Silent

H91 Capitalize *reverend* and *honorable* when they are used as titles; and always use them with a given name or initials as well as a surname.[26] They should not be used with a surname alone.[27]

the Reverend Aloysius Benton
the Honorable J. L. Byrne

H92 If an unhyphened compound title is to be capitalized, capitalize all the words in it.

Acting Secretary Smith	Recording Secretary Oglesby
Lieutenant Commander Hayes	Field Marshal Stitz
Radio Operator Tomlin	Chief Engineer Wilson
Rear Admiral Budde	Adjutant General Smally

H93 Capitalize only the first word of a hyphened compound title before a proper name, but do not capitalize *ex* and *pro.*

Actor-manager Gordon
Vice-president Alben W. Barkley
Governor-elect Shane

ex-President Hoover
pro-Ally August Romano

H94 Capitalize *Jr., Sr.,* and all other abbreviations of titles following a name.

Samuel Thompson, Sr.	Fletcher Stanton, Ph.D.
Samuel Thompson, Jr.	Lowell Winship, O.P.

---

[26] Do not capitalize initial *the* or conjunctions, articles, prepositions, within such names or titles.

[27] *Reverend* and *honorable* may be abbreviated within the heading and address of a letter. Within a sentence spell them out (F4).

H95 Capitalize *father, mother, brother, sister, uncle, aunt, cousin,* and other kinship names when they are used in direct address or as a substitute for a person's name or as part of a person's name.

In direct address or as a substitute for a person's name
You can't make *Mother* [that is, Mary or Mrs. Wilkes] rest.
That's *Dad's* [that is, James's or Mr. Wilkes's] umbrella.
See here, *Aunt* [that is, Agatha or Miss Wilkes], I love the girl.
Stay out of *Sister's* [that is, Betty's] room.
Is that *Junior* [that is, Harold or Harold Martin, Jr.] sitting there in the car?

As part of a person's name
His family calls him *Brother* George.
Here come *Aunt* Mary and *Uncle* Julian.
Is it true that *Cousin* John married in Kalupa?
This is *Mother* O'Meara, my wife's mother.

H96 Do not capitalize kinship names when they are used as common nouns; that is, not in direct address or as a substitute for a person's name or as part of a person's name.

Tell Walter's *father* to come to the phone.
Your *mother* certainly looks young.
A *sister* should not give away a *brother's* secrets.
The *uncle* is a director of some railroad or other.

H97 Sometimes you will have a kinship name that has a possessive in front of it and a person's name after it. In such cases capitalize the kinship name if you want to use it as a title, as part of the person's name; do not capitalize it if it simply means "uncle [or cousin, and so on] whose name is such-and-such."

You've met my *Grandfather* Monty, Gene; well, this is my *Grandfather* Ryan.

I've never gotten a kind word from my *grandfather* Monty [that is, from my grandfather whose name is Monty].

Our own dear *Cousin* Elbert has lentigo.

Our own dear *cousin* Elbert has lentigo [that is, cousin whose name is Elbert].

This will introduce my *Uncle* Henry, who wants to sell you a casket.

This will introduce my *uncle* Henry, who wants to sell you a casket [that is, uncle whose name is Henry].

My *sister* Nancy is a writer [that is, sister whose name is Nancy].

My *brother* Joe paints [that is, brother whose name is Joe].

Your *grandmother,* Sarah Green, and I are good friends [that is, grandmother, whose name is Sarah Green].

My *aunt,* Mrs. Willoughby Patterne, has trouble with poltergeists [that is, aunt, whose name is Mrs. Willoughby Patterne].

Your *uncle,* Commodore Squash, is seasick [that is, uncle, whose name is Commodore Squash].

Places, divisions, directions, buildings

H98 Capitalize the names of political and administrative divisions.[28]

Alaska	the Northwest Territories
the Archdiocese of St. Louis	the Philippines
Baton Rouge	the Republic [United States]
the British Empire	Sioux City
City of Chicago	the State of New Mexico
Diocese of Lafayette	Tenth Congressional District
the Dominion of Canada	the Twelfth Precinct
Fourth Ward	the United Kingdom
the Helenburg Deanery	United States of America
Louisiana	Vatican City
the Netherlands	Warren Township

I live in *Sioux City.*

The *Clayton County* sheriff became a Catholic yesterday.

H99 Do not capitalize the ecclesiastical term *parish* when it occurs in names such as those listed in H98.

We belong to Sacred Heart *parish.*

The *parish* of St. Gertrude has an active and rather celebrated little-theater group.

---

[28] Do not capitalize initial *the* or conjunctions, articles, prepositions, within such names or titles.
See H99 and H103.

H100 Capitalize the names of sections of states, cities, towns, and so on.[29]

Beacon Hill	Jackson Square
the Delta	the Left Bank
Fourth Ward	the Loop
the Gold Coast	the Seventh Precinct

We had a typical *Vieux Carré* meal.
Chicago also has a *Gold Coast.*

H101 Capitalize the names of streets, avenues, boulevards, and so on.[29]

Commercial Alley	Portland Place
Gracie Square	Regent Court
Highway 61	Sheridan Road
Lindell Boulevard	Sherman Parkway
Minnesota Avenue	Twelfth Street
Natchez Trace	U.S. Route 61

Are trucks allowed on the *Lincoln Highway?*
Harry is a *Park Row* cowboy.

H102 Capitalize geographical names.[29]

Adirondack Mountains	Gulf of Mexico
Aleutians	Gulf Stream
Alton Lake	Isle of Man
Arctic Zone	Japanese Currents
Atlantic Coast	Lake Erie
Bad Lands	Marquette State Park
Cumberland Gap	Mississippi River
Death Valley	Mount Hood
English Channel	Pacific Ocean
the Equator	Pikes Peak
Fly Creek	Rocky Mountain National Park
Gonzaro Pass	Torrid Zone

The *Japanese Currents* warm California, don't they?
Yes, Cap really was a *Mississippi River* pilot.

---

[29] Do not capitalize initial *the* or conjunctions, articles, prepositions, within such names or titles.
See H103.

H103 Do not capitalize *kingdom, empire, state, diocese, city, county, town, precinct, street, avenue, square, coast, stream, zone, island, mountain, lake, river, park, creek,* and like words unless they are used as part of a proper or official name.

Britain has liquidated her *empire.*
Our *ward* has suddenly gone Republican.
Tyrrell Street is really a broad *avenue.*
These *islands* cannot be the Aleutians.
This jagged, ugly *peak* is unlike anything in the Adirondacks.
Which is the largest of the three *lakes,* Lake Michigan?

The *State* of Illinois is prosecuting the murderers.
The *State* is prosecuting the murderers.
This is the Badger *State.*

The *state* of Idaho grows apples and other fruits.
Our *state* is not large, but it is progressive.
Totalitarianism believes in an all-powerful *state.*

Make your check payable to the *City* of St. Louis.
Make your check payable to the *City.*

Not many *cities* have grown as rapidly as the *city* of Houston.

H104 Capitalize the nouns *north, south, east, west,* and their noun combinations and derivatives only when they refer to a region of the nation or of the world, but not when they refer to direction.[30]

The civilization of the *East* is older than that of the *West.*

The *South* is the nation's winter playground.

The temperament of the typical *Northerner* is different from that of the typical *Southerner.*

Out of the *Middle West* comes food for the world.

We traveled *southwest* from the ranch.

To the *north* lay the mountains; to the *west,* the sea.

Most of us up-state North Dakotans do not realize that more than ninety per cent of the wheat used to make spaghetti is raised to the *south* of us, in the region below Grand Forks.

---

[30] See H105.

H105 Do not capitalize the adjectives or adverbs *north, south, east, west,* or their combinations and derivatives.[31]

Springfield is a few miles *east.*

But *eastern* civilization is older than *western* civilization.

He was naive enough to think that most *southern* planters have large homes.

I like the *northwest* section of the country best of all.

The wind is *southerly.*

H106 Capitalize the names of bridges, buildings, churches, chapels, clubs, libraries, and monuments.[32]

Hell Gate Bridge	St. Francis Xavier Church
Grand Central Station	Rogers Memorial Chapel
Humboldt Building	Racquet Club
Municipal Auditorium	Newberry Library
Museum of Modern Art	Lincoln Memorial

H107 Do not capitalize words like *bridge, building, church,*[33] *chapel, club, library, monument,* unless they are part of a proper name.

There should be a *bridge* near Southport.

Alice fell asleep in the *chapel.*

Organizations, institutions, schools

H108 Do not capitalize *federal government* or *government.*

The *federal government* exercises control over interstate commerce.

There is adequate housing for *government* workers.

The *government* of the United States cannot be sued except under certain restrictions.

The United States *government* has its own printing office.

The *government* of the state has decided that rural areas will have to suffer.

---

[31] See H104.

[32] Do not capitalize initial *the* or conjunctions, articles, prepositions, within such names or titles.
See H107.

[33] For capitalizing *church* when it means the Roman Catholic Church, see H64.

H109 Capitalize the names of political parties and their adherents (but not the word *party*).[34]

Democratic party	Democrats
Labor party	Laborites
Republican party	Republicans

Many a *Republican* holds the principles of the *Democratic party*.
Markoe is a *Labor party* hack.

H110 Capitalize such words as *democrat* and *republican* when they refer to the Democratic and Republican parties, but not when they are used in their general meanings.[35]

There's really not much difference between *Democratic* and *Republican* aims and promises in this election.

The king banished Lamberti because of his *republican* principles.
Fuller could be called an eighteenth-century *democrat*.

H111 Capitalize the names of all national, state, county, municipal, and town assemblies, departments, bureaus, commissions, offices, courts, and so on.[36]

Allen County Traffic Bureau	Hewesport Board of Aldermen
Bureau of Standards	House [of Representatives]
Cabinet	House of Commons
Circuit Court of Appeals	House of Lords
Civil Service Commission	Office of Education
Commons	Ohio House of Representatives
Congress	Parliament
Department of Public Works	Senate
Farm Labor Board	Senate Finance Committee
Federal Bureau of Investigation	State Department of Health
Foreign Office	Supreme Court

John Wesley Snyder was secretary of the *Treasury* in 1949.

Hiss had worked in the *Department of State* at the time.

You want to talk to the chairman of the *Board of Health*, a Dr. Gleason.

---

[34] See H110.

[35] See H109.

[36] Do not capitalize initial *the* or conjunctions, articles, prepositions, within such names or titles.
See H115.

H112 Capitalize the names of organizations, associations, foundations, societies, companies, railroads, and banks.[37]

American Association for the Advancement of Colored People	Knights of Columbus
	Legion of Decency
	New York Central Railroad
American Legion	Rockefeller Foundation
Bay Shore Traction	Society for the Prevention of Cruelty to Animals
Camera Club	
Catholic Rural Life Conference	Sock and Buskin
Chicago Community Trust	Station WEW
Eastman Kodak Company	Steuben Glass
First National Bank	Woods High School Fathers' Club
General Motors Corporation	

Herrick is going to be nominated for the *National Honor Society*.
I remember hearing that Toolen is a *Hodiak Mills* vice-president.

H113 Capitalize the names of educational institutions and of their schools and departments.[37]

Loyola University	Temple Hall
Pennsylvania State Teachers College	Ladue Grammar School
	Public School No. 8
Eden Seminary	Century Business School
Harvard Medical School	Miss Drane's Secretarial School
Campion High School	Department of Philosophy of Fordham University
St. Benedict Academy	

Gonzaga High School refuses to recognize any of my credits in home economics.

The *Wilson High* glee club—it has a resounding name that I've forgotten—is not very good.

My aunt, Helen Merkle, is head of the *Latin Department* at *Marlin*.

H114 Do not capitalize *freshman, sophomore, junior,* or *senior*.

I'm a *freshman* at Parkham.
The *sophomore* class is having a meeting today.
The *juniors* are giving a dance for the *seniors*.
On you, *seniors*, depends the quality of the student body.

---

[37] Do not capitalize initial *the* or conjunctions, articles, prepositions, within such names or titles.
See H115.

H115 Do not capitalize words like *club, assembly, bureau, commission, association, foundation, corporation, company, railroad, bank, university, college, department,* or *school,* unless they are part of a proper name.

Put your money in the *bank*—any *bank,* even Stillson's Bank of Commerce.

The *university* is going to finish the stadium next spring.

The Wilson High glee *club*—it has a resounding name that I've forgotten—is not very good.

A *commission* was set up to investigate the shock effects of fresh air on city dwellers who go to the country too suddenly.

What's the name of that *college* in Moorhead?

Military groups

H116 Do not capitalize the nouns *army* or *navy* unless they refer to the United States Army or Navy.[38]

The *Army* has worn a variety of uniforms since Washington's day [meaning the United States Army].

The *Navy* is sometimes almost absurdly jealous of its traditions [meaning the United States Navy].

A career in the *army* was all that Russia could offer him then.

The Brazilian *army* was represented by General Longino Finkler.

H117 Do not capitalize the adjectives *army* and *navy* when used without *United States,* and do not capitalize *naval.*

We spent the first three weeks in an *army* barracks on Hawaii, doing nothing but twiddling our thumbs and waiting.

Some years ago *navy* spokesmen were rather turbulent in protesting unification of the armed forces.

United States *naval* power has increased sharply since 1949.

An unidentified *United States Army* spokesman was credited with starting the rumor.

United States Navy personnel reported to the consulate.

---

[38] Do not capitalize initial *the* or conjunctions, articles, prepositions, within such names or titles.
See H117-18.

H118 Capitalize the names of military divisions, regiments, companies, and so on.[39]

This is a memorial to the dead of the *Rainbow Division*.

There is no word from *Company F*.

Jarkie had his share of experience in the *Medical Corps*.

Seven *Air Force* colonels are using your office, sir.

The *Marine Corps* has not enough marines to chance an engagement of that scope.

You will need a *Coast Guard* permit to visit Ship Island.

Under orders, the *Eighth Army* held off for three days.[40]

H119 Do not capitalize words like *division, regiment, company* when they are not part of a proper name.

Three *divisions* were strung along the Rhine.

The *cavalry*, as a matter of fact, hasn't ridden horses in years.

Just how much air power could accomplish without *infantry* is something we do not intend to find out just now.

Titles of works and events

PUBLICATIONS, WORKS OF ART

H120 Capitalize the first word and all other words except conjunctions, articles, and prepositions (C-A-P) in the titles of books, magazines, newspapers, essays, articles, poems, plays, motion pictures, paintings, and so on.[41]

The Life of Dr. Samuel Johnson [book]

"On the Extinction of the Venetian Republic, 1802" [poem]

Washington Crossing the Delaware [painting]

---

[39] Do not capitalize initial *the* or conjunctions, articles, prepositions, within such names or titles.
See H119.

[40] *Army* is here capitalized because it is used as part of the proper name of a military unit.

[41] For the capitalization of initial *the, a,* or *an* with such titles, see H121 and H150-51.
See also H122-24.
For italic with such titles, see D115-21. For quotation marks with such titles, see D102-7.
For capitalizing prepositions and conjunctions more than five letters long, see H149.

H121   Do not capitalize initial *the* in the titles of newspapers and magazines.

> This is the December 16 issue of the *Saturday Evening Post*.
> The story was carried by the *Times-Picayune*.

H122   If a hyphen occurs in the title of a book, poem, and so on, capitalize the word following the hyphen only if that word is ordinarily a noun or proper adjective.

> *Nineteenth-Century Science* [noun]
> "Some Thrills of Deep-Sea Fishing" [noun]
> "This Year's All-American Team" [proper adjective]

H123   If a hyphen occurs in the title of a book, poem, and so on, do not capitalize the word following the hyphen if it is a common adjective or if the hyphen merely joins a prefix like *ultra, co,* or *self* to the following word.

"Thirty-second Street's New Look"	*Second* is a common adjective.
The Case of the Dark-green Shade	*Green* is a common adjective.
Lives of Little-known Saints	*Known* is a common adjective or participle.
"Why Co-operate?"	*Co* is a mere prefix.
The Ultra-ambitious Oyster	*Ultra* is a mere prefix here.
How to Be Self-reliant	*Self* is a mere prefix here.

H124   Capitalize the titles of dictionaries, encyclopedias, indexes, directories, almanacs, and similar reference works.[42] (Do not use italic or quotation marks.)

Webster's New Collegiate Dictionary	Information Please Almanac
Catholic Encyclopedia	Americana Annual
Cumulative Book Index	the Roman Ritual
the Official Catholic Directory	Reader's Guide
	Code of Canon Law
	Who's Who

---

[42] Do not capitalize initial *the* or conjunctions, articles, prepositions, within such names or titles.

EVENTS AND ERAS

H125 Capitalize the names of historical events and eras.[43]

American Revolution	Dark Ages
Industrial Revolution	Middle Ages
the Flood	Elizabethan Age
Reformation	Christian Era
Renaissance	Victorian era
Reign of Terror	Revolutionary period
Revolution	Colonial days

H126 Ordinarily do not capitalize *day, era, period, epoch,* and *century* in the names of H125 unless they begin the title. But consult a dictionary when you are not sure.

H127 Capitalize the names of expositions, fairs, festivals, and so on,[43] but not the names of events that have only a very local and minor interest.

Century of Progress Exposition	amateur night
Humboldt County Fair	Mothers' Club card party
Olympic Games	our annual strawberry festival
Book Week	the turkey raffle

CHARTERS, ACTS, ALLIANCES, TREATIES

H128 Capitalize the titles of charters, acts, statutes, reports, and so on.[43] (Do not use italic or quotation marks.)

Act of Supremacy	Declaration of Independence
Atlantic Charter	Magna Charta
Constitution [of the United States]	Monroe Doctrine
	Stamp Act

H129 Capitalize the titles of alliances and treaties.[43] (Do not use italic or quotation marks.)

Articles of Confederation	Old Law
Balkan Pact	Quadruple Alliance
New Law	Treaty of Versailles

---

[43] Do not capitalize initial *the* or conjunctions, articles, prepositions, within such names or titles.

Languages, peoples, academic courses

H130 Capitalize the names of languages, peoples, races, and tribes, whether in noun or adjective form.[44]

Latin	Spanish	Bushmen
French	Caucasian	Iroquois
English	Indian	Mohawk
Spartan	Negro	Scandinavian

Howard thinks it incredible that the ancient *Romans* communicated in *Latin*.

I should like to take *Spanish* 3.

They used to converse in the *Greek* language—*Attic*, of course.

A *Frenchman*, Lauras, told me that *Russian* is the most euphonious of languages.

Crane studied *Romance* languages at Oxford.

As a child Sheila learned the *Cherokee* dialect—or is it a language?

There is good *Italian* cooking to be had here.

H131 Do not capitalize general terms that can be applied to several races or peoples.[45]

aborigine	half-breed	redskin
gypsy	mulatto	whites

There will be no segregation of *whites* from Negroes in heaven.

In Memphis there are Irish *gypsies* known as the Travelers.

In those days the *white man* was not very welcome in Japan.

H132 Do not capitalize *language, people, race, tribe,* and so on.[46]

Why not take a *language?*

Up there the Indians speak their own Taos *dialect.*

What's the origin of the French *language?*

The American *people* will stand for it.

These songs were produced by the Negro *race.*

Several *tribes* made up the Iroquois *nation.*

---

[44] Do not capitalize initial *the* or conjunctions, articles, prepositions, within such names or titles.
  See H131-32.
[45] See H130.
[46] See H130-31.

H133 Do not capitalize such words as *history, mathematics, chemistry, physics, religion,* and *algebra* unless they are used with a number to designate a specific course.

This year I'm taking *history* and *geometry,* but not Latin or *physics.* I'm taking *History* 6 and *Chemistry* 1.

I used to think *religion* a dull subject, but *Religion* 4 has begun to interest me.

Days, months, seasons, festivals

H134 Capitalize the names of the days of the week, the months of the year, holidays, holydays, and ecclesiastical seasons, feast days, and fast days.[47] (Do not use italic or quotation marks.)

Tuesday	Easter
January	Pentecost
Fourth of July	Advent
the Fourth	Feast of St. Agnes
Halloween	Gaudete Sunday
Labor Day	Holy Thursday
Lincoln's Birthday	Octave of the Feast
New Year's Eve	of St. John
Rosh Hashana	Rogation Days
Thanksgiving	Shrove Tuesday
All Saints' Day	Ash Wednesday
Ascension Thursday	Day of Atonement
Assumption	Ember Days
Christmas	Vigil of Pentecost

H135 Do not capitalize *day* when the name of a holyday or holiday makes sense without it.

Ed Buono's birthday is on Christmas *day.*	*Day* is not necessary.
March 25 is Lady *Day,* the Feast of the Annunciation.	*Day* is necessary.

---

[47] Do not capitalize initial *the* or conjunctions, articles, prepositions, within such names or titles.
See H135-36.

H136 Do not capitalize *day, week, month, year, century, era, epoch, aeon, period, age,* and so on, when they are not used as part of a title.[48]

Bills flood in with the mail every *day* of the *week.*

There have been many revolutions during the *month* of July.

Terence spouts glibly about the eighteenth *century* but says nothing of the present *year.*

Our *era* is quite properly called the Christian Era.

Beowulf is not an *epoch;* it's an epic.

During that *period* of the Stone Age, I imagine, dress design was sharply limited by the materials available.

In an *age* when everyone runs with the herd, Monica is quite content to please God and, incidentally, herself.

H137 Do not capitalize *spring, summer, winter, autumn,* and *fall* unless they are personified.

Mrs. Williams and the children go to Maine in the late *spring,* stay all *summer,* and return in the *fall.*

We must get ready for Old Man *Winter.*

Miscellaneous capitals

H138 Capitalize names that are clearly short forms of titles that must be capitalized.

The *Church* [the Roman Catholic Church] is a society.

The best place in the world to live is the *States* [the United States].

The *Street* [Wall Street] was in panic.

The *Terror* [the Reign of Terror] lasted from about March, 1793, to July, 1794.

The *Republic* was born in 1776.

At first he lived near Riverside Drive and then, later, on the *Drive* itself.

The *High School* [St. Benet's High School] cordially welcomes your Excellency.

---

[48] Quite often these terms are not capitalized even when they are part of a title. See H126 and H135.

H139 With the exception of those listed in H140, capitalize any word or its abbreviation that is followed by a numeral or a letter.

Act III	Lesson 7
Answer 10	List A
Appendix V	Number (No.) 7
Article II	Part IV
Book I	Question 6
Chapter V (5)	Room 16 (Room B)
Chart XVI	Rule 18
Exercise 19	Volume III (Vol. 3)

H140 Do not capitalize the following minor subdivisions.[49]

page 39	footnote 7
pp. 39-51	letter *b*
column 4	stanza 3
paragraph *a*	verse 3
line 18	v. 2
note 7	scene 2

H141 Capitalize the special adjective in a trade name, but not the common name it modifies.

Blue Label tomatoes	RCA radios
Café du Monde coffee	Stetson hats
Camel cigarettes	Sunrise bacon
Ivory soap flakes	Wrigley's gum

H142 Capitalize the names of ships, aircraft, trains, and so on.[50]

the *Queen Mary* [ship]
the *China Clipper* [airplane]
the *Empire Builder* [train]

H143 Capitalize *I* and *O*.[51]

I came; *I* saw; *I* conquered.
Hear me, *O* my friends!

---

[49] See H139.
[50] Do not capitalize initial *the* or conjunctions, articles, prepositions, within such names or titles.
[51] *O* (nowadays reserved for direct address in rather poetic language) is always capitalized and never followed by a comma. *Oh* is not capitalized and is usually followed by a comma.

H144 Do not capitalize *yes, no, oh, good-by, good morning, amen,* and so on, unless they begin a sentence.

Oh, Mike has a most pleasant way of saying *yes.*
A gentleman can always say *no* courteously.
I said *good-by* without regret.
Janice always added a smile to her *good morning.*
To that prayer we add a hearty *amen.*

In a faltering voice Grandpa answered, *"Yes."*

H145 Capitalize and italicize *whereas* and *resolved* in resolutions, and capitalize the first word following them.

Whereas, The fourth day of . . .
Resolved [or, *Be it resolved*], That the members . . .

H146 You may capitalize words for which special, usually humorous, emphasis is wanted. (Use this capitalization only very rarely.)

He looked with the greatest disdain upon the *Common Herd.*
She fell into theosophy on her way to the *Higher Things* in life.

H147 Capitalize words that are personified.

Man in the Moon   the Reaper

We must get ready for *Old Man River.*
The *Chair* recognizes the delegate from Puerto Rico.

> . . . bring with thee
> Jest and youthful Jollity,
>
> .   .   .   .
>
> Sport that wrinkled Care derides
> And Laughter holding both his sides.
>
> —MILTON

H148 Capitalize the names of the heavenly bodies and the signs of the zodiac, but not *sun* and *moon.*

Big Dipper   Saturn
Milky Way   sun
moon   Taurus

It is impossible to see the *Southern Cross* from here.
A circle with a dot in the center is the symbol for the *sun.*

274

H149 Do not capitalize conjunctions, articles, or prepositions (C-A-P) within titles, unless a conjunction or preposition is more than five letters long.

The preacher's sermon was on the Discourse *at the* Last Supper.

Let me read you the parable of the Friend Coming *in the* Night.

The article was entitled "Ups *and* Downs *of an* Elevator Man."

Mr. Sidney H. Coleman was then the executive vice-president *of* the Society *for the* Prevention *of* Cruelty *to* Animals.

I have returned *Costume Throughout the Ages* to the library.

H150 Except for the cases in H151-53, do not capitalize *the, a,* or *an* when it precedes a title or proper name. The article is not regarded as part of the title or name.

In *the* Bible are *the* Old Testament and *the* New Testament.

Let's say *a* Hail Mary.

When a priest says he's saying *the* Office, he means he's reading *the* Breviary.

Every Catholic is familiar with *the* Baltimore Catechism.

There in the stable *the* Magi found *the* Infant and adored Him.

Sister Mary had great devotion to *the* Sacred Heart.

June's father has been received into *the* Church.

The first part of *the* Mass, from the beginning to *the* Offertory, is called *the* Mass of the Catechumens.

Tonight *the* Holy Hour begins at half-past seven.

March 25 is Lady Day, *the* Feast of the Annunciation.

Did you have an audience with *the* Holy Father?

This article was written by *the* Reverend E. Irvin Burns, S.J.

Tell me who *the* Apostle of the Gentiles was.

Bob works for *the* Department of Commerce.

Where is *the* First National Bank?

I went through *the* Newberry Library.

It was dark when the men reached *the* Cumberland Gap.

Side by side on my desk are *the* American College Dictionary and *the* Concise Oxford Dictionary.

Describe *the* Industrial Revolution.

Today, *the* Fourth of July, is a great holiday.

H151 Capitalize *the, a,* or *an* as the first word in the title of a work of literature or art (book, play, short story, symphony, song, and so on)—any title in which the article is put in italic or quotation marks along with the rest of the title.[52]

Please get me *The Life of John Marshall.*

There is a delightful character sketch, "The Life and Times of a Small Waif," on page 16 of this book.

H152 Capitalize *the* when it is the first word in the heading or address of a letter.

H153 Capitalize *the* in a certain few place names. (They will be found in a dictionary or gazetteer.)

While in the Netherlands we made a trip to *The Hague.*
East of Portland is the city of *The Dalles.*

H154 Use no unnecessary capitals.

I Spelling

In general

I1 Practically every rule of spelling has exceptions. But the rules given in this book hold often enough to make them worth your while.

I2 When in doubt about the spelling of a word, consult a dictionary. Only the dictionary habit ensures correctness.

I3 American usage, in some instances, is different from British usage. British usage is best for Britons, American usage for Americans.

British usage	American usage
judgement	judgment
colour	color
analyse	analyze

[52] See D115 and D121.

Spelling rules[1]

I4 Form the plural of most nouns by adding *s.*

alley—alleys	chair—chairs
baboon—baboons	crowd—crowds

I5 When the singular of a noun ends in *ch, sh, s,* or *x,* add *es* to form the plural.

bench—benches	genius—geniuses
church—churches	Mass—Masses
crash—crashes	fox—foxes
rush—rushes	hoax—hoaxes

I6 When the singular of a noun ends in *y* preceded by a consonant, change *y* to *i* and add *es.*[3]

ally—allies	library—libraries
army—armies	mercy—mercies
lady—ladies	sky—skies

I7 When the singular of a noun ends in *y* preceded by a vowel, add *s.*[4]

alley—alleys	key—keys
alloy—alloys	monkey—monkeys
essay—essays	play—plays

I8 When a compound noun is written as one word, form the plural of the last word.

bathhouse—bathhouses	teaspoonful—teaspoonfuls

---

[1] For the proper spelling and punctuation of the possessive case of nouns and pronouns, see D128-38.

[2] For the plural of pronouns, see A29, A31, A37, and A55. For the plural of verbs, see A63-64.

[3] A consonant can be defined as a letter of the alphabet that is not *a, e, i, o,* or *u.* (More technically, it is a letter that cannot be named unless a vowel is pronounced with it; for example, *t* cannot be named without an *e* sound.) *U* preceded by *q* is considered a consonant: so the plural of *colloquy* is not *colloquys* but *colloquies.*

[4] The vowels are *a, e, i, o, u* (and, in some words, *w* and *y*). They are letters that can be sounded without the help of another letter.

I9 Generally, when a compound noun is written with hy-phens, form the plural of the first word. The rule, how-ever, does not hold where it would make for awkwardness or absurdity of pronunciation.

brother-in-law—brothers-in-law
passer-by—passers-by

But—

good-for-nothing—   *Goods-for-nothing* would be
   good-for-nothings   awkward.

two-year-old—two-year-olds   *Twos-year-old* would be alto-gether absurd.

I10 For the plural of nouns not covered by the rules, see a dictionary. The following is a list of some that may give you trouble:

A Words ending in *o:*

cameo—cameos   piano—pianos
curio—curios   solo—solos
dynamo—dynamos   soprano—sopranos

echo—echoes   potato—potatoes
hero—heroes   tomato—tomatoes
mosquito—mosquitoes   tornado—tornadoes
Negro—Negroes   torpedo—torpedoes

banjo—banjos, banjoes   halo—halos, haloes
buffalo—buffalos, buffaloes   hobo—hobos, hoboes
cargo—cargos, cargoes   volcano—volcanos, volcanoes

B Words that still keep a foreign ending:

alumna—alumnae[5]   curriculum—curricula,
alumnus—alumni[6]   curriculums
appendix—appendixes,   index—indexes, indices
  appendices   oasis—oases
beau—beaux, beaus   parenthesis—parentheses
chateau—chateaux   synopsis—synopses
ciborium—ciboria   tableau—tableaux, tableaus
crisis—crises   thesis—theses

[5] Rhymes with "a bum knee."
[6] Rhymes with "a bum eye."

c Words that end in *f, fe,* or *ff:*

belief—beliefs	fife—fifes
chief—chiefs	grief—griefs
dwarf—dwarfs	tariff—tariffs

beef—beeves, beefs	life—lives
elf—elves	loaf—loaves
half—halves	self—selves
hoof—hoofs, hooves	thief—thieves
knife—knives	wharf—wharfs, wharves
leaf—leaves	wolf—wolves

d *Child, ox,* and words that change the root:

child—children	man—men
gentleman—gentlemen	mouse—mice
goose—geese	ox—oxen
louse—lice	woman—women

IE AND EI

111 When spelling words with *ie* and *ei* in them, make use of the rhyme—

> *I* before *e*
> Except after *c*
> Or when sounded like *a*
> As in *neighbor* and *weigh.*

After letters other than c:

achieve	brief	grief	siege
apiece	chief	niece	sieve
belief	field	relieve	thief
believe	fierce	shield	yield

[Some exceptions:] *leisure, neither, seize,* and *weird*

After c:

ceiling	conceive	perceive
conceited	deceive	receive

When sounded like a:

freight	neighbor	rein	veil
heinous	reign	their	weigh

CEED, CEDE, AND SEDE

112 Memorize the spelling of these verbs:
Ceed:

exceed	proceed	succeed

Cede:

accede	intercede	recede
cede	precede	secede
concede		

Sede:

supersede

PREFIXES

113 A prefix is a syllable or a word added at the beginning of a word or root to change its meaning.

admit   readmit [admit again]

114 When adding a prefix to a word or root, do not double letters or drop letters.

antisocial	discharge	readmit
belabor	misshapen	re-enter
bemoan	misstate	reinforce
coerce	mistake	uncertain
coherent	occur	underrate
co-operate	overrun	understand
debase	oversee	unnatural
demonstrate	pre-eminent	withhold
disable	prelection	withstand

[Exception:] *all: already, although, altogether, always*

SUFFIXES

115 A suffix is a syllable or a word added at the end of a word or root to change its meaning.

cold   colder [more cold]

116 When adding a suffix to a word ending in a consonant, double the final consonant of the word if—

A The word is accented on the last syllable.[7]

bag   be*gin*

B The final consonant is preceded by a single vowel short in sound.

b*a*g   beg*i*n

C The suffix begins with a vowel.

-age	*-ing*
bag–baggage	occur–occurred
begin–beginning	plan–planned
clan–clannish	rebel–rebelled
control–controlled	refer–referred
get–getting	run–running
grab–grabbing	sad–saddening
hot–hotter	sit–sitting
impel–impelled	wed–wedding
infer–inferred	wit–witty

[Some exceptions:] *gaseous, transferable*

117 When adding a suffix to a word that ends in a double consonant, keep the double consonant.

add–added	full–fullness [*also* fulness]
address–addresses	odd–oddly
butt–butted	puff–puffy
dull–dullness [*also* dulness]	shrill–shrilly
ebb–ebbing	stiff–stiffness
embarrass–embarrassment	will–willful [*also* wilful]

118 Keep final *l* before a suffix beginning with *l*.

accidental–accidentally	occasional–occasionally
canal–canallike	real–really
casual–casually	soul–soulless
cool–coolly	tail–tailless
final–finally	usual–usually

---

[7] One-syllable words, of course, are accented on the last (the only) syllable.

I19 Except for the cases in I16, American usage does not double final *l* before a suffix that begins with a vowel.

apparel—appareled   travel—traveled, traveler,
equal—equaled   traveling

I20 Keep *n* before the suffix *ness*.

barren—barrenness   sudden—suddenness

I21 Keep silent *e* before a suffix that begins with a consonant.

docile—docilely   manage—management
hate—hateful   pale—paleness

[Some exceptions:] *acknowledgment, argument, judgment, truly*

I22 Keep silent *e* if it both—

A Follows soft *c* or *g*.

peace   advantage

B Precedes the suffix *able* or *ous*.

peaceable   advantageous

change—changeable   notice—noticeable
courage—courageous   outrage—outrageous
manage—manageable   service—serviceable

I23 Change final *ie* to *y* before the suffix *ing*.

die—dying   lie—lying   tie—tying

I24 In all cases not covered by I22-23, omit silent final *e* before a suffix that begins with a vowel.

argue—arguing   hope—hoping
arrive—arriving   judge—judging
come—coming   love—loving
desire—desirable   mistake—mistakable
dine—dining   please—pleasant
force—forcible   plume—plumage
give—given   purple—purplish
gore—goring   true—truer
guide—guidance   type—typing

[Some exceptions:] *dyeing* (tinting with dye), *hoeing, singeing* (burning slightly, as feathers), *tingeing* (staining)

125 If a word ends in *y* preceded by a consonant, change the *y* to *i* (unless the suffix begins with *i*).

anarchy—anarchical	duty—dutiful
body—bodily	hardy—hardiness
bounty—bountiful	mercy—merciless
busy—busier	sly—slily [*better* slyly]
cry—cried	study—studious
dry—drily [*also* dryly]	whinny—whinnied

[Exceptions:] Words formed from one-syllable adjectives like *dry, sly,* and *spry: dryness, slyness, spryly,* and *spryness*

126 If a word ends in *y* preceded by a vowel, keep the *y* before the suffix.

allay—allayed	gay—gayety [*better* gaiety]
annoy—annoyance	gay—gayly [*better* gaily]
buy—buying	joy—joyful
gay—gayer	obey—obeying

[Some exceptions:] *daily, laid, lain, paid, said, slain*

127 Add *k* to final *c* before the suffixes *ing, ed,* and *er*.

frolic—frolicking, frolicked, frolicker
picnic—picnicking, picnicked, picnicker
mimic—mimicking, mimicked
panic—panicking, panicked

128 Words ending in the sound *ize* are generally, in American usage, spelt *ize*.

Americanize	galvanize
apologize	harmonize
baptize	homogenize
canonize	modernize
catechize	organize
characterize	pasteurize
civilize	pulverize
criticize	recognize
devitalize	specialize
dramatize	sympathize

[Some exceptions:] *advertise, advise, chastise, compromise, despise, devise, enterprise, supervise, surprise; analyze*

Spelling lists

FIRST-YEAR SPELLING LIST

I29   This list of 250 words is partly the result of fifteen years of noting and checking the words most often misspelled by first-year high-school students. Fifty of the words have asterisks before them. According to Easley S. Jones,[8] if you master these you will eliminate about sixteen per cent of your spelling errors.

1 accept[9]
   accidentally
   *accommodate
   accumulate
   acquaintance
   *across
   adjective
   advice[10]
   affect[11]
   against

3 argument
   around
   article
   *athletic
   author
   awkward
   because
   becoming
   *before
   *beginning

5 chosen
   coarse[14]
   college
   committed
   committee
   conscience
   convenience
   couldn't
   deceive
   *decided

2 *all right
   almost
   already
   altogether[12]
   always
   among
   anyone
   anything
   *appearance
   aren't

4 *believed
   *benefited
   blasphemy
   breath[13]
   breathe[13]
   *business
   can't
   certainly
   characteristic
   choose

6 decision
   declarative
   *definite
   dependent
   describe
   *description
   desirable
   despair
   desperate
   determine

---

[8] Easley S. Jones, *Practice Handbook in English* (New York: Appleton-Century-Crofts, 1935), p. 167. By permission. Jones's complete list comprises one hundred spelling demons, the remaining fifty of which, with some exceptions, are dispersed through the second-, third-, and fourth-year lists in this book.

[9] *To receive with consent.* Do not confuse with *except*.

[10] Noun. Do not confuse with the verb *advise*.

[11] *To influence; to feign or pretend.* Do not confuse with *effect*.

[12] *Entirely.* Do not confuse with *all together*.

[13] *Breath*, noun; *breathe*, verb.

[14] *Unrefined, rough.* Do not confuse with *course*.

7 develop
development
device[15]
didn't
different
dining[16]
*disappeared
doctor
doesn't
dollar

8 don't
during
dying[17]
*effect[18]
eighth
embarrass
especially
Eucharist
everybody
everything

9 exaggerate
excellent

*existence
*experience
extraordinary
familiar
fatigue
finally
forgiveness
*forty

10 forward
four
friend
gallery
genuine
government
*grammar
group
guardian
hadn't

11 hasn't
haven't
*height
hoping[19]

humility
idle[20]
*imagination
imagine
*immediately
*independent

12 instead
*interesting
isn't
*its[21]
it's[22]
jealous
knowledge
laboratory
laid[23]
lead[24]

13 *led[25]
library
license[26]
lightening[27]
lightning[28]
loose[29]

---

[15] Noun. Do not confuse with the verb *devise*.

[16] Present participle of *dine (to take dinner)*. Do not confuse with *dinning* (from *din*).

[17] Present participle of *die (to cease to live)*. Do not confuse with *dyeing* (present participle of *dye*).

[18] Noun, *result;* verb, *to bring about, accomplish*. Do not confuse with *affect*.

[19] Present participle of *hope*. Do not confuse with *hopping* (from *hop*).

[20] Adjective, *useless, inactive;* also a verb. Do not confuse with *idol* or *idyll*, both nouns.

[21] Possessive case of *it*.

[22] Contraction of *it is*.

[23] Past and past participle of *lay (to set [something] down)*.

[24] Noun, the metal; pronounced to rhyme with *head*. Verb, present, *to conduct, to go ahead of those who follow;* rhymes with *need*.

[25] Past and past participle of *lead (to conduct, to go ahead of those who follow)*. Do not confuse with *lead*, noun, the metal, which is pronounced the same way.

[26] *License* and *licence* are almost equally common as verbs. *License* is distinctly preferred to *licence* as a noun.

[27] Present participle of *lighten*.

[28] *An electrical discharge as during a storm*.

[29] Adjective, *not fastened;* verb, *to undo*.

*lose[30]
lying[31]
many
meant

14 meddle
*minutes
morning[32]
mountain
mystery
*necessary
neighbor
night
noticeable
noun

15 nowadays
nuisance
*occasion
*occurred
occurrence
often
omitted
*opinion
*opportunity
opposite

16 original
paid
passed
past
peculiar

perform
perhaps
personally
persuade
pleasant

17 *possess
possible
preceding
preferred
present
*principal[33]
*principle[34]
*privilege
probably
procedure

18 proceed
professor
prominent
publicly
pursue
quantity
quarter
quiet[35]
quite[36]
really

19 *received
recognize
recommend
relief

religious
repetition
sacrament
sacrilege
sanctifying
scream

20 sense
sentence
*separate
shining
shriek
similar
since
sincerely
solemn
species

21 speech
stopped
stories
*stretched
studying
success
*successful
surely
*surprise
suspense

22 terrible
terrific
*their[37]

---

[30] Verb, *to fail to keep.*

[31] Present participle of *lie,* either sense.

[32] *Early part of the day.* Do not confuse with *mourning (sorrow, expression of grief).*

[33] Adjective, *chief, main;* noun, *official in a school, money drawing interest,* and so on.

[34] *A fundamental truth; rule of conduct.*

[35] *Free from noise or disturbance.*

[36] *Completely; exactly.*

[37] *Belonging to them.*

286

	there[38]	two[44]	*weird
	therefore	*until	where
	they're[39]	useful	
	thorough	using	25 *whether
	threw[40]		which
	through[41]	24 *usually	who's[48]
	title	village	whose[49]
		villain	winning
23	to[42]	visitor	within
	*together	wasn't	without
	*too[43]	waste[45]	wouldn't
	trait	weak[46]	writing
	tries	weather[47]	you're[50]
	*truly		

SECOND-YEAR SPELLING LIST

I30 This list is made up of 250 words, of which about a dozen are either newcomers to the language, born of the advances in technology, medicine, and so on, or else old words that have acquired a new prominence or a new twist of meaning to express new discoveries. All of the words in the list, or nearly all of them, are in your active vocabulary. That means that they are going to turn up regularly in what you write.

1	ability	accelerator[51]	addresses
	abundance	achieve	advertise[52]

---

[38] *In that place.*
[39] Contraction of *they are.*
[40] Past of *throw.*
[41] Preposition, *in at one side and out at the opposite side of.*
[42] Preposition, *in the direction of.*
[43] Adverb, *also; more than enough.*
[44] Adjective and pronoun, *twice one.*
[45] Do not confuse with *waist (the part of the body located between the chest and the hips).*
[46] Do not confuse with *week (a period of seven days).*
[47] Do not confuse with the conjunction *whether.*
[48] Contraction of *who is.*
[49] The possessive of *who* and *which.*
[50] Contraction of *you are.* Do not confuse with *your,* the possessive of *you.*
[51] *The foot-operated throttle of an automobile.*
[52] The spelling *advertise* is distinctly preferable to *advertize.*

	advise[53]	4	busier		deal[62]
	agriculture		buying		despise
	air-borne		carburetor		difficult
	allergy		casually		disable
			ceiling		disappoint
2	alley[54]		cellophane		discharge
	alleys[55]		chastisement		
	allies[56]		chief	7	distributor
	ally[57]		chiseled[59]		dramatize
	aluminum		chuckle		dyeing
	apiece				echo
	apologize	5	comfortable		echoes
	appendixes[58]		coming		elf
	appliance		comparison		elves
	arguing		compromise		embarrassment
			conceive		encouragement
3	armies		controlled		encyclopedia[63]
	authorize		convertible		
	baggage		coolly	8	enterprise[64]
	balloon		corpuscles		equaled[65]
	baptize		courageous		essays
	belief				exceed
	believe	6	crises[60]		field
	biology		criticize[61]		fierce
	bodily		cruise		foul[66]
	brief		daily		fowl[67]

---

[53] *Advise*, verb; *advice*, noun.
[54] *A very narrow street.*
[55] Plural of *alley.*
[56] Plural of *ally.*
[57] *Partner nation in a war.*
[58] Also *appendices.*
[59] *Chiselled* is acceptable American, and preferred British, spelling.
[60] Plural of *crisis.*
[61] *Criticise* is acceptable American, and preferred British, spelling.
[62] *Distribution of the cards in cardplaying; also a bargain.*
[63] Also *encyclopaedia.*
[64] *An undertaking; readiness to undertake things.*
[65] *Equalled* is acceptable American, and preferred British, spelling.
[66] *Very dirty; wicked.* When applied to weather, as in Shakespeare's "So foul and fair a day I have not seen," *foul* means foggy, rainy, or generally unpleasant. As a noun *foul* is used to name violations of the rules of an athletic contest.
[67] Singular or plural; *rooster, hen,* and so on.

	freight		hydrogen		lively
	frolicked		hymn		lives[74]
9	frolicking	12	indexes[70]	15	loaves
	frontier		industrial		lonely
	funeral		inquiry		loving
	garage		insurance		luxury
	gardener		interrupt		management
	gaseous		invisible		masses
	generous		island		medicine
	getting		jackknife		mercies
	ghost		jewel		miracle
	glasses		jeweler		mirror
10	gleam	13	joyful	16	mischief
	glimpse		judging		mistake
	gown		judgment[71]		monkeys
	grief		juice		mortgage
	grieve		keys		mosquitoes
	guidance		kindle		movement
	guide		kindred		negotiate
	guilty		knight		Negroes
	hair[68]		knitting		nephew
	handkerchief		labeled[72]		nervous
11	hasten	14	ladies	17	nevertheless
	hedge		lasso		niece
	heir[69]		laughter		noisy
	helicopter		lawyer		nostril
	heroes		leaves[73]		notable
	hesitate		leisure		nourish
	horizon		libraries		nursery
	hotter		liquor		obeying

[68] *The natural covering of the human head.*
[69] *One who inherits.* The *h* is not pronounced.
[70] Also *indices.*
[71] *Judgement* is acceptable American, and preferred British, spelling.
[72] *Labelled* is acceptable American, and preferred British, spelling.
[73] Verb, *departs;* noun, plural of *leaf.*
[74] Verb *(is alive* or *dwells),* rhymes with *gives;* noun (plural of *life*), rhymes with *wives.*

occasionally	quaint	theological
oddly	qualified	thief
	quartz	thieves
18 organize	quench	tobacco
originally	quietly	tomatoes
ornament		torpedoes
outrageous	21 quit[77]	transferred
overwhelm	quote	traveled[83]
oxygen	reconnaissance	
oyster	referred	24 traveler[83]
palm	reign	traveling[83]
parentheses[75]	relieve	truer
patience[76]	rifle	tying
	rivaled	uncertain
19 peaceable	rout[78]	understand
penance	route[79]	utensil
perceive		valiant
phase	22 said	valley
phenomenon	seize	vault
physician	shield	
pianos	should've[80]	25 veil
picnicked	signaled[81]	vilely
picnicking	singular	visible
pierce	slain	weigh
	sonar[82]	wheel
20 pigeon	squadron	willful
playwright	succeed	witty
potatoes		wolves
precede	23 sugar	writhe
psychiatry	surname	yield

[75] Plural of *parenthesis*.

[76] *The virtue of suffering quietly and cheerfully.* Do not confuse with *patients (persons under medical treatment).*

[77] *Stop* or *leave.* Do not confuse with *quite* or *quiet.*

[78] Rhymes with *out.* Verb, *to force out;* noun, *a disorderly retreat.* Do not confuse with *route.*

[79] Rhymes with either *boot* or *bout.* Verb, *to send along a certain road;* noun, *road, way to go.* Do not confuse with *rout.*

[80] Contraction of *should have.*

[81] *Signalled* is acceptable American, and preferred British, spelling.

[82] *A device for submarine detection.*

[83] *Travelled, traveller,* and *travelling,* are acceptable American, and preferred British, spelling.

THIRD-YEAR SPELLING LIST

131 The third-year list is made up of 250 words, some of which are a little more difficult, but no less common, than the words of the first- and second-year spelling lists.

1 absurd
accident
accustomed
achievement
acquire
acquitted
address
aerial
aggravate
airplane

2 altar[84]
alter[84]
amount
amusement
ancestor
answer
anxious
apology
apparently
appetite

3 approaching
arrange
arrangement
arrival
arrive

assistance
assistant
association
athlete
attacked

4 audience
authority
awful
balance
barren
based
beautiful
believer
boundary
bouquet

5 brilliant
burglar
buried
candidate
canoe
canvas[85]
captain
career
carrying
centigrade

6 changing
choice
clothes
colonel
column
common
compel
compelled
complement[86]
completely

7 compliment[87]
comrade
concern
confidence
confident
conquer
conqueror
considered
control
countries

8 course[88]
cries
crowd
cruelty
dealt

---

[84] *A structure on which sacrifices are offered.* Do not confuse with the verb *alter (to change).*

[85] *A coarse cloth.* Do not confuse with *canvass,* which may be used as a verb *(to go through a city or district asking for votes, orders,* and so on).

[86] Noun, *that which fills up or completes; the full number.* Verb, *to supply a lack.* Do not confuse with *compliment.*

[87] Noun, *an expression of approval;* verb, *to express approval of (someone).* Do not confuse with *complement.*

[88] Noun, *a track; part of a meal; series of studies;* and so on. Do not confuse with the adjective *coarse (unrefined, rough).*

debt
debtor
defendant
definition
depth

9 destroyer
dictionary
digging
discipline
discussed
discussion
disease
divide
divine
divisible

10 division
efficiency
efficient
emphasis
emphasize
encyclical
endeavor
enemies
entrance
espionage

11 evident
except
exercise
expense
expensive
explanation

Fahrenheit
February
forcibly
foreigner

12 forfeit
formally
formerly
forth[89]
fourth[90]
freshman
fulfill[91]
governor
guarantee
guess

13 handle
handsome
having
hear[92]
history
hungry
hurrying
imaginary
imitation
immense

14 immigration
incident
incidentally
independence
indispensable
innocent
instance

instant
interfere
invitation

15 itself
knew
know
known
later[93]
latter[93]
lieutenant
literature
magazine
maintain

16 maintenance
maritime
material
mathematics
merely
millionaire
mischievous
monkey
murmur
muscle

17 mysterious
naturally
necessity
neither
nickel
obedience
obedient
obliging

[89] *Forward.* Do not confuse with *fourth.*
[90] *Between third and fifth.* Do not confuse with *forth.*
[91] *Fulfil* is acceptable American, and preferred British, spelling.
[92] *To perceive by the ear, listen.* Do not confuse with the adverb *here.*
[93] The comparative of *late.* Do not confuse with *latter,* the opposite of *former.* (Some grammars and dictionaries, if superficially read, give the impression that *latter* is a synonym for *later* in certain circumstances. The impression is incorrect. Do not use *latter* as the comparative form of *late.*)

	o'clock		Protestant		strange
	officer		proved		strength
			pursuing		striking
18	oneself[94]		realize		suggestion
	operator		receiver		surround
	ostracize				tendency
	parallel	21	recollect		testimony
	particularly		recollection		till
	partner		relative		
	peace[95]		religion	24	tired
	perseverance		replies		toward
	persistent		representative		Tuesday
	perspiration		restaurant		twelfth
			ridiculous		typical
19	physical		sacrifice		undoubtedly
	physically		sacrificing		university
	piece[96]				unnatural
	plain[97]	22	safety		unnecessarily
	positive		scarcely		valuable
	possession		secretary		
	practice[98]		servant	25	varied
	preference		severely		variety
	premier		siege		vegetable
	preparation		smooth		velocity
			soldier		view
20	presence[99]		sophomore		violence
	priority		source		violet
	prisoner				Wednesday
	professional	23	speaking		woman
	pronunciation		statistics		women

---

[94] Also *one's self.*

[95] *A state of quiet or tranquillity.* Do not confuse with *piece (a part).*

[96] *A part.* Do not confuse with *peace.*

[97] *Clear.* Do not confuse with *plane (flat).* When using the words as nouns, remember that a level expanse of terrain is spelled *plain*, whereas the surface named in geometry or in rather scientific descriptions of objects is spelled *plane.*

[98] Sole spelling of the noun. The verb may also be spelled *practise.* For convenience' sake, it is a good idea to use the spelling *practice* invariably; for then you will never be troubled by having to notice whether you are using the noun or the verb and by having to remember which spelling or spellings are common for each.

[99] Singular noun, *state of being present.* Do not confuse with the plural noun *presents (gifts).*

FOURTH-YEAR SPELLING LIST

I32 The 250 words in the fourth-year spelling list are all words that you can reasonably be expected to use and to spell properly by the time that you leave high school. They are words that you will need more and more frequently to express your increasingly adult concepts. A few of them, like *ascension* and *sacrilegious,* you will probably use oftener than will most non-Catholics.

1		3		5	
	absence		appreciation		buoy
	abundant		appropriate		bureau
	accompanied		arithmetic		cafeteria
	achieved		aroused		calendar
	acquainted		ascend		capital[4]
	acquittal		ascension		capitol[4]
	actor		ascent		cemetery
	addressed		assurance		censure
	aisle[1]		attendance		chaperon[5]
	alliance		attraction		chauffeur
2		4		6	
	amateur		auxiliary		climbed
	ambassador		bachelor		commercial
	analysis		banana		commissioner
	analyze[2]		barbarous		comparative
	annual		bearing[3]		competent
	anonymous		beggar		competitive
	antarctic		Britain		competitor
	anxiety		British		conceit
	apparatus		Briton		concentration
	appreciate		bulletin		conscientious

---

[1] *A passage between chairs or benches.* Do not confuse with *isle (a small island).*
[2] Also *analyse.*
[3] *Carrying; enduring.* Do not confuse with *baring (uncovering, exposing).*
[4] Adjective, *of primary importance, initial;* noun, *accumulated wealth, chief city,* and so on. Do not confuse with *capitol (statehouse).* The easiest way to avoid confusion and consequent mistakes in spelling is to remember that *capitol,* meaning statehouse, is spelled with an *o,* and that in every other meaning you should use an *a.* This will give you only one thing to remember instead of dozens. Apply the same simplifying principle whenever you come across words related either in sound or meaning that have only one exceptional spelling.
[5] Also *chaperone.*

294

7   conscious
    continually
    continuous
    copies
    council[6]
    councilor[7]
    counsel
    counselor
    courteous
    courtesy

8   criticism
    crystal
    curiosity
    deceit
    deceitful
    descend
    descendant
    descent
    desert[8]
    dessert[8]

9   diphtheria
    disaster
    disastrous
    disobedience
    dissatisfaction
    dissatisfied
    dissipate
    dormitories
    ecstasy
    eligible

10 eliminated
    emigrant[9]

    eminent
    environment
    equivalent
    essential
    excel
    excellence
    exhausted
    exhilarate

11 fiery
    financial
    fragrant
    frantically
    fraternities
    fundamental
    furniture
    gallant
    gambling
    gauge

12 generally
    genius
    geyser
    goddess
    grandeur
    grievance
    grievous
    harass
    hindrance
    humorous

13 hundredths
    hurriedly
    hypocrisy
    hypocrite

    illiterate
    immigrant[10]
    increase
    incredible
    infinite
    influence

14 influential
    intelligence
    intelligent
    intentionally
    interpreted
    irresistible
    lacquer
    legitimate
    liable
    literally

15 livelihood
    loneliness
    loyalty
    manual
    marriage
    marries
    melancholy
    meringue
    metal
    miniature

16 miscellaneous
    momentous
    mournful
    nauseate
    nineteenth
    ninety

---

[6] *An assembly.* Do not confuse with *counsel (advice).*

[7] *Member of a council.* Do not confuse with *counselor (an adviser). Councillor* and *counsellor* are acceptable American, and preferred British, spelling.

[8] Noun, *due reward or punishment;* verb, *to abandon;* accented like *avert.* Noun, *arid region,* accented like *culvert. Dessert,* last course at a meal, accented like *avert.*

[9] *One who leaves one country to live in another.* Do not confuse with *immigrant.*

[10] *One who comes into a foreign country to live.* Do not confuse with *emigrant.*

     ninth

     obstacle

     offender

     omission

17 opponent

     optimism

     optimistic

     pageant

     pamphlet

     paralysis

     paralyzed

     parliament

     pastime

     perilous

18 permanence

     permanent

     perpendicular

     personnel[11]

     pneumonia

     politician

     politics

     porch

     possessor

     practically

19 prairie

     precedence

     precedent

     prejudiced

     prevalence[12]

     primitive

     proffered

     propeller

     prophecy[13]

     prophesied

20 prophesy[14]

     psychology

     purchaser

     questionnaire

     receipt

     reference

     remembrance

     reservoir

     respectability

     rheumatism

21 rhyme[15]

     rhythm

     righteous

     sacrilegious

     sandwich

     scenery

     schedule

     science

     scientific

     sentinel

22 sergeant[16]

     shepherd

     shone[17]

     shown[18]

     significance

     significant

     site[19]

     specifically

     specimen

     stationary[20]

23 stationery[21]

     strategy

     streaking

     suffrage

     summarize

     summit

     superintendent

     susceptible

     syllable

     symmetrical

24 synonym

     technical

     temperament

     temperature

     threshold

     tragedy

     traitor

     transferred

     translate

     treasurer

---

[11] *A body of persons employed in some service.* Do not confuse with *personal.*

[12] *Frequent occurrence; general acceptance.* From the verb *to prevail.*

[13] Noun, *prediction.* The *cy* rhymes with *sea.*

[14] Verb, *to predict.* The *sy* rhymes with *sigh.*

[15] Also *rime.*

[16] Also *serjeant.*

[17] Past and past participle of *shine.*

[18] Past participle of *show.*

[19] *A location.* Do not confuse with *cite (to quote)* or with *sight (vision).*

[20] *Not moving.*

[21] *Paper for writing.*

25	tyrannically	vigilance	welcome
	unconscious	vigilant	welfare
	vacancy	warrant	wondrous
	vengeance		

J Diagraming

In general

J1 A diagram of a sentence is a picture that shows the interrelation of the words, phrases, and clauses. Diagrams are a good way to analyze the structure of a sentence. They will frequently, though by no means always, reveal the grammatical flaw in a bad sentence; and they will untangle a complicated sentence so that one can see, for example, whether *who* or *whom* is required.

J2 If one gets the habit of diagraming on paper, soon one is able to diagram mentally, with the speed of thought.

J3 There are many good systems of diagraming. The system given here is one of them. Since it helps good order and efficiency for a whole class and a whole school to use the same system of diagraming, use the one given here.

Diagraming simple sentences

SUBJECT NOUN AND PREDICATE VERB

J4 Diagram a subject noun or pronoun and a predicate verb like this:

MODEL

subject noun | predicate verb

People are singing.

people | are singing

J5 Diagram a compound subject like this:

MODEL

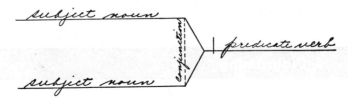

Johnson and Powers disappeared.

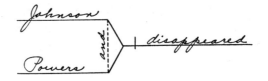

J

Men and women fainted.

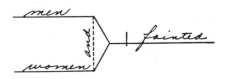

Either *Bill* or *John*, hardly
Kenneth, will do.

The diagram stresses the connective force of *hardly*.

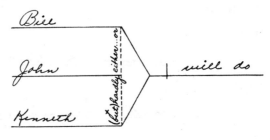

298

Either *Bill* or *John,* hardly *Kenneth,* will do.

The diagram stresses the adverbial force of *hardly.* (Compound elliptical sentence.)

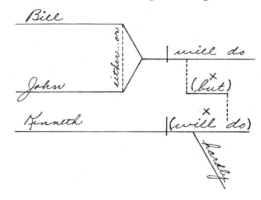

I, not *you,* am responsible.

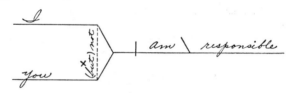

My *friend* and *neighbor,* Kittredge, is celebrating.

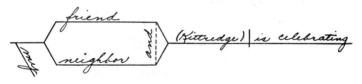

Raisins, peanuts, and *jelly* will mix.

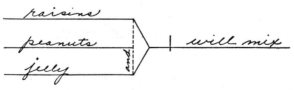

J6   Diagram a compound predicate like this:

Fairbanks *turned* and *ran*.

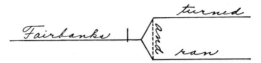

Fairbanks not only *turned* and *ran* but also *screamed*.

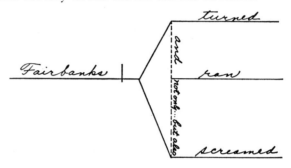

Fairbanks and Schlegel *turned* and *ran*.

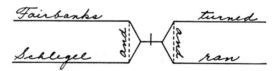

DUMMY SUBJECTS

J7   A dummy subject:

MODEL

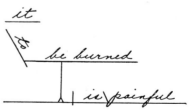

It is painful to be burned.

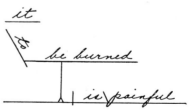

There came a man from afar.

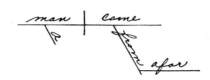

DIRECT OBJECTS

J8 A direct object:

MODEL

subject noun | predicate verb | direct object

Hilary is playing *golf*.

Hilary | is playing | golf

Mirabel likes *parades* and *pageants*.

Mirabel | likes | parades / and / pageants

J9 Two direct objects (not a compound direct object):

MODEL

subject noun | predicate verb | first object | second object

Mr. Claudel teaches *Adrian algebra*.

Mr. Claudel | teaches | Adrian | algebra

Hear *me* my *lessons*.

(you) | hear | me | lessons

301

INDIRECT OBJECTS

J10 An indirect object:

MODEL

Father Joe brought *Mother* Communion.

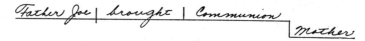

Dad got *Arnold* and *me* jobs.

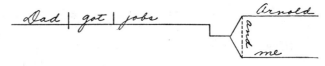

COMPLEMENTS

J11 A predicate noun, pronoun, or adjective:

MODEL

This is *milk*.

This is *milky*.

Raeburn is getting *tired* and *angry*.

Pitkin was named and was elected *chairman.*

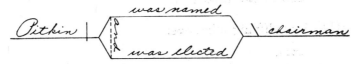

J12 An objective complement:

MODEL

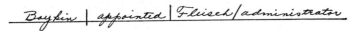

Boykin appointed Fleisch *administrator.*

I call that *ungrateful* as well as *selfish.*

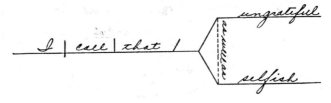

RETAINED OBJECTS

J13 A retained object:

MODEL

Vengarte has been given *money.*

MODIFYING ADJECTIVE

J14 A modifying adjective:

MODEL

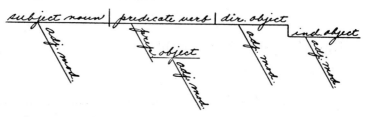

At *the morning* inspection *the* major gave *only* me *a second* glance.

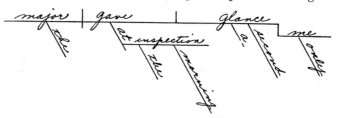

Whimpering and *barking*, the dog circled the porcupine.

ADVERBS AND ADVERBIAL NOUNS

J15 An adverb:

MODEL

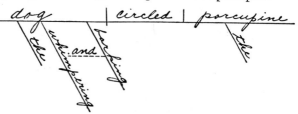

Very inexpensive books are *nowadays nearly everywhere* available.

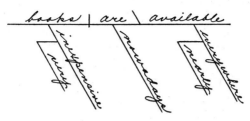

Hats get *more* and *more* absurd.

Friedel, groping *blindly* and *awkwardly, finally* found the light cord.

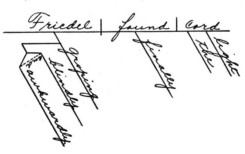

J16 An adverbial noun:

Dougherty went *home yesterday morning.*

Home, yesterday, and *morning* are adverbial nouns.

305

PHRASES IN GENERAL

J17 The subject noun or pronoun of a verbal is set off from
the verbal by the same perpendicular line, extended a
little below the horizontal line, that is used to set off a
subject noun or pronoun from a predicate verb (J4). The
direct and indirect objects, predicate complements, retained objects, and objective complements of verbals are
diagramed just like those of predicate verbs (J8-13).

NOUN PHRASES

J18 Prepositional noun phrases are not very common; but,
when they occur, diagram them like this:

Over the fence is out.

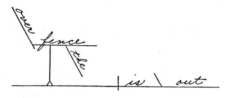

The smoke is coming from *under the house.*

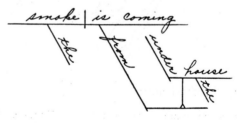

J19 A gerund noun phrase:

MODEL

306

Calling your enemy names is futile.

MODEL

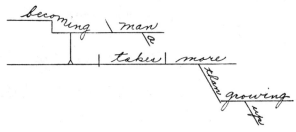

Becoming a man takes more than growing up.

MODEL

There is no doubt about *his being elected.*

The older children enjoy *shocking sorghum.*

Arguing with Linda is *fighting the wind.*

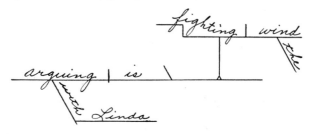

Your snubbing me and playing deaf only makes me persist.

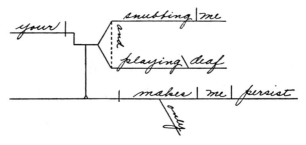

His swimming and Janet's won the meet.

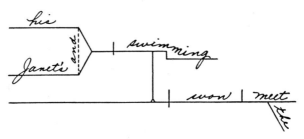

J20   An infinitive noun phrase:

MODEL

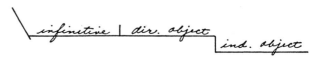

308

We had the waiter *bring Laury a bib.*

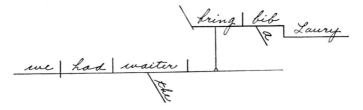

To object is reasonable this time.

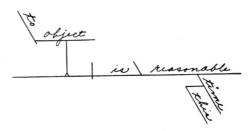

The girls are *to dress as Ubangis.*

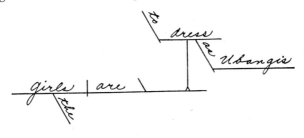

Someone ought *to tie the bell on.*

MODEL

We know *him to be a reader*.

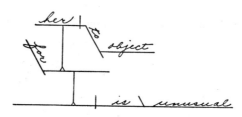

For her to object is unusual.

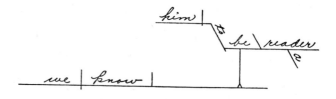

Your brother seems *to be restless*.

310

It is useless *to whine, to plead, or to argue with me.*

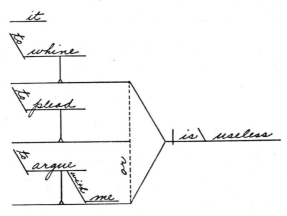

PREPOSITIONAL ADJECTIVE AND ADVERB PHRASES

J21 A prepositional adjective phrase:

MODEL

I prefer one *with a head.*

The chance *of surviving* seemed small indeed.

311

J22 A prepositional adverb phrase:

We swam daily *near the mouth.*

Wilton opened a window *in order* to dissipate the smoke.

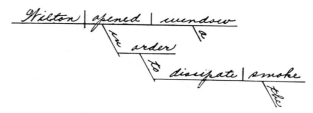

Gene plunged forward, sinking *to his knees.*

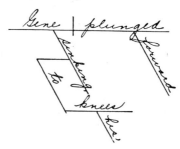

Who's afraid *of a striped kitten?*

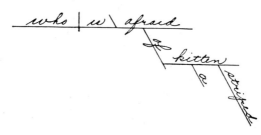

312

INFINITIVE ADJECTIVE AND ADVERB PHRASES

J23 An infinitive adjective phrase:

You appear *to be troubled.*

The will *to win* can be important.

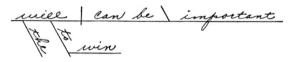

J24 An infinitive adverb phrase:

Put the pot on the stove *to boil.*

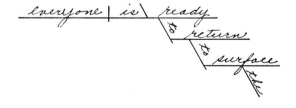

Is everyone ready *to return* to the surface?

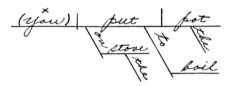

313

Afraid *to destroy the map,* I dropped it out the window.

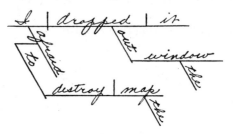

The beggar was too surprised *to say thanks or speak* at all.

PARTICIPIAL ADJECTIVE PHRASES

J25 A participial adjective phrase:

MODEL

Having given me another sly look, Mr. Snipe departed.

314

MODEL

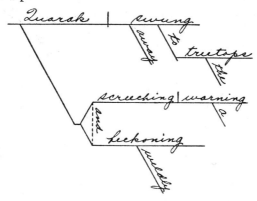

I noticed hundreds of men *standing idle.*

Quarak, *screeching a warning and beckoning wildly,* swung away to the treetops.

APPOSITIVES

J26 Place appositive nouns after and next to the head word in the diagram and enclose them in parentheses.

MODEL

My friend *Henry* is the man to see.

315

I have given years to my favorite occupation, *talking*.

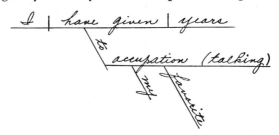

The manager's nephews—*Clem, Lem,* and young *Bartholomew*—all have good jobs.

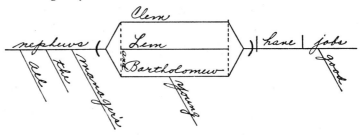

The regional sport, *racing jack rabbits,* is strenuous.

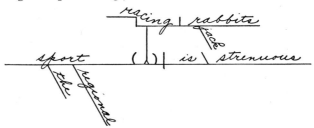

Andirons, or *firedogs,* sat in the center of the huge fireplace.

Or merely stresses the appositive and helps the rhythm.

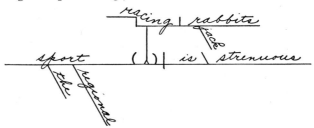

Another fact—namely, your *absence*—is against you.

MODIFYING POSSESSIVES

J27 Possessives are often adjectives. When they are so, diagram them like adjectives.

Calvin's doctrine is terrible.

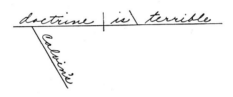

INDEPENDENT ELEMENTS

J28 Since independent elements have no grammatical connection with the rest of the sentence, they are diagramed by themselves, above or below the sentence or clause in which they appear.

J29 Independent words, phrases, or clauses are diagramed just like other words, phrases, or clauses.

J30 A nominative absolute:

MODELS

The battle won, the tanks retired.

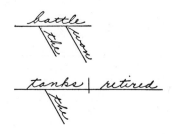

I'm glad, *no one needing the house,* to let you stay in it.

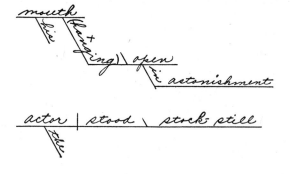

His mouth open in astonishment, the actor stood stock-still.

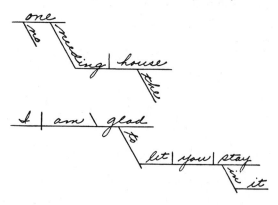

318

J31 A noun in direct address:

Mr. Froebes, have you anything to say?

Gentlemen, be seated.

J32 An exclamatory word:

Golly, I like the looks of the cow hand riding Terror!

J33 An absolute word, phrase, or clause:

Fetch me the candle snuffer, *please.*

319

Granting your facts, have you a solution?

By the way, has anyone found a license plate with an automobile attached?

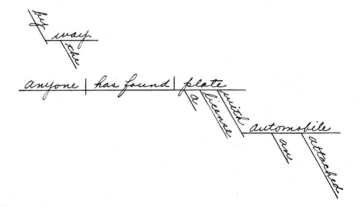

We all, *to be sure,* need mercy.

Who *do you suppose* ate the icing?

Consider *do you suppose* in this case to be merely thrown into the sentence. If it were not, it would be the independent clause with the *who* clause as its object.

This is the man whom *I imagine* we were to avoid.

Complex sentence.

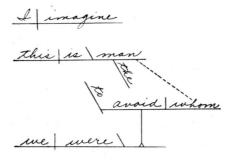

We found abalones among the rocks; *that is,* ear shells.

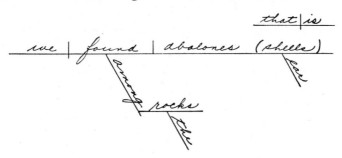

Helmer was a hero; *that is to say*, he did not let his fear rule him.   Compound sentence.

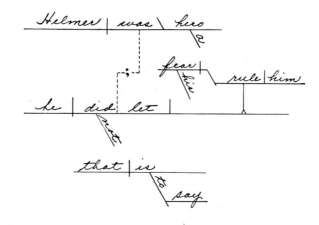

Fergen was a hobo or, *shall we say*, a gentleman of the road.

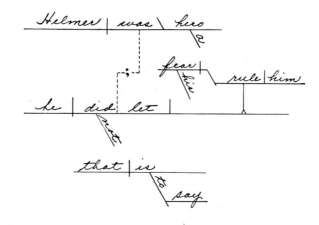

WORDS OMITTED

J34 In diagraming, replace an omitted word or group of words. Enclose it in parentheses, and put an x above it.

Bring me no more reports.

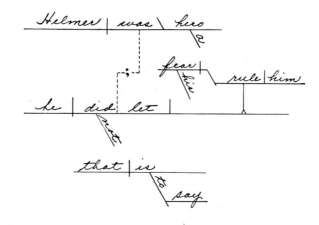

You are not so sensitive as I.   Complex sentence.

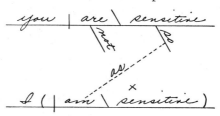

Diagraming compound sentences

J35 A compound sentence is made up of two or more clauses that could stand alone as simple sentences. So the diagraming of a compound sentence adds nothing to the diagraming of a simple sentence (J4-34) except the showing of connection between the clauses.

J36 When *and, or, nor, but,* or *for* is omitted between the clauses of a compound sentence, put a semicolon between them in the diagram, like this:

Everybody talks about the weather; nobody does anything about it.

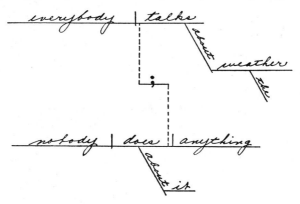

Everybody talks about the weather; still [conjunctive adverb], nobody does anything about it.

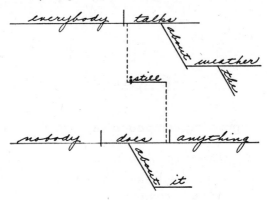

J37 When *and, or, nor, but,* or *for* is used between the clauses of a compound sentence, diagram the sentence like this:

Everybody talks about the weather, *but* nobody does anything about it.

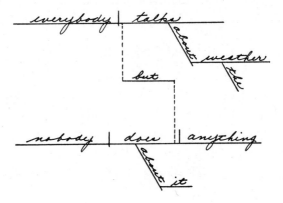

Everybody talks about the weather, *but* still nobody does anything about it.

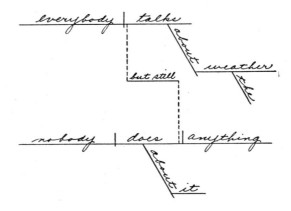

The Kenwigs family was not proud, *but* the neighbors ought to know about Morleena's French lessons; so she was told to mention them very humbly.

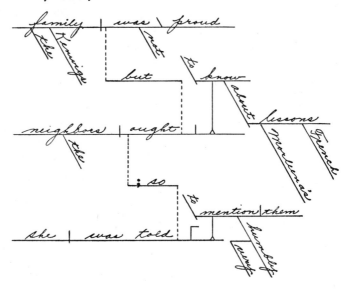

Diagraming complex sentences

NOUN CLAUSES

J38   Put a noun clause on a stilt.

MODEL

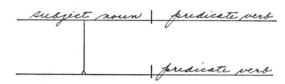

Sentences with subject noun clauses—
Whoever buys this car buys trash.

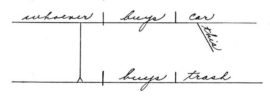

It was foretold in the Old Testament *that the Messias would be born in Bethlehem.*

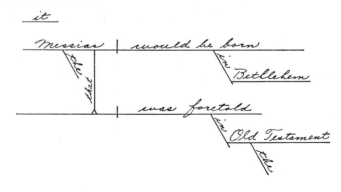

326

Where you have been and *what you bought there* are nobody's business.

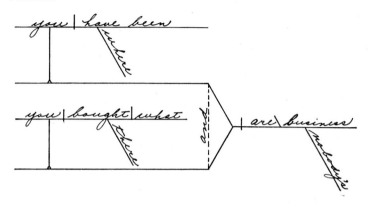

Sentences with object noun clauses—
Tell me *whether you will return in time.*

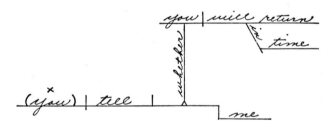

It is a question of *how we can raise the money* and *when we can have the hall.*

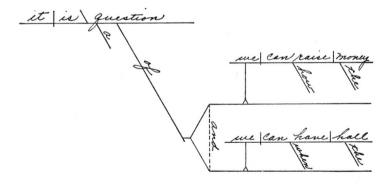

Ted, knowing only *what was required,* did not make a good record at college.

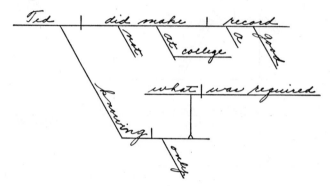

We had an argument about *whose snapshot should be submitted.*

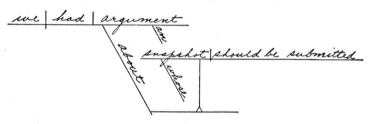

Sentences with noun-clause complements—
Holiness is *what we are striving for.*

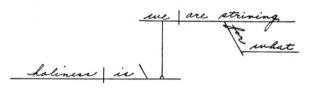

Rose discovered Mullen to be *what she least expected*—intelligent.

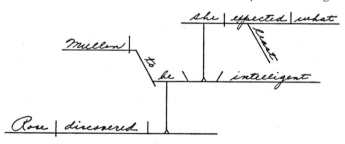

The question is, *who has the chipmunk.*

Sentences with noun-clause appositives—
Don's excuse, *that he had a flat tire,* sounded a bit thin.

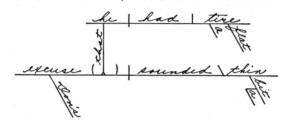

Everything—*whatever he earned* and *whatever came to him as tips*—he gave to his mother.

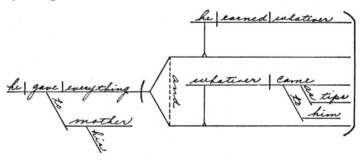

My Protestant friend is deterred by one difficulty; namely, *how can confession be necessary and good?*

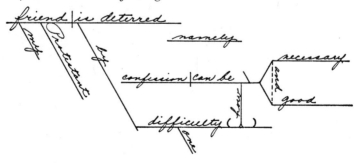

329

ADJECTIVE CLAUSES

J39 Draw a dotted line from the relative word in the adjective clause to the antecedent in the other clause. (Do not put the relative word on the dotted line.)

The Battle of Lepanto, *which Chesterton made the subject of this poem,* saved Europe from the Turks.

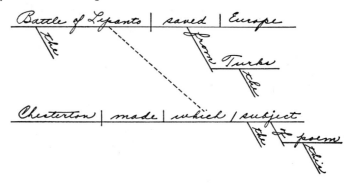

The sultan put his army through tactics *that would check the enemy's latest move.*

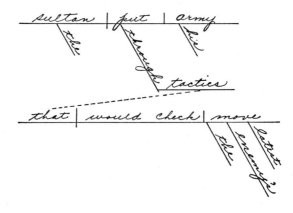

Conrad, *whose novel you just read,* died in 1924.

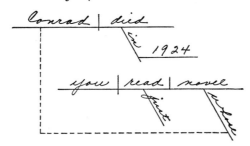

Holt told us the reason *why the fan belt had broken.*

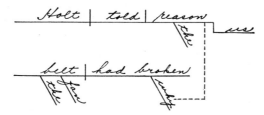

Tim was a man *who* we thought *would fight for us.*

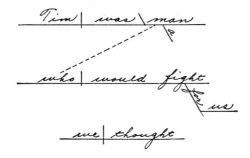

We spent more than seven years in Juarez, *in which city, by the way, we met Mark Tracy.*

The diagram treats *more* as an adjective used as a noun. *Than* is ordinarily a conjunction. But, in a sentence like this, in which no natural elliptical clause can be found, it seems to be felt as a preposition.

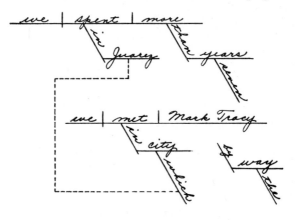

We spent more than seven years in Juarez, in which city, by the way, we met Mark Tracy.

This diagram of a portion of the sentence treats *more* as an adjective.

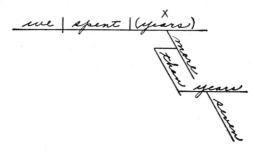

This is the lacquer *that we were waiting for* and *that arrived too late for use on our biggest contract.*

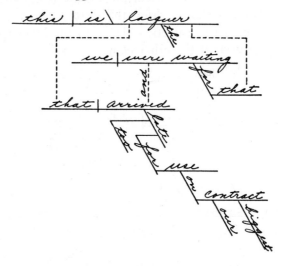

Alfredo is the uncle of Jake, *who is the cousin of Dubar, who in turn is my uncle.*

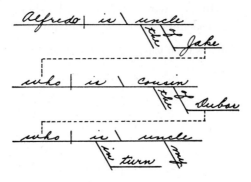

J40   On those rather rare occasions when a whole clause rather than an individual word or phrase is the antecedent of an adjective clause, draw the dotted line from the relative word in the adjective clause to the line under the predicate verb of the other clause.

Margaret threw away my pipe with the broken stem, *which annoyed me very much.*

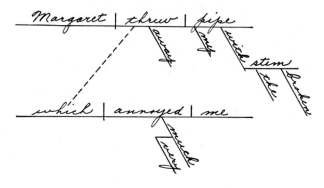

ADVERB CLAUSES

J41   Draw a dotted line from the predicate verb of the adverb clause to the word that the adverb clause modifies. On this dotted line, write the subordinating conjunction.

The latch was on *when I tried the door.*

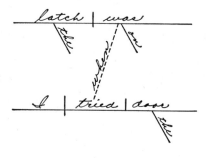

Charles behaved so badly *that we had to put him into a strait jacket.*

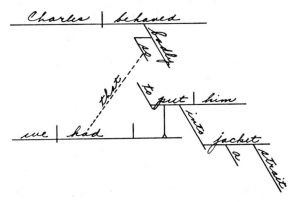

A diamond is harder *than any other precious stone.*

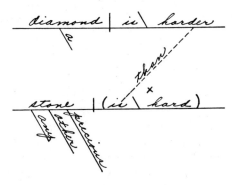

He sometimes acts *as though he were demented.*

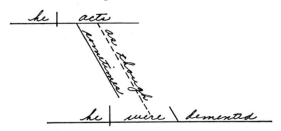

Had I the right, I would abolish advertising.

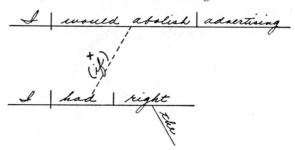

When one is tired and longs for rest, he can find repose at Slump-haven—*if he can pay for it.*

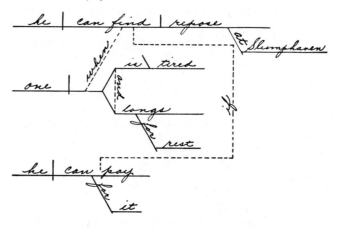

Where a million people blacken the sand like bees swarming thick on a limb and where every one of the million is in motion, there I lie and try to get a sun tan.

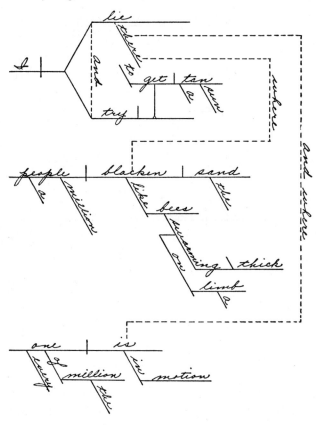

When Jason and I arrived at school and *then I remembered my books at home, seven miles away,* then I got a little upset—like a volcano.

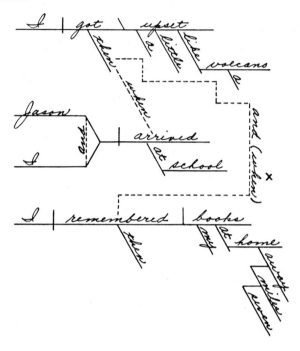

MIXED DEPENDENT CLAUSES

J42 Noun, adjective, and adverb clauses can often be found two kinds together or all three kinds together in one sentence. When this happens, diagram each kind according to its own form and rules. (Diagrams such as those in J42-43 are really virtuoso stunts, included in this book chiefly to convince the skeptical that complicated sentences can be diagramed. They are not, as a matter of fact, very useful, since their very complication makes them difficult to follow. Ordinarily one has little need to diagram more than one or two clauses at a time.)

338

The fact *that Renard was a journalist with whom I had become acquainted while I was taking a vacation in Santa Fe* was written down in my report.

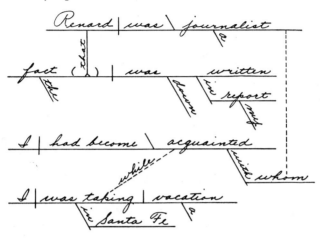

Diagraming compound-complex sentences

J43 A compound-complex sentence:

Don waited patiently for news; but, when they returned, the men had nothing to report about Miggy.

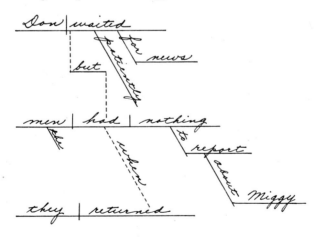

While Rome burned, Nero fiddled and his courtiers laughed.

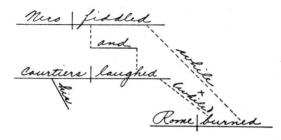

Vittorio fairly jigged with irritation when the bagpipes struck up, but McTavish seemed to enjoy the music.

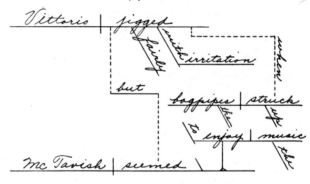

Magellan was killed in the Philippines; nevertheless, his companions, eager to prove that the world is round, continued their westward journey until their ships at length cast anchor off the coast of Spain.

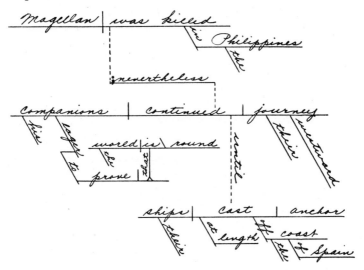

Among the pioneers in the modern French school of music was
Cesar Franck, the greatest and most famous composer that Belgium
has produced; in fact, musicians so esteemed him that they made
a cult of him and his music even before he died.

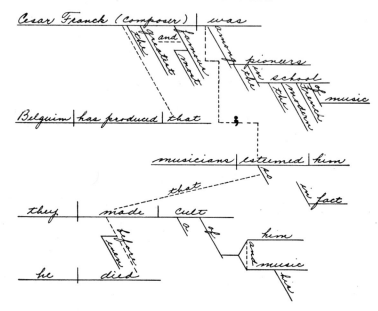

Diagraming direct quotations

J44 If a direct quotation is a half-sentence that can be considered part of the sentence or clause in which it stands,
diagram it as part of the sentence or clause.

Mr. Moulton shouted loudly that he was "plenty peeved!"

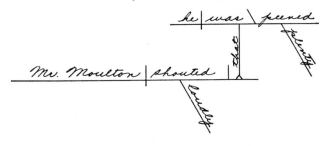

J45 If a direct quotation is not a half-sentence but a sentence,
diagram it as you would any other sentence. Diagram the
he said portion of the sentence independently of the
quotation.

"My people," said the chief, "do not wish to fight your people."

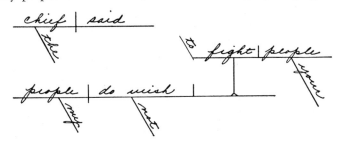

"Give us back our self-respect," shouted Tomanski, teetering on a rickety old chair, but maintaining his position above the crowd.

K The paragraph

K1 A paragraph is a sentence or a group of sentences separated by indention or by a similar device from other sentences in the same piece of writing.[1]

This is a paragraph. The first line is, as you see, indented, set back a little from the left-hand margin formed by the other lines. It is the technical essential of a paragraph that it be set off by indention or by some other device from the rest of the piece of writing. But, as other rules will indicate, a paragraph ordinarily corresponds to a unit of thought. In fact, the reason for the indention and, consequently, for the paragraphing is to set off one unit of thought from another. Thus the reader is prevented from mixing up things that should be kept separate, and the mind is given little rests between units.

---

[1] For paragraphs in dialogue see D95. For paragraphs in narratives see T21-29. For topic thoughts and topic statements, see M11-18. For unity, coherence, and emphasis in paragraphs, see M11-18, N19-27, and O19-23. For variety in paragraphs (methods of developing topic thoughts), see P15, P19, P22, P29, P34-35, P40, P43, and P46. For paragraphs as an emphasis device, see O34-35.

344

K2 In continuous composition, a good paragraph is a group of sentences that all develop a single topic thought[2] (although occasionally a paragraph will consist of only one sentence by itself).

Write your name and address in the upper right-hand corner of the page. In the center of the first line, write the title of your story. Skip two line-spaces and then indent for the first paragraph. Leave margins of an inch and a half at the sides and the bottom of the page.

The topic thought of the paragraph: *Here is the style your paper must follow.*

And now let us leave the style of the paper for a moment and consider its content.

This is a one-sentence paragraph, used as a bridge between parts of the theme.

K3 Occasionally a paragraph is complete in itself, and there results a one-paragraph composition like the ones to be found in some newspaper editorials or in the writings of some columnists. A paragraph, however, is generally a part—a new side or phase, a step forward: in brief, a division or a subdivision—of a larger composition.

K4 Except in the block form of typed letters,[3] in outlines,[4] in printed displays, and in certain kinds of technical writing, the first line of every paragraph should be indented; that is, the first line should be set in a little from the left-hand margin.[5] When indention is not used, paragraphs are indicated in some other way, usually by the insertion of extra space between them.

K5 The first line of a handwritten paragraph should be indented about one inch; of a typewritten paragraph, from three to eight characters.

---

[2] For topic thoughts see M11-18.
[3] For the block form of typed letters, see R105.
[4] For paragraphing and indention in outlines, see R32 and R46.
[5] For the indention of long quotations in, say, term papers, see R72.

K6 The first lines of all paragraphs in the same composition should be indented uniformly.

The indention of this first paragraph will govern the indention of those that follow.

This paragraph, as you see, is indented uniformly with the one immediately above. So with any others in the same theme.

L The theme

In general

L1 A theme is a group of paragraphs that all contribute to the development of one topic.[1]

To be perfectly candid, three things in this school cause me a good deal of concern.

One topic: *Three things in this school cause me a good deal of concern.*

The first is that the quickest to criticize are the slowest to lend a hand when an improvement is begun. For instance, all of the seniors made a great to-do about not having any privileges. But, when they were offered a lounge for their exclusive use on the condition that they furnish it themselves, only two men, Burns and Kauffmann, made any effort at all to bring anything in.

The topic of this paragraph, *the quickest to criticize are the slowest to lend a hand,* develops the topic of the whole theme, stated in paragraph 1.

The second disturbing thing is that most of the men think school spirit is just a matter of cheering at football games. Few of us consider turning this school into a Christian

Again, the topic of this paragraph, *most of the men think school spirit is just a matter of cheering at football games,* develops the topic of the whole theme.

---

[1] See also exposition, R3-82; description, S2; narration, T2-43; and argument, U3-42. For theme topics and topic paragraphs, see M19-22. For unity, coherence, and emphasis in themes, see M19-27, N28-44, and O24-43. For variety in themes (methods of developing theme topics), see P15, P20, P23, P30-31, P36-37, P41, and P44-46.

brotherhood in which every man but the bewildered freshman would consider it his Catholic job to help someone duller, weaker, or more friendless than himself—a fraternity in which the "big shots" would not be the athletes or the glad boys with smart cars; not the sophisticated drawlers or the bad, bad rebels; not the social lions who always have a date when stag fun like a class night is scheduled; but rather the men who couple brains and gaiety and goodness, the men who are worth following because they really are going somewhere.

And now the third disturbing thing is that Christ does not get from us the reception that He has a right to expect from Catholic students. We keep Him in the chapel. We do not let Him into the locker room, the cafeteria, the auditorium, the gymnasium. How many of us ever act as if He were walking among us, talk-

Again, the topic of this paragraph, *Christ does not get from us the reception that He has a right to expect from Catholic students,* develops the topic of the whole theme; namely, *three things in this school cause me a good deal of concern.*

ing with us, working with us, playing with us? This is His school. This is His money we are clinking. This is His food we are eating. This is His breath we are using. This is His truth we are learning. Yet some of us—only a few, but still some of us—push Him out the door. You know what I mean. And too many of the rest of us let Him go begging for friends.

L2 A theme may be thought of as a large paragraph that contains little paragraphs and follows nearly all the rules of paragraphs.

L3 Sometimes a theme will consist of only one paragraph. One-paragraph themes are rare except in such compositions as editorials, jokes, columns, and advertisements.

[One-paragraph theme in a box on the front page of a school paper:] All those interested in trying out for the junior basketball squad should meet Coach Drummond in the gym on Thursday, November 3, at 3:00 P.M. No experience is necessary. "If they're willing to work and ready to learn," says Drummond, "let them come, even if they think the game is played with a bat."

347

The introduction

L4   Do not use an introduction unless it will accomplish some useful purpose.[2] The topic paragraph,[3] especially in short themes, is often the best introduction in itself. Wordiness or a reluctance to get down to business will only bore the reader.

L5   Use an introductory paragraph or so—

A   To put your audience or readers in a receptive mood.

[Doubtful:] We have the worst spirit in the school. I have given this class a lot of thought, and I think I can tell you what is wrong with us and what we can do about it.

It may not be prudent to begin with this topic paragraph. The topic involves criticism, which few men take kindly unless it is softened. The audience or readers may be prejudiced from the start. Use an introductory paragraph or two, as just below.

[Better:] I think you all know my record—how little I have done to make this school and this class what they could be, and how much I have done to harm both. For example, you remember, I imagine, the time I broke up the rally before the Winston game, just to get a little attention from the crowd. You may recall that, up until two weeks ago, I had not attended a single class night this year. Oh, I've been no asset. Well, I've been doing some thinking—go on; laugh—and I've decided to change my tune. I think you'll take some plain talk from me, since you know that I am talking to myself just as much as to you.

We have the worst spirit in the school. I have given this class a lot of thought, and I think I can tell you what is wrong with us and what we can do about it.

B   To interest your audience or readers and make them want the rest of the theme.

---

[2] See L5. See also unity and emphasis in the theme, M22, O24-25, O27, O29, and O32; exposition, R33-34 and R36; narration, T16-19; and argument, U18 and U38-39.

[3] See M22.

| [Doubtful:] The effects of the Ten Commandments are not negative; they are positive. | This sounds very dull indeed, unless the audience or reader guesses at the implication. |

[Better:] If you are like most people, you think of the Ten Commandments as a series of frowning *don'ts* that restrict a man's liberty. But have you ever found yourself wondering what the world would be like if the Ten Commandments were simply disregarded? I don't mean that men would miss heaven or go to hell. I mean what *this* world would be like. One day I fell to speculating about this, and the speculation startled me. I found that the Ten Commandments are the basis of liberty, that the Ten Commandments set men free.

Put it this way: the Ten Commandments are really not negative; they are positive.

c To avoid an unpleasantly abrupt beginning.

| [Doubtful:] Three things in this school cause me a good deal of concern. | This would be a rather harsh and abrupt opening under most circumstances. |

[Better:] I know that you will excuse me if I do not this time pay my debt of praise to a school to which I owe as much as any of you. We are met for a different purpose now—not to congratulate ourselves on what we have, but to discover what we lack.

Three things in this school cause me a good deal of concern.

d To settle the doubts of the audience or readers about bringing up such a subject at such a time.

| [Doubtful:] Mallophaga, or bird lice, have some peculiar traits, several of which I shall discuss in this paper. | One can hear the groan of the audience or readers and the angry murmur: "Why bring *that* up?" Not everybody is automatically interested in bird lice. This is a very unfortunate opening. |

[Better:] Ordinarily I should not think of annoying you with the health problems of semidomestic fowl. But since the class is planning to raise pigeons and sell squabs to bring in money for the year-end picnic, I think I'll find you interested in Mallophaga.

Mallophaga, or bird lice, have some peculiar traits, several of which I shall discuss in this paper.

E To supply information that the audience or readers need at the very beginning of the theme.

[Doubtful:] Insofar as it assumes that man is purely material, cybernetics is doomed to failure.

Many readers would not understand this sentence because of the terms *cybernetics* and *material*. It is important, therefore, that before the theme goes very far these terms be explained; otherwise the author can write off his early paragraphs as total loss.

[Better:] There is a science—if one may use that word loosely—that has been attracting public notice of recent years in America: the science of cybernetics. "Cybernetics" is the comparative study of complex calculating machines and the human nervous system, with the hope that more may be learned about the operation of the human brain. Disciples of this science are fond of talking about machines as though they were human and about men as though they were machines. Some of these people apparently think that there is nothing essentially different between men and machines— that both are material only, that neither is partly spiritual.

Now, what I intend to try to show is that cybernetics, insofar as it assumes that man is purely material and not partly spiritual, is doomed to failure.

L6 It is a good idea to know exactly what you are introducing before you introduce it. Ordinarily, therefore, write the introduction last. It often happens, however, that an excellent introduction pops into one's mind before the theme itself is drafted. When this happens, write the introduction down on a separate piece of paper while it is still "hot." Then proceed to write the theme. Afterwards, read the introduction to see if it still fits. If it does, then use it. If it does not, jettison it and write another—if an introduction is needed.

L7 Unless there is good reason to the contrary, an introduction should answer all or some of these questions:[4]

---

[4] When it is a case of writing an atmospheric introduction to a story, a suspense-creating advertisement, or something of the kind, these questions—with

A What (and who) is going to be talked about? (This is answered when the theme topic is included in the introduction or is itself used as the introduction.)

B Why is it going to be talked about?

C Who is going to talk about it?

D What is he going to say about it?

E Why is he saying it to this particular audience or at this particular time, and so on?

F How is he going to talk about it? What divisions of the subject is he going to make, what is he going to include or exclude, and so on?

L8 The questions asked in L7 need not always be answered in a dry, straightforward manner.

The conclusion

L9 Often a theme does well to come to a close where its development stops. Do not use concluding paragraphs unless they will accomplish some useful purpose.[5] Wordiness or a reluctance to finish will only bore the reader and may spoil the effect of an otherwise good theme.

L10 It sometimes helps to use a concluding paragraph or so—

A To summarize the main points made in the body of the theme and leave them fresh in the reader's mind right at the very end.

Well, now, our time is up. This has been a lengthy and complicated discussion. Much that we have talked about needs further treatment. But two conclusions of major importance have been reached and should have immediate effect on our conduct: first, that discipline is a necessary condition of happiness and, second, that a man must forget himself to a large extent if he is to be himself to any extent at all.

---

the possible exception of the first—will not prove very helpful. But in the general run of informational and argumentative papers, they may help you to write an introduction that is organically connected with the theme. Use them where they help you and neglect them where they hinder you.

[5] See L10. See also exposition, R33-34 and R36; narration, T20 and T39; and argument, U21-22 and U42.

B To avoid an impression of abruptness or inconclusive-
ness, to keep the reader from asking, "What! Is that
the end?"

[Too abrupt:] ". . . If Horace is here, then I am saved," she
cried, turning to Mr. Klusterblum.

[Better:] ". . . If Horace is here, then I am saved," she cried,
turning to Mr. Klusterblum.

And so indeed she was saved, though not from Horace. For
this story ended as all such stories must. She and Horace were
married and quarreled happily ever after. And the moral of this
epic is: If you must climb cliffs, use a ladder.

C To finish on a rousing note and reinforce the persuasive-
ness of the whole theme.

Carry yourselves, then, like the gods that you are, and fear nothing but yourselves. "I have overcome the world." Remember that
God desires your happiness, that you are His adopted sons, that
you share the divine nature. Walk like brothers of Christ.

D To lower the reader gently from a highly emotional
state and ease him back into the calmer world he will
face when he looks up from your theme.

. . . as the bullet slammed into his chest.

So died, violently, a man who hated violence. Life has its ironies,
has it not? And hardly a man dies without some little irony at
the end to make a cynic mock and a saint smile with understanding
of the divine humor and the divine unexpectedness in things.

M Unity

In general

M1 Unity means oneness. In composition, unity is the principle that requires that there be only one main thought
and that all the other thoughts and words in a sentence,
paragraph, or theme directly or indirectly reinforce the
one main thought.

M2 Unity requires that thoughts and words that do not either directly or indirectly reinforce the main thought be omitted from the composition or be clearly marked off by parentheses or by expressions like *permit me to digress for a moment.*

M3 Unity requires that digressions be justified and that they be relatively few. Avoid them as a general rule.

M4 Clearness in writing is largely a matter of unity, coherence, and emphasis.[1] It is necessary, of course, that the writer's ideas be clear to begin with. But unity, coherence, and emphasis go far to make sure that these ideas will also become clear to the reader.

M5 What unifies a composition often also makes it coherent and lends it proper emphasis—and vice versa. Hence there is a certain amount of overlapping in fact and in rule.

Unity in the sentence

M6 Put into separate sentences ideas that are not plainly related.

Franklin D. Roosevelt had infantile paralysis and was president when the base at Pearl Harbor was attacked.	There is no relationship between the paralysis and the attack. So put the two ideas into separate sentences.

Franklin D. Roosevelt had infantile paralysis.

Franklin D. Roosevelt was president when the base at Pearl Harbor was attacked.

At the banquet of the Good Neighbor Club the toasts were in Spanish, the rest of the evening being spent in dancing.	There is no relationship between the toasts and the dancing. So put the two ideas into separate sentences.

At the banquet of the Good Neighbor Club the toasts were in Spanish. Once the toasts were over, there was dancing the rest of the evening.

---

[1] For coherence see N1-44. For emphasis see O1-43.

M7 If the sentence does not become unwieldy or cluttered, put into it all ideas that are closely related.

On the second floor, above the chapel, is the library. It contains about a hundred thousand books. It also subscribes to and circulates most of the current periodicals.

Let us suppose that the writer wants to say that there is a large library on the second floor. All of that can be put into one sentence with considerable gain in unity of impression. Below, the fragments are knit together into one clear statement.

On the second floor, above the chapel, is a library that houses about a hundred thousand books and nearly all the current periodicals.

M8 Do not write rambling, talkative sentences that include too many details.

When the wheezy old Ford had gasped its way up the dirt road of Mohawk Mound and then, with clanks and jolts, had tottered down the other side, through the cool dawn, into the valley through which the Saco Creek flowed, we piled together, beneath a big white oak where the Ford was left standing, our tent, duffel bags, cooking equipment, radio, fishing rods, and baskets, preparatory to taking a mile-and-a-half hike through thick, thorny underbrush to our camp site on the Creek where we were to fish for a long week end.

Although this sentence is talking about a lot of pleasant things of interest to everyone, the reader learns to hate it before it closes. It contains too many details. It rambles. It becomes a maze, a labyrinth, an endless passage in a nightmare. See how clear it becomes in the next example, where it is broken up into three sentences.

Through the cool dawn the wheezy old Ford gasped its way up the dirt road of Mohawk Mound and then, with clanks and jolts, tottered down the other side into the valley where flowed the Saco Creek. Beneath a big white oak, under which the Ford was left standing, we piled together our tent, duffel bags, cooking equipment, radio, fishing rods, and baskets. Our camp site on the Creek, where we were to spend a long week end fishing, was a mile and a half away through thick, thorny underbrush.

M9 Do not write tag-at-the-end sentences.

Summer is the time when the outdoors is most inviting, at least in good weather.	Just when the reader thinks he has the thought clear, the sentence reverses itself a little and confuses him. Give him the *at least* phrase early, where he expects it.

Summer—at least in good weather—is the time when the outdoors is most inviting.

M10 Save the independent clause of a sentence for the main idea; and do not put two ideas into two independent clauses unless the ideas are of equal or very nearly equal importance.

I entered the room, and Forhan was still sitting and staring at nothing.	Suppose that what Forhan was doing is the one main idea. Turn the first independent clause into something subordinate; say, a dependent modifying clause. That will make the sitting and staring at nothing stand out clearly.

When I entered the room, Forhan was still sitting and staring at nothing.

You are not permitted to kill a woman who has wronged you, but nothing forbids you to reflect that she is growing older every minute.[2]	In this sentence the writer wants to set forth two main ideas for the sake of humor: you may not kill a woman physically, but you may torture her mentally. He does well to put these two ideas into two independent clauses.

[2] *The Collected Works of Ambrose Bierce* (New York: Neale Publishing Company, 1911), Vol. 8, p. 379.

Unity in the paragraph

M11 The topic thought of a paragraph is the one clear, rather brief thought that answers the question *What is the paragraph about?*

Write your name and address in the upper right-hand corner of the page. In the center of the first line, write the title of your story. Skip two line-spaces and then indent for the first paragraph. Leave margins of an inch and a half at the sides and the bottom of the page. Do not let words wander into the margins.

The topic thought of the paragraph: *Here is the style your paper must follow.*

M12 Put one, and only one, topic thought into each paragraph.

It was Miss Murdstone who was arrived, and a gloomy-looking lady she was; dark, like her brother, whom she greatly resembled in face and voice, and with very heavy eyebrows, nearly meeting over her large nose . . . She brought with her two uncompromising hard black boxes, with her initials on the lids in hard brass nails. When she paid the coachman she took her money out of a hard steel purse, and she kept the purse in a very gaol of a bag which hung upon her arm by a heavy chain and shut up like a bite. I had never, at that time, seen such a metallic lady altogether as Miss Murdstone was. Murdstone—I thought this an odd name, one that sounded dark and forbidding. It was not a familiar English name, and I have never heard it since. It filled me with fear and made me, beforehand, uneasy about meeting its bearer.

As it is given here, this paragraph has two topic thoughts: (1) *Miss Murdstone was an unpleasant-appearing woman.* (2) *Murdstone was an unpleasant name.* When a paragraph is given to each topic thought, as in the presentation of the passage on the next page, each paragraph gains in unity of impression.

It was Miss Murdstone who was arrived, and a gloomy-looking lady she was; dark, like her brother, whom she greatly resembled in face and voice, and with very heavy eyebrows, nearly meeting over her large nose . . . She brought with her two uncompromising hard black boxes, with her initials on the lids in hard brass nails. When she paid the coachman she took her money out of a hard steel purse, and she kept the purse in a very gaol of a bag which hung upon her arm by a heavy chain and shut up like a bite. I had never, at that time, seen such a metallic lady altogether as Miss Murdstone was.[3]

Murdstone—I thought this an odd name, one that sounded dark and forbidding. It was not a familiar English name, and I have never heard it since. It filled me with fear and made me, beforehand, uneasy about meeting its bearer.

M13 Make each sentence of a paragraph develop the topic thought either directly or indirectly.

Mr. Claudius had a very elaborate funeral. There were great banks of flowers. I myself have never cared much for flowers at a funeral. At funerals they seem to raise a cloying sweetness that infects the good clean air. There were a great many mourners, enough to fill the great church. The music was of the finest, for the uncertain singers of the parish had made way for surer, grander voices hired for the occasion. The cortege was piloted to the cemetery by a whole platoon of motorcycle policemen. It all seemed singularly inappropriate to the character of Mr. Claudius, who had tried so hard all his life for the direct love and simplicity of Christ, only to have pomp thrust upon him at the very end.

This is not a good paragraph. The topic thought, not fully expressed in any one sentence, is: *Mr. Claudius's grand funeral did not fit him.* But the third and fourth sentences do not develop this topic thought either directly or indirectly. They should be put into another paragraph, if they are worth keeping, or dropped entirely. At the very least they should be put in parentheses— but only if they are very much worth keeping—to show that they interrupt the progress of the paragraph and are an aside, a digression.

---

[3] Charles Dickens, *The Personal History of David Copperfield* (Chicago: Weeks Publishing Company, no date), p. 56.

M14 If the paragraph does not become unwieldy or cluttered, put into it all the ideas that develop one topic thought.

My first glimpse of Europe was the shore of Spain.

The false stop after each paragraph here makes the reader think that the writer has done with the topic thought. He is consequently thrown off to find the writer taking it up again and again. The treatment in the passage below is much clearer.

Since we got into the Mediterranean, we have been becalmed for some days within easy view of it. All along are fine mountains, brown all day, and with a bloom on them at sunset like that of a ripe plum.

Here and there at their feet little white towns are sprinkled along the edge of the water, like the grains of rice dropped by the princess in the story. Sometimes we see larger buildings on the mountain slopes, probably convents.

I sit and wonder whether the farther peaks may not be the Sierra Morena (the rusty saw) of Don Quixote. I resolve that they shall be, and am content. Surely latitude and longitude never showed me any particular respect, that I should be over-scrupulous with them.

My first glimpse of Europe was the shore of Spain. Since we got into the Mediterranean, we have been becalmed for some days within easy view of it. All along are fine mountains, brown all day, and with a bloom on them at sunset like that of a ripe plum. Here and there at their feet little white towns are sprinkled along the edge of the water, like the grains of rice dropped by the princess in the story. Sometimes we see larger buildings on the mountain slopes, probably convents. I sit and wonder whether the farther peaks may not be the Sierra Morena (the rusty saw) of Don Quixote. I resolve that they shall be, and am content. Surely latitude and longitude never showed me any particular respect, that I should be over-scrupulous with them.[4]

M15 A topic sentence is the topic thought of a paragraph expressed in one sentence of the paragraph itself. (The topic thought may use up the whole sentence or only part of it.)

---

[4] James Russell Lowell, "Leaves from My Journal in Italy and Elsewhere," in *Fireside Travels* (Boston: Houghton Mifflin Company, 1892), pp. 157-58.

He is a swarthy browned man of fifty, well-made and good-looking, with crisp dark hair, bright eyes, and a broad chest. His sinewy and powerful hands, as sunburnt as his face, have evidently been used to a pretty tough life. What is curious about him is that he sits forward on his chair as if he were, from long habit, allowing space for some dress or accoutrements that he has altogether laid aside. His step too is measured and heavy, and would go well with a weighty clash and jingle of spurs. He is close-shaved now, but his mouth is set as if his upper lip had been for years familiar with a great mustache; and his manner of occasionally laying the open palm of his broad brown hand upon it, is to the same effect. *Altogether, one might guess Mr. George to have been a trooper once upon a time.*[5]

M16 Ordinarily express the topic thought of a paragraph in a topic sentence—unless, that is, doing so would hurt the paragraph (for example, give away too soon the secret that is creating suspense in a story).

M17 Ordinarily put the topic sentence at the beginning of a paragraph; occasionally—for, say, suspense or variety—put it at the end.

From her father Queen Elizabeth inherited her frank and hearty address, her love of popularity and of free intercourse with the people, her dauntless courage and her amazing self-confidence. Her harsh, manlike voice, her impetuous will, her pride, her furious outbursts of anger came to her with her Tudor blood. She rated great nobles as if they were schoolboys; she met the insolence of Essex with a box on the ear; she would break now and then into the gravest deliberations to swear at her counselors like a fishwife. But she was at once the daughter of Henry

The topic sentence is: *But she was at once the daughter of Henry and of Anne Boleyn.* Buried as it is at left in the middle of the paragraph, it does not contribute much to clearness. At the beginning of the paragraph, as in Green's original treatment on the next page, it makes a sharper impression on the reader's mind.

---

[5] Charles Dickens, *Bleak House* (Chicago: Weeks Publishing Company, no date), p. 352.

and of Anne Boleyn. Strangely in contrast with the violent outlines of her Tudor temper stood the sensuous self-indulgent nature she derived from Anne Boleyn. Splendour and pleasure were with Elizabeth the very air she breathed. Her delight was to move in perpetual progresses from castle to castle through a series of gorgeous pageants, fanciful and extravagant as a caliph's dream. She loved gaiety and laughter and wit. A happy retort or a finished compliment never failed to win her favour.

Queen Elizabeth was at once the daughter of Henry and of Anne Boleyn. From her father she inherited her frank and hearty address, her love of popularity and of free intercourse with the people, her dauntless courage and her amazing self-confidence. Her harsh, manlike voice, her impetuous will, her pride, her furious outbursts of anger came to her with her Tudor blood. She rated great nobles as if they were schoolboys; she met the insolence of Essex with a box on the ear; she would break now and then into the gravest deliberations to swear at her counselors like a fishwife. But strangely in contrast with the violent outlines of her Tudor temper stood the sensuous self-indulgent nature she derived from Anne Boleyn. Splendour and pleasure were with Elizabeth the very air she breathed. Her delight was to move in perpetual progresses from castle to castle through a series of gorgeous pageants, fanciful and extravagant as a caliph's dream. She loved gaiety and laughter and wit. A happy retort or a finished compliment never failed to win her favour.[6]

When I reached the Franklin place and walked up the path to the porch, there was no one about. The door hung by one hinge, and loosed its hold of that when I touched it, crashing to the floor with a clatter that sounded awful after the sunny stillness of the farmstead. I entered the living-dining room. The long trestle table had been flung over on

Here the topic sentence, *It was obvious that the raiders had gotten to the Franklins' before me,* is placed last in the paragraph with good effect. It rounds off the ideas of the paragraph like a little summary, and a certain amount of suspense is generated by saving it till the end. This sort of thing happens oftener in narratives than in other writing.

---

[6] John Richard Green, *A Short History of the English People* (New York: American Book Company, 1916), p. 370. By permission.

its side. What little furniture there had been—the two long benches, the fragile whatnot with sea shells and such in the corner, the one or two chairs—had all been toppled or smashed. Glass from the broken windows littered the floor. It was obvious that the raiders had gotten to the Franklins' before me.

M18 Some paragraphs cannot be expected to have a topic sentence. That is true of technical, dialogue paragraphs.[7] It is true also of some narrative paragraphs where the topic sentence would often have to be something like *Here is what happened in the next ten minutes.*[8]

Unity in the theme

IN GENERAL

M19 The theme topic is the subject matter of the theme, the one clear, rather brief thought that answers the question *What is the theme about?*

M20 A good theme has one and only one theme topic.

M21 Make sure that the theme topic is itself unified. If it contains more than one idea, make sure either that they are very closely related or that there is only one main idea to which the others are subordinate.

[Faulty:] The skyscraper capitol of Louisiana is in Baton Rouge, and the Standard Oil Company has an enormous plant there.

There conceivably could be something that relates the capitol and the plant more closely than does the fact that they are both in the same city. But, as far as one can tell here, the theme would profit if one or the other idea were dropped entirely.

[Good:] The skyscraper capitol of Louisiana is in Baton Rouge.

[Good:] The Standard Oil Company has an enormous plant in Baton Rouge.

---

[7] See D95.
[8] See T21-29.

[Faulty:] Boys enjoy making pocket money in many ways, but baby sitting is certainly not one of them.

This could lead the writer to develop two distinct topics without relating them: (1) *Boys enjoy making pocket money in many ways.* (2) *Boys do not enjoy baby sitting.*

[Good:] Baby sitting is not one of the ways in which boys enjoy making pocket money.

This theme topic will lead the writer to develop only one thought.

[Faulty:] Dickens was a great writer, but he failed to make a success of his family life.

This theme topic may lead the writer to develop two topics rather fully, when either of the topics would be more than sufficient for any theme.

[Good:] Dickens, the famous writer, failed to make a success of his family life.

Phrased thus, the theme topic will lead the writer to give no more than passing mention to Dickens's fame and to concentrate on his family life.

M22 It often starts both reader and writer well to state the theme topic in a topic paragraph near the beginning of the theme.

Educators are sharply divided on whether every high-school graduate or only a very few should be permitted to go to college.

Some people think that any control imposed on the press is a violation of freedom of the press; others maintain that freedom, even freedom of the press, can only be had where some control is imposed.

Some political theorists say that even an interim dictatorship over countries occupied by America after a war vio-

It is very difficult for the reader to guess what central idea holds these paragraphs together. The first talks about education; the second, the press; the third, defeated countries; the fourth, minorities; the fifth, raising children. Yet there is one main thought in these varied paragraphs. The puzzlement would disappear if the theme began with this topic paragraph: *Americans today are troubled by this question: How much control is healthy for people?*

lates the spirit of the Declaration of Independence and of the Constitution; others say that such temporary undemocratic government is essential to the creation of true democracy later on.

When they are in power, some politicians call for the suppression of any group that happens to criticize their foreign policy, on the ground that such criticism gives aid and comfort to the enemy. Some pundits and jurists, however, maintain that even parties like the Communists should not be curbed, much less suppressed, lest the freedom of minorities to exist and to become majorities should suffer injury.

Some parents seem to feel that they infringe the rights of their children if they punish them for neglect or disobedience. Others act as if children should never, under any circumstances, be allowed even to discuss a decision made by their elders, but should obey without any question whatever [and so on].

M23 Make every sentence develop its paragraph topic; make every paragraph develop the theme topic.[9]

M24 It is not always possible and it is never necessary that every paragraph develop the theme topic *directly*. Paragraph A, for example, may develop the theme topic, and paragraphs B and C may develop paragraph A. But do not carry such indirect development to the point where the reader loses the trail.

DIGRESSIONS

M25 In long and leisurely themes, it is all right to indulge in an occasional digression, provided that—

A There is some good reason for the digression, such as an attempt to put the reader in the mood to accept what you have to say.

B The reader is told in one way or another just when you leave the theme and when you come back to it.

c The digressions are relatively few and brief. (One digression of a sentence or so is about the maximum for a three- to five-hundred-word theme.)

---

[9] See M24.

INTRODUCTIONS

M26 Make sure that your introduction is closely connected with the rest of the theme and naturally leads into it.

> Thank you, John Edlegurt, for "them kind words."
>
> Ladies and gentlemen, I'm supposed to speak to you tonight on family allowances to supplement the living wage. Well, that reminds me. There was an old muskrat trapper (ha-ha) living along Bayou Bourboux down in old Louisiana who decided to "hire him a helper." Well, the helper

This introduction is very poor. It is connected with a theme on family allowances only in word and not in thought. Moreover, it is artificially introduced—does not grow out of the theme itself or out of the speaker's situation or any of the things naturally connected with the theme.

was a boy with "nimble fingers." Pretty soon the old trapper noticed that some of his pelts were disappearing, and it didn't take him long to make the obvious connection. When the boy came at the end of the month to collect his money, the trapper handed him about a tenth of what they had agreed upon. "Why," says the boy, "that ain't a livin' wage. The pope says you're supposed to pay me a livin' wage."

"Yeah?" answers the trapper. "You look in the Bible, son, and see what it says *there* about the wages of *sin!*"

> I think you all know my record—how little I have done to make this school and this class what they could be, and how much I have done to harm both. For example, you

This is a good introduction, closely and naturally connected with the rest of the theme.

remember, I imagine, the time I broke up the rally before the Winston game, just to get a little attention from the crowd. Well, I've been doing some thinking—go on; laugh—and I've decided to change my tune. I think you'll take some plain talk from me, since you know that I am talking to myself just as much as to you.

We have the worst spirit in the school. I have given this class a lot of thought, and I think I can tell you what is wrong with us and what we can do about it.

M27 Ordinarily an introduction will tend to be closely connected with the rest of the theme and to lead into it
naturally if it answers all or some of these questions:[10]

    A What (and who) is going to be talked about? (This
is answered when the theme topic is included in the
introduction or is itself used as the introduction.)

    B Why is it going to be talked about?

    C Who is going to talk about it?

    D What is he going to say about it?

    E Why is he saying it to this particular audience or at
this particular time, and so on?

    F How is he going to talk about it? What divisions of the
subject is he going to make, what is he going to include or exclude, and so on?

N Coherence

In general

N1 Coherence is the principle of composition that requires
that, for the sake of clarity, words and ideas follow one
another in an orderly manner and that the connections
between parts be made clear.

N2 If there is a reasonable chance that the relationship between words and ideas may be mistaken, the sentence,
paragraph, or theme is incoherent.

N3 Clearness in writing is largely a matter of unity, coherence, and emphasis.[1] It is necessary, of course, that the
writer's ideas be clear to begin with. But unity, coher-

---

[10] When it is a case of writing an atmospheric introduction to a story, a
suspense-creating advertisement, or something of the kind, these questions—with
the possible exception of the first—will not prove very helpful. But in the general
run of informational and argumentative papers, they may help you to write an
introduction that is organically connected with the theme. Use them where they
help you and neglect them where they hinder you; but never fail to keep the
general rule of introductions, M26.

[1] For unity see M1-27. For emphasis see O1-43.

ence, and emphasis go far to make sure that these ideas will also become clear to the reader.

N4 What unifies a composition often also makes it coherent and lends it proper emphasis—and vice versa. Hence there is a certain amount of overlapping in fact and in rule.

Coherence in the sentence

N5 Coherence in the sentence means that the parts of a sentence—words, phrases, and clauses—are rightly put together.

N6 The principal enemies of coherence in the sentence are misplaced, squinting, and dangling modifiers; unparallel structure for parallel ideas; faulty connectives and connections; and illogical expressions.

MODIFIERS

N7 Place modifying words, phrases, and clauses as near as you reasonably can to the words that they modify; and do not use dangling or squinting modifiers.[2]

PARALLEL STRUCTURES

N8 Where you can do so without forcing or awkwardness, express like ideas in like words and like constructions.

	Here are like ideas, but they are expressed in unlike words:
Just as Suarez High School is distinguished for its dramatics, so the students of Aquinas High School have become prominent in debating.	Suarez High School the students of Aquinas High School
	is distinguished for its dramatics have become prominent in debating

---

[2] See C323-31.

	Parallel ideas are given parallel expression:
Just as Suarez High School is distinguished for dramatics, so Aquinas High School is prominent in debating.	⎰ Suarez High School ⎱ Aquinas High School ⎰ is distinguished for dramatics ⎱ is prominent in debating
Just as the students of Suarez High School have become distinguished for dramatics, so the students of Aquinas High School have become prominent in debating.	⎰ the students . . . School ⎱ the students . . . School ⎰ have become distinguished ⎪ for dramatics ⎪ have become prominent in ⎱ debating

N9 Keep sentence parts parallel when they are joined by *and, or, nor, but,* and other co-ordinating conjunctions.

He was notified that he was drafted by the Army and to report for duty.	This sentence is incoherent. For no reason *and* is made to connect a dependent clause with an infinitive phrase. See how much cleaner an impression the sentence makes below, where *and* connects two dependent noun clauses.

He was notified that he was drafted by the Army and that he should report for duty.

Tommy rode not only through the city but also rode over the little rustic bridge.	This sentence is incoherent. *Not only . . . but also* is made to connect *through the city* and *rode*—a phrase and a predicate verb that are unlike not only in construction but also in thought. The sentence is less muddy below, where the conjunction connects two phrases and ideas that are somewhat alike.

Tommy rode not only through the city but also over the little rustic bridge.

For Denis, who had to regain his inn without attracting notice, there was real danger as well as merely feeling uncomfortable in the walk; and he went warily and with boldness at once, and at every corner pausing to make an observation.

This sentence is incoherent and, as a result, somewhat muddy. *As well as* connects the noun *danger* with the gerund phrase *feeling uncomfortable.* It is all right to connect a noun with a noun phrase when there is no noun ready to hand that will carry the thought. But here there is a noun ready to hand, and the reader is vaguely aware of the fact. Again, *and* is made to connect the adverb *warily* with the prepositional phrase *with boldness.* It is not a blunder to connect an adverb with an adverb phrase; but see how the sentence gains in sharp clarity below where two adverbs are used. Lastly, *and* is made to connect the predicate verb *went* with the participle *pausing;* and that is an out-and-out blunder that makes the sentence unpleasant and, to some degree, confusing. Below, *and* connects *went* and *paused;* and the sentence is pleasant and clear.

For Denis, who had to regain his inn without attracting notice, there was real danger as well as mere discomfort in the walk; and he went warily and boldly at once, and at every corner paused to make an observation.[3]

N10 Do not use *and, or, nor, but,* and other co-ordinating conjunctions between sentence parts that are not parallel in thought.

---

[3] Robert Louis Stevenson, "The Sire de Malétroit's Door," in *New Arabian Nights* (New York: Charles Scribner's Sons, 1895), p. 319.

I was punished for breaking silence and a cup.

True, *silence* and *cup* are both nouns. But the meaning of *break silence* and the meaning of *break a cup* are so divergent that they should not be connected as they are here. The sentence had better be rephrased as below.

I was punished for talking at the wrong time and for breaking a cup.

A man, tall and with a key, came up the stairs and let us in.

Tall is an adjective and *with a key* is an adjective phrase, but their meaning is so divergent that they should not be connected as they are here. The sentence had better be rephrased as below.

A tall man came up the stairs and let us in with his key.

Between the silver ribbon of morning and the green glittering ribbon of sea, the boat touched Harwich and let loose a swarm of folk like flies, among whom the man we must follow and who wore a beard was by no means conspicuous—nor wished to be.

[Whom] we must follow and *who wore a beard* are both adjective clauses, but their meaning is so divergent that they should not be connected as they are here. The connection is not natural. *Bearded man we must follow* would solve the difficulty nicely; or the beard could be saved for another sentence, as below.

Between the silver ribbon of morning and the green glittering ribbon of sea, the boat touched Harwich and let loose a swarm of folk like flies, among whom the man we must follow was by no means conspicuous—nor wished to be. . . . His lean face was dark . . . and ended in a curt, black beard that looked Spanish and suggested an Elizabethan ruff.[4]

---

[4] "The Blue Cross," p. 1. Reprinted by permission of Dodd, Mead and Company, from *The Innocence of Father Brown* by G. K. Chesterton. Copyright 1911 by Dodd, Mead and Company.

N11 Do not shift the idea in the subject needlessly.

Bravely the little boy spoke to the maid; but, instead of getting a reply, she slammed the door in his face.	The idea in the first subject is the boy; in the second it is the maid *(she)*. The sentence can be made to read much more smoothly (and, incidentally, the dangling phrase can be avoided) if the idea in the subjects is kept the same.

Bravely the little boy spoke to the maid; but, instead of getting a reply, he saw the door slammed in his face.

He was the sort of man whom anybody could lead on a string to the North Pole; it was not surprising that an actor like Flambeau, dressed as another priest, could lead him to Hampstead Heath.[5]	Here the idea in the subject changes frequently, but with good enough cause. Very awkward constructions and weak passives would result if the subject stayed the same. The sentence is coherent, clear.

N12 Do not shift voice needlessly.

Killian brought us food and medicines; but, best of all, we were given news of the rescue sleds by him.	The change to passive voice *(were given)* is scarcely necessary or helpful; and the sentence reads very much more smoothly (much more coherently) below, where the active voice is used and the idea of the first subject is retained in both clauses of the sentence.

Killian brought us food and medicines; but, best of all, he gave us news of the rescue sleds.

N13 Do not shift person or number needlessly.

Well, I like history because people interest me; and certainly history provides you with people of all types and classes.	The shift from *I* and *me* to *you* is unnecessary, troublesome, and incoherent. The sentence is a good deal smoother and clearer on the next page.

---

[5] *Ibid.*, p. 22. By permission of Dodd, Mead and Company.

[Good:] Well, I like history because people interest me; and certainly history provides me with people of all types and classes.

[Even better:] Well, I like history because I like to analyze people; and in history I certainly find people of all types and classes.

One went in, not as into most shops, in the mood of: "Please serve me, and let me go!" but restfully, as you enter a church; and, sitting on the single wooden chair, waited— for there was never anybody there.

You distracts. The sentence is more coherent below.

One went in, not as into most shops, in the mood of: "Please serve me, and let me go!" but restfully, as one enters a church; and, sitting on the single wooden chair, waited—for there was never anybody there.[6]

N14 Do not shift present and past time needlessly.

When at last I find him, Vladinov is very happy to see me, assures me that he can get papers for me and can smuggle me across the border without attracting notice, but wanted more money than he had already been paid.

The writer is using the "vivid present," which is quite all right—a good device if not overworked. But the shift to the past in *wanted* is unnecessary, jarring, distracting—incoherent. Say *wants more money than he has . . .*

He caught hold of a springy young sapling and to it he fastens his hunting knife, with the blade pointing down the trail; with a bit of wild grapevine he tied back the sapling.

The shift to the present in *fastens* is needless and distracting. Richard Connell's sentence, below, is very much better.

He caught hold of a springy young sapling and to it he fastened his hunting knife, with the blade pointing down the trail; with a bit of wild grapevine he tied back the sapling.[7]

---

[6] John Galsworthy, "Quality," in *The Inn of Tranquillity* (New York: Charles Scribner's Sons, 1914), p. 16. By permission.

[7] Richard Connell, "The Most Dangerous Game," in *The Golden Book*, Vol. 12, October, 1930, p. 49. Copyright 1924 by Richard Connell. By permission.

CONNECTIVES AND CONNECTIONS

N15 Use connectives that express your meaning precisely.

Andrew is slow, and he leads his class.	*And* hardly expresses the writer's idea plainly; and so there is a chance that the reader may be puzzled or annoyed.
Andrew is slow, but he leads his class.	*But* makes good sense and rules out misunderstanding.
Andrew is slow, and yet he leads his class.	*And yet* makes good sense and rules out misunderstanding.
I always felt a deep sympathy for the students, though I knew only their names; yet none of them was without trials and humiliations.	A faulty connective, *yet*, makes nonsense of an otherwise sensible sentence.
I always felt a deep sympathy for the students, though I knew only their names; for none of them was without trials and humiliations.	*For* makes the last clause the reason for the sympathy and pulls the meaning of the sentence together—makes the sentence coherent.
On the brown face of Velvet Pants there was not the slightest trace of fear, as he was smiling a slight, amused smile.	The meaning of *as* is muddy. Does it mean *while?* Does it perhaps mean *because?* As a matter of fact, neither *while* nor *because* makes perfect sense here. There is a much clearer sentence below.

On the brown face of Velvet Pants there was not the slightest trace of fear: indeed, he was smiling a slight, amused smile.[8]

N16 Occasionally *and* can be used without obscurity in the sense of *and yet* or *but*. For example, if a father said to his son, "I never heard of anyone your age camping out alone," the son might reply with perfect clarity, "Joe

---

[8] Richard Connell, "The Unfamiliar," in *The Century*, Vol. 106, September, 1923, p. 74. Copyright 1923 by Richard Connell. By permission.

Bergen is only twelve, and he camps out alone." Ordinarily, however, *and* is not an adequate substitute for *and yet* or *but*.

N17 Do not omit a word that is important to the clear and easy expression of your thought.[9]

They sell crabs at the Fulton Fish Market.	In this sentence *they* does not mean "people in general." It should be either given an antecedent, replaced by a noun, or eliminated altogether as in the construction below.

Crabs are sold at the Fulton Fish Market.

Hurried radio calls were sent out to all state policemen to stop the maroon convertible, but they were too late.	Which were too late, the calls or the policemen? *They* does not say which. The point is of no great consequence in this sentence; yet such little obscurities mark the incoherent—and unread—writer.

Hurried radio calls were sent out to all state policemen to stop the maroon convertible, but the calls were too late.

The elder Legruy seemed eager to get rid but not to pay for my services.	The sense is clear; but an important word has been annoyingly omitted.

The elder Legruy seemed eager to get rid of my services but not to pay for them.

My friend Mrs. Lummy has more fascinating ailments, like rushes of blood to the elbow, than anybody I know.	The sentence is absurd. Since Mrs. Lummy is "my friend," I must know her; yet the sentence says that I do not, since she has more ailments than "anybody I know."

My friend Mrs. Lummy has more fascinating ailments, like rushes of blood to the elbow, than anybody else I know.

---

[9] See C236-40, C271, C297-98, C300-301, C305, C307, C310, and C334-35.

N18 Phrase your sentences thoughtfully and logically so that they make sense and can have only one meaning.

Make yourself comfortable until half-past ten, when the moderator will begin his talk.	Grammatically this sentence is quite all right; nonetheless it is incoherent, thoughtlessly phrased. For it may mean simply that one should wait until the speech begins, or it may imply that once the speech begins all comfort will be at an end. As phrased below, the sentence does not insult the moderator.

Since the moderator's talk does not begin until half-past ten, you may as well make yourself comfortable during the wait.

The fireplace, which had not yet been lighted, made the room seem colder.	The fact that the fireplace held no fire is pushed into a subordinate nonrestrictive clause. This focuses attention on the independent clause—*the fireplace made the room seem colder*. That idea seems illogical. The sentence below would not puzzle the reader even for a moment.

The cold, black, fireless hearth only made the room seem colder.

The garret windows were opened, and pails were emptied, and there goes a new suit of clothes!	The writer of this became so carried away that he omitted a step or two from his narrative—a step or two that the reader would like to have; namely, that the clothes are on a man in the street below. In the sentence on the next page, Macaulay writes a more coherent, if less lively, sentence.

The garret windows were opened, and pails were emptied, with little regard to those who were passing below.[10]

Coherence in the paragraph

N19 Coherence in the paragraph means that the sentences of the paragraph are rightly put together and properly connected.

N20 When you are moving from sentence to sentence, keep the same voice, person, number, and time, and the same subject, unless the thought requires a change.[11]

N21 Establish clear connections where they are needed between sentences; and make sure that connectives are used with precision.

The rifle seemed to be in good condition. The bore was pitted with rust.

One could speak these two sentences and, by bearing down heavily on *seemed*, make the meaning of the paragraph clear. But when one puts them in writing, something is needed to bridge the gap between them. The two versions of the sentence given below will be clearer to readers.

At first the rifle seemed to be in good condition. However, the bore was pitted with rust.

At first alerts the reader for the change of thought in the second sentence; then *however* makes certain that he will not miss it.

At first glance the rifle seemed to be in good condition. On closer inspection its bore proved to be pitted with rust.

This is even clearer. *At first glance* and *on closer inspection* make the relationship of the two sentences altogether unmistakable.

---

[10] Thomas Babington Macaulay, *History of England from the Accession of James II* (Philadelphia: Porter and Coates, no date), Vol. 1, p. 281.
[11] See C145 and N11-14.

The pilgrims wound their way up the mountainside slowly, chanting the rosary and singing hymns. The way was long and the incline steep, but all of them kept up the steady pace and prayed and sang as though they had breath and to spare. In the meantime, the elderly bishop strode firmly along, carrying the heavy monstrance.

The writer does well to put a connective phrase at the beginning of the last sentence. One is needed, since there is a shift from the main body of the procession to the bishop at its end. But *in the meantime* does not express the relationship so precisely as the connective below. The bishop could be in another part of the state.

The pilgrims wound their way up the mountainside slowly, chanting the rosary and singing hymns. The way was long and the incline steep, but all of them kept up the steady pace and prayed and sang as though they had breath and to spare. At the end of the procession, the elderly bishop strode firmly along, carrying the heavy monstrance.

Hepner and Wolfram thrust aside the two retainers who guarded the door, strode into the center of the hall, and, standing back to back between the two rows of tables, smilingly faced the chieftains and lords, who had half risen from the benches and half stretched tentative fingers toward swords and knives. Then casually, quietly, he said, "My comrade and I will lop the first hand that touches a hilt."

The paragraph reads clearly enough until the fourth word *(he)* of the second sentence. Then the reader would like to know whether Hepner or Wolfram is doing the talking.

Hepner and Wolfram thrust aside the two retainers who guarded the door, strode into the center of the hall, and, standing back to back between the two rows of tables, smilingly faced the chieftains and lords, who had half risen from the benches and half stretched tentative fingers toward swords and knives. Then casually, quietly, Hepner said, "My comrade and I will lop the first hand that touches a hilt."

N22 When you are relating a series of events, put first what happened first, put second what happened second, and so on.

Serra and Portolá were right in thinking that their countrymen were at hand. The approaching Indians brought them the good tidings that San Diego was but a two-days' journey even for Portolá's tired men and still more tired beasts. The next day they were met by ten soldiers whom the *comandante*, Rivera y Moncada, had sent to escort them to their destination. The colonization of California had begun. The Indians had said that both ships were in port, that the first land expedition had arrived long since, and that there were many friars on the spot. Cheered and heartened, the company pushed on over a country so broken and rock-strewn that Serra—always a truth-teller—feared his heart would stop beating from sheer fright. It was the next day that the ten soldiers mentioned above met them. Under their guidance they encamped for the last night on level ground by running water, and in the morning, July 1st, 1769, they reached a gentle eminence from which they could see the ships riding at anchor, and the Spanish flag flying in the breeze. Portolá's soldiers fired a salute which was answered joyously from land and sea. The sacred expedition of Galvez had entered the promised land.

The time sequence of the paragraph at left is badly scrambled. Do not be surprised that it sounds as if it makes sense and yet confuses badly. See how much clearer, more pleasant, more interesting it is in the paragraph next below, where the events follow the order of time.

[Serra and Portolá were right in thinking that their countrymen were at hand.] The approaching Indians brought them the good tidings that San Diego was but a two-days' journey even for Portolá's tired men and still more tired beasts. They said that both ships were in port, that the first land expedition had arrived long since, and that there were many friars on the spot. Cheered and heartened, the company pushed on over a country so broken and rock-strewn that Serra—always a truth-teller—feared his heart would stop beating from sheer fright. The next day they were met by ten soldiers whom the *comandante*, Rivera y Moncada, had sent to escort them to their destination. Under their guidance they encamped for the last night on level ground by running water, and in the morning, July 1st, 1769, they reached a gentle eminence from which they could see the ships riding at anchor, and the Spanish flag flying in the breeze. Portolá's soldiers fired a salute which was answered joyously from land and sea. The sacred expedition of Galvez had entered the promised land. The colonization of California had begun.[12]

N23 When you are treating a series of things that can be located, start at the bottom and go to the top, or start at the top and go to the bottom, or start at the right and go to the left, and so on; or start at one end and go to the other, and so on; that is, proceed in an orderly fashion.

One sock drooped about the heel of his left brogue; the other sock was not visible, having no doubt slipped under the arch of his foot and bunched there uncomfortably. His nose was a mere indication, a reminder of what a nose is ordinarily like. A great rip in the seat of his trousers caused him some understandable concern; and this rip he was at pains to hold together with his unoccupied right hand, with a pathetic pretense of not noticing what he was doing, in the hope that no one else would notice, either. The top of one shoe had torn away from the sole and now presented the parody of an open mouth disclosing a thick brown tongue—his grimy big toe. In his left arm he cradled a shaggy, dispirited, dry-

This paragraph is annoyingly disordered. It is clear enough, for the subject being described is not difficult; but the reader's mind is made to return over and over again to a part of the boy's body (or to the dog) which should have been finished with once and for all. The mind's eye is jerked from shoe to nose to trousers to shoe to dog to eyes to torso to dog to shoes to dog. If this sort of thing continued for any length of time, any reader would soon weary of the effort to follow the writer. In the reorganization given on the next page, the writer selects a natural, coherent order (he might have used any one of several) and proceeds from bottom to top without any annoying and confusing twists, turns, and returns.

---

[12] From *Junípero Serra*, by Agnes Repplier, pp. 67-68. Copyright 1931 by Agnes Repplier. Reprinted by permission of Doubleday and Company.

nosed, small dog—of a black that was partly brown and a white that was gray. His eyes were the eyes of a boy twelve years old, which is to say that they were beautiful—as yet unglazed by the hardness and the fixity that comes with looking out always for the main chance. He wore no shirt despite the bite of the air, and so his cramped rib cage showed sickly white along the bones and sickly blue in the little hollows between them. Occasionally the dog would squirm and attempt to lick his face. There were no strings in his shoes. One of the dog's hind legs was splinted and bandaged, and that rather expertly.

The top of one stringless shoe had torn away from the sole and now presented the parody of an open mouth disclosing a thick brown tongue—the boy's grimy big toe. One sock drooped about the heel of his left brogue; the other sock was not visible, having no doubt slipped under the arch of his foot and bunched there uncomfortably. A great rip in the seat of his trousers caused him some understandable concern; and this rip he was at pains to hold together with his unoccupied right hand, with a pathetic pretense of not noticing what he was doing, in the hope that no one else would notice, either. In his left arm he cradled a shaggy, dispirited, dry-nosed, small dog—of a black that was partly brown and a white that was gray. One of the dog's hind legs was splinted and band-aged, and that rather expertly. Occasionally the dog would squirm and attempt to lick the boy's face. The boy wore no shirt despite the bite of the air, and so his cramped rib cage showed sickly white along the bones and sickly blue in the little hollows between them. His nose was a mere indication, a reminder of what a nose is ordinarily like. His eyes were the eyes of a boy twelve years old, which is to say that they were beautiful—as yet unglazed by the hardness and the fixity that comes with looking out always for the main chance.

The sand-hills here run down to the sea, and end in two spits of rock jutting out opposite each other, till you lose sight of them in the water. One is called the North Spit and one the South. Between the two, shifting backward and forward at certain seasons	Collins, the author of this passage, follows an easy order of place. He takes the reader's eye out along two parallel hills that can both be seen at once, to the quicksand between them, and out to the barrier that hems in the sand and walls out the sea.

of the year, lies the most horrible quicksand on the shores of York-
shire. At the turn of the tide something goes on in the unknown
deeps below, which sets the whole face of the quicksand quivering
and trembling in a manner most remarkable to see, and which
has given to it, among the people in our parts, the name of the
Shivering Sand. A great bank, half a mile out, nigh the mouth of
the bay, breaks the force of the main ocean coming in from the
offing. Winter and summer, when the tide flows over the quicksand, the sea seems to leave the waves behind it on the bank, and
rolls its waters in smoothly with a heave, and covers the sand in
silence. A lonesome and horrid retreat I can tell you! No boat ven-
tures into this bay. No children from our fishing-village, called
Cobb's Hole, ever come here to play. The very birds of the air,
as it seems to me, give the Shivering Sand a wide berth.[13]

N24   In a paragraph in which neither events nor localized
things are discussed, it is impossible to use the order of
time or place.[14] In such a paragraph it is good to use the
order of interest or importance.[15]

N25   After the topic sentence, if there is one, begin with the
least interesting or important idea, go on to a more interesting or important idea, and so on, and end with the
most interesting or important idea.

Many a man feels that his mother, the Church, is a slightly disreputable old lady, a little shabby, a little down at heel, a little foreign to the American notion that the best things in life are always bright and neat, like television sets. He feels that it would smarten the old lady considerably in America's non-Catholic eyes to concentrate on essentials and get rid of some hard-to-

The topic thought of the paragraph at left is: *It is a mistake to regret those parts of Catholic doctrine and practice that seem a little un-American.* The writer has no series of events to put before the reader; so he cannot use the order of time. He has no series of items that can be located in space for the reader; so he cannot use the order of place. He does have a number of

---

[13] Wilkie Collins, *The Moonstone* (New York: The Modern Library, 1937),
p. 24.
[14] For the order of time, see N22. For the order of place, see N23.
[15] See N25.

explain odds and ends like candles, indulgences, and the chanting of Masses by priests who could not sing well if their supper depended on it. Real abuses aside, I think that a Catholic in that frame of mind is in the wrong frame of mind. In the first place, it would never be possible to re-arrange the Church to suit every non-Catholic taste. Even Protestant churches find it im-possible—and no one could ac-cuse them of not trying. Again —and this is a more urgent point—as far as candles, indul-gences, private revelations, and so on, are concerned, we cannot blink the fact that things such as these are either directly given or at least al-lowed us by Christ for our comfort and help. It is a little ungrateful, to say the least, to hide the gifts one's lover has given, because some people do not think them very good. One need not flaunt them if he does not care to; but he should hardly hide them.

reasons for his stand to put be-fore the reader, and he quite properly elects to give them the order of interest or im-portance. He gives the least important first: it would be difficult if not impossible to adapt the Church to non-Catholic tastes. Then he gives a more important reason: it would be ungrateful to Christ to hide His good gifts. Then he gives his most important reason: it would be misleading to present the Church to non-Catholics as pleasant and neat, when Catholicism really is a terrible revolutionary force with little time for niceties. The mind of the reader re-ceives a clear impression from this order. There is a progres-sion, and a progression with a sense-making pattern. The human mind likes steps—and steps that go up or down, not steps that go up and down and up.

But perhaps the most important point is this: It would not prove wise in the long run to try to attract non-Catholics by neatness or any other minor come-on. Catholicism is a terrible religion that reaches down into the roots of a man and says, Take and drink, for the chalice is good and full of joy though often bitter to the first taste. If a non-Catholic looks to the Church for anything less than truth, power, joy, and life, he will be shocked as he comes to know her better. For Catholicism is not always pleasant; and it has little time for respectability, since it is a life and not a social manner. As Eric Gill says, God is not nice; and neither is the Cath-olic Church.

N26 When you are in control of the order, as in a fictional story, you can frequently make two or more of the orders of time, of place, and of importance or interest coincide, with consequent gain in clarity and interest.[16]

The new foreman of the road gang, Black Scott, was a stupid and cruel man. As the weeks of June passed, the road gang, fed to the teeth with his tyrannical way and vile tongue, grew lazier and lazier: the men loitered long at the water barrel, spent half hours cleaning their shovels and picks, continually rested what they claimed were strained backs and blistered hands, and often spent the day lying "sick" in their bunks. At mealtime, when Black Scott was with them, they said nothing, only asking for food in a mutter or with a sneer. After meals and at night, they gathered in little groups and cursed the food, the job, the weather—and especially Black Scott and his cruel, domineering ways. Thus passed June and July, the men simmering in a surly rage; and by the end of August hatred had rotted their hearts and evil taken full possession of their minds. Black Scott was in danger of his life.

N27 Most of the time it is quite justifiable to subordinate the order of time or the order of place to the order of interest or importance[16] in those paragraphs where the various orders are combined. But do not use an order or combination of orders that is not clear.[17]

Coherence in the theme

N28 Coherence in the theme means that the words, sentences, paragraphs, chapters, and parts of the theme are rightly put together and properly connected.[18]

N29 Arrange the main and subordinate parts of a theme in one of the following or similar orders:

A *The order of time.* First tell what happened first; second, tell what happened after that; third, tell what

---

[16] For the order of time, see N22. For the order of place, see N23. For the order of interest or importance, see N25.

[17] The treatment given in the preceding numbers considers some of the obvious orders of presentation. But any order may be used that will be clear and easy.

[18] See also narration, T13-15 and T39-41.

happened after that; and so on. (This order is particularly useful in narratives.)[19]

From the time that he left Alva, Wyck's progress was much more rapid than he had expected it to be. For once, reconnaissance had been wrong in the right way; the roads turned out to be in much better condition than reports had indicated. Moreover, the motorized units proceeded without the mechanical breakdowns so usual that commanding officers come to consider them inevitable—breakdowns that can snarl traffic for hours on narrow byways.

At 3:00 P.M., however, Wyck did run into trouble. A small party of Fascists fighting for the Germans—less than fifty—held up the advance for a little less than an hour with four machine guns, two of which swept the road where it passed through a narrow defile. They were finally cleared out without the loss of one American or allied soldier; and Wyck proceeded on his way, still well ahead of schedule.

The roads continued good; and so Wyck arrived at the southwestern approach to Templi well before his time, deployed his forces, and entered battle at precisely 8:00 A.M. the next day.

Within an hour it was apparent that he was meeting the full resistance of Templi. No one was creating a diversion at the eastern end of the little town. Hard pressed for a decision, Wyck fanned his men out in a quarter circle in the southwest and did what he could with what he had [and so on].

B *The order of place.* Start at the bottom and go to the top, or start at the top and go to the bottom, or start at the right and go to the left, and so on; or start at one end and go to the other, and so on. (This order is particularly useful in descriptions.)[20]

I was told to look for Mr. Forous on Salinas Street.

Salinas Street is a long, dirty, festering wound running through the south flank of Claymore from the river to the open prairie west of town.

At the river end it presents a pair of saloons, like gatehouses, on either side of the street. Dives they are, and look it; but they are the soundest edifices on the whole street and do not prepare one for the incredible squalor beyond.

---

[19] See T1-2.
[20] See S1.

After the saloons come two rows of hovels, gaping slack-jawed at each other across the wide, pitted, trash-strewn thoroughfare. "Hovels" has too grand a sound to describe the unbelievable jungle of drunken, staggering, slouching structures thrown together with wire, packing cases, sections of rusted metal culvert, cardboard, and old license plates nailed to overlap in pathetic parody of shingles and clapboard. These are the homes of the "Salinas Street Slush-Eaters," as the rest of Claymore cynically calls them—these foul and rickety nightmares that do not shelter the inmates from so much as a curious glance.

After several hundred yards of these, on the north side of the street there is a little clearing in the center of which rises—but not very high—Father Andreas's church: a shed, roofed with tin, open on three sides, and floored with dirt except for the platform under the "sanctuary" [and so on].

c *The order of interest or importance.* Start with the least important or interesting thought and move by degrees to the most interesting or important.

As a matter of fact, it was rather a full day. I spent several hours getting the dummy for the *Colombière Clarion* ready for the printer and another forty minutes working out that silly exercise in emphasis for English class tomorrow.

I spent another three hours doing something rather interesting: watching the men at D'Astignac Studios painting a backdrop for the school's production of *Everyman.* I found it amazing that they could work so quickly. Watching them slap paint on—mostly with ten-inch brushes—you would imagine that the result was going to look like something my manic-depressive little sister thinks up out of her water-color kit. On the contrary, they achieved a perfect copy of Laury's design and got it on a canvas twenty by forty feet in less than three hours.

But the thing that will make it a day to remember was something that happened down at the printer's. I was helping Mr. Shelton lay out our copy according to the dummy, when a rather fat, bald, tired-looking man came out of the office and walked over to the shop table where we were working. When he picked up a sheaf of *Clarion* copy and started reading through it, I felt rather annoyed that he hadn't asked anybody's permission. But I didn't say anything. He took advantage of a pause in the discussion I was having with Shelton to ask very curtly, "Who wrote this thing on the prize debates at Colombière?"

"I did," I said without looking up.

"You, eh?"

"Uh-huh."

"Well, son, when you finish high school and college, if you're still fool enough to like newspaper work, come down and get a job from me."

"Yes?" I said; "and who are you, mister?"

"Priestly," he answered; "R. C. Priestly, city editor, Wichita *Herald*. Darned good paper, and an excellent city editor."

D *The logical order.* Follow a series of causes and effects, circumstances and results, and so on.

It must not be understood that Joe was more of a coward than most boys. He could take a reasonable amount of physical punishment with a reasonable amount of suppressed whimpering. Joe's difficulty was pride.

Until the time that he was ten, he had lived in a rural area where he got his schooling at home and had the companionship of only two or three boys. He had learned to hunt, but not to shoot baskets. He had learned to plow a field, but not to field a ball. At the age of ten he came to live in the city and found that he was an ignoramus in all the sciences at which city boys excel. He could have learned them even then, but he was too proud. Pride kept him from courting the laughs and jeers that greet the late beginner. He pretended that he did not care for sports and spent his time watching the others and joining them only in those diversions at which they were no less green than he.

He had a glib and entertaining tongue; he was generous enough not only with possessions but with praise; and so he never lacked companions, friends, invitations. Indeed, whole days might pass during which he would account himself happy; but then would come one of those embarrassing incidents that he had learned to dread.

There was the time, for instance, when the coach, a kindly man with no knowledge of Joe's frame of mind, had tried to shame him, in front of a number of the school heroes, into going out for baseball. The coach was not entirely to be blamed. Joe did look like a ballplayer, and the technique of shaming a boy is not altogether bad pedagogy in some circumstances.

There were other embarrassing moments, too, when, for example, he had to pretend not to see a football that bounced his way, lest he should betray his girlish awkwardness in throwing it back to the players. Little by little he had learned a trick that absorbed the scorn of schoolmates and turned their jibes to friendly raillery. The trick was to anticipate the laugh against himself, to play for it. If he could not avoid returning a ball, he shouted: "Watch out! Here comes my spit ball." He would make elaborate show of spitting delicately on his finger tips. "It's illegal, but it's tricky. You'd better back up!" His wild and feeble peg would be greeted with mild merriment; and the impression would circulate that he could really do much better if he were not such a card [and so on].

E *The psychological order.* Follow the order that will make your matter more interesting, easier to understand, or more acceptable to a particular audience.

ANTONY: Friends, Romans, countrymen, lend me your ears;
I come to bury Caesar, not to praise him.
The evil that men do lives after them;
The good is oft interred with their bones.
So let it be with Caesar. The noble Brutus
Hath told you Caesar was ambitious:
If it were so, it was a grievous fault;
And grievously hath Caesar answer'd it.
Here, under leave of Brutus and the rest
(For Brutus is an honourable man;
So are they all, all honourable men,)
Come I to speak in Caesar's funeral.

At the beginning of this speech the crowd is hostile to Antony and the dead Caesar. Antony does not dare to give them his thesis right at the beginning, does not dare to say that Caesar was a great and just ruler and that he has been foully murdered. He would never get a hearing. He therefore begins most modestly. He carefully balances every item of praise of Caesar with the charge of ambition brought against him. He mentions traits of character that the crowd can accept without feeling disloyal to Brutus. Then he skillfully begins to set before them more sentimental facts, leading their emotions inch by inch, then foot by foot, then yard by yard away from the convictions that Brutus has planted in them a scant

He was my friend, faithful and
just to me:
But Brutus says he was ambi-
tious;
And Brutus is an honourable
man.
He hath brought many cap-
tives home to Rome,
Whose ransoms did the gen-
eral coffers fill:
Did this in Caesar seem am-
bitious?
When that the poor have
cried, Caesar hath wept:
Ambition should be made of
sterner stuff:
Yet Brutus says he was ambi-
tious;
And Brutus is an honourable
man.
You all did see that on the
Lupercal
I thrice presented him a kingly
crown,
Which he did thrice refuse:
was this ambition?

few minutes before. When he
has got them weeping with
him, he shocks them with
the sudden sight of Caesar's
shredded body. Then (near
the end of the speech, not
given here) he caps everything with what he has saved
till the last—the poorest argument against ambition, but the
argument that will mean most
to the crowd—the fact that
Caesar has left a little money
to every Roman citizen and
has willed his private estates
as public parks. The money
and the parks buy the mob
for Antony, and he sets it
to burning down Rome and
lynching his enemies. Had he
proceeded in any other way,
he would soon have lost his
hearing and possibly his head.
He used a psychological order,
adapted to his audience.

Yet Brutus says he was ambitious;
And, sure, he is an honourable man.
I speak not to disprove what Brutus spoke,
But here I am to speak what I do know.
You all did love him once, not without cause:
What cause withholds you, then, to mourn for him?
O judgment, thou art fled to brutish beasts,
And men have lost their reason!—Bear with me;
My heart is in the coffin there with Caesar,
And I must pause till it come back to me.
FIRST CITIZEN: Methinks there is much reason in his sayings.
SECOND CITIZEN: If thou consider rightly of the matter,
Caesar has had great wrong.
THIRD CITIZEN: Has he, masters?
I fear there will a worse come in his place.

FOURTH CITIZEN: Mark'd ye his words? He would not take the
   crown;
Therefore 'tis certain he was not ambitious.
FIRST CITIZEN: If it be found so, some will dear abide it.
SECOND CITIZEN: Poor soul! his eyes are red as fire with weeping.
THIRD CITIZEN: There's not a nobler man in Rome than Antony.
FOURTH CITIZEN: Now mark him, he begins again to speak.
ANTONY: But yesterday, the word of Caesar might
Have stood against the world; now, lies he there,
And none so poor to do him reverence.
O masters! if I were dispos'd to stir
Your hearts and minds to mutiny and rage,
I should do Brutus wrong, and Cassius wrong,
Who, you all know, are honourable men:
I will not do them wrong; I rather choose
To wrong the dead, to wrong myself, and you,
Than I will wrong such honourable men.
But here's a parchment with the seal of Caesar,
I found it in his closet; 'tis his will:
Let but the commons hear this testament,
(Which, pardon me, I do not mean to read,)
And they would go and kiss dead Caesar's wounds,
And dip their napkins in his sacred blood;
Yea, beg a hair of him for memory,
And, dying, mention it within their wills,
Bequeathing it, as a rich legacy,
Unto their issue.
FOURTH CITIZEN: We'll hear the will: read it, Mark Antony.
CITIZENS: The will, the will! we will hear Caesar's will.
ANTONY: Have patience, gentle friends, I must not read it;
It is not meet you know how Caesar loved you.
You are not wood, you are not stones, but men;
And, being men, hearing the will of Caesar,
It will inflame you, it will make you mad:
'Tis good you know not that you are his heirs;
For if you should, O, what would come of it!
FOURTH CITIZEN: Read the will; we'll hear it, Antony;
You shall read us the will; Caesar's will.
ANTONY: Will you be patient? Will you stay a while?
I have o'ershot myself to tell you of it:
I fear I wrong the honourable men,

Whose daggers have stabb'd Caesar; I do fear it.

FOURTH CITIZEN: They were traitors: honourable men!

CITIZENS: The will! The testament!

SECOND CITIZEN: They were villains, murderers: the will; read the will.

ANTONY: You will compel me, then, to read the will?
Then make a ring about the corse of Caesar,
And let me show you him that made the will.
Shall I descend? and will you give me leave?

CITIZENS: Come down.

SECOND CITIZEN: Descend. [*Antony comes down.*]

THIRD CITIZEN: You shall have leave.

FOURTH CITIZEN: A ring; stand round.

FIRST CITIZEN: Stand from the hearse, stand from the body.

SECOND CITIZEN: Room for Antony, most noble Antony!

ANTONY: Nay, press not so upon me; stand far off.

CITIZENS: Stand back; room: bear back.

ANTONY: If you have tears, prepare to shed them now.
You all do know this mantle: I remember
The first time ever Caesar put it on;
'Twas on a summer's evening, in his tent,
That day he overcame the Nervii—
Look, in this place, ran Cassius' dagger through:
See what a rent the envious Casca made:
Through this the well-beloved Brutus stabb'd;
And, as he pluck'd his cursed steel away,
Mark how the blood of Caesar follow'd it,
As rushing out of doors, to be resolv'd
If Brutus so unkindly knock'd, or no;
For Brutus, as you know, was Caesar's angel:
Judge, O you gods, how dearly Caesar lov'd him!
This was the most unkindest cut of all;
For when the noble Caesar saw him stab,
Ingratitude, more strong than traitors' arms,
Quite vanquish'd him: then burst his mighty heart;
And, in his mantle muffling up his face,
Even at the base of Pompey's statue,
Which all the while ran blood, great Caesar fell.
O, what a fall was there, my countrymen!
Then I, and you, and all of us fell down,
Whilst bloody treason flourish'd over us.

O, now you weep; and, I perceive, you feel
The dint of pity: these are gracious drops.
Kind souls, what, weep you when you but behold
Our Caesar's vesture wounded? Look you here,
Here is himself, marr'd, as you see, with traitors.
FIRST CITIZEN: O piteous spectacle!
SECOND CITIZEN: O noble Caesar!
THIRD CITIZEN: O woful day!
FOURTH CITIZEN: O traitors, villains!
FIRST CITIZEN: O most bloody sight!
SECOND CITIZEN: We will be revenged: revenge—about—seek—burn
—fire—kill—slay—let not a traitor live[21] [and so on].

N30 It happens often enough that one of the other orders listed in N29 is also the best psychological order for a certain audience under certain circumstances.

N31 Do not use the psychological order[22] as an excuse to throw away all order. Make sure first that you yourself have a plan that you can explain on demand and then take care that the reader always knows where he is and can see the connections between the parts of your theme.

N32 Supply the reader with all the information he needs for an easy following of the thought.

One fine day in late March, when it looked as if spring had decided to stay, Mark Hokins cut himself a generous slice from the flitch that hung in his smokehouse, took a loaf of bread from the box in the kitchen cupboard, filled a bottle with water, and set out at a good pace across the valley for Little Rawlings.

What makes the passage at left incoherent is the omission of one little bit of information that is important to the good order of the composition. In the revision on the next page, the missing information is supplied at the beginning of the second paragraph.

The supplies would hardly have been adequate for anyone else. But Hokins had taught himself to do with little—had even taught himself to enjoy doing with little. Looking at his tall leanness and

---

[21] William Shakespeare, *Julius Caesar*, Act III, scene 2.
[22] See N29.

the set of his jaw, you sensed immediately that this man was an ascetic, keeping himself in training against a day to come.

One fine day in late March, when it looked as if spring had decided to stay, Mark Hokins cut himself a generous slice from the flitch that hung in his smokehouse, took a loaf of bread from the box in the kitchen cupboard, filled a bottle with water, and set out at a good pace across the valley for Little Rawlings.

Since Little Rawlings was three days of good walking away, the supplies would hardly have been adequate for anyone else. But Hokins had taught himself to do with little—had even taught himself to enjoy doing with little. Looking at his tall leanness and the set of his jaw, you sensed immediately that this man was an ascetic, keeping himself in training against a day to come.

N33 Supply necessary information when or before the reader needs it. Do not use devices like *I forgot to tell you* or *it should have been mentioned earlier that . . .*

This is incoherent

Terrence McFarlane looked at the people around him. There were about thirty of them altogether, most of them dozing, lulled by the rhythmic sway as well as by the want of fresh air. McFarlane could stare at them without seeming impolite. Like everybody else over twenty-five, he enjoyed looking at people and trying to guess what sort they were and what had made them like that.

That sailor, for instance, had an interesting face. Even in sleep, which usually relaxes a man's features, the sailor looked hard. He was the youngest person on the bus and yet the bitterest-looking of the lot.

This is coherent

Terrence McFarlane looked at the people around him. There were about thirty of them altogether, most of them dozing, lulled by the rhythmic sway of the bus as well as by the want of fresh air. Mc-Farlane could stare at them without seeming impolite. Like everybody else over twenty-five, he enjoyed looking at people and trying to guess what sort they were and what had made them like that.

That sailor, for instance, had an interesting face. Even in sleep, which usually relaxes a man's features, the sailor looked hard. He was the youngest person on the bus and yet the bitterest-looking of the lot.

N34 To supply missing connections, to make vague ones more definite, and to smooth out abrupt transitions, use bridge words, phrases, sentences, and paragraphs.[23]

Without bridge words, phrases, sentences, or paragraphs

Anyone looking at Tim Peltier would have set him down as one of the most cheerful, generous hands that ever shouldered a big fat sack of cattle feed.

He had an easy way of talking through a constant grin, which made everything he said seem pleasant when you were looking at him. He put his hand on your shoulder when he asked you to do something for him, and you found yourself right complimented by the gesture.

He was the laziest, most malicious, and most calculating coyote it has ever been my misfortune to bunk with.

Tucker Langwood had a face always drawn into a scowl. His mouth seemed to remember dinner without relish. He had a beady pair of eyes, one of which swung well out to the left from time to time even when he was looking straight ahead.

Tucker Langwood was a fine man, the rare kind of hand that picks the worst bunk in the shack and acts as if he had the best.

With bridge words, phrases, sentences, and paragraphs

Anyone looking at Tim Peltier would have set him down as one of the most cheerful, generous hands that ever shouldered a big fat sack of cattle feed.

He had an easy way of talking through a constant grin, which made everything he said seem pleasant when you were looking at him. He put his hand on your shoulder when he asked you to do something for him, and you found yourself right complimented by the gesture.

That was Tim Peltier to look at. And Tim Peltier to live with—?

He was, *as a matter of fact,* the laziest, most malicious, and most calculating coyote it has ever been my misfortune to bunk with.

Tucker Langwood was in most respects Peltier's direct opposite. He had a face always drawn into a scowl. His mouth seemed to remember dinner without relish. He had a beady pair of eyes, one of which swung well out to the left from time to time even when he was looking straight ahead.

---

[23] See N35-44.

"Peltier," said the boss, "Sherrod's through. He turned up drunk again this morning. That makes you foreman. I expect you to get more work out of the men than Sherrod did" [and so on].

But Tucker Langwood was a fine man, the rare kind of hand that picks the worst bunk in the shack and acts as if he had the best.

Peltier and Langwood might never have tangled—for Langwood was not a tangler—if Peltier had not been made foreman just before the last spring roundup.

"Peltier," said the boss, "Sherrod's through. He turned up drunk again this morning. That makes you foreman. I expect you to get more work out of the men than Sherrod did" [and so on].

N35 Some common bridge words are *this, that; but, still, yet, however; then, next, first (second* or *secondly, third* or *thirdly,* and so on); *while, finally, meanwhile, afterward;* and *so, therefore, consequently.*[24]

N36 *Meanwhile* and similar connectives are very helpful in holding the reader on the track when the writer is keeping two or more series of events going at once.[25]

N37 Do not use *first* when no other items follow.

N38 Do not use *finally* when other items follow.

N39 Do not use *and* when you mean *but;* that is, when there is opposition to express.

[Wrong:] . . . only a very small expense to the season-ticket holders. So you can readily see the advantage of Mr. Shelton's plan. *And* now it is time to note some of the plan's defects . . .

[Right:] . . . only a very small expense to the season-ticket holders. So you can readily see the advantage of Mr. Shelton's plan. *But* now it is time to note some of the plan's defects . . .

---

[24] See N36-42.
[25] See T15.

N40 Do not use *therefore, consequently,* and so on, when what follows is not even in a wide sense a conclusion from what preceded it. Say *and now* or something of the sort.

Therefore, in conclusion let me say that it has been a pleasure to address such an intelligent and attentive audience.

Therefore is wrong here unless the speaker has been arguing to prove that he has enjoyed speaking to this audience—which is hardly likely. *And now* would be much better.

N41 Do not use *so* when a mere time connection or no connection at all exists between parts.

. . . told me to dress for dinner since she was having guests.

At
~~So at~~ eight o'clock the guests began to arrive [and so on].

. . . that finishes everything I have to say.

Well,
~~So~~ it has been fun chatting with you by mail [and so on].

N42 When using *this, that, he,* and other pronouns as bridge words, take care that it is always clear just what each one's antecedent is. When this is not clear, drop the pronoun in favor of some other word or phrase whose reference is not vague.

Preston took his place at my left, Henri at my right, and Piggot directly in front of me.

Piggot
~~He~~ snarled at me: "Dirty little sneak! What are you doing in a school with decent fellows?"

The boulder-strewn roads that wound over the ugly mountains were very hard on the jeeps, rattling them into junk heaps in two months or less. The altitude, also, seemed to affect the operation of the sturdy little cars. But perhaps the Greeks, with no touch at all for mechanical things and no skill in driving, caused more damage and breakdowns than the terrain and the altitude together.

These difficulties
~~This~~ finally made Major Shellabarger decide to call a conference of the American observers and General Karapopoloumenos's staff.

N43 Some common bridge phrases are *this* and *that* plus a noun, *on the other hand, on the contrary, after that, in the second place, in the last part, in the next part, in the meantime, as a consequence,* and *as a result.*

> Murca, we discovered, was fond of a noisome cheese that he had brought with him in considerable quantity.
>
> *This peculiarity* did not endear him to the others [and so on].

N44 Do not use bridge words, phrases, sentences, or paragraphs where they are not needed to make clear the connection and relationship between the parts of the theme. If you load your writing with unnecessary transitional expressions, you will slow its pace and make it sound windy.

O Emphasis

In general

O1 Emphasis means relative stress. In composition, emphasis is the principle that requires that more important thoughts be made to stand out from less important thoughts. Your composition is properly emphatic when your reader knows, without thinking the matter over, which thoughts you consider most important, which less, and which least important.

O2 Clearness in writing is largely a matter of unity, coherence,[1] and emphasis. It is necessary, of course, that the writer's ideas be clear to begin with. But unity, coherence, and emphasis will go far to make sure that these ideas will also become clear to the reader.

O3 What unifies a composition often also makes it coherent and lends it proper emphasis—and vice versa. Hence there is a certain amount of overlapping in fact and in rule.

---

[1] For unity see M1-27. For coherence see N1-44.

Emphasis in the sentence

IN GENERAL

O4 Save the independent clause of a sentence for the main
idea; and do not put two ideas into two independent
clauses unless the ideas are of equal or very nearly equal
importance.

I entered the room, and For- han was still sitting and star- ing at nothing.	Suppose that what Forhan was doing is the one main idea. Turn the first independent clause into something subordi- nate; say, a dependent clause.

When I entered the room, Forhan was still sitting and staring at
nothing.

You are not permitted to kill a woman who has wronged you, but nothing forbids you to reflect that she is growing older every minute.[2]	In this sentence the writer wants to set forth two main ideas for the sake of humor: you may not kill a woman physically, but you may tor- ture her mentally. He does well to put these two ideas into two independent clauses.

O5 Put emphasis in a sentence by arranging a series in the
order of climax: important idea, more important idea,
most important idea.

Willard is highly accom- plished: he can dance, play Mozart well on the piano, and wiggle his ears.	Unless the writer is striving for humor, this sentence is weak, unemphatic. The sen- tence below is emphatic—it distributes stress properly, ar- ranging Willard's accomplish- ments in ascending scale.

Willard is highly accomplished: he can wiggle his ears, dance, and
play Mozart well on the piano.

---

[2] *The Collected Works of Ambrose Bierce* (New York: Neale Publishing Company, 1911), Vol. 8, p. 379.

I came; I saw; I conquered.

> This sentence of Julius Caesar's is so handsomely emphatic that it has been worn out by frequent quotation. Though weary now, it remains an excellent example of climax.

O6 Do not admit a word by which a sentence does not gain in pleasant clarity.

[Unemphatic:] In a manner of speaking and, indeed, to put the thing plainly and as briefly as possible, the pie is truly and undeniably delicious, Mrs. Crane.

[Emphatic:] Mrs. Crane, the pie is delicious.

[Less emphatic:] Sunlight is poured out even on those who are wicked.

[More emphatic:] The sun shines even on the wicked.

[Emphatic, for every word works:] Especially was he beloved by the pretty girls along the Connecticut, whose favor he used to court by presents of the best smoking tobacco in his stock, knowing well that the country lasses of New England are generally great performers on pipes.[3]

Dog bit boy.

> This is clear and emphatic enough, but it is unpleasantly curt. The mind dislikes waste, but it does not like poverty of expression. *The dog bit the boy* is much better.

O7 Occasionally, but not regularly, give emphasis to an idea by saying in so many words that it is important.[4]

I have a skillet and a bass to fry in it.

> This sentence is clear. It may be made even clearer and more pleasant by the addition of *what is more important*.

I have a skillet and, what is more important, a bass to fry in it.

---

[3] Nathaniel Hawthorne, "Mr. Higginbotham's Catastrophe," in *Twice-Told Tales* (Boston: Houghton Mifflin Company, 1885), p. 127.
[4] See O11.

The house had a tall, narrow stone face pierced only by a door at street level and two eyelike windows under the roof with bars on them.

If the writer intends to make the bars on the windows an important part of his story, he had better emphasize them with two or three underscoring words, as below.

The house had a tall, narrow stone face pierced only by a door at street level and two eyelike windows under the roof with—remarkable fact—bars on them.

O8 Occasionally, but not regularly, give emphasis to a word or an expression by taking it out of its usual place in a sentence or clause and placing it at the beginning or at the end.[5] Take care to do this without awkwardness or loss of clarity.

Go I must and will; stay I cannot.

The usual order of such a sentence is *I must and will go; I cannot stay.* Place *go* and *stay* at the beginning of their clauses and you call attention to them, emphasize them.

I am a reasonable man, but this I will not tolerate.

The usual order of such a sentence is *I am a reasonable man, but I will not tolerate this.* Putting the object pronoun *this* before the subject pronoun gives it prominence.

Relentlessly the dentist drilled into Blake's tooth.

The usual order is *The dentist drilled relentlessly into Blake's tooth.* Putting *relentlessly* first gives it great prominence and strong emphasis.

Boundless and constant is the mercy of God.

The usual order: *The mercy of God is boundless and constant.*

An excellent athlete and a good scholar is Jonathan.

The usual order: *Jonathan is an excellent athlete and a good scholar.*

---

[5] See O9 and O11.

There had quietly entered the room a tall, poised, handsome woman—Lady Hitchcock.	The usual order: *A tall, poised, handsome woman, Lady Hitchcock, had quietly entered the room.* Placing the name last gives it prominence.

O9 There is a strong literary flavor about many inverted sentence orders.[6] In very natural, informal, conversational, or matter-of-fact writing, be careful to use only those that do not sound grand—too big for the subject matter, the mood of the piece, or the audience.

O10 Emphasize thoughts by repeating them; but do this only sparingly.

Kroner was hated throughout the ship, hated by the captain, hated by the second mate, and hated especially by the crew that he disciplined and worked without mercy.	In this sentence, *hated* receives great stress by being repeated four times.
"You are behaving ridiculously, quite ridiculously," he said with quiet venom.	The repetition implies that the speaker thinks the matter over and still reaches the same verdict. This lends force.
It's useless, useless, I tell you; it's completely useless.	Here the repetition of *useless* makes a very heavy sentence, with a note of despair.
First in war, first in peace, and first in the hearts of his countrymen, he was second to none in the humble and endearing scenes of private life . . .	These are the famous opening words of Henry Lee's funeral oration in honor of George Washington. Emphasis is got by repeating the words *first in* three times.
Alone, alone, all, all alone, Alone on a wide, wide sea!	These two lines—an elliptical sentence from "The Ancient Mariner"—contain a multiple repetition.

[6] See O8.

O11 The devices described in O7-8 and O10 should not be used in sentence after sentence. Ordinarily give your reader time to forget that you have used them before you use them again.

SUSPENSE SENTENCES

O12 Suspense could be defined as a state in which a person does not yet know, but wants to know, and feels that he will get to know. Its effect is to sharpen the impact, the importance, the appeal of the thing that one wants to know.

O13 Occasionally write a rather long sentence in which you do not release the predicate verb or (in the case of a complex sentence) the independent clause until the end or nearly the end of the sentence.

Under the brilliant lights of the marquee, huddling out of the rain after the play and waiting for his Cadillac to draw up to the curb, the fabulous Mr. Endacre was shot and killed.

Notice that you could not place a period at any point in this sentence until after the word *shot,* which occurs near the end. This is a suspense sentence. Compare it with the sentence below, which could be stopped very soon and which consequently does not arouse much suspense.

The fabulous Mr. Endacre was shot and killed under the brilliant lights of the marquee, huddling out of the rain after the play and waiting for his Cadillac to draw up to the curb.

There is no suspense in this sentence. The important information is released in the first six or seven words, before the reader's expectation and desire to know have been aroused. As a result, *the fabulous Mr. Endacre was shot and killed* does not here receive the prominence (emphasis) that it does in the sentence just above.

O14 A periodic sentence is a very long suspense sentence, usually rather grand and emotional in tone and ordinarily about something important.

> To bring under one yoke, after the manner of old Rome, a hundred discordant peoples; to maintain each of them in its own privileges within its legitimate range of action; to allow them severally the indulgence of national feelings, and the stimulus of rival interests; and yet withal to blend them into one great social establishment, and to pledge them to the perpetuity of the one imperial power;— this is an achievement which carries with it the unequivocal token of genius in the race which effects it.[7]

O15 A semisuspense sentence is a sentence that employs a suspense structure for a good part of the sentence and then adds further remarks. Semisuspense sentences are very useful.

> Near the mouth of the stream, at the foot of the cliff on Mount Durion, Jud the Trapper held his strange school; and here Jason spent ten years learning to wrestle, to box, to hunt, to play the fiddle, and to make the great pharmacy of the woods yield him its medicines to cure his hurts.

Suspense construction is used down through *strange school.*

O16 To get suspense in the structure of a sentence—

A Begin with modifiers—adjectives, adverbs, adjective and adverb phrases and clauses—or noun clauses.

> On the twelfth day of the search, near the head of the lake, in a kind of hollow, well screened from the shore by a growth of spruce, the McAllisters found the remains of a fire, and a message, still clear, scrawled in the dirt.

Adjective and adverb phrases.

[7] John Henry Newman, *The Idea of a University* (New York: The America Press, 1941), pp. 437-38.

Whenever I find myself growing grim about the mouth; whenever it is damp, drizzly November in my soul; whenever I find myself involuntarily pausing before coffin warehouses, and bringing up the rear of every funeral I meet; and especially whenever my temper gets such an upper hand of me that it requires a strong moral principle to prevent me from deliberately stepping into the street and methodically knocking people's hats off—then I account it high time to get to sea as soon as I can.[8]

If skillfully written, dependent clauses (adverb, adjective, and noun) can hold off the point of a sentence quite a while. It is possible to pile up a good number of them before releasing the independent clause. Some of the dependent clauses themselves can be rather long, provided that they remain clear. In this selection the adverbial *whenever* clauses and the other dependent clauses that they contain postpone the release of the independent clause until considerable suspense has been built up.

B Begin with an accumulation of subject nouns (and noun phrases or clauses) with or without modifiers.

The chair facing the door expectantly, the kettle steaming on the hob, the cups and silver laid ready for tea, the bread with one or two slices already cut and lying at the end of the loaf, the book open on the table—everything in the room seemed to be waiting, waiting—but not for me.

That a child of five should be lecturing their guests on geopolitics, that one of the adults of the family should be cutting out little dolls of paper and putting them to sleep with songs, that the ice cream should be kept in the oven, the car on the porch, the chickens in the master bedroom, and the guest of honor in the garage didn't seem at all strange to the strange McSwivverns.

C Begin with nominative absolutes.

The greatest prudes often being the greatest hypocrites and Fowler clearly being a great prude, it is little wonder that he gave everyone about him the devil of an itch to prick the outer bubble of his pietism and disclose his fraud.

---

[8] Adapted from Herman Melville, *Moby Dick* (New York: Dodd, Mead and Company, 1934), p. 1.

D Begin with direct objects.

The England that he loved so much, the England that had hunted him and tried its best to break his body on the rack, the England where a handful of Catholics stood firm in the sea of scorn and danger that lapped them round, the England that was home—that England Father Gerard would never see again.

E Put modifiers or appositives between the subject noun and the predicate verb.

And this corrupt politician, petty, in love with the dollar, faithless to every trust that has ever been given him, is now to decide what shall be law and what shall not?

A man, a stranger to me but very affable, really charming, who said he was an old friend of yours from your days at Wallace High, borrowed your car.

O17 A loose sentence is the opposite of a suspense sentence. It is a sentence of some length that could be stopped by a period a good deal before its end. (There are borderline sentences which might be described as either loose or suspense sentences.)

The fabulous Mr. Endacre was shot | and killed | under the brilliant lights of the marquee, | huddling out of the rain | after the play | and waiting | for his Cadillac | to draw up to the curb.

The sentence at left could be stopped by a period at any of the points indicated by the division lines. It is clearly a loose sentence.

Whenever there is time, I stop at Mrs. Welker's | on my way home | to exchange news | with her | and to find out how her arthritis is treating her.

This is predominantly a loose sentence, but the adverbial clause lends just enough suspense to make it a troublesome borderline case.

O18 A loose sentence is not inferior to a suspense sentence and may be every bit as soundly and as artfully constructed. The loose sentence is the backbone of most writing. Only when it is used over and over again without the relief of an occasional suspense sentence is it bad.

403

Emphasis in the paragraph

O19 Ordinarily place an important idea at the beginning or the end of a paragraph.

We very seldom realize that there are a great many things and persons at work for us. Animals, of course, work for us—horses and mules, even elephants and camels. But men work for us, too. Think of all the sailors on all the ships in the world doing a hard day's labor to bring us tropical fruits, foreign wines, English and Australian wool, oriental spices, and tons and tons of raw materials for our immense industries. Think of all the railroad men and truck drivers working day and night to bring us food and clothes and all kinds of necessities and comforts from every state. And God, more than any man or any group of men, is at work for us in His gifts. Are you lying in the shade? God is at work in the tree ever creating it anew, so that it may be, and so that it may be beautiful and useful. Did you say something? You could not, were not God busy making your tongue and teeth and lips do your bidding. Are you reading this paragraph? You can thank the God at work in you if smudges of ink are able to become the stuff of thought. Because He loves, God is constantly at work in all things for us.

This paragraph distributes its emphasis properly. The topic sentence, the sentence that carries the main idea of the paragraph, is ordinarily rather important. It certainly is so here, and so it is given prominence by being placed first: . . . *there are a great many things and persons at work for us.* But the most important idea in the sentence is that God works for us. That idea is not submerged in the middle of the paragraph but is given due prominence, given a chance to stand out, by being placed at the end of the paragraph.

O20 Put a series of ideas within a paragraph in the order of climax—least important or interesting, more important or interesting, still more important or interesting, most important or interesting.[9]

---

[9] See O21.

It seldom happens that we are unjustly charged with lying down on a job. But it does happen once in a while. When it does happen, what should we do? Of course, we can just sulk. Sulking, however, accomplishes nothing and is a kind of acid that eats away our own character; so it had best be left to ten-year-olds. Better, we can defend ourselves. Defense is a good and reasonable countermove, provided that we have evidence in our favor and that an unprejudiced judge will give us a fair hearing. That, unfortunately, is not often the case. The best thing to do most of the time is to remind ourselves that we are not working merely for the esteem of men. If we have it, good. If we don't, no great loss. Esteem is the gravy of this life: life tastes better with it, but it tastes all right without it. If we are not working for men—as slaves do—but only for men in Christ—as angels do—then we are certain that we are never misjudged by the one person who controls everything about us, the richest, the most powerful, the finest, the most loving person that ever was, and the person whose good opinion and bad opinion, whose rewards and punishments, are the only ones in the world that count. If everything is shipshape between Him and us, then to the devil with the judgments of little people.

O21 When applying O20 to a paragraph that begins with a topic sentence, use the order of climax in the sentences that follow the topic sentence—insofar as it is reasonable to do so.

O22 Occasionally emphasize an important idea by repeating it within a paragraph. Ordinarily repeat it in somewhat different words; rarely, in the very same words.

Finally, oppressed by the clatter, the blatting of the orchestra, the tinkle of insincere conversation, Fleurin made his way across the dance floor, through the French doors that gave on the lawn, across the lawn, across the highway, to the sea wall. Peace, he thought —I must find peace. Not the peace of emptiness, for that is only silence and silence can

The repetition of the words *love* and *peace,* and of the ideas of emptiness, fullness, and so on, in this paragraph seems justified and effective. For somehow the repetition conveys a bit of Fleurin's desperate hunger for a meaning and a purpose in life. The paragraph on the next page, which does not use repetition, loses in clarity and effect.

405

be fear. I must have the peace of fullness, and that means the peace of love. There can be love without peace, but there can be no peace without love. One must love the things that fill, not the things that empty, and then one will have peace. Then, Christ, I will have peace.

Finally, oppressed by the clatter, the blatting of the orchestra, the tinkle of insincere conversation, Fleurin made his way across the dance floor, through the French doors that gave on the lawn, across the lawn, across the highway, to the sea wall. Peace, he thought—I must find something to quiet my mind. But I don't want emptiness. I want fullness. That means that I want love. There can be some kinds of affection without rest of soul, but there can be no real tranquillity unless the heart has fastened on something. But if I love the things that enrich a man, not the things that beggar him, then, Christ, I may find satisfaction.

Great sin need not keep a man from finally getting to heaven. There was St. Peter, the chief of the apostles, for instance, who three times denied that he knew Christ— swore that he did not know Him at the very time when Christ, having been arrested, needed His friends. Then there was the Good Thief, St. Dismas, who had led, probably, a gangster's life. Another example is St. Augustine, who, as a young man—until he was thirty-three —lived a highly immoral life and defended heresy. Still others are St. John of God and St. Camillus of Lellis. St. John spent eighteen adventurous years as a free-lance trooper, hardened in body and soul; and St. Camillus, an Italian soldier, was for a long time a rakehell gambler. No; great sin does not prevent a man from getting to heaven, so long as he repents, walks away from his idiocy, and turns at last to God.

This paragraph uses one of the most emphatic repetition devices that there are. A thought is stated at the beginning. Then, after the point has been developed, the same thought is repeated—sometimes in the very same words; sometimes, as here, in slightly different words—at the end of the paragraph. This gives the same thought the benefit of the two most striking positions in the paragraph. What is more, it forges the paragraph together into one compact, sharp blade of thought that can hardly fail to penetrate the mind and leave an impression there.

406

O23 Occasionally put the idea that you wish to emphasize into a very brief sentence, and all the other ideas into rather long sentences. Place the brief sentence at the beginning or, often better, at the end of the paragraph. The difference in the length of the sentences will call attention sharply to the idea in the short one.

The torrential rain made an infernal racket on the dry palmettos that roofed the fragile half-shelter—roofed it so imperfectly, however, that little cascades of cold water often found the neck of a man's poncho and ran down his back, drenching him and leaving him shivering. What water missed the neck of one's poncho dripped, or ran, or somehow found its way to the ground, and there joined with the soft earth to make first a soupy gumbo and then a muddy lake most uncomfortable to sit in—and, of course, it was either sit in the muddy lake or stand up on the broken leg. All in all, Felito felt miserable.

All in all, Felito felt miserable gains considerable emphasis because it is a short sentence coming after two very long ones. Notice that the paragraph next below, which ends with a long sentence, fails to make so sharp an impression, even though it is a good paragraph.

The torrential rain made an infernal racket on the dry palmettos that roofed the fragile half-shelter—roofed it so imperfectly, however, that little cascades of cold water often found the neck of a man's poncho and ran down his back, drenching him and leaving him shivering. What water missed the neck of one's poncho dripped, or ran, or somehow found its way to the ground, and there joined with the soft earth to make first a soupy gumbo and then a muddy lake most uncomfortable to sit in—and, of course, it was either sit in the muddy lake or stand up on the broken leg. With all of these things to contend with and no means of contending with them except patience, poor Felito felt very miserable indeed and longed for some change, almost any change, in his circumstances.

Poor Felito felt very miserable is smothered a bit in this version, though not so badly that the thought is obscured.

It was half-way through the morning, and he had not breakfasted; the slight litter of other breakfasts stood about on the table to remind him of his hunger; and adding a poached egg to his order, he proceeded musingly to shake some white sugar into his coffee, thinking all the time about Flambeau. He remembered how Flambeau had escaped, once by a pair of nail scissors, and once by a house on fire; once by having to pay for an unstamped letter, and once by getting people to look through a telescope at a comet that might destroy the world. He thought his detective brain as good as the criminal's, which was true. But he fully realized the disadvantage. "The criminal is the creative artist; the detective only the critic," he said with a sour smile, and lifted his coffee cup to his lips slowly, and put it down very quickly. He had put salt in it.[10]

He had put salt in it gathers a great deal of emphasis from the contrast between its length and that of most of the sentences that have gone before. In fact, the sentence gains such emphasis that the reader would feel cheated if the salt turned out to be unimportant to the story. (It turns out to be important; for it is one of a trail of clues left by Flambeau's victim for the detective to follow, and it leads to Flambeau's capture.)

Emphasis in the theme

O24 Make clear the relative importance of thoughts in a theme.

O25 Give the most important thoughts the most space, the less important thoughts less space, and so on.[11]

O26 It sometimes happens that an important idea is so persuasive and so easy to understand in itself that to give it fuller treatment than less important ideas would be to blow it up with empty verbiage. When this happens, ignore O25 and use some other emphasis device.

---

[10] "The Blue Cross," pp. 8-9. Reprinted by permission of Dodd, Mead and Company, from *The Innocence of Father Brown* by G. K. Chesterton. Copyright 1911 by Dodd, Mead and Company.
[11] See O26-27.

O27 The introduction and the conclusion should be short in comparison with the body of the theme. In general, make the introduction and conclusion together one third or less of the whole theme.[12]

O28 Put important thoughts in emphatic positions.[13]

O29 The second most emphatic position in a theme is ordinarily near the beginning. For this reason it is often good to use the opening paragraphs to state the theme topic and to say something about it that will make the reader want to see it developed.[14]

O30 The most emphatic position in a theme is ordinarily near the end. The end of the theme is often, therefore, a good place (*a*) to restate the theme topic, (*b*) to summarize the main points of the theme, (*c*) to use your most telling argument or most striking presentation, (*d*) to introduce your most interesting incident, or (*e*) to release the reader from the suspense that has been building up by finally telling him what you want him to know.[15]

O31 After the topic paragraph, if there is one, start with the least important or interesting thought and move by degrees to the most interesting or important.[16]

As a matter of fact, it was rather a full day. I spent several hours getting the dummy for the *Colombière Clarion* ready for the printer and another forty minutes working out that silly exercise in emphasis for English class tomorrow.

I spent another three hours doing something rather interesting: watching the men at D'Astignac Studios painting a backdrop for the school's production of *Everyman*. I found it amazing that they could work so quickly. Watching them slap paint on—mostly with ten-inch brushes—you would imagine that the result was going to look like something my manic-depressive little sister thinks up out of her water-color kit. On the contrary, they achieved a perfect

---

[12] See O25.
[13] See O29-32.
[14] See O32 and L5.
[15] See O32 and L9-10.
[16] See O32.

copy of Laury's design and got it on a canvas twenty by forty feet in less than three hours.

But the thing that will make it a day to remember was something that happened down at the printer's. I was helping Mr. Shelton lay out our copy according to the dummy, when a rather fat, bald, tired-looking man came out of the office and walked over to the shop table where we were working. When he picked up a sheaf of *Clarion* copy and started reading through it, I felt rather annoyed that he hadn't asked anybody's permission. But I didn't say anything. He took advantage of a pause in the discussion I was having with Shelton to ask very curtly, "Who wrote this thing on the prize debates at Colombière?"

"I did," I said without looking up.

"You, eh?"

"Uh-huh."

"Well, son, when you finish high school and college, if you're still fool enough to like newspaper work, come down and get a job from me."

"Yes?" I said; "and who are you, mister?"

"Priestly," he answered; "R. C. Priestly, city editor, Wichita *Herald*. Darned good paper, and an excellent city editor."

O32 Sometimes clarity or some other important consideration makes it inadvisable to follow O28-31. For example, there are circumstances in which it is good to have a very unemphatic, gentle opening that promises very little. In such cases, use some other emphasis device.

O33 Get emphasis for a thought by contrasting its treatment with the treatment of the other thoughts around it.[17]

O34 Rarely, use visual devices like the setting off of a single brief statement in a paragraph by itself.[18]

It was obvious that a single extra division would turn the tide for us. We were doing well. We were holding Klavic's army longer than anybody had thought we could.

The sentence *But Tarleton never came* receives some emphasis in the first version as the last sentence in its paragraph, but more in the second as a paragraph by itself.

[17] See O34-37.
[18] See O35.

A single extra division would have given our left flank the strength it needed to advance. We all knew that that extra division, under Aubrey Tarleton, had been ordered up since the night before. We were all waiting tensely for it, hour after hour. But Tarleton never came.

It was Tarleton's unexplainable absence that finally broke [and so on].

It was obvious that a single extra division would turn the tide for us. We were doing well. We were holding Klavic's army longer than anybody had thought we could.

A single extra division would have given our left flank the strength it needed to advance. We all knew that that extra division, under Aubrey Tarleton, had been ordered up since the night before. We were all waiting tensely for it, hour after hour.

But Tarleton never came.

It was Tarleton's unexplainable absence that finally broke [and so on].

O35 Modern writers of the "popular" sort overwork the visual-contrast trick of O34. It is an obvious form of emphasis, and the reader does not like obvious tricks. So never use visual contrast to the point where the reader may come to notice what you are doing.

O36 Occasionally emphasize a thought by introducing it with an abrupt change of mood or atmosphere.

It was a mournful evening. Sheila sat in the window seat, staring out into the night. There was not enough light in the room behind her to make reflections on the panes, and so she could see out quite well; and what she saw was

The man and the boy are given importance and their entrance is pointed up sharply by the abrupt change of mood and atmosphere between the first and second paragraphs.

melancholy enough: a few giant cypresses starting up, stark and bare and grotesque, out of the black water of the swamp and gesticulating in silhouette against the faintly luminous sky. They shuddered a little when the wind came raging at them and howled on past the house and the window from which Sheila was looking out. Once she thought she saw something move in the dark water under the cypresses, but she could not be sure.

"Blow me for an empty bag," cried a voice behind her. "Here's a good room with a fine fire laid. Let's make port and drop anchor in here, Jackie—if, of course, the young lady over there in the window doesn't mind sharing this snuggery with us. The *pretty* young lady, I *should* say, Jackie; for the girl is pretty, though you're too young to notice—or are you, lad?" Sheila turned to find a great stout man and a boy in his teens standing in the doorway, both with their mouths open—the man's because he was talking and the boy's because he was gawking.

O37 Occasionally emphasize a thought by changes in rhythm, sound, sentence structure, and so on.

Laugh! Laugh loud! Be brittle and staccato. What you do, do quickly. Move along. Do, do, do. Never think. Achieve; win things; acquire things; fight for things; hold on to things. Never look at yourself. You won't like what you see. It will disturb you. Just get things for yourself. Pad yourself around with them. Insulate yourself against biting winds. And drink; above all, drink. Drink the sharp sting out of life. Soften the blinding light of life by looking at it through the bottom of a bottle.

Notice that in the first paragraph nearly all the sentences are brief and that the only two long sentences are loose sentences. Many of the words—for example, *brittle, do, think, fight*—have a sharp sound. The second paragraph is a long periodic sentence, containing a good many mouth-filling words of long, full, liquid, sonorous, or softened sound—for example, *overwhelm, drown, hush, rolls, flows, intones.*

But a quiet voice, a voice welling up in serenity to engulf the world's madness, to overwhelm it and drown it and hush it forever, a voice whose tide rolls out and laps the shores of eternity, a voice that flows some day into every heart, a voice raised in Galilee intones: "Thou fool, this night do they require thy soul of thee."

O38 Occasionally emphasize a thought by repeating it in the course of a theme. Sometimes, in very oratorical and emphatic themes, the thought may be repeated several times in exactly the same words. But usually the repetition must be dressed up a bit if it is to please and not seem too naked a device.

Catholics are not alert enough.

At a time when almost every other body, from Zionists to Jehovah's Witnesses, uses organized pressure to protect its rights and push its aims, Catholics act as if the safety and spread of their way of life should be left entirely to the miraculous intervention of the Holy Ghost.

Recently, when a prominent woman published a series of articles on her conversion to Catholicism, the magazine received thousands of letters—most of them, according to report, from communists—protesting the publication and canceling subscriptions, and almost none of them from Catholics approving it. It would not be astonishing if a long time passes before the magazine dares to publish such a Catholic piece again.

Communists read the article, were frightened—wrote letters and canceled subscriptions.

Catholics read the article, were pleased—did nothing.

A convert to Protestantism or Communism finds himself warmly welcomed into the social life of the group he has joined. His new coreligionists go out of their way to make it possible for him to enjoy a social happiness he did not have before. It is a pity that converts to Catholicism have to complain so often that they might almost have become Mohammedans for all the difference that their conversion makes to the parish. Many of them, who have given up their old associations to follow Christ, find themselves genuinely lonely in the midst of Christ's friends.

Catholics are not cruel, but they are often sleepy.

It happens too often that non-Catholic agencies come into a Catholic ward or district or county and clear up some social problem like juvenile delinquency that has been staring the parish in the face and that the parish could itself have taken care of with an increase of prestige for the cause of Christ and a possible increment to His kingdom.

Catholics are not alert enough.

O39 Occasionally get emphasis by stating that a thought is important, interesting, or something of the kind.[19]

And now we come to the most practical solution that I have to offer, an idea that I am sure is worth all my other suggestions put together . . .

---

[19] See O40-43.

O40 Of all the ways of getting emphasis, this by express statement (O39) is the most annoying when it is abused. The writer who abuses it is somewhat like the wit who ruins jokes by saying, "I want to tell you a story that will slay you. You'll die laughing." Keep the principles in O41-43.

O41 Do not say that a thought is important, interesting, or anything of the kind unless you are sure that it is.

O42 Do not say that a thought is more important, interesting, and so on, than it actually is.

> [An insult to the intelligence of reader or listener:] And now to the question that all America is asking: What cigarette guarantees the safest smoking enjoyment?

O43 Even if you have several very important or interesting points, do not *state* that more than one or two of them are important or interesting. Use other emphasis devices for the rest.

P Variety of development

In general

P1 Two qualities, chiefly, make a style adult: clearness and variety. Provided one's thought is clear, one's writing will also be clear if it has unity, coherence, and emphasis.[1] The following rules will help toward variety.

P2 Put variety into your writing by carefully mixing sentence patterns. Do not always write sentences of the same length and kind.[2]

P3 Put variety into your paragraphs by developing the topic thoughts in different ways. Do not develop every topic thought in the same way.[3]

---

[1] For unity see M1-27. For coherence see N1-44. For emphasis see O1-43.
[2] See P5-14, P18, P21, P28, P32-33, P38-39, P42, and P46.
[3] See P19, P22, P29, P34-35, P40, P43, and P46.

P4 Put variety into your themes by developing theme topics in different ways. Do not develop every theme topic in the same way.[4]

Combining sentences

P5 When sentences or independent clauses fall into a monotonous pattern because of uniform length and structure, the pattern can often be broken by combining some of the sentences or independent clauses according to the rules that follow.

P6 When two or more dull sentences or clauses have predicates that are identical or nearly identical in thought, combine them into one sentence or clause by using a compound subject.

> The Williamses have people over from the city every week end. The Carbanks have people over too. But Dad says we come to Florida to get away from people. Mother agrees with him. It's all very difficult for a nineteen-year-old daughter who must see men if she is to marry one some day.

> None of the sentences at left is bad in itself. But the first four work the same pattern to death for no reason. They are all short and choppy in rhythm. The brevity and choppiness do not echo the thought or serve any other purpose. In the next version below, a compound subject combines the first two sentences nicely and breaks up the monotony. (The second two sentences also could easily be combined.)

> The Williamses and the Carbanks have people over from the city every week end. But Dad says we come to Florida to get away from people. Mother agrees with him. It's all very difficult for a nineteen-year-old daughter who must see men if she is to marry one some day.

P7 When two or more dull sentences or clauses have subjects that are identical or nearly identical in thought,

---

[4] See P20, P23, P30-31, P36-37, P41, P44, and P46.

415

combine them into one sentence or clause by using a compound predicate.

Wintergalen was hesitant. He was indecisive. He was afraid to talk in public. But he was very intelligent. Melunas was aggressive. He always knew what he wanted. He loved an audience. But he was not precisely a thinker. The two men were born partners.	There is no reason for releasing the thought to the reader in these driblets or for wearying him with so many sentences of the same length. By combining predicates, in the version below the writer produces a pleasing arrangement of two long sentences and one short one.

Wintergalen was hesitant, indecisive, afraid to talk in public, but very intelligent. Melunas was aggressive, always knew what he wanted, loved an audience, but was not precisely a thinker. The two men were born partners.

P8 When one dull sentence explains a noun or pronoun in another dull sentence, turn the explanatory sentence into an appositive. (Use the same technique with dull independent clauses.)

Everyone else was happy. Everyone else had friends. But nobody noticed Benito. He was a hungry dreamer and a jailbird.	These sentences are so nearly uniform that monotony develops by the end of the paragraph. Turn the last sentence into an appositive.

Everyone else was happy. Everyone else had friends. But nobody noticed Benito—hungry dreamer and jailbird.

The boss of any business worries a lot. He feels it his duty to worry. No one can help him. But I heard a strange rumor today. There is a new machine to do his worrying for him.	An appositive noun clause can break the monotonous pattern at left.

The boss of any business worries a lot. He feels it his duty to worry. No one can help him. But today I heard the strange rumor that there is a new machine to do his worrying for him.

416

P9 Combine two or more dull sentences or independent clauses by means of the dummy-subject construction.

[Monotonous:] You have made up your mind. That is obvious. You are going to sing. No one can stop you. But the orchestra will not play.

[Better:] It is obvious that you have made up your mind to sing. No one can stop you. But the orchestra will not play.

P10 Combine two or more dull sentences or independent clauses by turning the less important into a nominative absolute.[5]

[Monotonous:] The Chrysler skidded up to the barrier. Its horn was blaring, and its tires were screaming. The driver jumped out.

[Better:] Horn blaring and tires screaming, the Chrysler skidded up to the barrier. The driver jumped out.

P11 Do not put the more important of two thoughts in a nominative absolute. The nominative absolute is a humble frame suitable only to secondary thoughts.

P12 It takes a trained eye and ear to discriminate between an awkward nominative absolute and one that is at home in its sentence. So (*a*) use nominative absolutes sparingly; (*b*) follow your teacher's taste until he tells you that your own is trustworthy; (*c*) read your sentences aloud to detect awkward sound or rhythm; and (*d*) note, when you read good authors, how they use nominative absolutes effectively.

P13 If one of a series of dull sentences or independent clauses tells when, where, how, or why, turn it into an adverb, an adverb phrase, or an adverb clause.[6]

[Monotonous:] One moment we were all standing around the skunk. It happened suddenly. The skunk was alone.

[Better:] One moment we were all standing around the skunk. Suddenly the skunk was alone.

---

[5] See P11-12.

[6] Subordinate only secondary thoughts in this way. Unity and emphasis require that, as far as possible, the independent clause or the subject noun and predicate verb of a simple sentence be reserved for the more important idea.

[Monotonous:] The infantry had a difficult time. They crawled through Huertgen's mud and mines. They crawled for endless, slow, and costly miles.

[Better:] The infantry had a difficult time. For endless, slow, and costly miles, they crawled through Huertgen's mud and mines.

[Monotonous:] Whites should not mind entering into brotherhood with Negroes. Christ Himself is proud to be their brother. What is good enough for Him is good enough for anyone.

[Better:] Whites should not mind entering into brotherhood with Negroes when Christ Himself is proud to be their brother. What is good enough for Him is good enough for anyone.

P14 Sometimes one or more of a series of dull sentences or independent clauses can be turned into an adjective, an adjective phrase, or an adjective clause.[7]

[Monotonous:] Toward the northeast, at daybreak, loomed Gibraltar. It was large. It was grand and gray.

There could be a reason in some contexts for breaking up the thought into such tiny fragments; for example, humor. But ordinarily such a pattern is irritating.

[Better:] Toward the northeast, at daybreak, loomed Gibraltar, large, grand, and gray.

[Monotonous:] This is an account of Mrs. Wendell Morgan. She is an elderly woman. She is known familiarly to all of lower Howard Avenue. She is of frowzy appearance, vague manner, and undiscerning look.

[Better:] This is an account of Mrs. Wendell Morgan. Elderly, of frowzy appearance, vague manner, and undiscerning look, she is known familiarly to all of lower Howard Avenue.

[Monotonous:] In my henhouse are two jumpy hens. At the slightest disturbance they panic the rest of the flock. Last night this proved fortunate. It saved my hens.

[Better:] In my henhouse are two jumpy hens that, at the slightest disturbance, panic the rest of the flock. Last night this proved fortunate. It saved my hens.

---

[7] Subordinate only secondary thoughts in this way. See footnote 6, page 417.

Developing thoughts

IN GENERAL

P15   In order to avoid monotony, develop the main ideas of sentences, paragraphs, and themes in a variety of ways.

P16   Some of the more serviceable ways of developing the main ideas of sentences, paragraphs, and themes are enumeration, giving circumstances, comparison and contrast, giving causes and effects, giving examples, and repetition.

P17   The following rules take up each of the methods of development listed in P16 and apply them to the sentence, the paragraph, and the theme. Of course, a combination of these methods is best for most compositions, since the steady use of only one would itself create monotony.

ENUMERATION IN THE SENTENCE

P18   Develop a sentence thought by dividing an idea in the subject or predicate into its parts.

[Thought:] Jerome Kern wrote some masterpieces of modern popular music.

[Development:] Jerome Kern, master of melody and boss of tricky rhythms, wrote some masterpieces of modern popular music.

The idea in the subject, Jerome Kern, is divided into parts, broken up into several notions that come to mind when one says "Jerome Kern."

[Thought:] Jerome Kern wrote some masterpieces of modern popular music.

[Development:] Jerome Kern wrote some masterpieces of modern popular music: "Ol' Man River," "Smoke Gets in Your Eyes," and "Long Ago and Far Away."

An idea in the predicate, masterpieces, is divided into parts, into a list of song titles—broken up into what comes to mind when one says "masterpieces of modern popular music."

419

[Thought:] I shan't easily forget that time aboard the *Nanette.*

[Development:] I shan't easily forget that time aboard the *Nanette,* when we ran for a glorious week before a spanking breeze, when the days were gold and blue and white, when the stars at night lay in the sky like diamonds bedded lightly in soot, and when, in shocking contrast, I lived in constant, nauseating terror of Captain Twilliger's great, hard fists.	An idea in the predicate, that time, is divided into parts, sliced into the several concrete, individual things that made up the time spent aboard the *Nanette.*

ENUMERATION IN THE PARAGRAPH

P19 Develop a topic thought by dividing an idea in the subject or predicate into its parts.

[Topic thought:] Jerome Kern wrote some masterpieces of modern popular music.

[Development:] *Jerome Kern wrote some masterpieces of modern popular music.* "Ol' Man River," for instance, seems fated not to die, though it has been mangled by singers who do not understand it; indeed, the artiest critics don't mind admitting that it deserves to live. "Smoke Gets in Your Eyes," though its lyrics are the sort to cloy after a time, is such good music that it survived even the lush treatment that Kostelanetz used to give it; and its appeal reaches lovers of Basin Street as well as those whose taste is just a little sentimental. "Long Ago and Far Away" has the

An idea in the topic sentence,[8] masterpieces of modern popular music, is divided into three of its parts in the subsequent sentences. It is broken up into "Ol' Man River," "Smoke Gets in Your Eyes," and "Long Ago and Far Away," with a few sentences showing how each is, in a sense, a masterpiece of modern popular music.

---

[8] A topic sentence is the topic thought of a paragraph expressed in one sentence of the paragraph itself. In the column at left, it is the sentence in italic. For topic thoughts see M11-12.

quality frequently described as "haunting" and "elusive," with this difference, that it continues to haunt and to elude after comparable songs have begun to bore. These three songs are outstanding, of course; but almost nothing that Kern wrote can be easily dismissed, and almost all of it promises to be here some time after this generation is gone. People are likely to be humming his tunes when they can no longer remember who wrote them.

ENUMERATION IN THE THEME

P20 Develop a theme topic by dividing an idea in the subject or predicate into its parts.

[Theme topic:] Jerome Kern wrote some masterpieces of modern popular music.

When Jerome Kern died not so long ago, the news of his death was news of a loss to America. Kern had not won a war, and he had not established peace; but he had paid rent for the time he had lodged on earth by making a rather substantial contribution to the fund of things that can pleasure a man's heart without poisoning it. For Jerome Kern wrote some masterpieces of modern popular music.

Topic paragraph.[9]

Take his "Ol' Man River." Compare it with the flood of noise about the Mississippi that has welled up in tin-pan alley in the last thirty years or so, rolled over America for a while, and then subsided, to the relief of everyone but the composers. Kern, of course, is no Schubert; and the score of "Ol' Man River" would scarcely sweep Toscanini into ecstasy. But as a certain kind of song it is a masterpiece, ranking with the rare best of its sort and rolling on to fuller and fuller popularity long after its rivals have quite trickled out.

The first paragraph of the development takes up the first division of masterpieces of modern popular music. This first division is "Ol' Man River." The topic thought of this paragraph is *In comparison with many other popular songs, "Ol' Man River" is a masterpiece.*

[9] The theme topic is the subject matter of the theme, the one clear, rather brief thought that answers the question *What is the theme about?* A topic paragraph is a paragraph that contains an explicit statement of the theme topic (M22).

Again, "Smoke Gets in Your Eyes" shows what Kern could do with the romantic sort of thing that others botch so badly. Here is swirling melody that triumphs over the lamentable pattern that many modern songs have fallen into—

The second paragraph takes up a second division. The topic thought: *In comparison with many other popular songs, "Smoke Gets in Your Eyes" is a masterpiece.*

strain, strain-repeat, break-strain, repeat. Its excellence is clearly proved by the fact that it can be sung by really good singers without reducing them to musical slummers and without itself sounding shoddy—something that cannot be said for the majority of pieces that make the *Hit Parade*.

As with these two songs, so it is with almost everything that Kern wrote. It is a pity

Conclusion.

that his work is not to be carried forward by anyone. With Berlin and Cole Porter aging, the great Gershwin gone, and the masters of jazz and Dixieland now just names in the history of music, the prospects of modern popular song are not so bright as they might be. There is no doubt about it, America will miss Kern.

CIRCUMSTANCES IN THE SENTENCE

P21 Develop a sentence thought by giving the circumstances related to it—by answering the question *When, where, how,* or *why is this?*

[Thought:] A laugh can be an empty thing.

[Development:] A laugh can be an empty thing, when the joy of Christ is not there to fill it with meaning.

The adverb clause answers the question *When?*

[Thought:] I'm afraid Tarky doesn't like me.

[Development:] I'm afraid Tarky doesn't like me, for I caught him in my closet putting ants and a caramel into the pocket of my coveralls.

The independent clause introduced by *for* answers the question *Why am I afraid?*

CIRCUMSTANCES IN THE PARAGRAPH

P22 Develop a topic thought by giving the circumstances related to it—by answering the question *When, where, how,* or *why is this?*

[Topic thought:] There is a new boy on our block.

[Development:] *There is a new boy on our block!* He arrived yesterday—he and his family—with a big moving van carrying a lot of furniture and (believe me; I saw it) a beautiful mahogany-and-white lake cruiser with a compact marine engine. He is going to live in the Lyons house, the one with the big side yard hidden away behind hedges. He arrived just in time; for, when the Lyonses moved, the neighborhood could no longer use the tree house in the yard nor the basement clubroom; and so the gang on the block was breaking up and joining other groups, having no place to get together. Now we'll be able to reorganize—and my term as president has not expired.

The first sentence (after the topic sentence), *He arrived yesterday . . . marine engine,* tells when and how. The second sentence, *He is going to live . . . behind hedges,* tells where. The last sentences, *He arrived just . . . has not expired,* tell when.

CIRCUMSTANCES IN THE THEME

P23 Develop a theme topic by giving the circumstances related to it.

[Theme topic:] Rear Admiral Jesse B. Oldendorf annihilated Nishimura's fleet.

Though it is not often that a classic textbook problem in naval warfare comes to life in actual battle, it certainly did happen once in recent times, when Rear Admiral Jesse B. Oldendorf annihilated Nishimura's fleet.

Topic paragraph.

The action took place on October 25, 1944, soon after MacArthur's return to the Philippines, at a time when a breakthrough by Nishimura would have jeopardized our chances of winning the war in the Pacific.

When?

Oldendorf's fleet was plugging the gap between Surigao Strait and the part of Leyte Gulf where American landing operations were proceeding under the protection of a number of inadequate old warships.

Where?

Nishimura, who might have skirted Surigao Strait and, going around on the outside of the islands, bottled up the whole American operation in Leyte Gulf and blasted it at will, chose rather to string out his fleet single file in the long narrow alley of Surigao. He lacked anything worthy the name of reconnaissance and did not suspect that the Americans lay athwart the end of the strait. Thus it happened that he steamed straight up to the center of Oldendorf's battle line and created the T-formation in which the perpendicular is subject to murderous cross fire.

How?

Because of the annihilation that followed, the Pacific war went to the Americans; and the tacticians will have something to talk about for years to come.

Conclusion.

COMPARISON AND CONTRAST IN THE SENTENCE

P24   Comparison consists in bringing out points of similarity between two or more things.

P25   Contrast consists in bringing out points of dissimilarity between two or more things.

P26   A contrast may be made only between things in which there are also some points of similarity obvious to the reader. It would be silly to say "Joe is not like the letter *r*," since the reader does not expect Joe to be like the letter *r*. But it is quite all right to say "Joe is not like Jim," because the reader knows that Joe is like Jim in many ways.

P27   In nontechnical talk the word *comparison* is frequently used to include contrast and to mean the showing of points of dissimilarity as well as of similarity between two or more things.

P28   Develop a sentence thought by using comparison, contrast, or both.

[Thought:] Hugh Bright is a flashy dresser.

[Development:] Hugh Bright is a flashy dresser, who, with his green hats, lemon ties, purple shirts, and fancy oxfords, looks like something out of a Technicolor nightmare.

Hugh Bright is compared to something out of a Technicolor nightmare.

[Thought:] Jack Dempsey was a fighter, not a boxer.

[Development:] Jack Dempsey was a fighter, not a boxer, who asked only to stand toe-to-toe and slug—unlike Joe Louis, who, by footwork, by strategy, and by tactical retreat, gained time to study and to wear down his adversary for the kill.

Jack Dempsey is contrasted with Joe Louis.

425

[Thought:] The ricksha is an oriental vehicle.

[Development:] The ricksha is an oriental vehicle that resembles a wheel chair, though unlike a wheel chair it has shafts like a carriage, with a man instead of a horse between them.

The ricksha is both compared and contrasted with first a wheel chair and then a horse-drawn carriage.

COMPARISON AND CONTRAST IN THE PARAGRAPH[10]

P29 Develop a topic thought by using comparison, contrast, or both.

[Topic thought:] God has left us free to love Him, to give Him our joyous suffering and work.

[Development:] If a man said that he loved his wife and yet never let her give him a thing, he would not be a very wise lover. He would soon reduce her to the status of a pauper with nothing to give,

The way in which God lets us love Him is made clear by comparison with the way in which a wise husband lets his wife love him.

nothing with which to assert her love and make it grow. If he never let her cook for him, never let her wash clothes for him, never let her share his worries or his fears, he would rob her of one of the deepest joys there is on earth—the joy of being needed by one's lover. A wise husband gives his wife a reasonable chance to work and suffer with and for him. This makes her happy. So, too, *God has left us free to love Him, to give our joyous suffering and work* in order to fill up what is missing from the suffering and work of Christ. He is a good lover, who understands us well. He will not have us beggars but friends.

[Topic thought:] The campus of Faber High is very quiet in the summer.

[Development:] The campus of Faber High is a very different thing in the winter

The campus in summer is contrasted with the campus in winter.

---

[10] For general notions of comparison and contrast, see P24-27.

from what it is in the summer. In the winter—from fall until late spring—it is a busy place, with five hundred boys milling over it all day long. Early in the morning they come, yelling and shoving, and spill over the lawns and sidewalks and playing fields. At recess, at noontime, and during the long afternoon, they're playing football, basketball, baseball, handball, and games without a name; they're getting into fights and shouting themselves hoarse. But the summer —how different. There is nothing on the campus then but the trees and the sunshine. The grass on the lawns gets thick and green; the weeds grow high on the football field and around the handball courts. The gymnasium, the auditorium, the swimming pool—all are empty caverns. And there is no sound, only silence all day long, deep and continuous silence, strange and out of place, silence that is startled by the sleepy chirp of a sparrow or the hum of a bee.

COMPARISON AND CONTRAST IN THE THEME[11]

P30 Develop a theme topic by using comparison, contrast, or both.

[Introduction:][12] Communists and other vicious groups are thinking about the Negro these days. In fact they have stopped thinking and are already acting to win him for themselves.

[Topic paragraph:] Catholics would do well to consider some facts about the Negro.

[Paragraph of comparison:] Outstanding American Negroes (like George Washington Carver and Booker T. Washington) compare favorably with outstanding American whites (like George Washington and Abraham Lincoln).

[Paragraph of contrast:] George Washington and Abraham Lincoln were permitted to become president of their country; George Carver and Booker Washington would still be kept even from voting in some states.

[Paragraph of comparison:] Christ makes no distinction between His white and black priests: He allows both to drink His precious Blood.

[Paragraph of contrast:] White priests are allowed to eat and drink in just about any restaurant they like; black priests are turned away from most restaurants.

---

[11] For general notions of comparison and contrast, see P24-27.
[12] Only skeletal development of this theme is given here.

[Paragraph of comparison:] The ordinary Negro, when he is given a chance at good education, sanitary facilities, a decent wage, and so on, turns out to be about as good and about as bad as the ordinary white.

[Paragraph of contrast:] The ordinary white American usually meets with as much justice and respect as he deserves and has a right to; the ordinary Negro American meets with contempt, coldness, or, sometimes, warmth in the guise of a blowtorch.

[Conclusion:] Catholics who say they love Christ had better reflect that Christ is in the Negro.

P31 In the example in P30 a theme topic is developed by a series of comparisons and contrasts. Another form of development is one long comparison or contrast running through a number or all of the paragraphs of a theme.

CAUSE AND EFFECT IN THE SENTENCE

P32 Develop a sentence thought by stating some of the effects or consequences of the truth or event in the sentence.

[Thought:] A great tree on the bank suddenly tottered and crashed to earth.

[Development:] A great tree on the bank suddenly tottered and crashed to earth, shattering the night quiet, with the result that Mack, startled, lurched heavily away from the noise, overbalancing the canoe and sending us, our clothes, provisions, guns, and the tent into the black, icy river.

The effects of the crash—the shattering of the quiet, the tipping of the canoe, the loss of the baggage, and the icy plunge—are used to build a very nice sentence.

P33 Develop a sentence thought by stating some of the causes of, or reasons for, the truth or event in the sentence.

[Thought:] The place was called Township—a confusing name.

[Development:] The place was called Township—a confusing name—not because anyone thought the word useful or

The original thought is developed by dismissing one reason for the rather odd name and giving another.

musical, but because an Alvin J. Township, lumberman, had built most of its public buildings out of his profits and had desired to stamp his generosity with his trade-mark.

CAUSE AND EFFECT IN THE PARAGRAPH

P34 Develop a topic thought by stating some of the effects or consequences of the truth or event it relates.

[Topic thought:] A twig snapped in the brush along the bank.

[Development:] *A twig snapped in the brush along the bank.* The frogs fell silent as if on signal. The three boys on the houseboat sat up rigid in their bunks, listening intently. Then Rob threw off his blanket, dropped noiselessly from his upper berth to the floor and, taking the shotgun from its hooks over the door, broke and loaded it with two shells from the box in the cupboard. Cleg and Hart joined him; and all stood silently trying to read reassurance in one another's faces, shivering a little because they were clad only in shorts and a bit more because they were frightened, and listening tensely for the next noise from shore.

The effects of the twig's snapping—the silence of the frogs and the actions and fear of the boys—are used to round out the topic thought into an effective paragraph.

P35 Develop a topic thought by stating some of the causes of, or reasons for, the truth or event it relates.

[Topic thought:] The twig snapped.

[Development:] The man had been careful to avoid any alarm that could alert the boys on the houseboat; and he had been skillful about it, too. But what is one to do when one steps on a snake and cannot tell, in the dark, whether or not it is a moccasin? He stepped back swiftly, of course, and in doing so placed the heel of a boot on a dry twig lying across a little hollow in the ground. *The twig snapped* with a noise as sharp as that of a small firecracker.

The causes of the twig's snapping—the snake, the position of the twig, the man's impulsive action—are used to develop the topic thought.

429

CAUSE AND EFFECT IN THE THEME

P36 Develop a theme topic by stating some of the effects or consequences of the truth or event it relates.

[Introduction:][13] In its relatively brief history, the United States Weather Bureau has recorded some sensational items.

[Topic paragraph:] In December, 1947, New York City was smothered under more than twenty-five inches of snow.

[Paragraph:] Traffic was strangled.

[Paragraph:] A fearful fire hazard was created (fire engines were snowed up in their garages).

[Paragraph:] Normal city life was in great part paralyzed.

[Paragraph:] The removal of the snow cost the city $232,170 for each inch of snow, or about $6,000,000 altogether.

[Paragraph:] But of course there were many who squeezed some fun out of the queer state of affairs.

P37 Develop a theme topic by stating some of the causes of, or reasons for, the truth or event it relates.

[Topic paragraph:][13] Brown, Lovett, and Driscoll do look a little weary this morning.

[Paragraph:] It seems that they attended the game last night in Driscoll's Model-A Ford—not a restful equipage.

[Paragraph:] Moreover, on the way home, the Ford began to disintegrate.

[Paragraph:] The boys left it and walked seven stumbling dark miles to a farm, where they rented a horse.

[Paragraph:] The horse, a spavined hack not up to pulling automobiles, soon collapsed and had to be put on top of the car to rest.

[Paragraph:] The boys pushed the car and the horse the remaining five miles to Houston.

[Paragraph:] In Houston they were arrested for trucking livestock without a license.

[Paragraph:] At 6:00 A.M. Driscoll's father bailed them out—just in time to get ready for school.

[Conclusion:] What wonderful times we have when we are young—and how tired we get having them.

---

[13] Only skeletal development of this theme is given here.

EXAMPLES IN THE SENTENCE

P38 Develop a sentence thought by giving particular instances or concrete examples of the general or abstract truth in the sentence.[14]

[Thought:] Man is always eager to blind himself to what is unpleasant.

[Development:] Man is always eager to blind himself to what is unpleasant; for example, after World War II, Americans put on rose-colored glasses to look at Russia and cried, "What a friendly democracy she is."	The general and abstract notion *man* is made particular and concrete by the example of Americans in the development, and the eagerness to blind oneself to unpleasant things is reduced to a particular example of what Americans did once World War II was safely concluded.

P39 It is by no means always necessary to use an expression like *for example* or *for instance* when developing a thought by giving examples.

EXAMPLES IN THE PARAGRAPH

P40 Develop a topic thought by giving particular instances or concrete examples of the general or abstract truth that it relates.[15]

[Topic thought:] It occasionally happens that, while a boy is in high school, he offers no accurate indication of his chances for the future.

[Development:] *It occasionally happens that, while a boy is in high school, he offers no accurate indication of his chances for the future.* G. K. Chesterton's experience is a	The general truth in the topic statement is developed by naming three men who were rather striking examples of it: G. K. Chesterton, Don Bosco, and Jean Vianney.

---

[14] For the notions of *general* and *abstract*, as the terms are used here, see Q21-22.
[15] See P39.

case in point. He was considered very dull and phlegmatic by his masters, one of whom delivered the crushing verdict that the boy's talent for English writing was negligible. Don Bosco is said to have been another who did not promise much in his early studies, except perhaps tenacity of purpose. And Vianney, the celebrated Curé d'Ars, was to all appearances such a numskull that he was ordained almost with reluctance and misgivings. No doubt their teachers should have been more alert to their capabilities. But the most alert teacher cannot always penetrate the defenses of a bashful student, and it requires special help from God to be able to say that a dullard like Jean Vianney will be transformed into the clairvoyant Curé d'Ars by the action of divine grace.

EXAMPLES IN THE THEME

P41 Develop a theme topic by giving particular instances or concrete examples of the general or abstract truth that it relates.[16]

[Introduction:][17] Those who refuse to accept Christ's word because "it's degrading to take things on faith" should notice what they are doing daily.

[Topic paragraph:] Even aside from the supernatural, man must live by faith.

[Paragraph:] It is only by faith in the testimony of witnesses that many of us know that there actually was an Abraham Lincoln, president of the United States.

[Paragraph:] We should all starve to death or go slowly mad if we did not believe that our restaurants and cooks use salt for seasoning, and not arsenic, when they say they use salt.

[Paragraph:] One who buys or sells stocks would be reduced to gibbering paralysis if he did not believe the quotations that come to him over the wires or in the newspapers.

[Paragraph:] Even the ordinary affairs of family life would become a nightmare if one did not accept on faith much of what his parents and others tell him.

[Conclusion:] If we believe so much on the word of mere human beings, we should not boggle at believing what Christ and His Church tell us.

---

[16] See P39.
[17] Only skeletal development of this theme is given here.

REPETITION IN THE SENTENCE

P42 Develop a sentence thought by repeating an idea in the subject or predicate in different words and with greater clarity or force.[18]

[Thought:] Paul Adams was no sycophant.

[Development:] Paul Adams was no sycophant, not the sort to trail behind campus playboys, waiting his chance to pat them on the back, not the sort to flatter their feeble wit with loud guffaws.

An idea in the predicate, sycophant, is repeated in a descriptive definition that to most readers will be clearer than the word itself.

REPETITION IN THE PARAGRAPH

P43 Develop a topic thought by repeating an idea in the subject or predicate in different words and with greater clarity or force.[18]

[Topic thought:] Mountains are to the earth's bulk what violent muscular activity is to a man's body.

[Development:] *Mountains are to the earth's bulk what violent muscular activity is to a man's body.* The earth's muscles and tendons and sinews are, in the mountain, brought out with fierce and knotted energy, full of expression, passion, and strength. The plains and the low hills are the earth at rest, with its muscles relaxed and concealed under curving, smooth skin. This is one of the first truths about the make-up of earth. The spirit of the mountains is action; the spirit of the plains is rest. The plains are asleep; the mountains with their swelling chests and plunging limbs, lift up their giant faces to heaven, crying, "I live forever!"

The second sentence repeats, more vividly, the notion that mountains equal muscular activity. The third sentence repeats the very same thing, but negatively, by a contrast. The fourth, fifth, and sixth sentences repeat the same notion, each with new clarity or force.

[18] See P45.

REPETITION IN THE THEME

P44 Develop a theme topic by repeating it with greater clarity or from a more interesting angle as the topic thought of subsequent paragraphs.[19]

[Introduction:][20] Too many people spend almost the whole of their brief lives before they discover a basic fact about human happiness.

[Topic paragraph:] We must love God or be unhappy.

[Paragraph:] To love evil is to be unhappy.

[Paragraph:] All human joy worthy of the name is founded in loving God.

[Paragraph:] If we do not love God, we really do not love anything, including ourselves.

[Paragraph:] If we do not love God, the universe is a shrieking nightmare or a cold waste.

[Conclusion:] Do not be dismayed; for to love God is to love and to get—now or later—everything that can satisfy and thrill the human heart.

P45 Greater care must be used with repetition than with the other methods of developing sentences, paragraphs, and themes; for cold, bald, useless repetition will bore a reader to death.

COMBINATION OF METHODS

P46 A combination of two or more of the methods explained in P18-45 can often be used effectively in developing a sentence, a paragraph, or a theme. Indeed, a combination of methods is more common than a single method in the development of themes, since continued use of one method would ordinarily produce monotony.

Introduction:[20] I was a witness to what happened at Tecky Mills last month.

Theme topic: One day "Mr. Smoothy" drifted into the plant.

---

[19] See P45.
[20] Only skeletal development of this theme is given here.

Development by giving circumstances

[Paragraph (when?):] He turned up right after the union at Tecky Mills had negotiated a fair contract with the management.

[Paragraph (how?):] He slipped right in without a stir at the router that old Jim Cabo had vacated when he was pensioned and retired.

Development by enumeration

[Paragraph:] "Mr. Smoothy" was a quiet fellow, rather well-mannered, whose real name was Joel Tollern.

[Paragraph:] He made friends easily.

Development by repetition

[Paragraph:] Yes; one day "Mr. Smoothy" drifted into Tecky Mills. [This is an effect paragraph, used to produce an atmosphere of suspense and slight foreboding, as well as to refocus the reader's attention.]

Development by giving effects

[Paragraph:] The atmosphere of the Mills began to change.

[Paragraph:] The men began to change.

[Paragraph:] Things began to happen to the work—annoying things, dangerous things.

Development by comparison

[Paragraph:] It was as though a kind of corruption had begun to stir and bubble in the Mills.

Development by giving causes

[Paragraph:] Why had "Mr. Smoothy" come?

Conclusion: What has "Mr. Smoothy" taught me?

Q Interest and force

In general

Q1 Interest is that quality of writing which attracts and holds a reader to what the writer is saying.

Q2 Force is that quality of writing which moves a reader to feel, judge, will, or act as the writer wants him to.

Q3 Interest and force are not merely a matter of the rules that follow. They are also a matter of unity, coherence, emphasis, and variety.[1]

Selecting words and expressions

THE RIGHT WORD

Q4 Use the right word or expression. This general rule is made practical in the following particular rules.

Q5 Use words and expressions clear to the audience for which the theme is intended.

It is my pleasant privilege to announce that on the imminent anniversary of the signing of that document by which our great nation threw off the yoke of a tyrannical mother country there will be a great pyrotechnical display in the

This speech, bad writing in itself, is hopelessly worded if it is intended for pupils in the fifth grade. But they could understand the version below without any difficulty.

vicinity of Moore's Wharf on Back Bay about eight-thirty in the evening. Billets admitting you to this extravaganza go at the ridiculously low tariff of ten cents each. But before I enter into commerce with you for the sale of these admissions to volcanic wonders, I must have the solemn pledge of this assembly of splendid little potential citizens of our commonwealth that not one of you will attempt to break through the cordon surrounding the men who will activate the instruments of the display, but that you will all content yourselves with the role of spectator. Ladies and gentlemen, will you gage me your honor for that?

I'm happy to tell you that on the Fourth of July there will be a big fireworks display near Moore's Wharf on Back Bay about 8:30 P.M. Tickets to see the fireworks cost only ten cents. But before I sell you any tickets, all of you must promise that you will not try to go beyond the lines and get close to the men who will be shooting off the fireworks, but will stand and watch where you are supposed to. Do you promise?

---

[1] See M1-27, N1-44, O1-43, and P1-46.

Q6 When you cannot tell, except in a very general way, who your audience will be, keep Q7-18.

Q7 Ordinarily use current words—words in common use. (This requires a good deal of reading; otherwise you will not know what words are in common use.)

[Doubtful:] In front of us stretched the serene.
[Better:] In front of us stretched the placid sea.

Q8 Ordinarily, when you use an uncommon word, make sure that other words around it can carry the main sense without it.

You will learn to add color and life to your themes, sparkle and verve.	Even if *verve* is not understood, the other words make the main meaning of the sentence clear.

Q9 Unless you have good reason for using them, avoid foreign words and phrases and those words that good dictionaries mark "archaic," "obsolete," "rare," "especially British," "dialect," and so on.[2]

Q10 You would have good reason to use the words and phrases discussed in Q9 if you could not express the thought adequately or accurately without them. You would not have good reason, you would merely be silly, if you used them to show off.

Q11 Use words or expressions suitable to the kind of theme you are writing: to its purpose, its mood, its atmosphere, and so on.[3]

Q12 In formal themes[4] ordinarily avoid colloquial words and expressions; that is, words marked "colloquial" in the dic-

---

[2] See Q10. For the use of slang, see Q16-17.
[3] See Q12-18.
[4] Formal themes are themes that, by reason of the subject matter, the occasion, the audience, or something of the kind, should be somewhat impersonal and rather dignified. Such are term papers; constitutions of an organization; speeches on formal occasions (valedictories, for example); impersonal reports, essays, and so on; ordinary business letters; letters to officials; letters of congratulations, acceptance, or condolence written to other than intimate friends.

tionary or expressions characteristic only of rather informal conversation.

We the people of the United States, in order to fix up the rather sloppy union we have had up to now, to make sure that everybody gets what's coming to him, that nobody gets funny at home, and that	The style of the paragraphs at left would be ill suited to the Constitution of the United States, of which they are a parody.

we won't be a pushover for a foreign enemy, that people get their big needs taken care of, and that we and our kids have a generous slice of freedom, do here set up this Constitution of the United States.

Section 1. When it comes to making laws, well, we'll just let Congress handle that.

Q13 Direct quotations within formal themes may, of course, contain colloquialisms.

Q14 In informal themes, use colloquial words and expressions where they best achieve your purpose—best carry the meaning, best establish the right mood and atmosphere, characterize a person or express an idea economically and vividly.[5]

The fact is, Jack was making a general nuisance of himself. So much so that Sheriff Bannock Burns, an advocate of stern and, always, singular justice, began picking vigilantes. Sheriff Burns had been	This quotation from a high-school student's composition uses colloquialisms to advantage, for it indirectly produces the atmosphere proper to a western by means of typically informal language.

_____

[5] See Q15. "Good English varies according to the occasion just as our dress varies according to the occasion. Evening dress would be out of place in playing a football game. Loose colloquial English . . . is frequently as appropriate as a loose-fitting garment in moments of relaxation. The lesser grammarians, who so generally present only one form of English, not only show their bad taste, but do a great deal of harm in that they impart erroneous ideas of language. . . . Those who always think of our popular speech as ungrammatical should recall that our present literary grammar was originally the grammar of the common people of England."—George O. Curme, *Syntax*, in "A Grammar of the English Language" (Boston: D. C. Heath and Company, 1931), Vol. 3, p. vi. By permission.

around quite a while. He was observant and pretty tolerant for a lawman. He had to be. But he knew the countryside well. He knew when somebody's yearlings got into the wrong corral, or why a local rancher was suddenly—and unexplainedly—well to do.

Q15 Great care is needed in the selection of colloquialisms. They must not clash with the rest of the theme, with the mood, with the occasion, and so on. For example, colloquial *ain't* might mar a good newspaper account of a game, whereas colloquial *youngster* would be quite in order.

Q16 Even in informal themes use slang only sparingly and judiciously; when, that is, nothing else would accomplish your purpose so well.[6]

Q17 Most new slang gets old quickly, and much of it dies altogether in a rather short time. It is therefore a good idea, generally, to avoid new slang fads even when they seem to serve your purpose. There are, moreover, degrees of respectability in slang.

Q18 Ordinarily do not use a big word or a sonorous, high-sounding expression where a little word or unpretentious expression will say the same thing as clearly, movingly, and economically.

[Ordinarily poor:] Decapitate the miscreant.
[Ordinarily better:] Cut the scoundrel's head off.

Q19 Use the accurate word or expression.[7]

For example, do not say "The scene was gorgeous," if there was nothing magnificent or resplendently beautiful about it. Content yourself with something like "The countryside was very pretty." Do not say "Then a marvelous thing happened," if the reader is going to discover that you really should have said "Then a surprising thing happened."

---

[6] Slang is not easy to define. Webster's New Collegiate Dictionary (1949) offers this definition: "Slang . . . 2. The jargon of a particular calling or class of society. 3. Language comprising certain widely current terms having a forced, fantastic, or grotesque meaning, or exhibiting eccentric humor or fancy."
[7] See Q20.

Q20 The accuracy required by Q19 is literary, not scientific. Scientific accuracy is ordinarily out of place except in scientific themes.

[Poor:] Tomlin was of average size, weighing about 160 pounds, standing 5 feet 10, and having a waistline of 29 or 30 inches.

[Better:] Tomlin was of average size, agreeably tall and slender but not remarkably so.

THE CONCRETE AND THE PARTICULAR WORD

Q21 A concrete word or expression presents persons and things as they really are. An abstract word or expression presents persons and things stripped down to a bare idea.

Abstract	*Concrete*
God created *man*.	God created *you*.
Age complains.	*An old man* complains.
Paul wanted *wealth*.	Paul wanted *a big bank balance, an estate, a fleet of Cadillacs, and a yacht.*
Justice must prevail.	Ward Riley must get back his stolen money.
Improvement results from constant effort.	With a lot of practice, you can correct that slice.

Q22 A particular word or expression calls to mind only one idea—or, at least, fewer ideas than a more general word or expression would. A general word or expression is one that could call to mind a number of ideas.

General	*Particular*
The man brought home a dog.	*Uncle Henry* brought home a dog.
People are waiting for you down in the drawing room.	*Janet and the electrician* are waiting for you down in the drawing room.
Stalin was ruthless.	To get his way, Stalin starved two million people.

A *dog* makes a good and faithful companion.	An *Airedale* makes a good and faithful companion.
The *noise* frightened him.	The *gunshot* frightened him.

Q23 Make liberal use of concrete and particular words and expressions.[8]

Q24 Concrete and particular expressions are not better than abstract or general ones for every purpose. The latter, while less vivid, have their important uses. Use abstract or general terms—

A To save words.

B For precise statements of principle or definition.

C To phrase brief, clear topic statements that will be made more concrete or particular in the development.

D In summaries of matter that has been or will be treated concretely and particularly.

E To avoid loading a paragraph with too much detail.

F To get contrast and relief from too much concreteness and particularity.

The manner of telling

IN GENERAL

Q25 The ordinary way to tell a thing is to say it straight out. Most of your writing should be like that. To go in for too many tricky expressions is to weaken your style and rob it of sincerity. On the other hand, although people admire what is solid and plain, they do not like too much of it. It is therefore necessary to vary plain talk with the little turns that bring pleasure if they are not used awkwardly or too often. The following rules consider such turns of speech.

---

[8] See Q24. Some words, while they are not actually abstract, have what has been called "the smell of abstraction." Technically, the italicized words in these sentences are both concrete: "*God* has been good to me"; "*The Deity* has been good to me." But *the Deity* brings with it a faint air of the abstract word *deity* (without the article) and hence lacks the vividness of the word *God*.

FIGURES OF SPEECH

Q26   A figure of speech is a change from the ordinary manner of expression, a change used for effect.

Q27   A simile is a comparison between things that are in general unlike, a comparison made with the use of *like, as,* or other comparative words. More briefly, a simile is an express comparison between unlike things.[9]

Thérèse has large, dark eyes.	This is a plain statement.
Thérèse's eyes are like the night itself, large and dark and full of soft mystery.	This is a simile. Eyes are compared to night in some points in which they are alike. Eyes on the whole are very unlike night (in fact the two differ entirely in nature, which is usually the case with the terms of a simile). And, the last essential, the comparison is made with a comparative word —in this case, *like.*

Q28   A simile may be short or long.

For example, many of our Lord's parables are long similes: some, for instance, that begin, "The kingdom of heaven is like . . ."

Q29   A simile may be negative.

Tracy could no more have written this note than a snake can cross its legs.

To put the matter gently and to avoid bruising your feelings—in my opinion this daub of yours resembles a painting about as much as a ten-watt bulb resembles a sunset.

Q30   The comparison in a simile should be better known to the reader, easier to see, or more appealing to the imagination than a plain statement of the thought.

---

[9] The comparison must be made between things that are in general unlike, or there is no figure of speech. For example, "Mary is as tall as Katherine" is not a figure of speech but an ordinary comparison.

He was as timid as a rabbit during the hunting season.	This is a good simile. It is probably more vivid and less vague than the plain statement "He was timid."
His eyes were like chrysolite.	Too few people know what chrysolite looks like. Unless written for mineralogists, this simile is of little value.

Q31 Similes are often awkward or too obvious. In such cases, use a metaphor.

[Awkward simile:] We could not hear above the wind, which was like a wild orchestra.

[Better:] We could not hear above the wild symphony of the wind.

Q32 A metaphor is a comparison between things that are in general unlike, a comparison made without the use of *as, like*, or other comparative words. More briefly, a metaphor is an implied comparison between unlike things.[10]

The night is in Thérèse's eyes, large and dark and full of soft mystery.[11]

You see, Michael's trouble is that he is a turtle. Whenever he sees the shadow of something that might be unpleasant, he quickly withdraws into his shell and holds himself close in nervous tension until pretty certain that the danger is past. In that way, it is true, he escapes a lot of the annoyances that plague other people; but he has more fears. Worst of all, he misses so much of the life he might enjoy if only he stuck his neck out a little more frequently. And it is ironic that, despite all his efforts to protect himself from harsh realities, he is almost fated to share the doom of turtles: to be stepped on, crushed, or tossed into the soup. For even turtles cannot protect themselves from big things. They can only take what God has in store for them—take it like turtles. It's a pity that Michael is not less of a turtle and more of a man.

Q33 Although similes and metaphors are at bottom the same, not every simile can readily be turned into a metaphor.

---

[10] What is said about the simile in Q27, footnote 9, and Q28-30 applies to metaphors as well.

[11] Compare this with the example of a simile under Q27.

Q34 Personification is a particular kind of metaphor. It is a figure of speech that gives the qualities or actions of persons to abstractions and other things that are not persons.

| History is not kind to conservative men. | History is treated as a person, since only persons can be kind in the strict sense. |

Fear lived with us in that house. It stared at us from the mirror in the morning. It gripped our throats when we tried to eat. It sat by our beds and caressed us with icy fingers when we tried to sleep.

Q35 Balance or parallelism can be considered a figure of speech, though not in the sense that it is to be used only occasionally. Ordinarily use like structures for like thoughts.[12]

Q36 When parallel structure becomes lengthy, it is often advisable to break it in order to avoid monotony. The break is usually, though not always, most effective if placed near the end.

Cissie was upstairs on the sleeping porch, and she heard nothing. David was drying dishes with Kathy in the kitchen, and they heard nothing. Mother was ironing in the basement, and she heard nothing. Aunt Sylvia was listening to a television show; and [break] whatever she heard, it was certainly not the howl of a jaguar.

Q37 Antithesis is a particular form of balance or parallelism. It is a figure of speech in which opposed ideas are balanced and placed next to each other or in parallel positions.

That isn't the truth; it's a lie.

You seem so wise, and yet how foolish you are.

Brake inspection costs you one dollar; an accident may cost you one life.

We thought him honest; he is deceitful. We thought him wise; he is only shrewd. We thought his own people esteemed him; they despise him. We thought he loved us; he hates us.

Q38 Antithesis is usually a very forceful, very striking figure. Do not use too much of it.

---

[12] See N8-14.

Q39 Climax is a figure of speech in which thoughts are arranged in ascending order of importance, interest, or effectiveness for a particular audience.[13]

Q40 Anticlimax is a figure of speech in which, for purposes of humor or scorn, climax is observed up to the end of a series of thoughts and then some unimportant idea is mentioned in the last, most important position.

> If you want to understand Daglesby's influence in the school, you must remember that he is no ordinary man made up, like you and me, of a soul, two arms, two legs, and so forth. You must realize that he belongs to a race apart, to the golden boys who represent the best that America can produce. You must weigh the fact that he is one of the demigods, a little larger than life and the dream come true of every man in the country. You must learn to accept this tremendous truth—he is a successful football player.

> Here thou, great Anna, whom three realms obey,
> Dost sometimes counsel take—and sometimes tea.[14]

Q41 Irony is a figure of speech in which one thing is said while obviously the opposite is meant.

> [Said to a man riding an ancient, spiritless hack, incapable of more than a painful walk:] Think you'll be able to bust that bronc?

Q42 Irony may be gentle or cutting. When it is cutting, it is called sarcasm.

> [Said to a bouncy partner at a dance:] I like to dance with you; but then, when I was a little girl, I liked to seesaw, too.

> [Said of England's most bloody executioner:] Gentle Topcliff!

Q43 Apostrophe is a figure of speech in which an absent or dead person or a personified thing is directly addressed.

> What, Washington, would you say now of "foreign entanglements" if you could see the world as it is today?

> Ambition, you have been a cruel master to me. I will serve you no longer.

---

[13] See O5, O20-21, and O31.
[14] Alexander Pope, "The Rape of the Lock," iii, 8. "Anna" is Queen Anne of England, reigning when this poem was written. *Tea* is pronounced *tay*.

Q44 Substitution[15] is a figure of speech in which, because they suggest each other or are otherwise closely associated—

A The maker or source is used for the thing made.

Along with many another illustrious, godly author, *Thomas Aquinas* was burned when Elstra made a bonfire of "subversive" books.	Thomas Aquinas, the writer or maker of the books, is substituted for the books.

B The thing made is used for the maker or source.

Capital has learned to sit down and talk with *labor*.	Capital, the thing, is substituted for the people who possess it. Labor, the thing, is substituted for the people who perform it.

C The sign is used for the thing signified.

I'm afraid we will have to punish those *sullen looks*.	Unless he is unreasonable, the speaker does not wish to punish the looks, which are only a sign, but the person who wears them or the attitude that they signify.

D The container is used for the thing contained.

Who steals my *purse* steals trash.	Iago does not mean the container—the purse itself—but the thing in the purse—money.

E A part is used for the whole.

We sailed for Barcelona in a good *bottom*.	Part of the ship, bottom, is used for the whole ship.
Drought gripped the land. Not a *green ear* stood on any *stalk* in all that country.	The species, ears of corn, is used for the general classification, vegetation.

---

[15] "Substitution" is a name coined by this series to replace the difficult *metonymy* and *synecdoche*. If your teacher prefers, use these definitions: Metonymy is a figure of speech in which a word is used for another which it suggests or which is closely associated with it. Synecdoche is a figure of speech in which the part is put for the whole or the whole for the part.

F The whole is used for a part.

The *nation* went to the polls that day to vote for spiritual life or death.	The whole nation is used for those that actually voted.
This *animal* builds great cities like London.	The general classification, animal, is used for the particular species, man.

G Similar substitutions are made.

Q45 Hyperbole is a figure of speech in which the writer exaggerates, not in order to deceive, but to emphasize a point, create humor, or achieve some similar effect.

An *endless* stream of wharf rats poured over the side the moment the ship docked at Suez.

Q46 Paradox is a figure of speech in which, to jolt the reader into a new realization, the writer states a seeming contradiction that will later be explained or that will yield sense on second thought.

He who loses his life for My sake will save it.

Q47 Onomatopoeia is a figure of speech in which words are used whose sound suggests their sense.

There broke on our ears the *clang* of *cymbals* and the *strident, brassy blasts* of *haughty trumpets.*

Q48 Do not strive for onomatopoeia unless you have good reason to think your audience or reader will be in the mood for it. It falls very flat when the context or the reader is not ready for it.

Q49 Alliteration is a figure of speech in which the same sound is repeated noticeably at the beginning of words placed close together.

*F*ull *f*athom *f*ive thy *f*ather lies.

Q50 Of all the figures of speech, alliteration should be used the most sparingly. Only reading aloud can teach a writer to use it well.

Q51 Make sure that every figure of speech is consistent with itself and consistent with the thoughts around it.

[Badly mixed figures:] Gentlemen, I smell a rat; I see it in the air; and I will nip it in the bud!

Q52 To avoid hackneyed, worn-out writing—

A Work out your own original figures to express your own thoughts.

B When unable to produce an adequate original figure or when the context deserves only a trite, dull figure, do not call attention to the one you have borrowed or emphasize it in any way.[16]

Q53 A great many figures of speech have become so common that they have passed beyond triteness into the very idiom of the language; for example, *best in the long run, right-hand man, as the crow flies.* There is no prohibition against these, unless you use many of them close together.

Q54 If you use figures of speech to "pretty up" your work, you will fall into what is called, without compliment, "fine writing." Follow Q55-59.

Q55 Do not think of figures as ornaments, as something added to a theme. Use them organically—not like clothes draped on a man, but like the organs that make him efficient, effective, and beautiful in himself and as a whole.

Q56 Rethink every thought that you write down. Make sure that it is now your own.

Q57 It often helps to write the first draft of a theme in the form of a letter to someone you know or at least to someone real, and then afterwards to remove the paraphernalia of the letter.

Q58 When writing the second draft of a theme, ask yourself constantly of each sentence, each figure—

A Does this directly or indirectly help the meaning of the main thought of the theme?

---

[16] See Q53.

B Does it help the central mood or atmosphere?
C Does it fit the audience for which I intend the theme?
D Does it fit the real or pretended writer?

Q59 Probe your mind and feelings until you find out why you like or dislike this or that passage in your own or in others' work and until you know whether your reasons are good or bad.

COLOR IN WRITING

Q60 Open your eyes to the colorful glory of God's good world, to the variety and shading. Make a color camera of your eye and turn your writing into a color production.

[Good, but wanting in color:] When she had been warped away from the dock, she flung out her great sails before the following gale, heeled a little under the impact, and then stood smartly down the bay. I tell you it made my heart stand still to look at her.

[With color:] When she had been warped away from the dock, she flung out her great crimson sails, quartered with gold crosses, before the following gale. Her black hull heeled a little under the impact, and then she stood smartly down the bay in the filtered-yellow afterrain. I tell you it made my heart stand still to look at her.

Q61 It is often good to determine color for a reader by appealing to something he is certain to know well.[17]

[Good:] His hair was brownish-red.
[Probably clearer:] His name, like his hair, was "Rusty."

[Good:] They used an ugly rough-finish brown tile in the shower room.
[Probably clearer:] They used an ugly rough-finish milk-chocolate tile in the shower room.

[Good:] Over her white shirt and dark slacks she wore a bright red jacket.
[Probably clearer:] Over her white shirt and dark slacks she wore a gay, neon-red jacket.

---

[17] See Q62.

Q62 Often it is not important that a reader get a definite notion of the color of an object. Do not slow your writing and bore your reader by going in for precision where precision is not necessary.

SUGGESTION

Q63 Do not always make things so plain for your reader that there is nothing for him to do but passively nod his head. Use suggestion now and then.

Q64 Suggestion is supplying the reader with sufficient, and only sufficient, information for him to make out the thought correctly and easily by himself.

[Plain statement:] Thompson is a coward.
[Suggestion:] Oh, Thompson talks a good fight.

[Plain statement:] The prisoner died at three o'clock.
[Suggestion:] By three o'clock the prisoner's soul, at least, had escaped its cell.

[Plain statement:] It looks as though the senator has been accumulating wealth unethically.
[Suggestion:] I'm afraid there's jam on the senator's fingers.

[Plain statement:] Hazel was a mediocre writer.
[Suggestion:] Hazel made the columns of the *New Yorker* once, when a critic recommended her novel to insomniacs.

[Plain statement:] Pearson sobbed out his plea. The judge was not impressed. He merely smiled thinly.
[Suggestion:] Pearson sobbed out his plea. The judge smiled thinly.

RHYTHM

Q65 Read your writing aloud to yourself; or, if you cannot yet read aloud intelligently, get someone to do so for you. Then revise your sentences according to the verdict of your ears.[18]

---

[18] Balance and antithesis (Q35-38), climax (Q39), anticlimax (Q40), onomatopoeia (Q47-48), and alliteration (Q49-50) are involved in rhythm.

Examples of good prose rhythm

If you would know what glory lodges deep in plain men's souls, come along my rounds with me tonight and see them die with courage, love, and dignity.

Far away rang the cry of Judith to the watchmen on the city walls, Open the gates! God is on our side. Open the gates! His power yet lives in Israel.[19]

In the common experience of misery, in the common sorrow of great catastrophes, in humiliation and distress, under the blows of the executioner or the bombs of total war, in concentration camps, in the hovels of starving people in great cities, in any common *necessity,* the doors of solitude open and man recognizes man.[20]

R Exposition

In general

R1 Exposition is that form of writing or talking whose purpose is to explain or inform.[1]

Common examples of exposition are most textbooks, how-to-do-it magazines like *Popular Mechanics,* the labels on canned goods, histories, dictionaries, the WRITING series, catechisms, and most business letters.

R2 A good exposition must have clarity, economy, accuracy.

A Clarity—because the purpose of an exposition is to give light, explanation, information.

---

[19] Judith 13:13. From the Old Testament, Vol. 1, in the translation of Ronald A. Knox. Copyright Sheed and Ward, Inc., New York, 1948.

[20] Jacques Maritain, *Ransoming the Time,* translated by Harry Lorin Binsse (New York: Charles Scribner's Sons, 1941), pp. 17-18. By permission.

[1] Almost always, the four forms of discourse (exposition, narration, description, and argument) are mingled in a composition of any length at all. Thus it happens that an exposition may contain narration, and so on.

If you wish to classify a whole theme, look at its main purpose. If its purpose is to relate a series of events, it is not exposition; if its purpose is to make a reader see, feel, or hear something just in order to entertain him, the piece is not exposition; if to convince or persuade him, not exposition. But if the main purpose is to explain something to him or to give him information, then the theme is exposition. The same thing holds true for portions of themes.

R

B Economy—because the reader's mind easily becomes clogged with too many details, and thus he misses what the writer is trying to explain.

c Accuracy—because misinformation or inexact information will either mislead your reader or cost you his respect, and because truth is godly.

The expository theme

R3 An expository theme is a theme whose purpose is to explain or inform.

CHOOSING THE GENERAL SUBJECT

R4 Not the subject, but the treatment must be new. There are very few new subjects under the sun; but the approaches to any given subject are practically limitless.

R5 When you have little time for study,[2] write about what you know.

R6 When you have sufficient time for study,[2] you may choose a subject that you would like to learn something about.

R7 Keep your readers in mind when you choose your subject. Will they be interested? Interested or not, will they benefit from being told something about this subject?

R8 Keep yourself in mind when you choose your subject. Will you be interested? Interested or not, will you benefit by writing about it? Will your readers accept a treatment of this subject coming from you?

For example, it might not be acceptable for a sophomore to choose "The Seniors Are Morons" as the subject of an editorial.

R

R9 Keep the occasion in mind when you choose your subject. Is it tactful or beneficial to bring up this subject at this time, under these circumstances? (Benefit outweighs tact.)

---

[2] The word *study* is here taken to include reading, interviews, experiments, experiences, and so on—research.

STEPS IN WRITING THE THEME

R10 Once you have chosen the general subject of an expository theme, this is ordinarily the best order to follow:

Step 1. Jot down what you yourself know about the general subject (R11-12).

Step 2. When you have finished jotting, put your notes in order, grouping them under appropriate headings (R13).

Step 3. Whenever necessary, fill out your knowledge of a general subject by means of interviews and reading (R14-22).

Step 4. Select a theme topic (R23-28).

Step 5. Outline the theme (R29-54).

Step 6. Write the rough draft of the theme (R55-57).

Step 7. Write the final copy of the theme (R58-82).

STEP 1. JOTTING

R11 Before you do any research, outlining, or composing, jot down what you yourself know about the general subject.

R12 Write these preliminary notes just as they occur to you, so that nothing may obstruct the free flow of your thought and nothing may distract your memory from the associations it is making.

STEP 2. PUTTING NOTES IN ORDER

R13 Put the notes of R12 in order, grouping related ideas under appropriate headings.

STEP 3. READING

R14 The notes of R11-13 will ordinarily bring to light weaknesses and shortcomings in your knowledge, proof, or authorities. Whenever necessary, fill out your knowledge of a general subject by means of interviews or reading.

R15 Use the services of the librarian. He knows his way through the various guides, indexes, and reference works; and he knows the books in his own library. He can help you track down information on almost any subject and can teach you to use the library intelligently.

R16 Here are some helpful standard reference works.[3]

Encyclopedias
AMERICAN PEOPLES ENCYCLOPEDIA, Sears, Roebuck and Company
BRITANNICA JUNIOR, Encyclopaedia Britannica Company
CATHOLIC ENCYCLOPEDIA, Robert Appleton
COLUMBIA ENCYCLOPEDIA, Columbia University Press
COMPTON'S PICTURED ENCYCLOPEDIA AND FACT INDEX, F. E. Compton and Company
ENCYCLOPAEDIA BRITANNICA, Encyclopaedia Britannica Company
ENCYCLOPEDIA AMERICANA, Americana Corporation
LINCOLN LIBRARY OF ESSENTIAL INFORMATION, Frontier Press
NEW INTERNATIONAL ENCYCLOPEDIA, Funk and Wagnalls Company
WORLD BOOK ENCYCLOPEDIA, Field Enterprises, Inc.

Yearbooks and almanacs
AMERICANA ANNUAL, Americana Corporation
BRITANNICA BOOK OF THE YEAR, Encyclopaedia Britannica Company
FUNK AND WAGNALLS NEW STANDARD ENCYCLOPEDIA YEARBOOK, Funk and Wagnalls Company
NEW INTERNATIONAL YEAR BOOK, Funk and Wagnalls Company
WORLD BOOK ENCYCLOPEDIA ANNUAL SUPPLEMENT, Field Enterprises, Inc.
THE AMERICAN YEAR-BOOK, Thomas Nelson and Sons
ECONOMIC ALMANAC, National Industrial Conference Board
INFORMATION PLEASE ALMANAC, The Macmillan Company
NATIONAL CATHOLIC ALMANAC, Saint Anthony Guild

Biographical dictionaries
AMERICAN CATHOLIC WHO'S WHO, Walter Romig
BOOK OF CATHOLIC AUTHORS, Walter Romig
CURRENT BIOGRAPHY: WHO'S NEWS AND WHY, H. W. Wilson Company
DICTIONARY OF AMERICAN BIOGRAPHY, Charles Scribner's Sons

---

[3] It is an excellent idea to make your own catalog of those books on this list that can be found in your school library.

DICTIONARY OF NATIONAL BIOGRAPHY, Oxford University Press

Thomas, Joseph, UNIVERSAL PRONOUNCING DICTIONARY OF BIOGRAPHY AND MYTHOLOGY, J. B. Lippincott Company

WEBSTER'S BIOGRAPHICAL DICTIONARY, G. and C. Merriam Company

WHO WAS WHO IN AMERICA, Vol. 1, 1897-1942; Vol. 2, 1943-1950; A. N. Marquis Company

WHO'S WHO (1848 to date), A. and C. Black, Ltd., London

WHO'S WHO IN AMERICA (1899 to date), A. N. Marquis Company

Dictionaries and books of synonyms

AMERICAN COLLEGE DICTIONARY, Harper and Brothers

CATHOLIC DICTIONARY, The Macmillan Company

CONCISE CATHOLIC DICTIONARY, The Bruce Publishing Company

CONCISE OXFORD DICTIONARY OF CURRENT ENGLISH, Oxford University Press

Fowler, H. W., A DICTIONARY OF MODERN ENGLISH USAGE, Oxford University Press

NEW CENTURY DICTIONARY OF THE ENGLISH LANGUAGE, Appleton-Century-Crofts Company, Inc.

NEW OXFORD DICTIONARY (Murray's, N.E.D., New English Dictionary), Oxford University Press

NEW PRACTICAL STANDARD DICTIONARY OF THE ENGLISH LANGUAGE, Funk and Wagnalls Company

THORNDIKE-BARNHART COMPREHENSIVE DESK DICTIONARY, Doubleday and Company

WEBSTER'S NEW INTERNATIONAL DICTIONARY OF THE ENGLISH LANGUAGE, G. and C. Merriam Company

ROGET'S INTERNATIONAL THESAURUS, Thomas Y. Crowell Company

WEBSTER'S DICTIONARY OF SYNONYMS, G. and C. Merriam Company

Gazetteers and atlases

LIPPINCOTT'S COMPLETE PRONOUNCING GAZETTEER OR GEOGRAPHICAL DICTIONARY OF THE WORLD, J. B. Lippincott Company

WEBSTER'S GEOGRAPHICAL DICTIONARY, G. and C. Merriam Company

WORLD ATLAS, Encyclopaedia Britannica Press

WORLD ATLAS, Rand McNally Company

Histories of literature and similar books

CAMBRIDGE HISTORY OF AMERICAN LITERATURE, The Macmillan Company

CONCISE CAMBRIDGE HISTORY OF ENGLISH LITERATURE, The Macmillan Company

OUTLINE HISTORY OF AMERICAN LITERATURE, Barnes and Noble, Inc.

OUTLINE HISTORY OF ENGLISH LITERATURE, Barnes and Noble, Inc.

OXFORD COMPANION TO AMERICAN LITERATURE, Oxford University Press

OXFORD COMPANION TO CLASSICAL LITERATURE, Oxford University Press

OXFORD COMPANION TO ENGLISH LITERATURE, Oxford University Press

READER'S ENCYCLOPEDIA OF WORLD LITERATURE AND THE ARTS, Thomas Y. Crowell Company

Mythology and antiquities

Gayley, Charles M., CLASSIC MYTHS IN ENGLISH LITERATURE AND IN ART, Ginn and Company

Hamilton, Edith, MYTHOLOGY, Little, Brown and Company

Peck, Harry T., HARPER'S DICTIONARY OF CLASSICAL ANTIQUITIES, American Book Company

Books of quotations

Everett, Christopher and Louella, BARTLETT'S FAMILIAR QUOTATIONS, Little, Brown and Company

Mencken, H. L., A NEW DICTIONARY OF QUOTATIONS ON HISTORICAL PRINCIPLES FROM ANCIENT AND MODERN SOURCES, Alfred A. Knopf, Inc.

Indexes to books and periodicals

CUMULATIVE BOOK INDEX (1928 to date), H. W. Wilson Company

GUIDE TO CATHOLIC LITERATURE, Walter Romig

THE UNITED STATES CATALOG (books in print January 1, 1928), H. W. Wilson Company

ANNUAL MAGAZINE SUBJECT INDEX, F. W. Faxon Company

CATHOLIC PERIODICAL INDEX, H. W. Wilson Company

INTERNATIONAL INDEX TO PERIODICALS (1907 to date), H. W. Wilson Company

READER'S GUIDE TO PERIODICAL LITERATURE (1900 to date), H. W. Wilson Company

R17 If there is a great deal of material available on your general subject, choose one aspect of the subject and read with that as a guide. Select articles that seem likely, from their listing in the index and from other indications, to treat your angle of the subject. Omit or read quickly portions of books that do not treat your angle.

R18 When you are reading in order to write, keep with you a pencil or pen, a packet of cards 3 x 5 or 4 x 6 inches in size, and some ordinary paper. Use them as directed in R19-22.

R19 When in your reading you come across a passage that bears on your subject and looks as if it may be useful as a reference, put a code number for that particular book, article, or pamphlet in the upper right-hand corner of the card. It does not matter what the number is so long as it is not repeated on any other card.

R20 Next make a reference for the book, article, or pamphlet on the card. These are the various forms:

For reference to books
Name of author
Title of the book, underlined
Place of publication, publisher, and date of publication (or—if that is missing—of copyright). Enclose all these in one set of parentheses followed by a period.
Library call number

```
                                                    13

   Hilaire Belloc,

   Joan of Arc

   (London: Cassell and Company, Ltd., 1929).


   BJ 572 Be

```

For reference to magazine articles
Author of the article (if the name is given)
Title of the article, in quotation marks
Name of the magazine, underlined; the volume; the date between
parentheses; the pages; a period following the last item

```
                                                        6


    Herbert Elliston,

    "Jim Forrestal, a Portrait in Politics,"

    the Atlantic Monthly, Vol. 188 (November,
    1951), pp. 73-80.
```

For reference to newspaper articles
Headline or title of the article, in quotation marks
Name of the city (and state, if necessary) in which paper is published; name of paper, underlined; date; page; column; a period
following the last item

```
                                                        8


    "Educational TV? 20-Odd Colleges Plan
    Own Stations,"

    New York, the Wall Street Journal,
    June 5, 1952, p. 1, col. 1.
```

For reference to articles in encyclopedias
Author of the article (if you can find his name)
Title of the article, in quotation marks
Title of the encyclopedia, without underlining or quotation marks;
the year or edition; the volume; the pages; a period following the
last item

```
                                                        10


    Frederick Barton Maurice,

    "Lee, Robert Edward,"

    Encyclopaedia Britannica, 1950, Vol. 13,
    pp. 862-64.
```

R21 It is best to make out the cards in R18-20 immediately,
while you are working through indexes, guides, and bibli-
ographies, whenever you find a likely looking article or
book. Even if you do not use the cards directly in your
theme, they will furnish you with a bibliography.

R22 When reading a book or article listed on your card, if you
come to a pertinent passage, make a brief summary of it
on the ordinary paper (or, if you intend to quote it, copy
it word for word) and add the card code number and the
pages on which the passage appears in the book.

STEP 4. SELECTING A THEME TOPIC

R23 Select a theme topic and write it out.[4]

R24 Writing out the theme topic often exposes weaknesses in
it. A written theme topic, moreover, lying on your desk

[4] For the notion of theme topic, see M19-21.

before your eyes, is a constant reminder of what the theme is supposed to be about and keeps you from straying off into useless digressions.

R25 If it is at all possible to do so—and it almost always is—state your theme topic in a single, uncomplicated, declarative sentence:

    A A single, uncomplicated sentence, because the briefer and less complicated the theme topic, the easier it is to develop it coherently.

    B A declarative sentence, because questions do not indicate and limit development. There are innumerable developments possible if the theme topic is "How did Denton beat Plainville?" But the two chief parts of the theme are already plain if the theme topic is "Denton beat Plainville by using a modified T and concentrating on Joe Jacoby."

    C A complete sentence, because half-sentences and very elliptical sentences cause the same trouble that questions do.

R26 Limit the general subject sharply when stating the theme topic.

For example, if a student has Russia as his general subject, he will get into difficulties if he makes his theme topic "The history of Soviet Russia is interesting." The development could easily run to many volumes. The student will probably write a hop-skip-and-jump theme in which he touches many topics and handles none of them well or an unfinished theme with only "The End" to show that he meant to conclude it. He would do much better to use a topic like this, "At the United Nations during 1950, Russia acted on the principle that truth means whatever may help the Communist party."

R27 Avoid extravagant and superlative terms when stating the theme topic.

For example, it is easy to show that Da Vinci's *Last Supper* is a well-beloved masterpiece. It would be very difficult indeed to show that it is the greatest painting in the world.

R28 Make the theme topic as definite as you reasonably can.

[Vague, leading to uncertain planning and development:] There are several steps in cracking petroleum.

[Definite, leading to clear-cut planning and development:] There are five steps in cracking petroleum.

STEP 5. OUTLINING

R29 An outline is a sketch showing the theme topic and the main points of its development.[5]

R30 The outline is not merely a helpful adjunct to the writing of expository themes; it is also a useful form of exposition in its own right. It is sometimes the clearest way in which first to present a difficult subject to a reader, since it gives him an uncomplicated, over-all view. It offers a convenient set of hooks on which to hang an extempore talk. Lastly, an outline can be a help to study. When, for example, you have to put great masses of matter into your head to pass an examination, you would do well to outline the material and then study the outline.

R31 Two kinds of outline are particularly useful in planning an expository theme: the topic outline (R32-50) and the sentence outline (R51-52).

R32 A topic outline is a list of the points a theme will discuss, arranged to show their equal or unequal importance and expressed (with the exception of the theme topic) in incomplete sentences.

Theme topic.—Interscholastic football is not the sport for four classes of boys.
  I. Some boys occupied with more important things
 II. Some boys unfit physically
III. Some boys unfit intellectually
 IV. Some boys unfit emotionally

---

[5] In this book *outline* is a technical term reserved for exposition. The sketch of a narrative is called a plan or a plot, and the sketch of an argument or persuasive speech is called a brief. (In popular speech *outline* is often used for all three and even for summaries and condensations.)

Except in the case of very short themes without much development, an outline such as the one just above, which gives only the main heads, does not serve very well. Usually subheads are needed, as shown below.

Theme topic.—Interscholastic football is not the sport for four classes of boys.

   I. Some boys occupied with more important things
      A. Earning their education
      B. Developing intellectual abilities
  II. Some boys unfit physically
      A. Injuries and diseases
      B. Slow co-ordination
III. Some boys unfit intellectually
      A. From viewpoint of the team
      B. From viewpoint of the boy
         1. Cannot spare time from studies
            a) Long practice
            b) Utter weariness
            c) Constant distraction
         2. Cannot keep football in its proper place
         3. Cannot get benefits of training
 IV. Some boys unfit emotionally
      A. From viewpoint of the team
         1. Irresponsible
         2. Indecisive
      B. From viewpoint of the boy
         1. Strain
         2. Abnormal reactions
            a) Depression
            b) Elation
            c) Fear
               (1) However, football sometimes a diagnosis
               (2) However, football sometimes a cure
                  (a) Much depends on coach
                  (b) Much depends on other boys
                  (c) Much depends on boy himself

Note that by no means must all heads have subheads or sub-subheads. Only so many should be used as the author wishes or the matter requires.

R33 If you wish, you may indicate the introduction or the conclusion or both in the outline.

> *Theme topic.*—Interscholastic football is not the sport for four classes of boys.
> *Introduction.*—This article necessary though unpopular
>   I. Some boys occupied with more important things
>   II. Some boys unfit physically
>   A. Injuries and diseases
>   B. Slow co-ordination
>   III. Some boys unfit intellectually
>   IV. Some boys unfit emotionally
> *Conclusion.*—This article intended to help, not to stir controversy

R34 Do not use any letters or figures with the headings "theme topic," "introduction," and "conclusion." But you must italicize them and follow them with a period and a dash.

R35 Do not bother to use the heading "body." The Roman numerals are sufficient indication of the body of the theme, and "body" would only clutter the outline.

R36 Ordinarily the headings "introduction" and "conclusion" should be written in last; otherwise you may give in to the inclination to conceive a brilliant introduction and make the rest of the theme fit it, instead of the other way round as good sense requires.[6]

R37 Begin each heading of an outline with a capital.

R38 Do not use a period after the headings of a topic outline unless they make complete sentences.[7] You may use a question mark or an exclamation point if either is needed for clarity.

R39 Label the heads and subheads with these alternating figures and letters in this order: I. II. III.; A. B. C.; 1. 2. 3.; a) b) c); (1) (2) (3); (a) (b) (c); i. ii. iii.[7]

R40 Put a period after all the letters and figures in R39 that are not followed by a mark of parenthesis.

---

[6] See L6.
[7] See the second example under R32.

R41   Do not put a period after the letters and figures in R39 that are followed by a mark of parenthesis.

R42   The heads in each series marked with the same kind of letter or figure should be of equal or nearly equal importance. For example, Head II should be equal or nearly equal to Head I; Head B under Head I should be equal or nearly equal to Head A, but not equal to Head I; and so on.

R43   Whenever it can reasonably be done, begin each head in the same series with the same or an equivalent part of speech.[8] This verbal parallelism aids the mind in remembering the headings and in perceiving immediately which are of parallel importance.

  I. Noun . . . .
      A. Verb . . . .
         1. Preposition . . . .
         2. Preposition . . . .
      B. Verb . . . .
 II. Noun . . . .
      A. Adverb . . . .
      B. Adverb . . . .
         1. Verb . . . .
         2. Verb . . . .

Note that all Roman-numeral heads are in the same series. A and B under Head I are in one series; A and B under Head II are in another; and so on.

R44   Whenever you can easily carry parallelism beyond the first word of a heading, do so.

R45   Do not cling to parallel form at the expense of clarity or efficiency.

R46   Indent heads labeled A, B, C; indent 1, 2, 3, more deeply than A, B, C; and so on. Line up vertically all heads that have the same kind of number or letter.

---

[8] Gerunds and pronouns may be considered parallel with nouns, adjectival participles with adjectives, and so on.

```
I.
    A.
    B.
        1.
        2.
            a)
            b)
                (1)
                (2)
                    (a)
                    (b)
                        i.
                        ii.
II.
    A.
    B.
        1.
        2.
```

R47 Do not ordinarily use a single subhead under any head. A single subhead can usually be combined with its head, with benefit to the arrangement and logic of the outline.

Wrong	*Right*
I. The panic	I. The panic, July, 1742
A. July, 1742	II. The rebellion
II. The rebellion	

R48 Make each head and subhead as definite as you can without being wordy. Use statements instead of questions.

Wrong	*Right*
I. The loss of Balny	I. The loss of Balny
A. When?	A. At the beginning of the war
B. How?	B. Through Marvin's treachery
C. By whom?	C. By General Jasper Clark

R49 Do not give details.

R50 The heads of the outline may in some cases coincide with the topic thought of paragraphs written from the outline. But there need not be one paragraph or only one paragraph for each head or subhead of the outline.

R51 A sentence outline is a list of the points a theme will discuss, arranged to show their equal or unequal importance and expressed in sentences.

Theme topic.—Interscholastic football is not the sport for four classes of boys.

Introduction.—This article is necessary though it will probably be unpopular.

   I. Some boys are occupied with things more important than football.
      A. Some are earning their education.
      B. Some are developing their intellectual abilities.
  II. Some boys are unfit physically.
      A. Injuries and diseases disable some.
      B. Slow co-ordination hinders others.
 III. Some boys are unfit intellectually.
      A. Some are unfit from the viewpoint of the team.
      B. Others are unfit from the viewpoint of the boy.
         1. They cannot spare time from their studies.
           a) Long practice fights study.
           b) Utter weariness fights study.
           c) Constant distraction fights study.
         2. They cannot keep football in its proper place.
         3. They cannot get the benefits of the training.
 IV. Some boys are unfit emotionally.
      A. Some are unfit from the viewpoint of the team.
         1. They are irresponsible.
         2. They are indecisive.
      B. Others are unfit from the viewpoint of the boy.
         1. They undergo too much strain.
         2. They experience abnormal reactions.
           a) They experience depression.
           b) They experience elation.
           c) They experience fear.
              (1) However, football sometimes diagnoses fear.
              (2) However, football sometimes cures fear.
                 (a) Much depends on the coach.
                 (b) Much depends on the other boys.
                 (c) Much depends on the boy himself.

Conclusion.—This article is intended to help, not to stir up controversy.

R52 The statements in R33-37 and R39-50 apply to both topic and sentence outlines.

R53 Remember that a very few headings in an outline can turn into a very long theme.

R54 Do not hesitate to alter the outline while you are writing the theme; but show the alterations on paper, and do not work without a written outline.

STEP 6. THE ROUGH DRAFT

R55 When you have completed your outline, write a rough draft of the expository theme.

R56 Space the lines of the rough draft very widely and leave abundant margins at the top, bottom, and sides for corrections and insertions. If you are using lined paper, it is usually a good idea to skip every other line. A crowded and messy rough draft can treble your work and lead to disorganized writing.

R57 When you transfer to the rough draft a direct quotation or a fact or an idea from the notes described in R18-22, put after it the code number of the card and the pages of the book from which you borrowed the material. Encircle the code and page numbers.

> "The King's Men played on no bare boards; the throne of Denmark was no chair. Renaissance stagecraft was quite elaborate. It included nearly everything that the lighting and machinery of those days could produce." (Card 7, page 102)

STEP 7. THE FINAL COPY

R58 The following regulations will produce a neat, legible final copy that teachers will enjoy correcting and others will enjoy reading. The rules are for typewritten copy, but with obvious changes most of them apply to handwritten copy also.

R59 Write on only one side of each sheet.

R60 Leave a margin of at least an inch and a half at the top, bottom, and left of each page and a margin of at least one inch at the right.

R61 Double-space your typing.[9]

R62 Place your name, the course, the date, and other pertinent information in the upper right-hand corner, but inside the margins, of the first page.[10] Put the name on its own line, the course on its own line, and so on.[11]

R63 Halfway down the first page, center the title of the paper between the side margins.[11]

R64 Type the title all in capitals, with or without underlining, or in capitals and small letters, with underlining. Do not use quotation marks unless *part* of the title is a quotation from some other work.

<u>TROUBLE IN SONORA</u>   TROUBLE IN SONORA   <u>Trouble in Sonora</u>

<u>The Meaning of Lady Macbeth's "We Fail"</u>

R65 After the title skip two line-spaces and center your by-line under the title.[11] (A by-line is the word *by* followed by the name of the author. It may ordinarily be omitted. It should be included if the article is to be published and the by-line is copy for the printer, especially if the author writes under a pen name different from the name in the upper right-hand corner of the first page.)

R66 After the by-line (or after the title if there is no by-line), skip three line-spaces and begin the first paragraph.[11]

---

[9] This rule does not apply to a direct prose quotation that runs to two or more sentences and at the same time to four or more typewritten lines (R72), to quotations of more than one line of poetry (R74), to notes grouped together at the end of a theme (R80), or to footnotes (R81)—all of which are to be single-spaced in order to set them off from the rest of the text.

[10] "Other pertinent information" means whatever is necessary for the reader to identify the paper at a glance. If you are writing for publication, the editor will want to know the number of words; so put that in too. But do not clutter this corner with any unnecessary information.

[11] See illustration under R68.

R67 The first lines of all paragraphs should be uniformly indented. Indent not less than three and not more than eight typewriter characters. In handwritten copy indent not less than half an inch and not more than an inch. Less is usually undiscernible; more is usually ugly.

R68 On the first page, midway between the last line of type and the bottom edge of the paper and midway between the left and right margins, center the Arabic numeral *1*. Do not use the word *page*.

Ethel B. Terry
English 3
Term paper for Mr. Walsh
January 16, 1955

Trouble in Sonora

By Ethel B. Terry

One would hardly expect an incident that took place in
Sonora, Mexico, to affect the course of American literature. The incident I have in mind probably would have been
recorded only in Spanish-language chronicles if James M.
Race--an American tourist sojourning in a Mexican village--
had not witnessed it. Because Race was there, because he
owned a newspaper in Axton, Wyoming, to which he wired an
account of what he saw, and because a young American writer
of promise noticed the account and was aroused by it, there

1

R69   Number pages 2, 3, 4, and so on, with an Arabic numeral just inside the right-hand margin, midway between the top edge of the paper and the first line of text. Do not use the word *page*.[12]

```
                                                               2



            exists today a body of writing that would not otherwise have

            come to be.

                 The incident took place on July 25, 1879, in the village

            of Corrubias, Sonora, Mexico. At a time of day not specified

            in Race's account, shots were heard in the vicinity of a

            wine shop at one end of the Calle Fortinbras. The police of
```

R70   If you wish or are required to do so, use a running head from page 2 to the end of the theme. Starting just inside the left-hand margin, on the same line with the page number,[13] write your name in capitals and small letters; then a comma; and then the title all in capitals, with or without underlining, or in capitals and small letters with underlining. If the title is too long for the space, use a shortened form. The running head should stop at least five typewriter characters before the page number.

```
            Ethel B. Terry, Trouble in Sonora                   2


            exists today a body of writing that would not otherwise have

            come to be.

                 The incident took place on July 25, 1879, in the village

            of Corrubias, Sonora, Mexico. At a time of day not specified

            in Race's account, shots were heard in the vicinity of a

            wine shop at one end of the Calle Fortinbras. The police of
```

R71   Direct prose quotations, except for those mentioned in R72, should be inserted right into the text of the theme and enclosed in double quotation marks.

---

[12] *Page*, though common enough, is unnecessary.
[13] See R69.

R72 When a direct prose quotation runs to two or more sentences *and at the same time* to four or more typewritten lines, it should be indented in its entirety eight typewriter characters from the left-hand margin and typed single-space. Paragraphs should be indicated by indenting the first line an additional three typewriter characters. No quotation marks should be used except those that are in the original text.

```
it became quite clear that he was interested in the transfer

only because it meant a saving of some thousands of dollars

to his firm of importers. In the signed minutes of the meet-

ing held on January 2, 1948, the stenographer reports Bullock

directly as saying--

          Frankly, I don't care whether these children are
     returned to Frankfort or not. I want the use of my
     warehouse, and I want someone else to take over the
     task of feeding them. Each of them is costing us
     from fifty cents to a dollar a day for food. You can
     talk all you want about "the Christian attitude," as
     Mr. Pollet so beautifully puts it; I'm a hardheaded
     businessman, and I just don't put out money where
     none comes in.26

     It was at this point that Mr. Pollet, seconded by the dele-

gate from England, made a motion to expel Mr. Bullock from
```

It is permissible (indeed, some college style sheets require it) to indent long quotations an equal distance from the left- and right-hand margins.

R73 Quotations of only one line of poetry should be inserted right into the text of the theme and enclosed in double quotation marks.

R74 Quotations of more than one line of poetry should be set off from the text by single-spacing and centered between the left and right margins. No quotation marks should be used except those that are in the original poem.

R75 Unless your theme is very informal indeed, you will want to acknowledge the source of any direct quotations in it and also of ideas and information not directly quoted but nonetheless borrowed from some other writer.

R76 The acknowledgment called for in R75 is not ordinarily made right in the text itself. It is made either in notes at the end of the theme[14] or in footnotes at the bottom of the same page on which the end of the quotation or borrowed material appears.[15] The purpose is to avoid interrupting the text with dull and complicated references.

R77 At the place in the text where you wish to introduce a note or a footnote, write a superior figure. On an ordinary typewriter a superior figure is written by turning the platen back half a space and holding it there with the left hand and striking the number key with a finger of the right hand. Place the superior figure always immediately after the quotation or words to which the note belongs.[16]

R78 The first superior figure to appear in the theme should be *1*, the second should be *2*, and so on down through the theme.[17]

R79 A superior figure in the text should be placed immediately after a word, with no intervening space, unless punctuation follows the word. If punctuation follows the word, the figure should be placed immediately after the punctuation, with no intervening space.

```
The second book9 had not yet been published.
```

```
As a friendly critic of Mr. Danesly's theories insists,
"Danesly always expressed himself badly. He was not so
foolish as his writing makes him seem."10
```

[14] For notes at the end of the theme, see R80.

[15] For footnotes see R81-82.

[16] See R78-79.

[17] When you are using footnotes (rather than notes grouped together at the end of the theme), it is permissible to start over with superior-figure *1* on each page. For the sake of uniformity, however, number your notes consecutively throughout the theme unless the school or your teacher directs otherwise.

In many books, footnote numbers begin again at *1* with each chapter or section. The object is to make sure that footnote numbers never go above 99. Three-figure numbers are rather noticeable. They tend to interrupt the text and make a page of type matter look less pleasant.

R80 When footnotes are not used,[18] but rather all the notes are grouped together at the end of the theme—

   A Do not start these notes on the page on which the theme ends but on the next page.

   B On the first line under the top margin write *Notes* with a capital and small letters and underline it. Center the word between the left and right margins.

   C After the title *Notes*, skip two line-spaces, indent as for paragraph, and then write the number of the first note. (Write the number on the line; do not turn the platen back half a space as for a superior figure.) Follow the number with a period. Hit the space bar once and then copy the note from the card according to R81, G. Do the same for subsequent notes.

   D Single-space the notes.

   E Skip a line-space between notes.

14

Notes

   1. Hilaire Belloc, Joan of Arc (London: Cassell and Company, Ltd., 1929), pp. 134-35.

   2. Herbert Elliston, "Jim Forrestal, a Portrait in Politics," the Atlantic Monthly, Vol. 188 (November, 1951), p. 75.

R81 When footnotes are used—[19]

   A Make sure that the footnotes do not run into the bottom margin of the page. When footnotes and text cannot be perfectly fitted, it is better to let the text fall short than to invade the margins.

---

[18] Readers do not like to turn back and forth to relate notes and text. They much prefer to find a note at the bottom of the page to which it is pertinent. For this reason, many college style books instruct the student to use footnotes instead of a note section at the end of a theme. Unless your teacher directs otherwise, use footnotes exclusively.

[19] The treatment of footnotes given here is by no means exhaustive. It gives only the basic notions that a student is expected to bring with him to college. In difficulties that go beyond the rules in this book, consult your teacher or work out your own solution. Moreover, this is only one of several common systems of writing footnotes. It is, however, a good one.

B Separate the first footnote from the text by a line twenty typewriter characters long.

C Separate the first footnote from the line mentioned in B, just above, by a line-space.

D Separate one footnote from another on the same page by a line-space.

E Single-space each footnote.

F Before writing the superior figure at the beginning of each footnote, indent the same number of spaces as for a standard paragraph of the text.[20] Then turn the platen back half a space and write the footnote number. The first word of the footnote follows the number immediately, without intervening space.

G Copy the information from the card,[21] adding the page number from the rough copy.[22] Do not use the library call number in the footnote.

H When two or more footnotes that are identical (or identical except for the page numbers) follow one another consecutively, give full information only in the first; use *ibid.* (short for *ibidem,* in the same place) for the others. Underline *ibid.* and use the abbreviation only. Put a comma after *ibid.* and write the page numbers if they differ from those of the footnote immediately above.

I When two or more footnotes that are identical (or identical except for the page numbers) do not follow one another consecutively, use the author's last name, a comma, and *op. cit.* (short for *opere citato,* in the work already quoted). Underline *op. cit.,* use the abbreviation only, and always put a comma and the page numbers after it.

---

[20] This refers to the ordinary paragraph discussed in R67, not to the indented quotations discussed in R72 and R74.

[21] See R19-20. If the information on the card has been properly punctuated and capitalized according to the models in R20, then you need only copy it in run-on lines and it will appear in proper footnote form. Of course, you must insert the pertinent page numbers of your quotation just before the period. Do not give the general page numbers on the card, for they indicate where the *article* may be found rather than where the particular quotation you have used may be found.

[22] See R22 and R57.

J *Op. cit.* may not be used if two works by the same author have already been cited in the theme, for the
reader would not readily know to which one it referred.
If two authors cited in the theme have the same last
name, then in *op. cit.* footnotes the first name or the
initials must be used as well as the last name.

```
        so that the connection between raising doves and Shakespeare
        is not so remote as it might at first seem.


            ⁶Robert P. Brooks, Shakespeare's Stage (Boston: T. McGill
        and Sons, 1936), p. 103.

            ⁷Ibid.

            ⁸Ibid., p. 23.

            ⁹Ibid., p. 25.

            ¹⁰William L. Tremont, "Raising Doves," Backyard Life,
        Vol. 36 (December, 1949), p. 124.

            ¹¹Ibid., p. 126.

            ¹²Brooks, op. cit., pp. 109-10.

            ¹³Harrison J. Tremont, Fine Feathers (Raleigh: Bardun and
        Baines, 1953), p. 112.

            ¹⁴William L. Tremont, op. cit., p. 125.

            ¹⁵Ibid.
```

R82 Footnotes are not reserved exclusively for bibliographical
reference. They may be used for editorial comment or for
information that should not be allowed to interrupt the
text and yet may be useful to the reader. In the ordinary
theme, however, there should not be many nonbibliographical footnotes; for footnotes annoy some readers,
who cannot resist reading them and yet find them distracting. If, therefore, there is any doubt about the usefulness of a nonbibliographical footnote, omit it. For every
reader that it pleases, there will probably be three others
that it will annoy. In matter that is not intended to be
read consecutively—such, for example, as the rules in this
book—abundant footnotes are not a hazard; indeed, they
are welcomed if, by cross references and similar appara-
tus, they help the reader to find what he wants.

Definitions

IN GENERAL

R83 Definition is the explanation of the meaning of a word or phrase.

R84 A good definition explains a word in terms that are better understood by the reader than the word to be defined.

[Not a good definition for most readers:] Mallophaga are an order or suborder of ametabolous insects with mandibulate mouth, valvate labium, shovel-shaped head, and flat body.

[A better definition for most readers:] Mallophaga are bird lice.

R85 Two of the most common and useful forms of definition are synonym and the logical definition.

DEFINITION BY SYNONYM

R86 A synonym is a word that has the same or nearly the same meaning as another word in the same language.

R87 Define a word by giving a synonym that is better known to the reader.

An apothecary is a druggist.
He complained of vertigo; that is, dizziness.

R88 Find the most exact synonym you can.

[Not very good:] A condor is a bird.
[Better:] A condor is a vulture.

[Not very good:] A buccaneer is a robber.
[Better:] A buccaneer is a pirate.

[Not very good:] A dwelling is a building.
[Better:] A dwelling is a house.

R89 Keep parallelism between the word to be defined and its definition.

[Wrong:] "Chanting" [gerund] means to sing [infinitive].
[Right:] "Chanting" [gerund] means singing [gerund].

[Wrong:] "Oaf" [noun] means stupid [adjective].
[Right:] "Oaf" [noun] means blockhead [noun].

[Wrong:] "Rapture" [abstract noun] means a mystic [concrete noun].
[Right:] "Rapture" [abstract noun] means ecstasy [abstract noun].

[Wrong:] "Chants" [present] means sang [past].
[Right:] "Chants" [present] means sings [present].

R90 Verbal parallelism must sometimes yield to parallelism of thought. For example, if a noun, like *narration,* has an action sense, then it may be defined by a gerund: "Narration is telling." In a context where a participle has a descriptive rather than an action sense, it may be defined by an adjective: " 'Enervated' means weak" (instead of " 'Enervated' means weakened").

R91 Advantages of definition by synonym: (*a*) It is often the easiest method of definition for the writer—and often the easiest for the reader, since a synonym is brief, easy to remember, and does not clutter the mind with details. (*b*) It is often the more informal way of defining a term; it defines without halting the composition.

He was an apothecary—one of those chemists who fill physicians' prescriptions and sell drugs, medicines, and allied chemical preparations—but he earned many a guinea on real-estate deals undertaken for the great lords of his day.	This is rather formal. The full definition between the dashes tends to halt the easy flow of the composition.
He was an apothecary—a druggist—but he earned many a guinea on real-estate deals undertaken for the great lords of his day.	This is informal. The synonym between the dashes slows the reader scarcely at all.

R92 Disadvantages of definition by synonym: (*a*) Definition by synonym is often very inexact. (*b*) Moreover, synonyms often do not supply very much information. If, therefore, you need greater exactness or more information than can be supplied by a synonym, use a logical definition instead.[23]

For example, to define a chair as a seat does not say exactly what a chair is; for a sofa or a bench is also a seat, and yet it is not a chair. Again, to say that a condor is a vulture does not offer a great deal of information. There are vultures that are not condors, and condors have a number of interesting characteristics that such a definition omits. If the reader did not know what a condor is and if condors played a considerable part in the theme, he might have reason to wish for a fuller definition.

THE LOGICAL DEFINITION

R93 Define a word by giving (*a*) its general class and (*b*) the characteristics that make it different from the other things of that class.

Word to be defined	*Class*	*Distinguishing characteristics*
chair[24]	seat	with a back, for one person
exposition	that form of writing or talking	that has for its purpose explaining or informing
boy	male human being	between the ages, roughly, of one and twenty-one
brittleness	quality of material substances	that renders them easily broken or snapped
creeps	moves along	with the body prone and close to the ground, or slowly or stealthily or timidly
spasmodically	in a manner	that is fitful, lacks continuity, or is intermittent
monotonous	occurring	without change or variety

---

[23] See R93-100.

[24] In a theme, logical definitions would not appear in the telegraphic style in which they are given here. They would be phrased something like this: "A chair is a seat that has a back and that is intended to hold one person."

R94 Do not give the widest, but the narrowest, general class the reader may be expected to know.

For example, in defining *man,* do not ordinarily say that man is a being. For, from God, who is a being, to electrons, which also are beings, man shares the word with too many things for this to be a useful class in most contexts. Say man is an animal.

R95 Do not use the pronoun *one* as the general class.

[Too vague:] A rifle is one that has grooves in the barrel to rotate the bullet.

[Better:] A rifle is a shoulder firearm that has grooves in the barrel to rotate the bullet.

[All right, since here *one* clearly means "a person" and is not vague:] An emperor is one who rules an empire. A renegade is one who deserts to the enemy.

R96 Keep parallelism in your definitions.

[Not parallel:] "Brittle": that quality of material substances that renders them easily broken or snapped.

[Parallel:] "Brittle": possessing that quality of material substances that renders them easily broken or snapped.

R97 Except for the cases in R98-99, do not repeat, in the definition, the word to be defined.

[Wrong:] An anthology is an anthology of poems or other literary compositions.

[Right:] An anthology is a collection of poems or other literary compositions.

[Wrong:] "Healthful": conducive to health.

[Right:] "Healthful": conducive to the well-being and vigor of the body.

R98 When the term to be defined is made up of two words one of which is already well known to the reader, it is quite usual and correct to repeat the well-known word in the definition.

For example, readers may ordinarily be presumed to know what a rifle is; so this definition of an automatic rifle is in order: "An automatic rifle is a rifle whose recoil rejects the used shells, replaces them with new bullets, and fires the new bullets as long as the trigger is held in firing position."

R99   When the purpose of a definition is to show that the unknown word is merely a variation of a known word or a word built from a well-known root, repetition is quite all right.

"Terrible": inspiring terror.
"Informal": not formal.

R100   Over and above the general class and the necessary distinguishing characteristics, add other distinguishing characteristics and other information as you like or as the matter requires.

For example, you need not content yourself with this definition: "Mary is the mother of God." You may add, for example, that she was ever virgin, that she was immaculately conceived, that she co-operated in our redemption, and that graces come to us through her hands—as you like or the matter requires. In this connection, note that a definition need not be confined to a single sentence. Moreover, it may be so interwoven with other matter that the writer defines only obliquely, while directly discussing something else; for example, see the examples under R91.

Business letters

FORM[25]

R101   Make your letters clean—free of smudges, visible erasures, mistakes, crossouts, corrections, and strike-overs.

R102   Use white unruled paper, 8½ x 11 inches. Use only one side of each sheet.

R103   Use a black typewriter ribbon or blue, black, or blue-black ink.

R104   Center your letter on the paper so that the margins are balanced all around it.

---

[25] For punctuation of the various parts of letters, see D14-16 and D65. For capitals see H13-15.

R105 Use block form—no indentions—for typewritten letters. Leave a line-space between the paragraphs.[26]

St. Thomas More High School
Tower Hill, Massachusetts
May 28, 1954

The Holmes Advertising Agency
139 West 152 Street
New York 20, New York

Gentlemen:

At the advice of one of your copy writers, Mr. Harvey P. Morton, I am writing to inquire whether you will have an opening in your office next fall for a high-school graduate.

During my four years here at St. Thomas I made English my major subject. In my senior year I edited our literary magazine, the <u>Utopian</u>, and won the Chancellor Essay Award. I worked for three summers in the offices of a country newspaper.

If you want to make inquiries about me, let me suggest that you speak to Mr. Morton or write to the Reverend John Fisher, Principal of St. Thomas More High School.

Sincerely yours,

David Masterson

David Masterson

David Masterson
St. Thomas More High School
Tower Hill, Massachusetts

The Holmes Advertising Agency
139 West 152 Street
New York 20, New York

---

[26] It is still rather common to use indented form for the paragraphs within the body of a typewritten letter. You may do so, indenting the first line of each paragraph from five to ten characters, unless your teacher directs otherwise. But do not use indented form for headings, addresses, signatures, and so on, in typewritten letters, even though you indent the paragraphs in the body.

R106   Single-space typewritten letters that run to more than four or five lines. Leave one line-space between single-spaced paragraphs, two between double-spaced paragraphs.[27]

R107   Leave three line-spaces between the date and the first line of the address.[27]

R108   Leave a line-space between the address and the salutation and between the salutation and the first paragraph of the letter.[27]

R109   Leave two line-spaces between the last paragraph and the complimentary close, and four line-spaces between the complimentary close and the typed signature.[27]

R110   When the first page of the letter carries a printed letterhead, then only the date is typed by the writer.

R111   The complimentary close may be placed laterally anywhere to the right of an imaginary line drawn down the center of the letter. It is good form and looks nice to place the complimentary close so that it lines up, flush left, with the typewritten date at the top of the letter.[27] But always place the complimentary close far enough to the left so that the handwritten signature does not have to run into the right-hand margin.

R112   Unless you have already written several times to the same correspondent and have excellent reason to know that he will have no difficulty whatever in deciphering your handwritten signature, always add a typewritten signature. But never use a typewritten signature only.[28]

R113   If it is pertinent and if it is not already found on the letterhead, you may type your office or position in the organization or firm directly under the typewritten signature and lined up with it, flush left.

---

[27] See the illustration under R105. Except for R112, these directions are somewhat arbitrary. Styles of spacing and placement differ. But the main objective of all of them is to present a pleasing picture and to separate clearly the various parts of a letter. The directions given here accomplish that end.

[28] Sometimes, usually in circulars, the name of the firm is typed after the complimentary close and followed by the written signature of the individual writer,

R114 Use indented form for handwritten business letters.

3458 Clarendon Avenue
Drayton, Oregon
April 7, 1945

Mr. James B. Harkins
395 East 64 Street
Millvale, Ohio

Dear Mr. Harkins:

On March 10 I ordered a set of your precanceled jubilee stamps. My letter contained a money order for one dollar. Nearly a month has passed; the stamps have not come, nor have I heard anything from you.

Will you please let me know whether you received my order? If you did not get it, I shall try to trace it.

Yours truly,
Henry J. Burke

Henry J.
3458 Cla
Drayton,

Mr. James B. Harkins
395 East 64 Street
Millvale, Ohio

R115 Correct forms of address and salutation in business and formal letters are given on pages 484-87. (There are other, equally correct forms; but these will suffice.)[29]

---

[29] For punctuation of addresses and salutations, see D14-15 and D65. For capitals see H13-14.

Cardinal archbishop
His Eminence John Cardinal Hamilton
Archbishop of Hammondsport
135 Valley Drive
Hammondsport 3, Arizona
Your Eminence:

Cardinal
His Eminence Jules Cardinal Bourget
1492 West 63 Street
Kalmath Falls, New Hampshire
Your Eminence:

Archbishop
The Most Reverend Archbishop Henry McHarris, D.D.
16 Houston Avenue
Abilene 2, Texas
Your Excellency:

Bishop
The Most Reverend Nicholas Allen, D.D.
222 McKinley Place
Great Forks, Minnesota
Your Excellency:

Monsignor
The Right Reverend Monsignor Baffin Powell
221 North Main Boulevard
Portsmouth, Florida
Right Reverend Monsignor:

The Very Reverend Monsignor Herbert Holm
1459 Clement Street
Stillwater 7, Nevada
Very Reverend Monsignor:

Provincials of religious orders and congregations,
rectors of seminaries
The Very Reverend Herbert Neill, S.J.
4715 Central Avenue
Phoenix 6, Arizona
Very Reverend Father Neill:

Priest
The Reverend John Campbell[30]
2049 Parkside Boulevard
Toledo 7, Ohio
Dear Father Campbell:

Religious Brother
Brother Charles R. Skipwith, S.M.
Washington College
Washington Springs, Arkansas
Dear Brother Skipwith:

Nun
Reverend Mother M. George, S.H.C.J.
St. Mary's Convent
Albion, Kentucky
Dear Reverend Mother:

Sister M. Elizabeth, S.H.C.J.
Lady College
Trent 3, Iowa
Dear Sister Elizabeth:

Senator (national or state)
The Honorable John H. Madison[31]
The United States Senate
Washington, D.C.
Dear Sir:

Representative (national or state)
The Honorable Hugh A. Bradley[31]
The House of Representatives
Washington, D.C.
Dear Sir:

Governor
The Honorable Paul H. Bates[31]
Governor of Illinois
Springfield, Illinois
Dear Sir:

---

[30] The forms *Reverend Campbell, Dear Reverend Campbell,* or *Reverend* by itself are never to be used.

[31] The form *Honorable Madison, Bradley,* or *Bates* is never to be used.

Mayor
The Honorable Ferris Payne[32]
Mayor of the City of Penceford
Penceford, Oregon
Dear Sir:

Judge (federal, state, and so on)
The Honorable Matthew Huntingdon[32]
United States District Judge
501 South Norton Street
Weaversville, Michigan
Dear Sir:

A senator, representative, and so on, and his wife
Honorable and Mrs. H. A. Bradley
Apartment 2B
12 Sheraton Square
New Bedford 17, Virginia
Dear Mr. and Mrs. Bradley:

Doctor
Dr. Colfax Twilliger
Medical Arts Building
4939 Maryland Avenue
New Orleans 12, Louisiana
Dear Dr. Twilliger:

A doctor and his wife
Dr. and Mrs. Colfax Twilliger[33]
The Cliff House
16 Bronson Road
William's Mills, Missouri
Dear Dr. and Mrs. Twilliger:

Dean
Mr. Hobart Lane
Dean of the College of Arts and Sciences
St. James University
St. James, Idaho
Dear Dean Lane:

---

[32] The form *Honorable Payne* or *Huntingdon* is never to be used.
[33] The form *Mrs. Dr. Twilliger* is never to be used.

Business house
The American Soap Company
Stoddard Building
13-21 South 143 Street
Wrenton, North Carolina
Gentlemen:

Several men
Messrs. Mark and Cross
Roan and Seventh Avenues
Harpersburg 2, Wisconsin
Gentlemen:

One man
Mr. Lawrence Johnston
Humboldt Building
New Alton 6, Maine
Dear Mr. Johnston: (*or* Dear Sir:)

Several women
The Misses Templar
Templar Secretarial School
503 Iron Row
Norman 13, Illinois
Dear Ladies:

Mrs. Allen J. Crosby
Miss Ellen R. Scheinuk
16 Westpark Freeway
Clary, Minnesota
Dear Ladies:

One woman
Mrs. J. G. Barringer
3811 Cates Avenue
Chicago 25, Illinois
Dear Mrs. Barringer:

R116 There are a number of acceptable forms of complimentary close for business and formal letters. But those on page 488 are common and good and will suffice.[34]

---

[34] For punctuation of a complimentary close, see D16. For capitals see H15.

Letters to clerics and members of religious orders
Respectfully yours,
Sincerely yours,

Letters to civil authorities
Very truly yours,
Sincerely yours,

Letters to all other persons
Sincerely yours,

CONTENT

R117 Be brief.

A Ordinarily keep your letter to one page or less in length.

B Do not become chatty.

C Confine yourself to one easily digested topic per letter. If there are several scarcely related topics, it is better to send several letters at once. This makes for brevity and easy reading, and permits the routing of different matters to different departments.

D Long compliments at the beginning or end of a business letter usually defeat their purpose by making the reader impatient. A short complimentary paragraph, provided you really have something to say, is in order. But avoid such bromides as *with every good wish* or *we hope that this finds you in good health.*

R118 Be plain.

A Do not use the peculiar jargon and wordy padding sometimes affected in business letters: *yours of the 7th inst. to hand; in reference to the matters that we have had under discussion, let me say that;* and so on.

B Avoid pomposity, ornament, gush, breeziness, involved sentence structures, long sentences, and much use of the passive voice.

[Poor:] It is certainly hoped that our merchandise will meet with your complete satisfaction.

[Better:] I hope you will like the samples.

C Use a straightforward *I* whenever you can (rather than *the writer,* a passive form, or *we*). *We,* however, is in order whenever you are expressing notions that clearly pertain to the organization rather than to an individual; for example, *we do not publish comic books.*

D Avoid technical terms unless you have good reason for using them and are certain that your reader will recognize them.

[Poor:] The young man in question had a standard secondary education with the usual curriculum.

[Better:] He had an ordinary high-school education.

R119 Be accurate.

A Supply all the information you should.

B State definite qualities, quantities, order numbers, catalogue numbers, catalogue descriptions, dates, academic grades, places, names, ages, addresses, and so on.

C Ordinarily acknowledge a previous letter received from your correspondent and give its date accurately. He will want to look up the carbon in his file and check what he said to you.

R120 Be prompt. Answer at the first reasonable opportunity.

S Description

In general

S1 Description is that form of writing or talking whose purpose is the creating of pictures, sounds, smells, and touch sensations in the imagination of the reader.[1]

S2 Pure description is description for its own sake and is nowadays seldom found except in books analyzing works of art, travelogues, and so on.

---

[1] For matters not treated in this section but involving description, see Q26-65 and T30-38.

S3 Running description is description used more or less incidentally to dress, enliven, or enrich narration, exposition, or argument. The description may be long (several paragraphs) or very short (just a word or two).

The viewpoint

S4 A viewpoint is the actual or imaginary position from which a writer or speaker sees what he is describing.

S5 Select a viewpoint and describe only what can be seen from it.

S6 Follow S5 with regard to the mental viewpoint or attitude of mind.

For example, the appearance and character of a man are likely to seem very different to one who loves him, to one who hates him, to his valet, to his employer, to his dog, to a newsboy, to a man he has injured, and to a man to whom he has loaned money.

S7 When there is need, change the viewpoint.

S8 When you think that your reader might otherwise be confused, indicate that the viewpoint is changing.

From where we stood at the edge of the woods in front of it, we saw that the house was set in a clearing in the firs, halfway up the hillside, and that this gave it an air of privacy and rest. It was a large three-story frame building, whose weatherboarding had achieved by exposure to the

From where we stood at the edge of the woods in front of it states explicitly what the first viewpoint is; the two expressions *inside* and *at the rear of the house* give unmistakable notification of a change in the writer's viewpoint.

elements that shade known in Dallas as Lambert green, which makes houses look old, cool, and substantial. The front supported twin gables, each with its dormer window, one at either end of the gray slate roof. Tall chimneys rose above the ridge of the roof. There was nothing in the ensemble that an architect would care to sign his name to; but the house presented an agreeable, quiet welcome when first we came upon it in the clearing.

S
T
U

490

Inside, we were to discover, it was a pleasant-enough house if one intended to stay only the summer. The rooms were large and cool, the furniture plain but comfortable. The kitchen, a large, old-fashioned affair, was full of shining copperware hung on a rack above the table and on hooks about the walls. We liked it particularly.

At the rear of the house was a kind of patio with a little pool in the center, a place that invited me to set up my typewriter and table at once and get to work.

S9 Unless there is very good reason for not doing so,[2] finish with one viewpoint before going on to the next. Do not flit back and forth from one viewpoint to another.

S10 There is occasionally—not often—good reason for flitting back and forth from one viewpoint to another.

[In this passage, the writer wants sharp contrast. He has taken care, however, that there is no confusion:] I can explain the discrepancy, Your Excellency. Hale was in the hollow. I was on the hill. Hale saw only the cloud of dust that hung above the desert; I saw the flash of the sun on red tunics and gold braid. Hale heard only the faint sounds of a wagon caravan; I heard the staccato mutter of Spanish orders and Spanish replies. Hale smelled only the still air of the hollow; my nose was offended by the reek of the corpses jolting along in the last wagon. When I add that Hale had strictest orders not to leave the hollow in any contingency, it must be clear that this court-martial is doing him the gravest injustice, especially now that he is dead and can offer no defense.

The basic image

S11 In descriptions of some length or complication, ordinarily begin with the basic image.[3]

S12 In visual description, the basic image usually consists of the general size, shape, and color of the object.

It was a large white house, modeled on Mount Vernon and set in a great sweep of lawn.

---

[2] See S10.
[3] See S12-18.

He was a great, dark brute of a man, with a huge torso balanced on absurdly inadequate-looking legs.

S13 Often enough, the size, the shape, or the color is omitted from the basic image when one or another of them is of no significance to the description.

He was a great brute of a man, with a huge torso balanced on absurdly inadequate-looking legs.

S14 In auditory description, the basic image usually consists of a general classification of the sound that is heard.

As we turned the corner, our ears were assailed by a loud roar compounded of many noises, all fierce and frightening.

I noticed at first that it was a kind of light tapping, a sound I had never heard before, but similar to something I had heard.

S15 In tactile description, the basic image usually consists of a general classification of the touch sensation.

I felt something wet and viscous, and wondered for a moment whether I had put my hand into one of the still-warm pots on the stove.

Steve felt the dry, ropelike thing stir and writhe in his grip.

S16 In olfactory description, the basic image usually consists of a general classification of the smell as strong or faint, pleasant or disagreeable, and so on.

It was a pungent, disagreeable odor that seemed to envelop the whole quarter of town where the stockyards lay.

S17 In the description of things that are not experienced by the external senses (for instance, a mood or a person's character), the basic "image" is usually a general classification of the thing as good, bad, timid, dull, weary, hopeless, uneasy, cheerful, or something of the kind.

Von Tolen wasn't at all what you would expect a Prussian general to be. He was a nervous little mouse of a man, quite afraid of the world.

I can describe the feeling only as a special sort of uneasiness, a pleasantly unpleasant expectation that something exciting was going to happen.

492

S18 Occasionally it is quite reasonable to begin even a long or complicated description with something other than the fundamental image of the object.

> What I noticed first was an eyebrow—a most imperious eyebrow, raised above a cold blue eye. When finally I was able to detach my attention from the eyebrow, I found that the eye was contemplating me steadily over a frond of one of those potted plants that some hotel managers still use to underscore the general ugliness of lobbies.

> In this passage the writer has decided to make capital of one feature of his character—an eyebrow. He intends to harp on that eyebrow from time to time in the course of his story and so begins his description with it.

Filling in the picture

S19 Once you have the basic image, set down the most striking features of the object and then fill in a few minor details, if they are necessary to the description or will enrich it.

[Basic image:] One's first impression of Mr. Starrett was of a tall, dark, very slender man—with teeth. [Most striking features:] These teeth were not crooked, did not protrude, lacked none of their lawful number. Those above meshed nicely with those below. All of them were Mr. Starrett's own. Indeed, they were such unexceptional teeth that it is a wonder that they were the first thing about him that one noticed. One noticed them because they were always, always visible, gleaming and resplendent, between lips fixed in a perpetual, mocking smile—a smile quite without common mirth but full of relish for some secret joke that Mr. Starrett found in everything he looked upon. The smile disappeared only when he gazed into a mirror. He seemed to find no joke there, and so the teeth retreated for the nonce to well-earned privacy and concealment.

[Minor details:] The rest of Mr. Starrett was good to look at. There were no unseemly bulges to betray his forty years. His handsome head was set with becoming features: intelligent-seeming eyes; a nose not too thin, not too gross; a manly chin. His hands were as slender as he and as graceful. He wore his comfortable clothes comfortably and looked like neither a movie star, nor a stuffy bourgeois, nor an eccentric. If it had not been for his smile, one would have found him pleasant to behold and would have been mildly interested in making his acquaintance.

S20 Occasionally, especially for reasons of emphasis, it is best to save your most striking detail till the last.

The mother superior was an energetic, intelligent woman, rather small in size and small in feature, movement, and gesture. She was more than approachable and genuinely interested in nearly everyone she met. She inspired respect and confidence; no one was ever known to treat her casually. This agreeable composition of qualities and appearance became remarkable when one finally noticed that she was blind—more so when one was told that she had been blind for thirty years.

The town was just as I had remembered it: the one dusty-yellow street with a line of stores on each side, gat-toothed with vacant lots; the church and the courthouse facing each other near the middle of town; and the water trough, dry for years, in front of the post office. There was one difference. The place was deserted.

BRIEF SKETCHES

S21 Often the full technique—basic image, striking details, and minor details—cannot be used without halting the theme objectionably. When this happens, do a brief sketch, selecting one or two striking or fundamental features of the object and letting them suggest the rest.

Brown entered a room that was *all glitter and gleam, from the chandeliers to the men's shirt fronts and the women's jewelry.* He hurried in the wake of his *frenzied* hostess from group to group, murmuring in response to introductions and moving on before he could make sure of a single name or face. Finally he was deposited near the refreshments with a trio that Mrs. Daggers seemed to think he might complement: *an empty-headed blonde occupied in saying nothing and sweeping the room with a selective eye; a handsome man who looked like an executive* and who turned out to be an executive's secretary; and Miss Dutreil. He would hardly have noted Miss Dutreil, *fortyish, mousy, and dowdy,* if she had not said a remarkable thing.

She said, "Mr. Brown, you were not in Mexico City last November, as you said you were."

That startled Brown into rudeness. "Just what are you talking about?" he asked.

T Narration

In general

T1 Narration is that form of talking or writing that has for its purpose the relating of a series of events.[1]

The narrative theme

T2 A narrative theme is a theme whose purpose is the relating of a series of events.

CHOOSING A SUBJECT

T3 Not the subject, but the treatment must be new.

T4 When the subject of a narrative theme has not been assigned or has not suggested itself naturally, jotting down the answers to these questions may stimulate your imagination a bit:

A What happened to me during the first eight years of my life that impressed me or others as interesting, strange, humorous, puzzling, difficult, or splendid? What happened during the second eight years?

B What problem, interest, amusing thing, hope, fear, fascination has occupied my mind a good deal lately?

---

[1] Almost always, the four forms of discourse (exposition, narration, description, and argument) are mingled in a composition of any length at all. Thus it happens that a narration may contain exposition, and so on.

c What have I read, heard, or seen that stirred, delighted, or amused me or that made me think?

d What do I dislike heartily?

e What do I like particularly?

f What have I discovered about living that is different from what people have told me it is or should be?

g What is there worth remarking about my dog or cat, my enemy, my friend, my father, my mother, or someone or something else that plays a large part in my life?

h What would I like to do with my life?

i What would I care to change in the world at large or in my world?

j What is that unusual life, so different from my own, that attracts me, even though the possibility of my living it is remote or nonexistent?

T5 Once you have a central idea for a narrative, start thinking around the subject that has occurred to you. Start doodling; that is, start writing down the fragmentary ideas that occur to you.

[Central idea:] Pirates

[Doodling:] I like pirates. I like pirates?

Why? Costumes? Life they lead? Their morality? I wouldn't want to be a pirate in real life. Stinking ships. Godlessness. Why do I like pirates? Ah, because they did brave deeds gracefully.

I'll bet they seldom did. Or very few of them. My whole idea is based on Francis Drake, Rafael Sabatini, Hornblower stories, and Hollywood pirates.

I could *play* a pirate in Hollywood. Fun. Well, I could be an extra, anyway. Wear a cutlass and swing it. Imagine playing a pirate-extra in Hollywood and then having to come home each day to ordinary life.

Could do that. Have character play pirate-extra, then come home to drab, lonely life. Decides he will live like pirate. Turns home into ship. Builds crow's-nest atop chimney. Makes dog walk plank. Gets into trouble with neighbors for running up Jolly Roger on television aerial and striding up and down on front porch with patch over one eye, hailing passing pedestrians with "Ship ahoy!" County-asylum people arrive.

THE THEME TOPIC[2]

T6 When you have a subject and some ideas about it, select a theme topic.

T7 Upon the selection of your theme topic will depend to some extent the kind of treatment your narrative is to get: humorous, acid, sympathetic, and so on. On it will depend what you are going to stress: action, character, atmosphere, and so on.

Five ridiculous things happened when John Curlew tried to play pirate.[3]

This theme topic stresses events. In the development character will probably turn out to be secondary.

John Curlew was born out of time, as he discovered when he tried to play pirate.

This stresses character. In the development events will probably turn out to be secondary, though not unimportant.

There is no room for fools like Mr. J. Curlew, pirate, in this modern world.

This is unsympathetic—even acid. The emphasis will probably be on character.

Playing pirate, Mr. Curlew found himself beset by a world hostile to simple delight.

This is sympathetic to the main character—even sentimental. The treatment may be rather whimsical.

Against the drabness of a suburban neighborhood, John Curlew flashed madly for a moment, then was abruptly extinguished.

This stresses atmosphere, impressions, emotional reactions, and that sort of thing.

T8 Write out the theme topic. Writing it out often exposes weaknesses in it. A written theme topic, moreover, lying on your desk before your eyes, is a constant reminder of what the theme is about and keeps you from straying off into useless digressions.

---

[2] For the notion of theme topic, see M19-21.

[3] The theme topics given here are all based on the doodling that illustrates T5.

T9 If it is at all possible to do so—and it almost always is—state your theme topic in a single, uncomplicated, declarative sentence:

 A A single, uncomplicated sentence—because the briefer and less complicated the theme topic, the easier it is to develop it coherently.

 B A declarative sentence—because questions do not indicate and limit development. There are innumerable developments possible if the theme topic is "How did Denton beat Plainville?" But the two chief parts of the theme are already plain if the theme topic is "Denton beat Plainville by using a modified T and concentrating on Joe Jacoby."

 C A complete sentence—because half-sentences and very elliptical sentences cause the same trouble that questions do.

T10 Limit the range of your ideas sharply when stating the theme topic, or you will find yourself writing an endless narrative.

T11 Make the theme topic as definite as you reasonably can.

[Vague, leading to uncertain planning and development:] It required several things to bring Dan McKay to terms.

[Definite, leading to clear-cut planning and development:] It required four attacks to force Dan McKay to resign.

THE PLAN OR PLOT

T12 Once you have written down your theme topic, write a plan or plot:[4]

 A List and number the main events of your narrative in the order in which you wish to present them.

 B Under each of these main events, list circumstances that contribute notably to it.

 C Do not go into detail.

---

[4] The outline of a narrative is called a plan when it is the skeleton of a straight narrative (T42) and a plot when it is the skeleton of a plot narrative (T43).

498

D To avoid complications use the vivid present whenever you can. (In developing the plot or plan into a full narrative, ordinarily use the past.)

Plan of a narrative letter

Theme topic.—I am quite all right after being lost for a night.

1. I meet Eileen and make a date with her.
   In front of the church, on Wednesday.
   As I am bringing boys from my camp to Mass.
2. I set out Thursday evening in a canoe for Eileen's camp.
   It is two miles away directly across the lake.
   From there we are to use her car to drive to town for a **movie**.
3. I am taken from my course by a bonfire.
   I think it is directly in front of Camp Moony.
   It is either to the east or to the west of Moony.
   It is deserted.
4. Lost now, I paddle in one direction for a while.
   There is nothing by which to take a bearing.
5. I enter an inlet.
   The night is so dark that I cannot see anything but the shore that I am keeping on my right.
   As a result, I enter inlet after inlet, without knowing that I am doing so.
6. I discover that I am hopelessly lost.
7. I decide to tie up for the night.
   The night is long, but I have cigarettes; the night is cold, but I have a jacket.
8. At dawn, I find my way to Eileen's camp.
   She has aroused both camps.
   A search for me is on.
9. There are no bad aftereffects to the misadventure.

Letter developed from the plan above

Camp Woogwooly
Oskwog, Maine
July 6, 1954

Dear Mom,

Now that you are hearing from me in person, you will have to believe that I am quite all right. I am glad that Mr. Twiller's telegram reached you in time to keep you from making a useless trip up here. It was silly of Joe to alarm you with his telephone call. Of

499

course, I'd like to see you; but I know that you would hardly welcome the expense of an unnecessary trip, especially now that things are not going well with Dad.

Here is the correct version of what happened, Joe's hysterical account notwithstanding. (Joe loves drama; you should know that.)

Since I'm the only Catholic counselor here, I round up all the Catholic boys and take them to Mass on Wednesdays and Sundays. Last Wednesday—that was July 3—I met Eileen Kirsch just as we were going into the church. I had had no idea that she was up in this neck of the woods; and, as you can imagine, I was quite surprised and delighted to see her. It turns out that she is a counselor at a girls' camp near here, a much ritzier place than ours, situated just across the lake from us. Well, we made a date for the following night. Both of us welcomed the prospect of one evening away from the brats. (I like the kids in my cabin: they're fun and as interesting as ants under glass. They can teach me at least as much as I can teach them. On the whole they're well behaved, too; so I really can't complain. But once in a while I want to get away from their treble squeak. They sound like mice on a hot griddle.)

On Thursday, then, I set out in one of our canoes for Eileen's camp, Moonetonkwonk. (These pseudoaboriginal names!) Eileen has a car up here with her, and we intended to use it to drive into town for a show. The movie and a drugstore are all that Oskwog has to offer in the way of night life—which is monotonous but convenient for my wallet. Now the camp lies just across the lake, not more than two miles from us. I should have been able to hit it swimming blindfold under water. And I *would* have hit it, had I not been seduced from my course by the flickering of a bonfire.

"Moony," I thought, "is the only place hereabout that would build a bonfire; so that must be Moony."

I steered for the fire and was right upon it before I realized that it must be a good distance either to the east or to the west of Moony, since there was no sign of the camp. There wasn't so much as a star overhead; and, looking back across the lake, I found I couldn't see even the glimmer of a lamp at Woogwooly from which to take a bearing. I realize now that a little hill to the west of us must have come between me and the lights in the boys' cabins.

For a minute or so I sat staring across the bow at the bonfire. It was utterly deserted. The girls must have set it earlier and gone off and left it—bad woodcraft, even for a girls' camp. (To be quite

500

frank, they're usually much more careful about that sort of thing than we are.)

"Well," I thought, "there's nothing to do but to try the east or the west; and, since I don't know where the camp is, I'll go on in the direction in which the canoe is drifting." So, not alarmed but merely anxious not to be very late for my date, I struck out into the darkness ahead, keeping the shore on my right.

The night was really very dark; otherwise I would have noticed that I was leaving the lake and entering an inlet. As I know now, the inlet opened into other inlets and sloughs. By keeping a shoreline always on my right, I found my way—without realizing what was happening—from one pass to another, until I was trapped in a labyrinth of small waterways. It was not until, after some time, I had decided that I had gone east far enough, and had reversed my course, that I discovered what had happened to me. Almost immediately I was confronted by a shoreline that should not have been lying across my bow. For a moment I was confused, then I understood the situation. I paddled a bit longer to see if I could find a way out; but every five minutes or so brought me up against banks or shore that were unfamiliar, until it was painfully clear that I no longer knew north from nougat. It seemed foolish to spend the night threshing about in a maze; so I tied the canoe to a willow, put on my jacket and pulled the collar up about my ears, and spent the night smoking cigarettes and sleeping. To be quite candid, I did a good deal more sleeping than smoking. The bottom of the canoe was not altogether uncomfortable; there was plenty of room to stretch out; there was a cushion for my head.

At dawn I found my way, without much difficulty now that I could see, to Moonetonkwonk to let Eileen know what had happened. It was then that I found out that she had become alarmed, had phoned our camp, alarmed Joe, and started that torchlight boat-search on the lake that he told you about. I'm afraid the brats enjoyed looking for my body a great deal.

So there's the whole thing. You will want to know if I was cold. Not very. The nights up here, even in July, are not warm; but I had my jacket. Was I frightened? Yes, but not very much. Were there any aftereffects? Well, I was hungry from doing a lot of paddling I had not expected to do.

All my love to you,

PETER

501

TWO SERIES OF EVENTS

T13 Whenever you can do so without injury to the content or the reader's interest, write a separate narrative for each series of events. But it sometimes happens that two series of events that come together at one or two points must be kept going in the same narrative.

T14 Draw a two-column plan or plot, one column for each series of events. Box and connect those events in which the two series converge.

Wyck series	*Alfredo series*
1. General Wyck and General Alfredo plan to converge on Templi. Alfredo from east, Wyck from southwest. Rendezvous set for 8:00 A.M. the next day.	1. General Wyck and General Alfredo plan to converge on Templi. Alfredo from east, Wyck from southwest. Rendezvous set for 8:00 A.M. the next day.
2. Wyck makes better time than he had expected. Roads in better shape than reported. No mechanical trouble in motorized units.	2. A bridge halts Alfredo for four hours. Patrols had mistakenly reported it safe. It must be shored up.
3. At 3:00 P.M. of first day, Wyck meets and overcomes resistance. Ambush by small party causes delay of one hour.	3. Unmapped Fascist mine field delays Alfredo another three hours. Several casualties.
4. Nonetheless Wyck manages to arrive at rendezvous on time.	4. Alfredo arrives at Templi at 3:00 P.M. of second day, seven hours late for rendezvous. Hears no firing. No sound of Wyck.
5. At 8:00 A.M. sharp, Wyck attacks Templi. Meets full resistance. No diversion from the east.	5. Decides not to attack but to make contact with Wyck. Circles wide to southwest.

6. After five hours he retires. Four fifths of his troops are casualties.
7. At safe distance he sits down to wait for word of Alfredo.

> 8. Alfredo meets Wyck.
> 9. They decide to combine forces and attack again from southwest.
> 10. They are routed.

11. Wyck is killed.

> 6. Alfredo meets Wyck.
> 7. They decide to combine forces and attack again from southwest.
> 8. They are routed.

9. Alfredo leads remnant of forces back to Alva. Two thirds casualties.
10. Alfredo thinks it would have been better to halve forces after making contact and follow original plan.

Narrative developed from the plan above

The loss of Templi did not receive much publicity during the war, presumably for reasons of security. After the war, as far as I have been able to discover, it received no attention whatever. Yet it is a rather interesting episode in the fierce battle for the Micarno region.

Two identical forces—each a mixture of Italian and American infantry complemented by American tanks and other motorized units, one under the command of Brigadier General Maurice L. Wyck of the United States Army, the other under General Almiral Alfredo of the friendly Italian forces fighting with the Americans in Italy—planned to converge on the little but strategic town of Templi for a concerted attack at eight the following morning.

Wyck was to attack from the southwest, Alfredo from the east—the only other approach offering good cover.

Their divergent routes were about equal in length; so the two forces set out for Templi at the same time.

From the time that he left Alva, Wyck's progress was much more rapid than he had expected it to be. For once, reconnaissance had been wrong in the right way; the roads turned out to be in much better condition than reports had indicated. Moreover, the motorized units proceeded without the mechanical breakdowns so usual that commanding officers come to consider them inevitable—breakdowns that can snarl traffic for hours on narrow byways.

At 3:00 P.M., however, Wyck did run into trouble. A small party of Fascists fighting for the Germans—less than fifty—held up the advance for a little less than an hour with four machine guns, two of which swept the road where it passed through a narrow defile. They were finally cleared out without the loss of one American or allied soldier; and Wyck proceeded on his way, still well ahead of schedule.

The roads continued good; and so Wyck arrived at the southwestern approach to Templi well before his time, deployed his forces, and entered battle at precisely 8:00 A.M.

Within an hour it was apparent that he was meeting the full resistance of Templi. No one was creating a diversion at the eastern end of the little town. Hard pressed for a decision, Wyck fanned his men out in a quarter circle in the southwest and did what he could with what he had.

Where was Alfredo? Shortly after setting out from Alva, he had run into a serious annoyance. A bridge, the only crossing of the Laruna within miles, lay in his path. Whether through mistake or carelessness, patrols had reported the bridge to be in good shape. Alfredo discovered that it practically required rebuilding before it could sustain his vehicular traffic. Quite understandably loath to abandon his motor units, he spent four precious hours shoring up the supports with timbers and laying steel mats across its rotted, sagging floor.

Hardly had he crossed the bridge and once more achieved a good forward pace, when the head of his column tripped the first of the mines that Fascists had laid both across the road and a good distance to either side of it. Progress was agonizingly slow as his men cautiously picked their way, not without casualties, through the mine fields. To hurry the men would have been to murder a good number of them. His tension and irritation mounting as the precious moments fled by, Alfredo finally had to resign himself to arriving at least seven hours late for his rendezvous.

Meanwhile, at Templi, Wyck's unsupported troops were getting a very bad worst of it. By one o'clock four fifths of his men were casualties. He then made a decision that he would have made hours before had he not momently expected the arrival of Alfredo in the east. He withdrew to a safe distance and sat down to wait for word of Alfredo.

Some two hours after Wyck's withdrawal, Alfredo arrived at the eastern approach to Templi. There was, of course, no sight or sound of Wyck, since firing had ceased a good deal earlier. At this juncture, Alfredo proceeded more wisely than had Wyck. He determined to make contact with the latter before attacking the town.

504

Consequently, he circled widely to the southwest until he came upon Wyck with the remaining fifth of his forces.

At the conference that ensued, three possible plans lay before the generals: to give up Templi as lost; to combine forces and attack at one point; to divide their combined forces in two and proceed on the original plan of simultaneous attacks from the east and southwest.

It is a credit to their valor—though perhaps not to their military acumen—that they never seriously considered their first plan. They chose the second. But now, with the element of surprise gone and their total troops reduced almost by half, the attempt ended in a complete rout of the Americans and their allies and in the death of Wyck, who was killed in his command car. Alfredo limped back to Alva with only one third of the men who had set out from there two days or so before.

Assessing the defeat afterward, Alfredo said that he was now convinced that he and Wyck had made the wrong decision, that it would have been better to halve forces and follow the original plan of simultaneous attacks from two approaches.

Be that as it may, it is clear even to the layman that the battle of Templi was fought with a shocking disregard for elementary communications between separated groups. Had Alfredo been able to warn Wyck that he would be seven hours late in reaching the town, Wyck would have been able to hold his attack. Military men whom I quizzed about the affair were inclined, almost to a man, to shrug their shoulders and remark that not even in World War II were communications always what they should have been. In the case of Templi, that fact spelled disaster.

T15 When treating two separate series of events in the same narrative—[5]

   A Change from one series to the other no oftener than is necessary.

   B But do not let one series go unmentioned so long that the reader may forget about it.

   C Announce the changes from one series to another by bridge expressions like *meanwhile, on the other side of the river,* and so on.[6]

---

[5] See the example of a theme under T14.
[6] For a treatment of bridge expressions, see N34-44.

INTRODUCING AND CONCLUDING A NARRATIVE[7]

T16 Ordinarily introduce a narrative in which initial suspense
is not a major factor in one of these ways:

A By stating the theme topic in palatable fashion.

[Theme topic:] I have found a friend.

[Introduction containing theme topic:] We use a lot of words
carelessly, and one of them is loneliness. Until I came to live alone
for five years under the cold eyes of the Tarrana Indians, I had
no idea what it meant. And that is why the next sentence has
enormous significance for me. Today I have found a friend.

B By answering the questions *who, what, when, where,
how,* and *why*—or as many of them as you find useful.

After trailing Saulter High School for three quarters, the Bishop
High School Marauders managed to salvage a 7-6 victory in the
last three minutes of play this afternoon at Barry Stadium. Ten
thousand prep-football fans watched the thrilling close of the game,
as the Marauders uncorked everything they had in a desperate but
successful effort to keep the state-championship trophy for another year.

T17 When your story is such that it would gain by being lively
from the first word on, start it in one of the following ways
and *only then* use one of the introductions of T16.[8]

A Start the story with an incident.

Petrie had been watching for an hour, but nothing had happened in the tall gray house across the street. No matter; he had
at his disposal all the hours that he would need, and he was determined to spend them in patience. He had come to the end of a
long quest, and his quarry was in the gray house across the street.
It would be silly, he thought, to let himself become impatient now
after having been patient for so very many years. But he had to
own to a certain excitement now that the end had come. He could
not afford that excitement. His finger must be steady on the trigger.
No slips.

---

[7] For general notions about introductions and conclusions, see L4-10 and O27.
[8] See T18-19.

Quite suddenly, without warning, the blank face of the gray house took on expression. The front door was opening. It did not open wide. Someone, standing in the shadow of the hall beyond the door, was looking out carefully before venturing on to the porch. "But he can't see me," thought Petrie, and the corners of his mouth rose in the faintest parody of a smile.

Now the person, apparently having discovered nothing to suggest retreat, stepped out on the porch. When the morning sunlight fell full across his face, Petrie gazed at it in unbelief and dismay. The wrong man! And yet he knew for certain that there had been only one man in the house. Then his eyes narrowed. No. Of course. The fellow had simply shaved off the beard. This was his man.

The man took a packet of cigarettes from his pocket, fished in it for a moment very deliberately, turning his head meanwhile to take in the whole length of the street, and finally put a cigarette into his mouth. His hand went back to his pocket for a match.

Petrie fired. The man crumpled to the floor of the porch, kicked grotesquely for a moment, and then lay still.

[The methods of T16 start here:] It was a long road that had led Petrie to the window across the street from the tall gray house where a man now lay dead on the porch. It began in Harley, Connecticut, where Petrie—Hale Petrie, quite respectable then before things had begun to happen to him, and a man who had never thought of killing—had worked behind the soda fountain of the only drugstore in the village and dreamed of marrying Cally Ralls [and so on].

B Start the story with a conversation.

"It is too bad, isn't it," sighed Letitia, "that whenever a really eligible man finds his way by accident to Bancroft, he is bagged by the Daltons before he can get to know any of the rest of us charming people."

"Eligible?" inquired Alice Train, as sharp and angular a woman as Letitia was round and placid.

"Eligible for Helen and Esther, of course." Letitia's candor was by turns amusing or disconcerting. "You do know, my dear—let's not pretend that you don't; we've known and liked each other too long for that—that I have two daughters who are of no earthly use to me and whom I should like to marry off to two pleasant, guileless, unsuspecting, well-to-do Catholic men."

507

"Why guileless and unsuspecting, Mamma?" asked Esther, stepping inopportunely from the house to the terrace where Letitia and Alice were sitting in the sun.

"You weren't supposed to hear that, my love," sighed Letitia.

"But I did hear it. So you might as well tell me. Why guileless and unsuspecting?"

"Well, then, my sweet—because someone not guileless and unsuspecting might discover, before he married you, that you, my dove, are a shrew; and that your sister, for all her appearance of cheerful vigor, has the backbone of an oyster and the same colorful personality."

[The methods of T16 start here:] Meanwhile, at the other end of town, the eligible young man most recently bagged by the Daltons was just waking from a prolonged rest in the comfortable bed in the best Dalton guest room. He was Herbert Q. Waterman— and looked it, right down to the Q. He understood very well that in Bancroft he was a catch, and he intended to do nothing to dispel that notion. The fact that his total wealth [and so on].

T18   Not every story should begin briskly, and so an incident or a conversation is not to be used in every case. Gauge the mood of your narrative.

T19   You must not keep the reader waiting too long before you use one or both of the introductions of T16. So keep the opening incident or conversation short. How short depends on the length of the story. A reader does not mind waiting as much as a chapter or two in a long novel; but in a rather short story—say, five hundred words—he ordinarily does not care to wait beyond a few paragraphs.

T20   Ordinarily conclude a straight narrative[9] in one of the following ways or by a combination of two or more of them:

A   By giving a variation of the introduction.

[Introduction:] We use a lot of words carelessly, and one of them is loneliness. Until I came to live alone for five years under the cold eyes of the Tarrana Indians, I had no idea what it meant. And that is why the next sentence has enormous significance for me. Today I have found a friend.

---

[9] See T42.

[Conclusion:] And so I have a friend. Xuatl has all the filthy customs and manners of his people. When he grins at me with his filed teeth, he looks more like hunger than benevolence. But he has offered me a precious gift. He is sincere; he is good. God make me worthy of his trust. I need his friendship; and he, poor man, has need of the sacraments, of the life I can give him.

B By pointing a moral, a lesson, or a conclusion, from the events related in the theme.

His had been what many an unthinking man would call a full life. Yet, when he came to die, he could not look back on a single act that would bring him comfort in his last conscious moment, ease his passage into eternity, or give him something to say to his judge. In the next world he must stand mute before Christ—he mute, who had so many frivolous things to say as he wasted away his precious years entertaining his pathetic little coterie.

C By recapitulating the main events of the narrative.

That is my story. It differs strikingly from the wild tales circulated by my adversaries. I was in France working on the *Herald* at the time that they claim I was in Moscow. From France I went to China to cover the fall of Nanking. From China I returned to California, where I have lived in retirement and silence until this moment, when the FBI has permitted me to speak and set the record straight.

D By speculating about subsequent events.

There you have the situation at the present time. No one would care to risk his reputation on a flat statement of what tomorrow will bring. But I am willing to hazard a guess, if it will be accepted as a guess and nothing more: Within thirty-six hours Paneast-Falton will sit down with union officials to write a new contract that will involve considerable compromise on both sides.

E By an observation not closely, yet not too remotely connected with the events of the narrative.

As the roar of that holocaust died and the gruesome work of separating bodies from the debris began, a boy who could hardly have been more than seventeen years old looked at me and said, "Golly, what a show!" He seemed pleased. I can only hope that he was hysterical.

509

PARAGRAPHING NARRATIVES[10]

T21 Many a narrative paragraph cannot be said in any strict sense to have a topic thought.[11] You will therefore need the following rules and suggestions.

T22 In general: when you are not dealing with topic thoughts, group in paragraphs those events and thoughts that go together naturally.

T23 Start a new paragraph when the focus shifts to another character or set of characters.

> By half past ten, though Elise had left, it seemed that the bickering would go on all night. Groot, as usual, spoke right on without listening to anyone else. Aunt Tib made querulous little side remarks that sounded like the piping of a frightened bird above the storm. Peleas and Melisande added to the din by barking through the windows at the sort of thing that dogs see and bark at in the night.
>
> [Focus shifts; so a new paragraph:] William, in the meantime, had said nothing. "It is not my quarrel," he thought, "and any attempt to get into it will be resented as an intrusion."

T24 Start a new paragraph when there is a shift in mood or atmosphere.

> The little girl's face was, to be sure, a picture of woe. If she had been the sort to cry, she would have been crying; and somehow it pierced the heart of the bystanders the more deeply that she was not crying. The whole thing was the more poignant because we did not know her language and could not help her at all.
>
> [Mood shifts; so a new paragraph:] Quite without prelude to prepare us for the change, all shadows fled from her face and were replaced by a smile so warm and a glance so bright that one felt as one does when a fire is lighted in a cold and lonely cabin in the wilderness.

T25 Start a new paragraph when events take a turn from the line that they have been pursuing.

---

[10] For the punctuating and paragraphing of dialogue, see D95.
[11] See M11-16 and M18.

It was an ordeal for which they were not prepared, that trek through the desert. For days without end, it seemed, they made their way through all but intolerable heat and then at night sat or lay half frozen as close as they could get to the fire.

[Events take a turn; so a new paragraph:] About the seventh day Stebbins made a proposal that was to render life easier for a time but was eventually to lead them into disaster. He suggested that they sleep by day inside and underneath the wagons and travel by night.

T26 Start a new paragraph when there is a lapse of time.

He bade farewell several times to Miss Lindsey, started out the wrong door, found the right one, hooked his sleeve on its knob, disentangled himself, tripped over his own feet, and finally took his departure.

[Lapse of time; so a new paragraph:] Fifteen minutes later he was back again to retrieve his hat, which Miss Lindsey handed him without a word. She was quite afraid to speak.

T27 Start a new paragraph when there is a break in the action.

Hurtling down the slope, it crashed from boulder to boulder with harsh rending and pounding noises, and finally disappeared over the brink. After several moments there came from below the faint sound of a splash. Then all was still.

[Break in the action; so a new paragraph:] We looked at one another stunned.

T28 Start a new paragraph when there is a change of setting.

Altogether it was an unlovely forest whose great trees lifted their arms above us not so much, it seemed, in benediction as in a gesture of menace and oppression.

[Change of setting; so a new paragraph:] At length we emerged from the woods onto the plain. Here an immense prospect lay before us, apparently bounded only by the horizon and rolling away in gentle swells to the west.

T29 Start a new paragraph when there is a change from one series of events to another.

Hard pressed for a decision, Wyck fanned his men out in a quarter circle in the southwest and did what he could with what he had.

511

[Change from one series of events to another; so a new paragraph:] Where was Alfredo? Shortly after setting out from Alva, he had run into a serious annoyance. A bridge [and so on].

DESCRIPTION IN NARRATIVES

T30 Narratives that neglect the help of description are bare, colorless, dead. They are suitable only for reports in which dryness is at a premium. Ordinarily it is not enough to relate what people do, say, or think; you must often tell how they do, say, or think it.

T31 To make a narrative vivid, give dramatic details of bodily action.[12]

[Without details:] Jack gave an utterly inadequate answer.

[With details:] Jack flushed to the roots of his hair. He dropped his gaze to the floor, ran his finger around the edge of his collar, coughed once or twice, and finally stammered out an utterly inadequate answer.

T32 To make a narrative vivid, give dramatic details of sense perception. In other words, tell what your character sees, hears, feels with his sense of touch, and—if it will help— what he smells and tastes. Do not exhaust one sense and then go on to the next. Mingle the sensations in the same way in which one experiences them in real life. Combine this method with T31.[12]

[Without details:] With a great effort Hawkins jumped, caught the top of the wall, and pulled himself up.

[With details:] Hawkins leaped mightily for the top of the wall. His upflung right hand slapped smartly on the ledge and found a grip. The gulp of air that had been burning his lungs rushed through his lips in a tearing gasp. Dangling from a wrist already aching and beginning to swell, he cautiously brought his other hand up and rubbed in the loose cement at the top of the wall for a grip. He stayed there a moment, his head hanging back and his face turned upward, the sweat running into his eyes and turning

---

[12] See T36.

greasy and chill on his cheeks, where the fitful and ironically play-ful breeze kissed them for a moment. He clawed at the wall with his bare feet and heard the disgusting scrape of his nails against the bricks. Finally his toes found a crevice. Summoning his strength in a second effort that ran like fire down his arms and cut like a knife through his toes, he pulled himself to where he could get one leg over the wall, and then the rest of his body to the ledge. For a moment he lay there, his face in the dusty, crumbling cement still warm from the sun that had gone down hours before. The salt sweat ran into his mouth, mitigating the dryness but not the thirst.

T33 To make a narrative vivid, give dramatic details of emo-tional reactions. In other words, tell in some detail what your character feels.[13]

I was no sooner certain of my opponent's death than I began to feel sick, faint, and *terrified.* The hot blood was running over my back and chest. The dirk, where it had pinned my shoulder to the mast, seemed to burn like a hot iron; *yet it was not so much these real sufferings that distressed me, for these, it seemed to me, I could bear without a murmur; it was the horror I had upon my mind of falling down from the crosstrees into that still green water beside the body of the coxswain.*

I clung with both hands till my nails ached, and I shut my eyes as if to cover up the peril. Gradually my mind came back again, my pulses quieted down to a more natural time, and I was once more in possession of myself.[14]

T34 To make a narrative vivid, give dramatic details of think-ing and speaking. In other words, you can often improve a passage by telling not only what your character does, senses, and feels, but also what he thinks or says, or both—quoting his thought and speech either directly or indirectly.[15]

[Without details:] The boys went down to the junk yard and sold the car.

[With details:] The boys went down to the junk yard and sold the car. Gol-lee! thought George; fifteen dollars. That will pay the

---

[13] See T36.

[14] Robert Louis Stevenson, *Treasure Island* (New York: The Heritage Press, 1941), pp. 156-57. Italic not Stevenson's.

[15] See T35-36.

whole debt and leave two dollars to spend after the dance. But since he knew how Tracy felt about giving up the jalopy, he kept the elation out of his face and merely muttered, "Well, that's that. Let's get out of here."

T35 Direct quotation (the speaker's own words) is usually more vivid than indirect quotation *(he said that, they asked whether)* and therefore better in climaxes. But either sort becomes obvious and monotonous if it is used almost exclusively.

T36 How much detail[16] you should use depends upon the importance to the story of what you are describing. Do not detain your reader with a detailed treatment of unimportant matters.

SUGGESTION IN NARRATIVES

T37 Occasionally, when you are certain that your reader will not miss your meaning, suggest character, mood, atmosphere, or incident rather than state it plainly.

[Plain statement:] It was on Tuesday of that week that I first met Mr. Helmuth. He turned out to be a mean, crabby old man. If that were all, it would be enough. But he turned out to be dangerous as well.

[Suggestion:] It was on the Tuesday of that week that I first met Mr. Helmuth. I had strayed through a breach in the wall where a freshet had dislodged some of the loosely laid stones and effected a rough gate. I found the estate on the other side very beautiful but in pitiful disrepair. The grass needed cutting, the flower beds were choked with weeds and dotted with blooms dead on their stalks, and the house that I could glimpse through the elms and evergreens could have done with a coat of paint. I came upon Mr. Helmuth very suddenly, as I turned the corner of an untrimmed hedge much higher than a man. He had obviously seen me before I caught sight of him, for he showed no surprise.

"You're trespassin'," he said.

"I know it." I managed a laugh, but it was embarrassed and apologetic. "I hoped you wouldn't mind. You're Mr. Helmuth,

---

[16] See T30-34.

aren't you? It was time to pay you a call anyway, since we're going to be neighbors."

"I'm Helmuth. I take it you're Fax. Well, Mr. Fax, I ain't much given to payin' or receivin' calls. You're trespassin'." His pale watery eyes looked resolutely over my shoulder. The weathered, loose skin of his face was crisscrossed with cracks like a piece of old leather. Some twenty years before, when he had been fifty, he must have been a great hulking man. But now he was stooped; all muscle tissue and fat seemed to have melted from his frame; for, wherever skin was visible—at his face, his neck, his forearms and hands—it hung loose, mottled, and heavy-veined, with scarcely anything between it and the bones to give it contour.

"I apologize, sir," I said, since he was technically in the right, "for trespassing. But now that I'm here, perhaps you'll let me look around your beautiful place. I especially envy you your elms."

He drew a revolver from the pocket of his trousers, flicked open the breech and turned it toward me. "What do you see?" he asked, his lip lifting slightly over one yellow fang.

"Why," I stammered, looking at the six brassy heads in the chambers, "why, a revolver, a loaded revolver."

He flipped the breech closed with his finger and pointed the gun at me. "Get goin'."

"What?"

He shot at the ground near my feet. "Get goin'."

T38 Suggestion is useful for putting the reader in the mood for what is going to happen and for intensifying his feeling of suspense.

Ta-ra-*rah*. The drumbeat is followed by an interval of silence in which is heard only the shuffle of feet. Ta-ra-*rah*—then the shuffle of feet. Ta-ra-*rah*—then the shuffle of feet. It is a dead march, or at least a march of the dead. Over the heads of the long column slowly streaming through the dusk, the angry heavens thrust out long menacing fingers of cloud, their edges smeared with blood by the dying sun. Round about them in the valley, the breeze sighs, rouses itself to a sobbing wail, to a scream, and dies. Along the narrow clay road, the poplars stand at attention, somber and inscrutable, as the doomed march forward to the beat of the dead march. The faces of the men are white and drawn. They know what awaits them. They feel that it is inevitable, and they march like a hypnotized battalion to meet what they cannot escape.

CLIMAX

T39 In narratives in which the order of events is under your control and particularly in plot narratives,[17] place your most interesting or most important event at or very near the end.

T40 Perhaps the easiest way to make sure that your plot narrative[17] will have climax is to plan it backwards from the most interesting or important event.

T41 As far as the circumstances of your composition permit, keep O30-32.

STRAIGHT NARRATIVE AND PLOT NARRATIVE

T42 Straight narrative records a series of events without introducing complications and solutions. It is the form of narrative found in most news accounts in newspapers, in most history books, and so on. It may be lively or quiet, factual or fictional.

T43 Plot narrative deliberately introduces complications and obstacles that the characters in the story must overcome if they are to meet success, happiness, and so on. Plot narrative is usually fictional—though not always. It always makes use of suspense and climax.[18] It usually stresses cause and effect in human beings.

Personal letters[19]

T44 Make your letters clean—free of smudges, visible erasures, mistakes, crossouts, corrections, and strike-overs.

T45 Write personal letters on white or light-colored stationery. The paper may be a single unfolded sheet varying in size

---

[17] See T43.

[18] See T39-41.

[19] For punctuation of the various parts of letters, see D14-16 and D65. For capitals see H13-15.

from 5½ x 7 inches to 8½ x 11 inches; or the stationery may be in the form of a booklet.

T46 Use a black typewriter ribbon or blue, black, or blue-black ink.

T47 Use block form—no indentions—for typewritten letters. Leave a line-space between paragraphs of block-form letters. Use indented form for handwritten letters.[20]

T48 Center your letter on the paper so that the margins are balanced around it. The margins should never be less than half an inch wide; they may of course be wider if the message is short.

T49 Do not crowd the writing at the bottom of the page.

T50 If you use booklet paper, and the message is long enough to run to four pages, start at page 1 and go straight through to page 4. When the message is short, write on page 1; on pages 1 and 3; or on pages 1, 3, and 4.

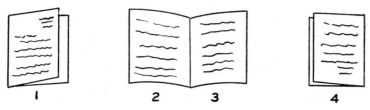

1 2 3 4

T51 It is customary to begin the letter with a heading in the upper right-hand corner. Write your street address on the first line; the city, zone number, and state on the second; and the date on the last. The rest of the heading may be omitted and only the date given if the recipient is certain to know your address or if the address is printed on the stationery.

---

[20] It is still rather common to use indented form for the paragraphs within the body of a typewritten letter. You may do so, indenting the first line of each paragraph from five to ten characters, unless your teacher directs otherwise. But do not use indented form for headings, addresses, signatures, and so on, of typewritten letters or envelopes.

See R105 and T52 for examples of block-form and indented letters.

T52   Do not give the address of the recipient on the first page.

Ozark Park

Blue River, Missouri

June 21, 1945

Dear Bob,

        The directions you gave us for getting to the Park were helpful, all right. If we hadn't had them, we might find ourselves in Arkansas now — and still going. The detours we had to make were many, as you said, and rough, but we got along without trouble and arrived on time.

        Will you do me a favor, Bob? Phone Mother and tell her we're all well. I should have written a letter to her yesterday but was too late for the mail. If she asks whether there's anything we want, tell her there is: some candy. Not chocolates, though; the weather is too warm.

        Be sure to let us know when you're coming. We'll meet you at the train.

Yours sincerely,

Tom

T53 These are correct forms of salutation in personal letters:

Dear Archbishop McHarris,	Dear Mayor Payne,
Dear Monsignor Powell,	Dear Dr. Twilliger,
Dear Father Campbell,	Dear Mr. Macklin,
Dear Brother Basil,	Dear Mrs. Barringer,
Dear Reverend Mother,	Dear Miss Templar,
Dear Sister Francis Regis,	Dear Tom,
Dear Senator Madison,	Dear Mother,

T54 The salutation beginning *My,* though somewhat more formal than the ones in T53, may be used in personal letters: *My dear Archbishop McHarris.*

T55 Never use *Sir* or *Madam* in a personal letter.

T56 *Dear Friend* and *Dear Miss* are not good form.

T57 The complimentary close should be in harmony with the salutation and tone of the letter.

   A *Sincerely yours* and *Yours sincerely* are the most formal.

   B *Sincerely yours in Christ, Yours in our Lord, Yours in the Sacred Heart,* and so on, suit any sort of letter.

   C *Cordially yours, Affectionately yours, Your loving son,* and so on, suggest a degree of affection and intimacy.

T58 A thank-you note may close with *Gratefully yours.*

U Argument

In general

U1 Argument is that form of talking or writing whose purpose is to convince another of the truth of some statement.[1]

---

[1] Persuasion is that form of talking or writing whose purpose is to make another feel or do what you want him to. Argument addresses itself to the intellect; persuasion, to the feelings or to the will. Ordinarily you must persuade your hearer as well as convince him; and hence, except in philosophy and mathematics classes, pure argument—an appeal to the intellect only—is seldom used. A mixture of argument and persuasion is the usual thing. For this reason the two are treated together in this book.

U2 Argument makes use of exposition, description, and narration, but for its own purpose.

Planning the argument

THE THESIS

U3 The theme topic[2] of an argument is called a thesis or proposition.

U4 A truth thesis states that a thing is or is not so.

God exists.
Americans do not love money.
Felicity Frisbie was a victim of circumstances.

U5 An action thesis states that something should or should not be done.

Alaska should be admitted as the forty-ninth state.
Congress should not adjourn before passing the Lytton Bill.
You should vote for Ed Roberts for secretary of the Salamanders.

U6 Write out your thesis.[3]

U7 If it is at all possible to do so—and it almost always is— state your thesis in a single, uncomplicated, declarative sentence.[3]

U8 Avoid extravagant and superlative terms when stating your thesis.[3]

U9 Make your thesis as definite as you reasonably can.[3]

U10 Make sure that your thesis states a truth or advocates a course of action that is good.

[Bad:] Animals think.
[Bad:] The United States government should take over all schools.

U11 Make sure that your thesis states only certain truths as certain.

---

[2] For the notion of theme topic, see M19-21.
[3] For further treatment see R24-25 and R27-28. The rules and examples given there for theme topics apply to theses as well.

For example, unless the thing is certain, say, "It is probable that fifty per cent of all Americans suffer from self-induced ailments." If the thing is not even probable, but merely possible, say so.

U12 Make sure that your thesis does not commit you to prove more than you have to prove, more than you should, or more than you can.

For example, if your purpose were simply to clear a friend of charges of incompetence in office, you would do badly to state this thesis, "Jack White has performed the duties of treasurer in a competent manner and is, in fact, the most able member of this organization." If you fail to prove that he is the most able man, that failure may reflect on your proof of his competence, when you might with ease have carried the point of his competence alone.

U13 Make your thesis as clear and concise as you can. If either you or your audience is vague about what is to be proved or what is to be done, you will probably lose their support. If your thesis rambles, it will be difficult for you or them to keep it in mind.

THE BRIEF

U14 Write an outline of your argument.

U15 The outline of an argument is called a brief. Since it has a different purpose from that of the outline of an exposition or the plan or plot of a narrative, it also has a different form.[4]

U16 Always write a brief in complete sentences only.

U17 A brief has three principal parts: the introduction, the proof, and the conclusion.

U18 The introduction—[4]
   A States the thesis.
   B Defines any terms that have more than one meaning or that might not be understood.

---

[4] See the example under U21.

c Gives any explanation or background necessary to the understanding of the argument.

D States the issues.

U19 The issues are the major points on which the truth or falsity of the thesis hangs. It is of the greatest importance that both the writer and his audience understand what the issues are. Confusion often conquers truth when the issues are not stated clearly and when the opposition is permitted to evade them.

U20 The proof once again states each issue, following it with the word *for* and reasons.[5]

U21 The conclusion recapitulates the issues as briefly as possible and restates the thesis.

> I. Introduction
> A. *Thesis.*—H. B. Stenson is guilty of plagiarism.
> B. *Definition.*—"Plagiarism" is the passing off as one's own the stolen writing of another.
> C. *Explanation.*—The victim of the plagiarism is Talbot Sparks.
> D. *Issues.*—I will prove my case by establishing the following issues:
>   1. The two stories are identical.
>   2. Sparks's story was written three months before Stenson's.
>   3. Stenson had access to Sparks's story.
>   4. Stenson made use of Sparks's story.
> II. Proof
> A. The two stories are identical, *for*—
>   1. Mr. Judson, authorized by this court, has pronounced them so.
>   2. Your own eyes will prove them so.
> B. Sparks's story was written three months before Stenson's, *for*—
>   1. Three reliable witnesses testify that Sparks's story was written by July 3, 1949.
>   2. Stenson's own admission and the testimony of a reliable witness show that his story was not written before October 7, 1949.

---

[5] See the example under U21.

    C. Stenson had access to Sparks's story, *for* Sparks had given it to him for two days to criticize.

    D. Stenson made use of Sparks's story, *for*—

       1. There is no other reasonable explanation of the identity.

       2. Stenson admitted to a reliable witness that he had copied the story and published it as his own.

  III. Conclusion

    Since the stories are identical, since Sparks's story was written before Stenson's, since Stenson had access to Sparks's story, and since Stenson made use of Sparks's story, therefore H. B. Stenson is guilty of plagiarism.

U22 If you are going to use the brief as the outline for a written speech, you need not write out the conclusion as shown in U21, since the matter it contains is already stated in the issues. But if you are going to use it for making an extempore talk, then you should write out the conclusion; for there will be no time to leaf back through pages looking for the issues and the thesis.

SOURCES OF PROOF

U23 Argue from the statements of a reliable witness. Man is not a natural liar; hence his statement that a thing is so (his testimony) is excellent proof.

U24 Your audience must grant you, or you must prove, these four things:

  A That there is nothing to show that your witness is given to lying. (If possible, show that your witness has a reputation for telling the truth or, better, is a man of outstanding integrity.)

  B That your witness has no reason for lying in this particular case (that is, that it would be of no advantage to him to lie).

  C That your witness has enough understanding to repeat accurately what he saw and what he heard.

  D That your witness was careful and attentive in watching or listening.

U25 Immediate (eyewitness) testimony is the more readily convincing; but mediate testimony, coming through several witnesses in turn, is quite good, provided it fulfills the four conditions of U24.

U26 Argue from accepted or established general truths or principles.

> I believe, gentlemen, that all of us hold the principle that one may not do evil even in order to accomplish good. It is true that Nevvers is slowly strangling decency and freedom in the city and the county. It is true, too, that it has proved impossible to pry him loose with any legitimate wedge. It is temptingly true that God has now delivered him into our hands and that, if I tell only one little lie on the witness stand tomorrow morning, I can send him to rot in jail where he belongs and assure the election of an honest man. But if I did so, I would forsake one of the precious principles that should separate men like us from men like Nevvers. I will not fight evil with evil. I will not become what I hate. And you will not ask me to.

U27 The argument in U26 can be reduced to this: It has been proved (or will be proved, or is accepted by all of you) that General Principle A is true (or good). But Particular Instance B is merely a form of General Principle A. Therefore Particular Instance B is true (or good).

U28 Appeal to an accepted authority. An authority is a person whose views on a subject are generally acceptable because of his known and proved knowledge of the matter and because of his integrity.

> For example, God is the supreme and infallible authority except with the poseurs who call themselves atheists. God's word is, therefore, the perfect proof of anything. Others, however, are authorities in this or that particular field of knowledge. Thus it happens that you may call on the views of Planck to prove a point in physics; you may call on the authority of the popes to prove a point in faith or morals, especially when they have spoken *ex cathedra;* you may call on the authority of the coach to prove a statement about the athletic ability of a member of his team or about changes that should be made in the rules of a sport; and so on.

U29 When appealing to an accepted authority, remember—

A A man who is an authority in one field is not automatically an authority in another. For example, the fact that Einstein is an authority in physics does not make him an authority in theology.

B When the declarations of authorities conflict, the argument from authority must be dropped or must be bolstered by other arguments to prove the superiority of the authority you have selected. Authority is not a matter of majority rule, and so sometimes a single authority may outweigh a host of others.

C Whatever your audience may think, the value of an authority's statement is conditioned by his fallibility.

D When all the authorities agree, that adds immeasurably to the strength and effectiveness of your argument.

U30 Argue from a cause to an effect. Causes produce effects; so, if you can show that the cause of a thing exists, you will prove that the effect exists or will exist. However, if such an argument is to give a certain conclusion, there must be a necessary connection between the cause and effect; that is, the cause must be such that only this effect can flow from it. If there is not a necessary connection between the cause and the effect, the conclusion will vary in value from mere possibility to high probability.

You say, Joe, that you murdered this man deliberately, with full knowledge of what you were doing, with premeditation and utter willingness.

[Certain conclusion because of necessary connection:] That means, Joe, that you have scraped the image of Christ from your soul. That means that you have fouled the temple of the Holy Ghost and have given over His dwelling to darkness, to cold, to echoing emptiness.

U31 Argue from effect to cause.

For example, if you came upon a skyscraper in the wilderness, you would at once conclude that either human beings or some higher agency had been at work; that is, from the effect you would correctly and with certitude conclude to the cause.

U32 Argue from the evidence of circumstances. Circumstantial evidence, more often than not, affords only probability of high or low degree.

For example, if a man were seen to enter a café and, two hours later, to stagger away from it, bawling a song at the top of his voice in the public street, one might conclude with some justice that these circumstances—the bar, the staggering, the loud singing—point to a bout of drinking.

U33 Argue from specific instances.

A This argument must be founded on the examination of a great number of particular cases under a wide range of circumstances.

B Such an examination, however, can rarely be related to an audience in detail. It usually has to be summarized in a sentence or so.

In scientifically controlled and tabulated interviews with several thousand applicants for jobs in every region of the country, it was discovered that only 40 per cent of all American men have anything, or can formulate anything, but a materialistic purpose in applying for work. The other 60 per cent were unable to name anything but money and what money can buy as the object of work. For further details of the survey on which this figure is based, see [and so on].

C With some audiences it often suffices for conviction to supply only one appealing example.

I strongly urge you not to buy Rigomort theater seats for your auditoriums. I sat in, or rather thrust myself into, one of them the other day and found myself embraced with alarming and acutely uncomfortable pressure by the arms of the thing. When I tried to stand up to let a patron of the theater pass in front of me, one of the arm brackets tore away the pocket of my coat; and the hat gadget on the bottom of the seat clawed a vicious rip in my trousers. Yet I am of average size.

The audience takes it for granted that the speaker, a man of integrity, would not condemn all Rigomort seating facilities unless he had made a prudent sampling of them all or knew in some other way that they were all defective.

U34 Argue from common experience.

We all know that during our waking hours our minds are never entirely vacant, empty of thought. We are aware of things about us and we are accepting and rejecting them. It is absurd, therefore, to talk about keeping a child's mind empty and letting him grow up to the age of thirteen or so before he chooses his own religion. He will have been choosing all along; and, if we have not been supplying his mind with the warm, rich truth during that time, he will have been choosing cold, bare, pale reflections of it. You might as soon speak of not feeding a child until he can decide for himself what he wants for dinner. Your child is like you, and you know no one could have kept your mind blank for thirteen years.

U35 Argue from analogy. The argument from analogy means that, if two things are alike in some particulars, then they will be alike in others.

To me, at least, it is almost inconceivable that a boy so very like his great-souled father could have done the crime with which you charge him. No one would have dared to accuse his father of such a thing, for the world would have laughed the accuser to scorn. Well, this boy and his father were cut by God on the same pattern. Every presumption is against his having done or said an ignoble thing.

U36 Use the argument from analogy charily, for it can readily lead to false conclusions. It is best used as a merely persuasive proof; and, of course, it should not be proposed to an audience as conclusive by itself.

Writing the argument

U37 In general, argument will make use of everything that you have learned about the other three forms of writing. An argument fleshes the skinny bones of its brief with exposition, description, and narration. The points in the following rules, however, are worth mention.

U38 Occasionally circumstances will be such that you can confine the introduction of your argument to the items listed in the introduction of its brief.

527

U39 Most of the time you should use the opening paragraphs of your argument to catch your audience's interest and make them like you. (After this is done, take up the items listed in the introduction of the brief.)

   A Concede something that they hold and that they do not expect you to grant.

> There was a time when I was stupid enough to think that there could be no circumstances in which a man was justified in going to a non-Catholic college. I have since come to realize that, if he can get an education in no other way and if he takes certain precautions like regular conferences with a priest to make the danger to his faith remote, then he may go to a non-Catholic college. There was also a time when I thought that every non-Catholic college was waiting to choke a Catholic's faith out of him. Since then I have heard of two cases in which men *found* the true faith in secular colleges. It is therefore without prejudice, it is with my eyes as open as yours, that I still insist that you gentlemen, if you can possibly arrange to do so, should attend a Catholic college.

   B Amuse them.

   C Compliment them. Be sincere and specific. Insincerity, whether detected or not, degrades the speaker; and it is often detected. General compliments do not impress.

   D Use a humble, straightforward, manly tone where they expect sarcasm, reproach, or invective.

U40 Except when you have good reason to be impersonal—as, for instance, when you are trying to give the impression that you are merely presenting truth, not attempting to persuade anyone to anything—

   A Use direct address (the second person), but judiciously.

   B Use direct questions, but sparingly.

U41 In writing an argument, consider the brief to be the outline of the proof, of the evidence, rather than an outline of the presentation. In the presentation, use all that is of advantage in exposition, description, and narration.

U42 In a closely reasoned argument that is rather complicated, it is usually good, near the end, to recapitulate the issues and the thesis so as to leave with the audience as clear a notion as possible of what you have accomplished. The treatment, however, need not be dry.

There, then, you have the case against H. B. Stenson. It has brought me no pleasure to make this charge against the man, to prove it so conclusively, to shock the many people who hold his name in esteem, to brand him with the stigma of meanness, of pettiness, of selfishness. I feel as did the old man who worked for my father when I was a boy. "Don't fight with little people, boy," he told me. "Little people are sufficiently punished by what they are." However, the rights, the name, and the property of another man were at stake in this case; and so I am glad that the truth against H. B. Stenson stands so firm and clear that you can come to judgment against him without hesitation. For, as I have shown, the two stories are identical; Sparks's story was written three months before Stenson's; Stenson had access to Sparks's work; and, by Stenson's own admission, repeated under oath by a reliable witness, Stenson made use of Sparks's work. The conclusion, of course, is clear: H. B. Stenson is guilty of plagiarism. May you find your certain duty of bringing judgment against him less unpleasant than was my task of bringing proof. Pleasant or not, it is a duty you must perform as good men and good citizens. Your distaste, I trust, will not outweigh your convictions.

Fallacies

U43 A reasoning process that is not logical is called a fallacy. You should know the common fallacies so that you may avoid them in your own work and detect them when you are refuting the arguments of others.

IGNORATIO ELENCHI

U44 Mistaking the question is arguing for or against something other than the thesis, motion, or resolution actually proposed for discussion.

[This speaker, supposed to be arguing the question "Military service is good character training," has mistaken the question and is arguing against drafting boys under eighteen:] To draft a boy under eighteen years of age is a crime against human nature! Until the time that he is at least eighteen a boy has need of the atmosphere, the guidance, the will training, the example that only a home can afford. After he is eighteen, perhaps the time has come to throw him from the nest and let him try his wings; but before that the risk of dashing his young soul to death is too great. I am against this iniquitous proposal.

U45 To refute an argument that mistakes the question, call the attention of your opponent and the audience to the mistake and restate the actual question.

Mr. Clay has argued eloquently and at some length against drafting young men before they are eighteen. I find no difficulty in agreeing with him. But let me remind him that his eloquence was scarcely related to what is before the house this evening—the proposition that "Military service is good character training." I wish that Mr. Clay had brought his mind to bear on that topic, since that—and not the draft age—is what we came here to discuss. Let us reserve the draft age for another evening. Tonight let us talk about the effect of military service on a man's character.

PETITIO PRINCIPII

U46 Begging the question is taking for granted what you ought to be proving.

I want to propose Helen Murchison as the best-dressed girl on the campus. She wears smarter clothes than anyone else here at Sarat and is therefore fully entitled to the distinction "best-dressed." Now that I have proved her the one most worthy of the honor, I am sure that you will all give her your votes.

U47 The common refutation of an argument that begs the question is to show your opponent and the audience that he has not proved, but merely stated, the question.

I hope that neither Miss Murchison nor Miss Peters will take offense when I point out that the latter has offered no evidence, but has merely stated, that Miss Murchison is the best-dressed girl at Sarat. In a momentous matter of this sort we must have a better guide to a decision than mere statement. Now *my* candidate, as I shall *prove* [and so on].

VICIOUS CIRCLE

U48 A vicious circle is proving *A* by *B* and *B* by *A*.

It is easy to see that *cow* is a noun in this sentence. Look, it is modified by an adjective, *sprightly*. Adjectives, you know, modify only nouns or noun substitutes; and, of course, there is no question of a noun substitute here. *Sprightly*, I'll admit, looks like an adverb, since it ends in *ly*. But it is clearly an adjective here, for it modifies the noun *cow*.

U49 An effective way of refuting a vicious circle is to strip it of verbiage and present it in all its naked illogic.

Joe, you have proved that *cow* is a noun because it is modified by the adjective *sprightly* and that *sprightly* is an adjective because it modifies the noun *cow*. No, Joe. You could prove Gromyko to be papal secretary of state in that fashion.

POST HOC, ERGO PROPTER HOC

U50 False causality is assuming that, since one thing happens after another, it is therefore caused by that other.

I will never drink milk again. Last night, just before I went to bed, I drank a glass of milk. Then this morning, when I tried to get up, I found that I had a bursting head and that my stomach was one great ache.

U51 A simple question will often refute false causality.

Could nothing else have made you feel ill? Do you think that you should conclude that milk was the culprit without looking for a more likely suspect?

FALSE ASSUMPTION

U52 False assumption is taking something to be true that is not true and building an argument on it.

The presence of Jacob O'Neill in this hall tonight gives some notion of the unbridled boldness, of the shamelessness, of the arrogance of the man; of his utter disregard for what decent people

531

like yourselves think of him. You see with what sort of person you have to deal, my friends. He defies you to your face! What will be your answer?—Excuse me. What's that? You say Mr. O'Neill is not in the hall tonight!

U53 False assumption is such bad gaffe that the best refutation, ordinarily, is to call attention to it without gloating. Occasionally, however, it is necessary to be severe about it, lest the audience be misled.

FALSE APPEAL TO COMMON KNOWLEDGE

U54 False appeal to common knowledge or consent is using a phrase like *as everybody knows* or *only a fool would deny that*, when the point in question is not a matter of common knowledge or consent and may even be untrue.

I don't have to take time out to prove to people as enlightened as you that American-style democracy is the only good form of government. Only power-mad rulers and benighted Europeans, long accustomed to the surrender of their freedom of thought, would dare to offer any rebuttal.

U55 False appeal to common knowledge or consent is one of the more vicious fallacies when used deliberately. For it plays upon that snobbishness in people which makes them reluctant to admit that they do not know something or that they are peculiar enough to think differently from their neighbors.

U56 The refutation of false appeal to common knowledge or consent is (*a*) to point out that you, at least, do not know or do not consent to the statement of your opponent, and (*b*) to cite men of excellent knowledge and authority who disagree with it or deny it.

ARGUMENT BY UNFAIR IMPLICATION

U57 Argument by unfair implication is the stating of a fact or a truth but using it to imply something that does not follow from it.

532

The other day I was talking to a Catholic, and a rather intelligent one. I asked him whether there was any basis for the doctrine of the infallibility of the pope besides the fact that some pope decided that it would be nice to be infallible. This Catholic couldn't give me an answer. Now that's Catholicism for you—authoritarian nonsense.

The implication in this argument is that, if a presumably intelligent Catholic cannot explain a doctrine, then there is no explanation.

U58 The refutation of argument by unfair implication is to examine your opponent's statement and the conclusion he draws from it, and to show that the connection he implied between the two does not exist.

Mr. Glenn seems to feel that if a Catholic does not know the answer to a question, then there is no answer. I'll wager that Mr. Glenn does not know the answer to 12364 multiplied by 7463. Yet I do not think that Mr. Glenn would dare to say that there is no answer. I am sorry and a little embarrassed that his Catholic friend did not know something of the answer—not the more intricate aspects, but at least something. But I am dismayed to find that Mr. Glenn would use one man's ignorance to mislead you.

AMBIGUITY OF TERMS

U59 Ambiguity of terms is an illogical shifting of the meaning of words.

Catholics maintain that their popes are infallible. Let me show you how silly this is. They themselves admit that one of their popes—I've forgotten which—died of poisoning. Now if he had been infallible, do you think he could have made a stupid little mistake like taking poison? It beats me how Catholics can swallow such—excuse the word, please; but I get worked up about this thing—such hogwash.

U60 The refutation of an argument based on ambiguous terms is to redefine the terms.

DEFECTIVE INDUCTION

U61   Defective induction is an argument based on too few instances or on an examination made unscientifically, without sufficient variation of circumstances or controls.

> Sheep, my friends, are all white. I know. I have two sheep, and they are both white.

U62   The refutation of defective induction is either to show that too few instances have been examined or that the examination was unscientific, or else to bring up a fact that refutes the induction, according to the old dictum, "An argument cannot batter down a fact" *(Contra factum non valet illatio).*

> The gentleman who spoke just before me proved, or seemed to prove, that all sheep are white. I should hesitate to attack his conclusion were it not that I happen to have a sheep with me—a sheep that is black. Bill, will you please bring in that sheep?

FALSE ANALOGY

U63   False analogy is arguing that, because two things are alike in some particulars, they will therefore certainly be alike in others.

> For example, in a widely current television commercial, the salesman dips two sponges in water, one coated with a water-resistant material. The uncoated sponge becomes soft. Then he says that the same thing happens to whiskers that have been cleared of water-resistant film by his product. He often concludes with remarks implying that he has *proved* that his product softens whiskers.

U64   The refutation of false analogy is to point out the differences between the two things that are compared and to show how these must be taken into consideration no less than the similarities.

Index

539

Biblical characters, descriptive names of, capitals, H31
Biblical references (chapter, verse, and so on), colon, D66
Biographical dictionaries, list, R16
Bishop
  form of address, salutation, and complimentary close in business and formal letters, R115-16
  form of salutation and complimentary close in personal letters, T53-54, T57
Blessed Virgin, capitals, H48-53
  adjectives and adverbs accompanying names of, H48, H52
  "blessed," H48
  descriptive substitute names (epithets), H50
  "mother," H53
  simple descriptive appositive or predicate names, H51
  "virgin," H49
Block form, K4
  business letters, R105
  personal letters, T47
Body and blood of Christ, capitals, H41-42
Book of Common Prayer and its parts, no italic or quotation marks, D107, D118
Books
  capitals
    for "chapter," "page," and so on, H139-40
    general rule of titles, H120
    particular rules of titles, H21, H23-25, H32-33, H122-24, H149, H151
  for reference, list, R16
  numbers with "chapter," "page," and so on, G13
  punctuation
    titles in italic, D115
    titles in quotation marks, D102, D104, D115
    titles with no punctuation, D105-7, D116-18
  reference cards for, R18-22
  research for themes, R14-22
"Boulevard," abbreviation, F8
Boulevards, capitals, H101, H103
Brackets, D88, D113
Breviary
  capitals, H32

no italic or quotation marks, D107, D118, H32
Bridge (transitional) words, phrases, sentences, and paragraphs
  for coherence, N15-16, N34-44
  in a narrative theme, T15
Bridges, capitals, H106-7
Brief of an argument, U14-22
  conclusion, U17, U21-22
  definition, U15
  introduction, U17-18, U38
  issues, U19
  outline of proof rather than of presentation, U41
  proof, U17, U20
  sample brief, U21
  to be stated in complete sentences, U16
  to be written out, U14
Brief sketches, S21
British usage, spelling, I3
Broadcasting stations, abbreviation without period, F10
"Brother," capitals, H95-97
Brother (religious)
  abbreviation (error), F9
  capitals, H88
  form of address, salutation, and complimentary close in business and formal letters, R115-16
  form of salutation and complimentary close in personal letters, T53-54, T57
"Brothers," abbreviation, F8
"Building," abbreviation, F8
Buildings, capitals, H106-7
Bureaus, capitals, H111, H115
Business and formal letters, R101-20. *See also* Letters (correspondence).
Business houses, form of address, salutation, and complimentary close in business letters, R115-16
"But"
  bridge (transitional) word, N15-16, N35, N39
  conjunction, A151. *See also* Conjunctions, co-ordinating.
  preposition, A144
"But not"
  co-ordinating conjunction, A151
  introducing contrasting expressions, comma, D49
By-line, R65-66

"Cabinet," capitals, H111, H115
Call numbers, R20, R81
"Can" and "could," A72, C38, C91-95
Capitals, H1-154
  abbreviations of titles following a
    name, H94
  academic courses, H130, H132-33
  acts, alliances, charters, reports, stat-
    utes, and treaties, H128-29
  adjectives and adverbs
    accompanying names of Blessed
      Virgin, H48, H52
    accompanying names of God or
      referring to God, H37-38, H44,
      H46
    derived from titles of sacred writ-
      ings, H22, H26
    modifying "Mass" and the names
      of the Eucharist, H67, H70
    proper adjectives, H18-20
  "aeon," H136
  after colon, H11-12
  "age," H126, H136
  aircraft, H142
  almanacs, H124
  angels, H58
  "anti-," H19
  "apostles," H75
  "Apostolic See," "Holy See," "Chair
    of Peter," H79
  "army," H116-17
  art, works of, H120
  articles ("a," "an," "the")
    in titles, H120-21, H149-51,
      H153
    "the," first word in headings and
      addresses of letters, H152
  articles (essays), H120, H122-23
  assemblies, H111, H115
  associations, H112, H115
  avenues, H101, H103
  banks, H112, H115
  "beatific vision," H61
  Bible, H21-28
  biblical characters, descriptive
    names of, H31
  Blessed Virgin, H48-53
  body and blood of Christ, H41-42
  books, H120, H122-24
  boulevards, H101, H103
  Breviary and its parts, H32
  bridges, H106-7
  buildings, H106-7
  bureaus, H111, H115

"cabinet," H111, H115
catechisms, H33
"century," H126, H136
chapels, H106-7
"church" and churches, H64-65,
  H106-7
church members, H63
church services and devotions,
  H72-74
cities and sections of cities, H98,
  H100, H103
classes and orders of people within
  the Church, H75-78
clubs, H106-7, H112, H115
colleges, H113, H115
"column," H140
commissions, H111, H115
companies, H112, H115
compound words in titles, H92-93,
  H122-23
confessions of faith, H33
congregations, religious, H76-77
"congress," H111, H115
congressional districts, H98, H103
conjunctions in titles, H120, H149
continents, H102-3
counties, H98, H100, H103
countries, H98, H102-3
courses, academic, H130, H132-33
courts, H111, H115
creeds, H33
creeks, H102-3
"cross," H43
"day," H126, H135-36
days of the week, H134
"democrat," "democratic," and so
  on, H109-10
departments of government, H111,
  H115
departments of schools, H113,
  H115
devil, H60
devotions, H72-74
dictionaries, H124
dioceses, H98, H103
direct questions within a sentence,
  H3
direct quotations, D96-97, H5-6
directions ("north," and so on),
  H104-5
directories, H124
"disciples," H75
discourses, biblical, H27
"doctors of the Church," H75

ecclesiastical seasons, H134
educational institutions, H113,
H115
empires, H98, H103
encyclopedias, H124
epithets, H90
for God, H35-39
for the Blessed Virgin, H50
"epoch," H126, H136
eras of history, H125-26, H136
essays, H120, H122-23
Eucharist, H69-71
events
in the life of our Lord or our
Lady, H55-56
major (historical), H125
minor, H127
fairs, festivals, expositions, H127
fast days, H134-36
"fatherhood" (of God), H40
"fathers of the Church," H75
feast days, H134-36
"federal government," H108
first word
of direct quotation, D96-97,
H5-6
of indirect quotation (error), H7
of sentence, H1-2
of unspoken thoughts, or words
directed by a person to himself, D91, H4
"footnote," H140
for emphasis, H146
foundations, H112, H115
"freshman," H114
geographical names, H102-3
God, H34-47
adjectives accompanying names
of, or referring to, H37-38,
H44, H46
adverbs in names of, H38
body and blood, H41-42
"divinity," "providence," "deity,"
H39
false deity, H47
"heart" and "Sacred Heart," H42
"humanity" and "hypostatic union," H43
"name," "holy name," "fatherhood," "sonship," H40
names used as descriptive predicates or appositives, H36
pronouns and adjectives referring
to, H44-46

proper names, H34
substitutes for proper names, H35
"gospel," H25-26
"government," H108
governmental assemblies, bureaus,
commissions, courts, departments, offices, and so on, H108,
H111, H115
gulfs, H102-3
half-sentences corrected by capitalization, B6
headings in outlines, R37
"heaven," H61
heavenly bodies, H148
"hell," H61
historical events and eras, H125-26
holidays, H134-35
Holy Eucharist, H69-71
"Holy Family," H54
"holy name," H40
"Holy See," "Apostolic See," "Chair
of Peter," H79
holy souls, H59
holydays, H134-35
"host," "sacred host," "sacred
species," H71
"House of Representatives," H111,
H115
"humanity" (of Christ), H43
"hypostatic union," H43
"I" (personal pronoun), H143
indexes, H124
indirect quotations, H7
islands, H102-3
"junior"
school term, H114
title following a name, H94-95
kingdoms, H98, H102-3
kinship names, H95-97
lakes, H102-3
"language" and languages, H130,
H132
"letter," H140
letters (correspondence), H13-15
addresses, H13, H152
complimentary close, H15
headings, H13, H152
salutations, H14, H85
libraries, H106-7
"line," H140
line and sentence, H1-16
magazines and periodicals, H120-23
Mass and its parts, H66-67
military groups, H116-19

Capitals—*continued*
  Missal and its parts, H32
  "monk," "priest," "nun," and similar
      words, H78
  "month" and months, H134, H136
  monuments, H106-7
  "moon," H148
  "mother"
    Blessed Virgin, H53
    kinship name, H95-97
  motion pictures, H120, H122-23
  mountains, H102-3
  musical works, H120, H122-23
  mysteries of the rosary, H74
  "mystical body" and "mystical un-
      ion," H43
  "name" (of God), H40
  "navy," H116-17
  newspapers, H120-21
  nicknames, H90
  "non-," H19
  "north," "south," "east," "west,"
      H104-5
  "note," H140
  "Notes," heading in expository
      theme, R80
  "nun," "monk," "priest," and similar
      words, H78
  "O" (exclamatory word), A162, H143
  oceans, H102-3
  offices, H111, H115
  "oh," H144
  operas, H120
  orders, religious, H76-77
  "organization" and organizations,
      H108-13, H115
  outlines, R37
  "page," H140
  paintings, H120, H122-23
  "papacy," H80
  parables, H28
  "paradise," H62
  "paragraph," H140
  parenthetical sentences in paren-
      theses, D83, D87, H1-2
  "parish" and parishes, H98-99
  parks, H100, H102-3
  "patriarchs," H75
  "people" and peoples, H130-32
  "period," H126, H136
  personal titles, H81-97
    abbreviations following name, H94
    "brother," H95-97
    "Brother" (religious), H88

  civil, H81
  compound, H92-93
  "father," H95-97
  "Father" (priest), H88
  followed by proper names, H81-83
  "His Eminence," "His Excellency,"
      "His Holiness," "His Honor,"
      and like titles, H89
  "honorable," H91
  in direct address, H84-88, H95
  indicating position or occupation,
      H82-83
  "Jr.," H94
  kinship names, H95-97
  military, H81
  "mister," "master," "miss," not
      followed by proper names, H86
  "mother," H95-97
  nicknames and epithets, H90
  not followed by proper names,
      H85-89, H95-96
  religious, H76, H78, H81, H88-89
  "reverend," H91
  "sir," "madam," "gentlemen,"
      "ladies," "children," and so on,
      H85
  "sister," H95-97
  "Sister" (religious), H88
  social, H81
  "Sr.," H94
  terms of address used opprobri-
      ously, H86
  personifications, H137, H147
  plays (dramas), H120, H122-23
  poetry, H8-10, H120, H122-23
  political and administrative divisions,
      H98-99, H103
  political parties, H109-10
  prayers, H29-30
  precincts, H98, H100, H103
  prepositions in titles, H120, H149
  "priest," "monk," "nun," and similar
      words, H78
  "pro-," H19
  pronouns referring to God, H44-46
  proper adjectives, H18-20
  proper nouns, H17, H19-20
  "prophets," H75
  "purgatory," H61
  "race" and races, H130-32
  radio stations, H112, H115
  railroads, H112, H115
  "real presence," H71
  "redemption," H55-57

reference works, H124
regions, H102-5
religions and their members, H63-65
religious orders and congregations,
H76-77
religious terms, H21-80. *See also the particular term; for example,* Capitals, dioceses.
"republican," H109-10
"Resolved" (in resolutions) and the first word following it, H145
rivers, H102-3
Roman Catholic Church, H63-65
rosary, H30, H74
running heads for themes, R70
"sacrament" and sacraments, H68-70
"Sacred Heart" and "heart," H42
sacred writings, H21-28
"Satan" and its synonyms, H60
"scene," H140
school subjects, H130, H132-33
school terms, H114
schools, H113, H115
seasons
    ecclesiastical, H134
    "spring," "summer," and so on, H137
sections of states, cities, towns, and so on, H98, H100, H103
"senate," H111, H115
"senior"
    school term, H114
    title following a name, H95
sentence and line, H1-16
sentences in parentheses, D83, D87, H1-2
"service" and "devotion," H72
ships, H142
short forms of titles, H138
societies, H112, H115
"sonship" (of Christ), H40
"sophomore," H114
"stanza," H140
states and sections of states, H98, H100, H102-3
streets, H101, H103
"sun," H148
"Supreme Court," H111, H115
television stations, H112, H115
territories, H98, H102-3
"the," H120-21, H149-53
titles, H16, H120-24, H128-29
    articles ("a," "an," "the") in, H120-21, H149-51, H153

conjunctions in, H120, H149
for themes, R64, R70
personal. *See* Capitals, personal titles.
prepositions in, H120, H149
short forms, H138
word following hyphen in, H93, H122-23
See also Capitals, books; Capitals, essays; Capitals, paintings; *and so on.*
See also classification of particular name you are concerned with. For instance, if you wish to know whether "Elks Club" should be capitalized, see Clubs, capitals.
towns and sections of towns, H98, H100, H103
trade names, H141
trains, H142
"transubstantiation," H71
"tribe" and tribes, H130-32
"un-," H19
unnecessary capitals, H154
unspoken thoughts, D91, H4
verse, H8-10, H120, H122-23, H140
"week," H136
"Whereas" (in resolutions) and the first word following it, H145
word following hyphen in title, H93, H122-23
word following "Whereas" and "Resolved," H145
words directed by a person to himself, D91, H4
words followed by numeral or letter, H139-40
"year," H136
"yes," "no," "oh," "good-by," "good morning," "amen," and so on, H144
zones, H98, H100, H102-3
Cardinal and cardinal archbishop
    form of address, salutation, and complimentary close in business and formal letters, R115-16
    form of salutation and complimentary close in personal letters, T53-54, T57
Cardinal numeral adjectives, A133
Case, C186-90
    after "it is" in informal speech and writing, C168, footnote 50

case not affected by parenthetical
clauses, C264-65
See also Case, nominative; Case,
objective; *and* Case, possessive.
retained objects, C105, footnote 36
subject pronouns
of gerunds, C225, C389, C393
of infinitives, A181, C224
of nominative absolutes, C203,
C223
of predicate verbs, C222
"who" for "whom" in informal
speech and writing, C159, footnote 48
with gerunds, C159-60, C163, C225,
C228-31, C389, C393
with infinitives, C159-60, C163,
C224, C227, C229-31
with nominative absolutes, C203,
C223
with participles, C159-60, C163,
C203, C223, C229-31, C389,
C393
with predicate verbs, C159-60, C163,
C168, C222, C226, C229-31
with prepositions, A143, C232, C389,
C393
Catechisms
capitals, H33
no italic or quotation marks, D107,
D118, H33
Cause and effect
false causality (*post hoc, ergo
propter hoc,* fallacy), U50-51
for variety in developing main ideas,
P16
in the paragraph, P34-35
in the sentence, P32-33
in the theme, P36-37
in plot narratives, T43
logical order for coherence, N29-30
sources of proof in argument, U30-31
"Ceed," "cede," and "sede," spelling,
I12
Cents, numbers, G9
Centuries, numbers, G5
"Century," capitals, H126, H136
Chapels, capitals, H106-7
"Chapter"
abbreviation, F8
capitals, H139
Chapters
numbers, G13
titles, quotation marks, D103

Characteristics, distinguishing, in log-
ical definitions, R93, R100
Charters
capitals, H128
no italic or quotation marks, D106,
D117, H128
"Choose," taking both direct object and
objective complement, C157
Christ, capitals, H34-38, H40-46. *See
also* Capitals, God.
Chronological order. *See* Events, in
chronological (time) order.
"Church" and churches, capitals, H64-
65, H106-7
Church members, capitals, H63
Church services and devotions
capitals, H72-74
no italic or quotation marks, D107,
D118
Circle, vicious (fallacy), U48-49
Circumstances, for variety in developing main ideas, P16
in the paragraph, P22
in the sentence, P21
in the theme, P23
Circumstantial evidence, source of
proof in argument, U32
Cities and sections of cities, capitals,
H98, H100, H103
Civil titles, capitals, H81
Clarity
comma for, D53
hyphen for, D150
in exposition, R2
in general, M4, N3, O2, P1
See also Clear reference.
Clauses, C397-421
absolute, diagraming, J33
adjective (dependent, relative),
C411-16
as misplaced modifiers, C328-29,
N6-7
definition, C411
diagraming, J39-40, J42
in series, punctuation, D18, D21-
24, D28, D57, D63
relative adjectives in, A124, A126,
C403, C412, C416
relative adverbs in, A159, C403,
C412-13
relative clauses, C412
relative pronouns in, A43-49,
C260-65, C322, C403, C412,
C414-15

550

551

Conjunctions—*continued*
  definition, A3, A148-49
  disjunctive ("or," "either . . . or,"
    and so on), A152
  affecting agreement with anteced-
    ent, C245
  affecting verb agreement, C32-33,
    C35
  definition, C245, footnote 72
  "neither . . . or" (error), A153,
    C362
  in titles, capitals, H120, H149
  precision in use of, N15-16, N21,
    N39-41
  relative adverbs, A159, C403, C412-
    13
  subordinating, A156-59
  "as," "as if," and "as though"
    in noun clauses (error), C367
  "as," case of pronoun after, C233,
    C302
  "as fast as" for "all the faster,"
    and so on, C303
  "as" in comparisons, C297, C371
  "as" used ambiguously (error),
    C373
  "because" in noun clauses (error),
    C363-64
  "being as" or "being that" for
    "since" or "because" (error),
    C368
  "directly" or "immediately" for
    "as soon as" (error), C376
  "except" for "unless" (error),
    C369
  "if" sometimes omitted in con-
    ditional clauses, C421
  in adverb clauses, A158, C368-80,
    C418-19, C421
  in dependent clauses, C403
  in noun clauses, A157, C363-67,
    C407
  "like" as conjunction, C350
  list, A157-59, C407
  "on account of" as conjunction,
    and "on account of because"
    (error), C374
  relative adverbs, A159, C403,
    C412-13
  "so" in comparisons, C297
  "so that" preferred to "so," A155,
    footnote 63; C377
  "than," case of pronoun after,
    C233, C302

"than" for "from" or "to" after
  "different" (error), C340, C380
"than" in comparisons, C295,
  C297, C372
"when" and "where" to introduce
  predicate complements (error),
  C365
"when" preferred to "than" after
  "scarcely," "hardly," "barely,"
  C378
"where" for "that" in object
  clauses (error), C366
"while" for "although" (ambiguous use, error), C375
"without" as conjunction (error),
  C370
  See also Connections and connectives.
Conjunctive adverbs, A154-55, C401,
  C419
Connections and connectives
  between parts of sentences, N9-10,
    N15-17
  between parts of theme, N31-44, T15
  between sentences, N21
  See also Conjunctions, Prepositions,
    and Pronouns.
"Consequently," bridge (transitional)
  word, N35, N40
"Consolidated," abbreviation, F8
Continents, capitals, H102-3
"Continue on," C353
Contractions, apostrophe, D139
Contrast
  definition, P25-27
  emphasis device, O33-37
    changes in mood or atmosphere,
      O36
    changes in rhythm, sound, struc-
      ture, O37
    visual devices, O34-35
  See also Comparison and contrast,
    for variety in developing main
    ideas.
Contrasting expressions, commas, D49
Conversation, introducing a narrative
  theme, T17-19
Co-ordinating conjunctions, A150-53.
  See also Conjunctions, co-ordi-
  nating.
Correlative co-ordinating conjunctions,
  A152-53, C362, J5-6
"Could," substitute for subjunctive,
  C121

Italic—*continued*
  letter used only as a letter, D125
  letters used in place of names
    (error), D126
  magazines, D119-20
  Mass and its parts (error), D107,
    D118, H66
  Missal and its parts (error), D107,
    D118, H32
  motion pictures, D115
  musical works, D121
  mysteries of the rosary (error),
    D107, D118
  name of city in which newspaper or
    magazine is published (error),
    D120
  newspapers, D119-20
  op. cit., D124, R81
  operas, D121
  paintings, D121
  pamphlets, D115
  parables and biblical discourses
    (error), D107, D118, H27-28
  part of a larger work (error), D102
  plays, D115
  prayers (error), D107, D118, H29
  radio programs, D115
  railroads (error), D123
  reference works (error), D105,
    D116, H124
  "Resolved," H145
  sacred writings (error), D107, D118,
    H21, H23-25
  ships, D122
  sparing use, D127
  statues, D121
  steamship lines (error), D123
  story, musical work, poem, and so
    on, not long enough to make a
    book (error), D103
  television programs, D115
  trains, D122
  "Whereas," H145
  word used only as a word, D125
  works of art, D121
"Its" and "it's," D138-39

Joint possession, D135
Jotting, Step 1 in writing expository
    theme, R10-12
"Jr."
  abbreviation, F5
  capitals, H94
  commas with, D27, F5

Judge
  form of address, salutation, and com-
    plimentary close in business and
    and formal letters, R115-16
  form of salutation and complimentary
    close in personal letters, T53-54,
    T57
"Junior" (school term), capitals, H114

"Kind of" and "sort of" as adverbs
    (error), C277
Kingdoms, capitals, H98, H102-3
Kinship names, capitals, H95-97

Labor unions, abbreviation without
    period, F10
"Ladies," capitals, H85
Lakes, capitals, H102-3
"Language" and languages, capitals,
    H130, H132
Latin words
  abbreviation, F1
  in footnotes, R81
  italic, D124, R81
  use in composition, Q9-10
"Lay" and "lie," C173
"Lead," with two direct objects, C156
"Learn" and "teach," C178
"Leave" and "let," C180-85
"Less" and "fewer," C267, C292
"Let us" (hortatory subjunctive), C111,
    footnote 42
"Let's us" (error), C219
"Letter," capitals, H140
Letters
  in an enumeration, punctuation, D80-
    81
  in outlines, R34, R39-42
  used for names, no italic or quota-
    tion marks, D126
  used only as letters
    formation of plural, D141
    italic, D125
  words preceding, capitals, H139-40
Letters (correspondence)
  business and formal, R101-20
    accuracy in, R119
    address and salutation, R107-8,
      R115
    block form, R105
    complimentary close, R109, R111,
      R116
    content, R117-20
    form, R101-16

564

handwritten, R101-4, R114
heading, R105, R107, R110, R114
indented form, R114
ink or ribbon, R103
margins, R104
paper, R102
signature, R109, R111-13
spacing and placement, R104-9,
  R111, R113
typewritten, R101-13
capitals, H13-15, H85, H152
personal, T44-58
  address, T51-52
  block form, T47
  complimentary close, T57-58
  handwritten, T46-47
  heading, T51-52
  indented form, T47
  ink or ribbon, T46
  margins, T48
  salutation, T53-56
  spacing and placement, T47-51
  stationery, T45, T50
  typewritten, T46-47
punctuation, D14-16, D27, D65
Librarian, R15
Libraries, capitals, H106-7
Library
  call numbers, R20, R81
  reading, R14-22
  reference works
    general list, R16
    in school library, R16, footnote 3
"Lie" and "lay," C173
"Like" as conjunction, C350
"Limited," abbreviation, F8
Limiting adjectives, A109-11. See also
  Articles ("a," "an," "the"),
  Demonstrative adjectives, Indefinite adjectives, Interrogative adjectives, Numeral adjectives,
  Possessive adjectives, and Relative adjectives.
"Line," capitals, H140
Linking verbs, C166-72
  adjectives after, C166-67, C169-70
  definition, C166
  "do good, bad, nice" (error), C171
  "feel badly, rightly" (error), C170
  list, C172
  test of, C169
  with complements, C166-70
Litany of Loretto, names of Blessed
  Virgin in, capitals, H50-51

Literary accuracy of expression, Q19-20
Literary titles. See Titles.
Logical definitions, R85, R93-100
  distinguishing characteristics, R93,
    R100
  general class, R93-95, R100
  parallelism, R96
  repetition of word to be defined,
    R97-99
Logical order in themes, N29-30
Logical phrasing of sentences, N18
"Loose" ("loosen") and "lose," C177
Loose sentences, O17-18

"Madam," capitals, H85
Magazine articles
  capitals, H120, H122-23
  quotation marks, D102-3
  reference cards for, R18-22
Magazines
  capitals, H120-23
  italic, D119-20
  reference cards for articles in, R18-22
Main idea in the sentence, M10, O4.
  See also Emphasis, Theme topic,
  and Topic thoughts.
Main verbs, affecting tense of subordinate verbs, C141-44, C146-50
"Manufacturing," abbreviation, F8
Margins
  business and formal letters, R104
  personal letters, T48
  themes, R60
Marks of ellipsis, D12-13
Marks of parenthesis, D77-87. See also
  Parenthesis, marks of.
Mary (Blessed Virgin), capitals, H48-
  53
Mass and its parts
  capitals, H66-67
  no italic or quotation marks, D107,
    D118, H66
"Master," capitals, H86
"May" and "might"
  helping verbs, A72, C38, C84-90
  in expressions of permission, C85-86
  in expressions of possibility, C87-89
  in expressions of purpose, C90
  in sentences with "if" clause, C88-89
  substitutes for the subjunctive, C121
Mayor
  form of address, salutation, and com-
    plimentary close in business and
    formal letters, R115-16

565

Mayor—*continued*
form of salutation and complimentary
close in personal letters, T53-54,
T57
"Meanwhile," bridge (transitional)
word, N35-36, T15
Measurements, numbers with, G10, G15
Mediate and immediate (eyewitness)
testimony, source of proof in
argument, U23-25
Men
form of address, salutation, and com-
plimentary close in business and
formal letters, R115-16
form of salutation and complimentary
close in personal letters, T53-54,
T57
"Messrs.," abbreviation, F3
Metaphor, Q31-34
Metonymy, Q44, footnote 15
"Might." *See* "May" and "might."
Military bodies, numbers, G5
Military groups, capitals, H116-19
Military titles, capitals, H81
Misplaced modifiers, C328-29, N6-7
"Miss," capitals, H86
Missal and its parts
capitals, H32
no italic or quotation marks, D107,
D118, H32
Mistaking the question (*ignoratio
elenchi*, fallacy), U44-45
"Mister," capitals, H86
Mixed dependent clauses, diagraming,
J42
Modifiers, A103
as part of appositives, C211
as part of phrases, C383, C387,
C391, C395
compound
hyphen, D145-48, D152
in titles, capitals, H92-93, H122-
23
dangling, C323-27, C420, N6-7
misplaced, C328-29, N6-7
restrictive and nonrestrictive, C312-
22
adjectives, C312-17
adverbs, C312-15, C318-19
articles, C317
punctuation, D38-40, D74, D79
test of, C315
"that" preferred to "which" in
restrictive clauses, C262, C322

squinting, C330-31, N6-7
used for suspense, O16
See also Adjectives; Adverbs;
Clauses, adjective (dependent,
relative); Clauses, adverb (dependent); Phrases, adjective;
and Phrases, adverb.
"Modify," definition, A103
Money, numbers, G9-10
"Monk," capitals, H78
Monsignor
form of address, salutation, and complimentary close in business and
formal letters, R115-16
form of salutation and complimentary
close in personal letters, T53-54,
T57
"Month," capitals, H136
Months
abbreviation, F7
capitals, H134
Monuments, capitals, H106-7
Mood, C108-21
definition, C108
imperative, C109, C111-12. *See also*
Imperative mood.
indicative, C109-10. *See also* Indicative mood.
optative, C109, footnote 39
potential, C109, footnote 39
subjunctive, C113-21. *See also* Subjunctive mood.
"Moon," capitals, H148
"More than," affecting agreement of
predicate verb, C19
"Most" for "almost" (error), C272
"Mother," capitals
Blessed Virgin, H53
kinship name, H95-97
Motion pictures
capitals, H120, H122-23
italic preferred to quotation marks,
D115
Mountains, capitals, H102-3
"Mr.," "Messrs.," "Mrs.," F3
Musical works
capitals, H120, H122-23
italic, D121
quotation marks, D103
"Must," helping verb, A72, C38, C58-61
Mysteries of the rosary
capitals, H74
no italic or quotation marks, D107,
D118

prayers (error), D107, D118, H29
radio programs, D115
reference works (error), D105, D116, H124
sacred writings (error), D107, D118, H21, H23-25
series of books, D104
short stories, D103
single, D90
something mentioned as part of a larger work, D102
statues, D121
technical words or terms, D110
television programs, D115
titles of themes, R64
with other punctuation marks, D98-100
words followed by their definition or explanation, D109
words that need setting off for clearness, D108
words used ironically, D112
works of art, D121
Quotations
books of, list, R16
dialogue, paragraphing and quotation marks, D95
direct, D89-91, D93-101
brackets in, D88, D113
broken by "he said" expressions, punctuation, D101
capitals, D96-97, H5-6
colon before, D60
comma before, D51
diagraming, J44-45
dialogue, paragraphing and quotation marks, D95
in expository themes, quotation marks, R71-74
in narrative themes, T34-35
quotation marks with, D89. *See also* Quotation marks.
indirect
capitals, H7
comma before (error), D52
definition, D92, footnote 32
in narrative themes, T35
with quotation marks, D92

"Race" and races, capitals, H130-32
Radio programs
capitals, H120, H122-23
italic preferred to quotation marks, D115

Radio stations
abbreviation, F10
capitals, H112, H115
Railroads
abbreviation, F8
capitals, H112, H115
no italic, D123
"Raise" and "rise," C176
"Re-," hyphen, D149
Reading, Step 3 in writing expository theme, R10, R14-22
"Real" for "really" or "very" (error), C278
"Real presence," capitals, H71
"Recall of" (error), C347
Recapitulation in argument, U21, U42
Reciprocal pronouns, A60-61, D137
number, A61
possessive, D137
"Recollect of" (error), C347
Redemption, events of, capitals, H55-57
Reference, clear. *See* Clear reference.
Reference cards for expository themes, R18-22
Reference works
capitals, H124
list, R16
no italic or quotation marks, D105, D116, H124
References
biblical, colon, D66
commas, D27
notes and footnotes, R76-81
Reflexive pronouns, A39-40
Regions, capitals, H102-5
Relationship (kinship) names, capitals, H95-97
Relative adjectives, A123-26
apostrophe with (error), D138
in dependent (adjective) clauses, A124, C403, C412
"which," A126, C416
Relative adverbs, A159, C413
in dependent (adjective) clauses, C403, C412-13
Relative clauses, C411-16. *See also* Clauses, adjective (dependent, relative).
Relative pronouns, A43-49
agreement of predicate verb with, C12
agreement with antecedents, A45-47, C12, C242, C249
apostrophe with (error), D138

583

Relative pronouns—*continued*
  case, A43, D138
    complicated by parenthetical expressions, C160, C230, C264-65
    not affected by antecedent, C241, C263, C415
    See also Case.
  gender, A45-47
  person, A48
  requiring antecedent in another clause, A49, C261, C414
  singular and plural, A43, A48
  test of, A49, C261, C414
  "that" preferred to "which" in restrictive clauses, C262, C322
  used only in dependent (adjective) clauses, A44, C260, C403, C412. *See also* Clauses, adjective (dependent, relative).
Reliable witness, source of proof in argument, U23-25
Religions and their members, capitals, H63-65
Religious (Brothers, Sisters, and so on)
  capitals, H76, H78, H81, H88
  form of address, salutation, and complimentary close in business and formal letters, R115-16
  form of salutation and complimentary close in personal letters, T53-54, T57
Religious orders and congregations
  abbreviation, F5
  capitals, H76-77
Religious services and devotions
  capitals, H72-74
  no italic or quotation marks, D107, D118
Religious terms, capitals, H21-80. *See also the particular term; for example,* Capitals, dioceses.
Religious titles, capitals, H76, H78, H81, H88-89
"Remember of" (error), C347
Repetition
  in definitions, of the word to be defined, R97-99
  in paragraphs, O22, P43, P45
  in sentences, O10-11, P42, P45
  in themes, O38, P44-45
Reports
  capitals, H128
  no italic or quotation marks, D106, D117, H128

Representatives
  form of address, salutation, and complimentary close in business and formal letters, R115-16
  form of salutation and complimentary close in personal letters, T53-54, T57
"Republican," capitals, H109-10
Requests phrased as questions, D4
"Resolved," capitals and italic, H145
"Rest, the," agreement of predicate verb with, C17
Restrictive and nonrestrictive appositives, C212-15. *See also* Appositives, restrictive and nonrestrictive.
Restrictive and nonrestrictive modifiers, C312-22. *See also* Modifiers, restrictive and nonrestrictive.
Retained objects, C105-7
  case, C105, footnote 36
  diagraming, J13
"Reverend"
  abbreviation, F4
  capitals, H91
Rhythm in composition, Q65
Right word and expression in composition, Q4-20. *See also* Interest and force, right words.
"Rise" and "raise," C176
Rivers and streams, capitals, H102-3
Roman Catholic Church, capitals, H63-65
Rosary
  capitals, H30, H74
  no italic or quotation marks, D107, D118
Rough draft, Step 6 in writing expository theme, R10, R55-57
Rules for spelling, I4-28. *See also* Spelling, rules.
Running description, S3
Running heads, R70
Runovers (run-on or run-together sentences), B7-12

Sacraments, capitals, H68-70
"Sacred Heart," capitals, H42
Sacred writings
  capitals, H21-28
  no italic or quotation marks, D107, D118, H21, H23-25
Salutation of letters
  business and formal letters, R115

capitals, H14, H85
colon after, D15, D65
comma after, D15
personal, T53-56
"Same" used as pronoun, C217
Sarcasm, Q42
"Satan," capitals, H60
"Scene," capitals, H140
School subjects, capitals, H130, H132-33
School terms, capitals, H114
Schools, capitals, H113, H115
Scripture references, colon, D66
Seasons, capitals
    ecclesiastical, H134
    "spring," "summer," and so on, H137
Second-year spelling list, I30
Sections of cities, states, towns, and so
    on, capitals, H98, H100, H103
Self-adjectives, A111, footnote 52
Self-pronouns, A37-42
    agreement with antecedents, A38,
        C242
    gender, A38
    intensive, A41-42
    misspellings, C259
    person, number, case, A37
    reflexive, A39-40
    used where personal pronouns would
        suffice (error), C258
Semicolon, D55-58
    before "namely," "for example," "for
        instance," and so on, D58
    in compound sentences, D31-32,
        D55-56
    in direct quotations, with "he said"
        expressions, D101
    in series, D57, D63
    with other punctuation marks, D63,
        D84, D99
Semisuspense sentences, O15
"Senate," capitals, H111, H115
Senator
    form of address, salutation, and com-
        plimentary close in business and
        formal letters, R115-16
    form of salutation and complimentary
        close in personal letters, T53-54,
        T57
"Senior" (school term), capitals, H114
Sentence fragments, B4-6
    capitals, H6
Sentence outlines, R31, R51-52. *See
    also* Outlines.

Sentences, B1-25
    bridge (transitional), N34, N44
    capitals, D83, D87, H1-7
    coherence in, N5-18. *See also* Co-
        herence, in the sentence.
    combined for variety in composition,
        P5-14. *See also* Variety, com-
        bining sentences and independ-
        ent clauses.
    complex, B23-24
        diagraming, J38-42
    compound, B22
        diagraming, J35-37
        punctuation, D30-32, D55-56
    compound-complex, B25
        diagraming, J43
    declarative, B14
        in outlines, R48
        in theme topics, R25, T9
        in thesis or proposition of an
            argument, U7
        period, D2
    definition, B1
    elliptical, B2-3
        dependent clauses in, C404
    emphasis in, O4-18. *See also* Em-
        phasis, in the sentence.
    end punctuation, D1-13
    enumeration in, P16, P18
    exclamatory, B17, D8
    half-sentences, B4-6
    imperative, B16, D3-4, D9
    incomplete (elliptical sentences and
        half-sentences), B2-6
    interrogative, B15, D4, D6-7
    interrupted, punctuation, D11-13,
        D67
    inverted
        agreement of predicate verb, C8
        used for emphasis, O8-9, O11
    loose, O17-18
    order of climax in, O5
    parallelism in, N8-14
    parenthetical, D83, D87, H1-2
    periodic, O14
    repetition of words and ideas in,
        O10-11, P42, P45
    runovers (run-on or run-together
        sentences), B7-12
    semisuspense, O15
    simple, B19-21
        diagraming, J4-34
    suspense, O12-18
    topic, M15-18, O21

Theme topic
  definition, M19
  for unity in themes, M19-24
  in argument, U3
  in expository themes, R11, R23-28
  in narrative themes, T6-11, T16
  in outlines, R33-34
  placement, M22, O29-30
  variety in development of, P4. *See
    also* Variety.
Themes, L1-10
  coherence in, N28-44. *See also* Co-
    herence, in the theme.
  conclusions, L9-10. *See also* Conclu-
    sions (themes).
  definition, L1
  digressions, M2-3, M25
  emphasis, O24-43. *See also* Em-
    phasis, in the theme.
  expository, R3-82. *See also* Exposi-
    tory themes.
  formal, Q12-13
  in general, L1-3
  informal, Q14, Q16
  introductions, L4-8. *See also* Intro-
    ductions (themes).
  narrative, T2-43. *See also* Narrative
    themes.
  one-paragraph, K3, L3
  topic. *See* Theme topic.
  unity, M19-27. *See also* Unity, in the
    theme.
  variety, P15-17. *See also* Variety.
  *See also the particular entry in which
    you are interested:* Final copy
    of expository theme; Footnotes;
    Rough draft, Step 6 in writing
    expository theme, *and so on.*
"There"
  dummy subject, A163
    agreement of verbs after, C9, C19,
      C36
    used for variety, P9
  with "that" and "those," A121,
    C256-57
"Therefore," bridge (transitional)
  word, N35, N40
"Theres" or "there's" for "theirs"
  (error), C254
"These" with "here," A121, C256-57
Thesis or proposition, U3-13. *See also*
  Argument, thesis or proposition.
"They," "we," "you," meaning "people
  in general," C237-38

Third-year spelling list, I31
"This"
  bridge (transitional) word, N35, N42
  for "so" or "very" (error), C284
  with "here," A121, C256-57
  See also Demonstrative adjectives
    and Demonstrative pronouns.
"Those" and "them," A120, C255
Thoughts, unspoken
  capitals, D91, H4
  no quotation marks, D91
Time of day
  colon, D64
  numbers, G8, G16
Titles
  articles ("a," "an," "the") in
    capitals, D119, D122, H120-21,
      H149-51, H153
    italic, D119, D122
  capitals, H16, H120-24, H128-29,
    H138
  conjunctions in, capitals, H120, H149
  exclamation points, D17
  in themes, R63-64, R70
  italic. *See* Italic.
  personal. *See* Personal titles.
  plural, agreement of predicate verb
    with, C28
  possessive case, D133-34
  prepositions in, capitals, H120, H149
  question marks, D17
  quotation marks. *See* Quotation
    marks.
  short forms, capitals, H138
  word after hyphen, capitals, H93,
    H122-23
  See also Names *and the particular
    kind of title or point about titles
    that you are interested in.*
"To," A144. *See also* Prepositions, "to."
"Too" before a past participle, C281
Topic. *See* Expository themes, choosing
  a general subject; Narrative
  themes, subject; Theme topic;
  Topic paragraphs; Topic sentences; *and* Topic thoughts.
Topic outlines, R31-32, R52. *See also*
  Outlines.
Topic paragraphs, L4, M22, O29, O31-
  32, T16
Topic sentences, M15-18, O21
Topic thoughts, K2, M11-18, M23
  and headings in outlines, R50
  in narrative paragraphs, T21-22

About this book

The *Writing Handbook* was designed by William Nicoll of EDIT, INC. It was set in the composing room of LOYOLA UNIVERSITY PRESS. The text is 11 on 13 Caledonia; the reduced matter, 9 on 12. The display type is Spartan Heavy and Futura demibold, bold, and medium.

It was printed by C. O. OWEN AND COMPANY from nickeltypes made by the CENTURY ELECTROTYPE COMPANY. The diagrams and handwritten corrections were reproduced from zincs made by the ADVANCE ENGRAVING COMPANY, INC., and STEARNS AND COMPANY. The book was printed on WARREN's 45-pound English Finish paper and bound by the ENGDAHL BINDERY in BANCROFT cloth.